LANGUAGE, CAPITALISM, COLONIALISM

LANGUAGE, CAPITALISM, COLONIALISM: TOWARD A CRITICAL HISTORY

Monica Heller and Bonnie McElhinny

UNIVERSITY OF TORONTO PRESS

Copyright © University of Toronto Press 2017
Higher Education Division

www.utppublishing.com

All rights reserved. The use of any part of this publication reproduced, transmitted in any form or by any means, electronic, mechanical, photocopying, recording, or otherwise, or stored in a retrieval system, without prior written consent of the publisher—or in the case of photocopying, a licence from Access Copyright (the Canadian Copyright Licensing Agency) 320–56 Wellesley Street West, Toronto, Ontario, M5S 2S3—is an infringement of the copyright law.

Library and Archives Canada Cataloguing in Publication

Heller, Monica, author
    Language, colonialism, capitalism : toward a critical history/Monica Heller and Bonnie McElhinny

Includes bibliographical refereneces and index.
Issued in print and electronic formats.
ISBN 978-1-4875-9416-9 (hardcover).—ISBN 978-1-4426-0620-3 (softcover).—ISBN 978-1-4426-0621-0 (PDF).—ISBN 978-1-4426-0622-7 (EPUB)

    1. Sociolinguistics. I. McElhinny, Bonnie S., 1966–, author II. Title.

P40.H45 2017   306.44   C2017-903607-6
                                    C2017-903608-4

We welcome comments and suggestions regarding any aspect of our publications—please feel free to contact us at news@utphighereducation.com or visit our Internet site at www.utppublishing.com.

North America
5201 Dufferin Street
North York, Ontario, Canada, M3H 5T8
2250 Military Road
Tonawanda, New York, USA, 14150

ORDERS PHONE: 1–800–565–9523
ORDERS FAX: 1–800–221–9985
ORDERS E-MAIL: utpbooks@utpress.utoronto.ca

UK, Ireland, and continental Europe
NBN International
Estover Road, Plymouth, PL6 7PY, UK
ORDERS PHONE: 44 (0) 1752 202301
ORDERS FAX: 44 (0) 1752 202333
ORDERS E-MAIL: enquiries@nbninternational.com

Every effort has been made to contact copyright holders; in the event of an error or omission, please notify the publisher.

This book is printed on paper containing 100% post-consumer fibre.

The University of Toronto Press acknowledges the financial support for its publishing activities of the Government of Canada through the Canada Book Fund.

Printed in the United States of America.

CONTENTS

List of Figures ix
Acknowledgements xi
Preface: Hope xiii

1 **LANGUAGE, CAPITALISM, COLONIALISM: WALKING BACKWARD INTO THE FUTURE** 1
   Language and Inequality: A Wary Approach to a Red Thread World 2
   Red Flags: Keywords, Hegemonies, Ideologies, and Warty Genealogies 4
   Language Out of Place 12
   Knotted Histories: Following the Threads through the Book 15
   The End of the Beginning 22

PART I: LANGUAGE, INTIMACY, AND EMPIRE

2 **LANGUAGE AND IMPERIALISM I: CONVERSION AND KINSHIP** 27
   "The First Nations Bible Translation Capacity-Building Initiative" 28
   Colonialism, Imperialism, Postcolonialism, Decolonization 30
   Intimacy and Connection Across Five Continents 32
   Reduced to and by Christian Love: Missionary Linguistics 35
   Family Trees, Comparative Philology, and Secular Religion 42

3 **LANGUAGE AND IMPERIALISM II: EVOLUTION, HYBRIDITY, HISTORY** 57
   "Mixing Things Up" 58
   Imperialism and Industrial Capitalism 60
   Evolutionary Theory: Language and/as Race 63
   Slavery, Plantation Labour, Trade, and "Mixed" Languages 71
   Americanist Anthropology: The Limits of Cultural Critiques of
      Evolutionary Racism 77
      American Modern: Assimilating Blackness, Disappearing Indigeneity 81
      American Primitive: Extracting Language 84
   Linguistic Relativity, Colonial Ambivalence, and Modern Alienation 87

PART II: THE CONTRADICTIONS OF LANGUAGE IN INDUSTRIAL CAPITALISM

4 LANGUAGE AND EUROPEAN NOTIONS OF NATION AND STATE 93
   "Le Symbole" 94
   The Emergence of the Nation-State in Europe 94
   Markets and Liberal Democracy 96
   Making Subjects through Language 98
   　Regimentation: Census, Standardization, Literacy 102
   　Standardization: Grammars, Dictionaries, Canons, Pedagogies 106
   Language and Differential Citizenship 108
   Creating Peripheries 110
   Regulating Relations in Industrial Capitalism 113
   Making Scientific Linguistic Expertise 117

5 INTERNATIONALISM, COMMUNISM, AND FASCISM: ALTERNATIVE MODERNITIES 123
   "Visions of the Future" 124
   Peace, Geopolitics, and International Auxiliary Languages 126
   Making Communist Linguistics 135
   　Marrism 139
   　The Bakhtin Circle 141
   　From Language as Action to Language as Tool in the Cold War 142
   Language and Fascism 144
   　National Socialism in Germany 146
   　Language and Race: Yiddish and Esperanto 149
   　Race, Propaganda, and Mass Media 150
   Fault Lines 155

PART III: BRAVE NEW WORLDS: LANGUAGE AS TECHNOLOGY, LANGUAGE AS TECHNIQUE

6 THE COLD WAR: SURVEILLANCE, STRUCTURALISM, AND SECURITY 159
   "Black Out" 160
   Battles for Hearts and Minds 162
   The Investigation of Linguists during the McCarthy Period 164
   Suspicious Words, Suspicious Minds 168
   　The Prague Linguistics Circle 168
   　Fear of the Translator 171
   Infrastructure and Institutionalization: Communication Studies, Area Studies, Linguistics, Applied Linguistics 176
   Machine Translation and the Rise of Syntax 181
   　Rational and Universal Principles for Linguistic Analysis: Late Structuralist Linguistics 182
   　Freedom, Creativity, and Human Nature: The Rise of Generative Linguistics 184
   Nineteen Eighty-Four as a Weapon of the Cold War 188

7	ON THE ORIGINS OF "SOCIOLINGUISTICS": DEMOCRACY, DEVELOPMENT, AND EMANCIPATION 192

"A Dialectologist in India" 193
Engineering Language: Literacy, Standardization, and Education 196
Language Policy and Planning: Technocratic Solutions 199
Domestic Development and American Sociolinguistics 201
    Challenging 'Deficit': Three Approaches 205
    Fear of the Political 212
Challenging Consensus 214
    Feminist Linguistics 215
    Difference and Domination: Anti-Racist Critiques 217
Pidgins, Creoles, and New Nationalisms 219
The Rise of Sociolinguistics in Europe: Class and Conflict 221
The End of the *Trente Glorieuses* 225

8	LANGUAGE IN LATE CAPITALISM: INTENSIFICATIONS, UNRULY DESIRES, AND ALTERNATIVE WORLDS 227

"Nayaano-nibiimaang Gichigamiin" 228
Late Capitalism: The Expanding Reach of the Market and the
    Neoliberal State 230
Language, Inequality, and Ideology 235
Managing Your Assets: Language Quality, Linguistic Diversity,
    and Citizenship 238
Brave New Selves: "I Am a Business, Man!" 242
Affect, Authenticity, and Embodiment 244
Recapturing the Commons 252
Reclamation, Redress, Refusal, and Reimagining 254
This Is How We Hope 257

References 261
Index 295

FIGURES

0.1	Por un mejor 2017	xiii
1.1	Red thread world	1
1.2	"We must create a new future." Philosopher's Walk/Taddle Creek, Toronto, 2016	23
2.1	Canadian Bible Society: Ojibwe Bible and Tagalog Bible. North York, 2017	27
2.2	Biblical geneaology as social and spatial relations: Noah's descendants	48
2.3	Language relationships as family tree	51
3.1	Diversity? Unity? Hybridity? Race	57
3.2	Wave theory model of linguistic change	77
4.1	"Le symbole." Morbihan, early twentieth century	93
5.1	"Espéranto. La langue équitable"	123
5.2	A Movado watch, La-Chaux-de-Fonds, Switzerland, 2016	126
6.1	A page from Roman Jakobson's FBI file	159
6.2	"Happy linguists make a diagram": Example of a syntactic tree	185
7.1	John Gumperz with two as yet unidentified colleagues, India, 1956	192
8.1	Nayaano-nibiimaang Gichigamiin (the Great Lakes) in Anishnaabewomin (Ojibwe)	227
8.2	Workers in a call centre	245
8.3	"cé faitte icitte/not made in china": mugs made in Québec by Hugo Didier	247
8.4	Trees versus rhizomes	254

ACKNOWLEDGEMENTS

We would first like to thank our editor at University of Toronto Press, Anne Brackenbury. Anne first approached us with a somewhat different idea; this book is the result of many discussions amongst the three of us. Anne's openness to the idea of what this book has now become, her support, her excellent questions—all have been vital to this project.

There is a second set of people whose work has been crucial: our graduate assistants at the University of Toronto. Their research skills, sharp eyes, inquiring minds, and enthusiasm for the project have sustained the book in countless ways and taught us a great deal. Thanks, then, to (in alphabetical order): Andrea Derbecker, Erika Finestone, In Chull Jang, Eun Yong Kim, Kate Morris, Kyoko Motobayashi, Norielyn Romano, Emily Sheppard, Leah Shumka, Jinsuk Yang, and Han Zhang. Valérie Dailly provided technical support, for which we are deeply grateful.

Margaret Hogan, Lead Archivist at the Rockefeller Archives, provided crucial support for the research we undertook for Chapter 7.

Andrea Derbecker rendered the beautiful hand-drawn trees, rhizomes, and waves in figures in Chapters 2, 3, 6, and 8.

Reviewers at two crucial stages of the book's development provided important critiques and extremely helpful suggestions. They gave both the proposal and the manuscript a close, engaged, and detailed read, for which we are grateful.

We have been fortunate to have been able to present parts of this work at various conferences and in the form of invited talks, where we have benefited from insightful comments and critiques. Finally, we have had the support and feedback from a variety of students and colleagues, some of whom have commented on drafts of chapters, and others of whom have provided key information at critical moments (and of course sometimes both): Kori Allan, Peter Auer, Sandra Bamford, Lindsay Bell, Annette Boudreau, Josiane Boutet, Cécile

Canut, Eva Codó, Christine Connelly, Jenny Cook-Gumperz, James Costa, Gary Coupland, Michelle Daveluy, Alfonso Del Percio, Aaron Dinkin, Alexandre Duchêne, Claude Gacon, Pedro Garcez, Maria Rosa Garrido, Mireille Grosjean, Louis Hébert, Kaitlyn Heller, Emily Hofstetter, Paul Hopper, Christopher Hutton, Kenneth Huynh, Nicolas Kaiser, Ivan Kalmar, Ron Kassimir, Ken Kawashima, Georg Kremnitz, Chris Krupa, Normand Labrie, Mika Lähteenmäki, Patricia Lamarre, Imanol Lamea Mendizabal, Xavier Lamuela, Richard Lee, Jean-Léo Léonard, Ed Liebow, Paul Manning, Jeff Martin, Marinette Matthey, Mireille McLaughlin, Claudine Moïse, Salikoko Mufwene, Xosé Núñez Seixas, Jeremy Paltiel, Lilli Papaloïzos, Alejandro Paz, Sari Pietikäinen, David Price, Joan Pujolar, Alessandra Renzi, John Rickford, Peter Sawchuk, Mark Solovey, Daniel Stotz, Miquel Strubell, Valérie Symaniec, Sally Thomason, Humphrey Tonkin, Bonnie Urciuoli, Jacqueline Urla, Saskia Witteborn, and Ruth Wodak.

PREFACE: HOPE

FIGURE 0.1: Por un mejor 2017. From José Antonio Millán, Bruno Millán, and Susana Narotzky (Photo: J.A. Millán and S. Narotzky): Graffiti in Cacilhas, Lisbon Metropolitan Area, Portugal. Taken on December 18, 2016.

Monica received this season's greeting card in her email at the end of 2016, as she was sitting in her living room editing this preface. She was contemplating the two quotes below—quotes Bonnie had found that spoke to both of them.

> Hannah Arendt ([1951] 1968): This moment of anticipation is like the calm that settles after all hopes have died. We no longer hope for an eventual restoration of the old world order with all its traditions, or for the reintegration of the masses of five continents who have been thrown into a chaos produced by the violence of wars and revolutions and the growing decay of all that has still been spared.... Never has our future been more unpredictable, never have we depended so much on political forces that cannot be trusted to follow the rules of common sense and self-interest—forces that look like sheer insanity. ... Desperate hope and desperate fear often seem closer to the center of such events than balanced judgement and measured insight. (*Origins of Totalitarianism*, vii)

> Junot Díaz (2016): For those of us who have been in the fight, the prospect of more fighting, after so cruel a setback, will seem impossible. At moments like these, it is easy for even a matatana to feel that she can't go on. But I believe that, once the shock settles, faith and energy will return. Because let's be real: we always knew this shit wasn't going to be easy. Colonial power, patriarchal power, capitalist power must always and everywhere be battled, because they never, ever quit. We have to keep fighting, because otherwise there will be no future—all will be consumed. Those of us whose ancestors were owned and bred like animals know that future all too well, because it is, in part, our past. ... But all the fighting in the world will not help us if we do not also hope. What I'm trying to cultivate is not blind optimism but what the philosopher Jonathan Lear calls radical hope. "What makes this hope *radical*," Lear writes, "is that it is directed toward a future goodness that transcends the current ability to understand what it is." Radical hope is not so much something you have but something you practice; it demands flexibility, openness, and what Lear describes as "imaginative excellence." (*The New Yorker*, November 21, 2016, 65).

Here are two weary writers, separated by 66 years, writing from difficult moments of social change, when hatred and distrust, violence and fear risk overwhelming us—one of those moments is ours. But they are talking to us about a struggle for equality and for peace, talking to us about the role of hope—and about what hope might be, what it might need in order to emerge, to flourish.

They point to a strategy for navigating this particular difficult moment, and those that will inevitably come. We don't mean a grand strategy, we mean one for everyday life, everyday work. We understand radical hope to combine both Arendt's "balanced judgement and measured insight" against "desperate hope and desperate fear," and Diaz' invocation of Lear's "imaginative excellence."

Our work is constructed around the question of what language has to do with social difference and social inequality. This, centrally, is what this book is about. Once again, not for the first time in history, language is coming to the fore in struggles for power. People are attentive to how you speak and how you look, regimenting your body and your tongue in all kinds of ways, from the hyper-institutional to the everyday. You can be refused asylum, arrested, or yelled at while trying to pay for your purchases at the supermarket. Muslims are accused daily of being "terrorists" in North America and Europe, elected female officials are greeted with chants of "lock her up!", and swastikas are spray-painted on doors and windshields. Again.

At the same time, there is pushback, there is refusal. It may take generations to heal the trauma wrought by the instruments of colonialism and empire, but there are attempts at truth and reconciliation from South Africa to Canada. And there is refusal to engage in processes that reproduce old harms, even if they do so in new ways. These involve language, too. These processes sometimes need dialogue, and they sometimes need silence. They unfold in struggles over what to name things, over what names mean: refusals to use a term such as "alt-right" for political movements that are racist and sexist, or movements to change racist names of American sports teams. They unfold in struggles to reclaim linguistic forms and practices stamped out by the repressions of colonial regimes.

Language is not peripheral to any of these phenomena; it is crucial to understanding them. We therefore turned to looking for a way to think about sociolinguistics and linguistic anthropology in which such issues *are* of central concern. That is how we hope.

Tracks and Traces

Looking for such a way has meant excavating both the approaches that marginalize such questions and those who seek to raise them. It has meant asking why language becomes salient at specific times, in specific places. Why does that salience result in the emergence or circulation of certain ideas about language and its relationship to social order, and the marginalization, even active repression, of others?

We started from the position that we would have to understand the relationship between language and social order through linking the value and meaning of language to the value and meaning of the rest of the resources that count in society, and so to the basic working of the economic and political order. To do so means telling stories and writing histories about language, colonialism, and capitalism that have been infrequently told in mainstream linguistic anthropology or sociolinguistics. Our approach is historical, though there are several places where we need to tell the story from more than one angle and need to retrace our steps.

We are interested in understanding when, how, and where projects to challenge inequity have been delimited, or interrupted, by prevailing ideologies and practices, or by forms of violence, verbal and physical. Throughout, we attend to which actors were interested in or developed certain approaches to language, explaining how they became involved through their positions in political economic processes. We track what kinds of people do not participate, as well as those who try to but are marginalized or silenced—though silence leaves few traces.

The stories are sometimes scattered, made incoherent by the ways we often narrate histories of the field. Often enough, these have been nationalist histories narrated in ways that have made more international and imperial connections invisible or illegible or unintelligible. Often enough, there are ways of narrating this history that are principally supportive of capitalism or communism or fascism, in obvious but also subtle ways that need to be challenged. Sometimes we are tracing tracks that run cold. Sometimes the tracks end abruptly. Some of these stories are going to need a lot of work to track down.

Stories are Telling

We are interested in which stories are told and which ones are not told, but also in who tells the stories. This is an epistemological and a political point. Our field (any field) will never be neutral or objective, but it may be more equitable when a wider range of voices are included, and when we work on the systemic forms of exclusion that have led to the centring of certain kinds of people, and thus certain kinds of questions. We will see some of the dramatic ways that the field changes when groups or political perspectives that were previously excluded or even repressed enter the field.

Therefore, we would like to lay out what we bring, and also what we don't bring, to this project. Our voices, too, will be inadequate for the task we have undertaken for ourselves in this book. We want to explain how and why we came to write this book, as well as think about what lacunae it may have as a result. We are white and able to speak English, and we are working at a major Canadian research university, so we can be understood to be of the centre. At the same time, our biographies each mark certain frailties in those central positions, and positions in some kinds of powerful peripheries as well.

We have an ambivalent relationship to the centres of thinking about linguistic anthropology and sociolinguistics. We write from, live in, and teach in and about Canada. Canada is a powerful periphery, a white settler colony shaped by the empires of Great Britain and France and their wars with each other, and engaged in ongoing negotiations with Indigenous groups; it is a neighbour to the United States imperial behemoth and a site for migration from many former colonies and other, less powerful, peripheries.

From Toronto, we see the workings of the U.S. and European markets intimately, but at the same time from a distance. The questions we ask, and that make sense to us in the context of our transnationally Canadian lives, don't quite fit their frames. Canadian lives are leaky—that is, their boundaries are not tight, and their content is fluid. The status of French and English in Canada minimally requires a recognition that there is knowledge production going on somewhere that maybe not everyone participates in. The increasing resurgence of Indigenous groups, and the rapidly changing notions of who counts as a "majority" in major cities, is also significant. We experience this daily where we live: in Toronto, 50 per cent of the population is classified as "foreign-born" (i.e. they are new migrants to Canada), and 47 per cent of the population is, problematically, called "visible minorities" in the 2006 Canadian census statistics (Good 2009, 42). In Toronto, we are also on the land called "Dish with One Spoon," a covenant for sharing resources between the Indigenous nations (Anishinaabe, Haudenosaunee, Wendat) who overlapped here in this place.

Neither one of us was born or raised in Toronto, though. Like so many others, we came here as adults, because this is where we got a job. We entered networks where most of the people we met had the same story, although the specifics differed. Here are ours.

Bonnie: I was born in 1966, the eldest of six sisters, and grew up on a farm in Western Pennsylvania in the United States, an area that is in the rolling foothills of Appalachia, but often doesn't understand itself as such. My mother was a secretary for Heinz (the major food industry company) before she married (her father didn't believe girls needed a university education), and a mother and active community volunteer after that (PTA president, adult literacy tutor, food bank coordinator …). My grandfather was a migrant from Slovakia who worked in the Pittsburgh steel mills all his life. His father, my great-grandfather, died in an industrial accident in the mills; when my grandfather was about 11, he was called in to identify the body. My father is from a family of 12, and co-owned a farm with two of his brothers; my Irish-American grandfather had bought it after losing money working in construction in Pittsburgh; he tried the mines and mills, and didn't like them, feeling confined by them.

Both sides of the family were Catholic, but seasonal or shift-based ones; work always took first priority. I have worked all my life, starting in Grade 5. I worked long days in the summer, starting at 4 in the mornings to pick corn to get it to retail markets, selling corn at a small roadside stand from 10 to 6, sometimes accompanying Dad or Uncle Spike or a cousin to sell corn in farmers' markets in Pittsburgh until 9 pm. I liked the corn stand best: I could read books there between customers. When there was work to be done, everyone was expected to chip in. Kids, adults, my elderly Aunt Belle. Still, there were moments when my male cousins were given certain privileges ("You jump up there and drive that truck"), and my sisters and I were angry, complaining to Mom. We were proud of how strong we were, after lifting sacks with five dozen ears of corn all summer long. Most holidays were a party at the farmhouse, with 100 or so people, virtually all of whom were aunts, uncles, or cousins; most everyone lived within walking distance.

I went to an almost exclusively white high school, in which the graduating class had 420 students, one of whom was black. The one black student seemed to survive in part by becoming a comedian; he performed at our high school prom. The high school was named Seneca Valley High School, after the Seneca Nation, who share this traditional territory with the Lenape, and it had (and still has, as many American high schools and universities do) an Indigenous[1] native mascot—controversial in many discussions now, never mentioned in that area then. Spring plowing on our farm often turned up stone points ("arrowheads"). The creek that runs through is the Connoquenessing (a Lenape word local historians say means "a long way straight").

I received a full academic scholarship to attend the University of Pittsburgh. My parents, and most of my aunts and uncles, didn't go to university; my sisters, and many of my cousins, did. Once Mom, and then I, cried, worried that the more immersed I was in university, the further away I would be, physically and emotionally, from my family.

These experiences with work led me to a focus on gender and working-class work in my dissertation, which was on attempts to transform a traditionally white, working-class workplace in Pittsburgh (the police department) with an affirmative action system that required hiring more black men, black women, and white women as officers. I patrolled with the police

---

[1] In this book we use a variety of terms to refer to indigenous peoples, including First Nations, Indigenous, and Native American. The terms in use have varied across time, and still vary across place, with, for example, different uses in Canada and the United States. In this book, we use "Indigenous" as the most widely accepted term in contemporary, international settings. However, because there is a history of usages, we also use "Native American" and "First Nations" or the name of the relevant nation/tribe where this is the term most relevant for the period and territory in question.

department for a year. The work remained a valuable, unionized job, attractive even to college graduates, in a deindustrializing, former steel city. I studied in France as an undergraduate, and had a Fulbright fellowship in Helsinki as a postdoc—these international experiences also decentred American traditions of learning.

I was interviewed for a Rhodes scholarship once, and was quiet and awkward at the reception where we were supposed to display our social ease—it felt competitive, empty, and shallow. I didn't grow up going to receptions. I remember a party at the house of John Bowen, my postdoctoral mentor, where his son, then about seven, introduced me to his little brother ("Bonnie, have you met …") with an ease and fluency that bespoke multiple such experiences. I had spent so much of my time before age 18 with extended family only.

I migrated to Canada when I received a job at the University of Toronto, a privileged migrant, though because I am white I am rarely addressed as an immigrant, and rapidly became a Canadian citizen. Being a mother has also shaped my work. My first post-maternity leave project looked at the work done by women travelling from the Philippines to care for other people's children, asking how American colonialism in the Philippines, especially health and educational discourses and interventions into Filipino child-rearing practices, had shaped these forms of migration.

Also relevant, in addition to these familial and intellectual geneaologies, are academic ones. Though I was drawn to philosophy and literature (and did undergraduate degrees in them), they still felt a bit frivolous for a farmer's daughter. The applications of sociolinguistics to social problems were more readily apparent, and allowed the same play with language. Linguistics seemed more democratic—open to a wider range of genres, and speech as well as writing. I did an undergraduate thesis on pidgins and creoles and international auxiliary languages at the University of Pittsburgh with Sarah Thomason, a historical linguist and specialist on pidgins and creoles; in the thesis I considered some of the ways ideologies and features of each were shaped by oral and written language norms. Later, I did graduate work at Stanford University with John Rickford, a specialist on pidgins and creoles, Penny Eckert, a feminist variationist, and Gregory Guy, a variationist interested in studies of class and phonology (all students of William Labov; see Chapter 7), as well as with Shirley Brice Heath (a student of Dell Hymes who works on literacy and literature, race, and class; see also Chapter 7). I benefited from being in the Bay Area; there was a rich community of graduate students and faculty at Stanford, Berkeley, and the University of California, Santa Cruz who regularly met at the Gender and Language conferences at Berkeley. We created our own community, our own sense of peer review, and our own venues for publication; I later was the founding co-editor of a new journal on gender and language that grew out of those conversations.

Monica: I was born in 1955 in Montréal, Québec, a city understood both as a cosmopolitan, multilingual metropole and as the cultural capital of a francophone Canadian (eventually "Québécois") nation. The east was French, the west was English, immigrants like my paternal grandparents came up the middle. Though the city is on traditional Mohawk territory, we whites learned to see the Mohawks as far away in time and place: depicted greeting the French in the paintings of Montréal history in the "chalet" at the top of the mountain, or understood to be unreachable on the reserve across the river.

My father's parents came to North America in the decade before World War I as part of the large wave of Yiddish-speaking Jews fleeing pogroms in Eastern Europe in the late nineteenth and early twentieth centuries. My mother arrived in 1940 with her family, having fled Nazi Germany through Switzerland and France. She and her sisters spoke German and French (their brother and their parents also spoke English, and their Warsaw-born mother spoke Polish and Russian as well). They had been schooled by Catholic nuns in Switzerland, and in a private school in Paris—only to find francophone Montréal closed off to them as Jews (and anglophone Montréal not exactly thrilled about them either; even Jews like those on my father's side of the family found them strange).

Education, then, was in English. It was also our job. My father, stereotypically for that second generation of North American Jewish males, became a doctor. Women were not exempted from the duty of educational success, albeit also crazy-makingly expected to take care of family and home. My paternal grandmother regularly dragged me by the upper arm into her bedroom for an inquisition about my grades (and eventually also about my boyfriends).

I grew up well aware of silences and absences. My paternal grandparents refused to talk about the places and the people they had left behind; family was limited to the siblings of my grandparents and their descendants. My mother's large, close-knit extended family was blown apart by Nazism. Many survived, but scattered quite literally around the globe. The central lesson transmitted to my generation was to learn whatever languages you have to, get a good education (they can't steal that), and be prepared to run. On my mother's side, this was underscored by a deep mistrust of mass movements, especially those animated by nationalism or religious fervour (turned equally on all religions, including Judaism). In this my father joined them, having become an atheist in a time and place where everyone had to have a religion, and having become involved in a variety of causes connected to what he felt he learned as a doctor; foremost among these was the struggle for socialized medicine and for the legalization of abortion.

This is the position from which I encountered the social movement against francophone inequality of the 1960s, known as the Quiet Revolution, though it wasn't always so quiet. Not firmly anchored on one side or the other, I sought to understand why the same events could be narrated so differently in English and in French, why no shared frame seemed available. I also had to figure out, as did everyone else, what language to speak to the bus driver. I must have become obsessed with this language thing, because one day my father brought me home a magazine featuring an article about Noam Chomsky. It turned out there was a discipline called "linguistics" that might have tools for grasping that kind of phenomenon.

I was lucky enough to be able to get the education in linguistics (and anthropology) that magazine held out for me (even though Chomsky, in the end, was not at all helpful for addressing the questions that were bothering me). I studied first at Swarthmore College and then at the University of California, Berkeley. That period at Berkeley was characterized by intense interdisciplinary collaboration among linguists, anthropologists, psychologists, and philosophers, allowing me to learn from such figures as my thesis supervisor, John Gumperz, the anti-Chomskyans George Lakoff and Charles Fillmore, the feminist linguist Robin Lakoff, the psychologist and theorist of bilingualism Susan Ervin-Tripp, and the philosopher of language as social action John Searle.

At the same time, in Montréal, I participated in sites of discussion on variationist sociolinguistics (Gillian Sankoff, at the Université de Montréal, generously allowed me to attend doctoral seminars and conferences) and language policy (through the sociolinguistics research department of the Québec language policy agency, l'Office de la langue française, where I was an intern for six months in 1978, mentored by Pierre Laporte and Denise Daoust). I also had access to flourishing Montréal-based work on the social psychology of bilingualism (notably by Wallace Lambert, Donald Taylor, and Taylor's student, Alison d'Anglejan). My thesis focused on the role of the state and Canadian political economy in shifting relations of ethnolinguistic/class power in the private sector, through an ethnography of a large factory owned by anglophones, with almost exclusively francophone workers (almost all male at all ranks).

I was unhappy with the traditional linguistic and anthropological academic mode of separating home, work, and field site, and headed back to Canada. For complicated reasons having everything to do with the political economy of language in Canada, I landed first a postdoc and then a job in Toronto. Teaching in French and English, I had to work to discover what had been going on in francophone Europe, and to compare what kinds of questions and approaches emerged in the literature in each language.

Since schooling was a key site of struggle for minority language rights, I spent a dozen years doing school ethnographies, which taught me about the role of schooling in social selection, and about the challenges to dominant ideas of nationhood presented first by immigration and by the integration of francophones into an increasingly globalized market, and by Indigenous struggles for sovereignty. This led to a long series of projects on the conditions that allow for or destabilize the production of discourses of language and nation in francophone Canada, all undertaken in close collaboration with teams of colleagues and students from across Canada and from Europe. My networks and my questions, like Bonnie's, shape and are shaped by how we intersect(ed) with questions of language and inequality on material terrains, and by how we were able to gather the wherewithal to be able to spend our lives asking them.

Bonnie and Monica: Each in our way, then, we have come to a certain critical stance on taken-for-granted principles of social organization, and the ideologies of language and culture, class, gender, race, and nation that legitimize them. Our institutional and national base has given us more affordances than obstacles in the end (after all, it is our university press that is publishing this book). We have brought slightly different sets of orientations and sensibilities to this project, in ways that have certainly shaped the selection of issues and cases. But both of us studied workplaces at moments of demographic change. And we share the fundamental goal set out above: to develop an approach to linguistic analysis in which political economy, social difference, and social inequality are at the centre.

The experience of writing this book has been eye-opening. We have more questions than when we started out, we know much more about what we don't know. Looking for the alternative genealogies has, of course, proved particularly difficult, since those are the ones that leave the fewest traces. But excavating has been exhilarating. As Leonard Cohen said: "There is a crack in everything, that's how the light gets in."

Toronto

CHAPTER 1

LANGUAGE, CAPITALISM, COLONIALISM: WALKING BACKWARD INTO THE FUTURE

FIGURE 1.1: Red thread world (© Amid | Dreamstime.com)

Language and Inequality: A Wary Approach to a Red Thread World

> So it is not, as people try here and there conveniently to imagine, that the economic position produces an automatic effect. Men make their history themselves, only in given surroundings which condition it and on the basis of actual relations already existing, among which the economic relations, however much they may be influenced by the other political and ideological ones, are still ultimately the decisive ones, forming the red thread which runs through them and alone leads to understanding. (Friedrich Engels 1894)

The core of this book is an account of how ideas about language play a central role in the making of social difference and social inequality. Our starting point is our present and our future: we are looking for ways to understand what is happening around us now, and to develop the tools we need in order to participate in making our world more equitable—and therefore safer. To get there we need to go first to the past, in order to understand how it came to pass that we have inherited both specific conceptual tools and the conditions that make us want to use and refine them, or possibly pick up or make new tools altogether.

But we are wary of a linear, progress-oriented understanding of the relationship between past and present. We conceptualize our approach here as "walking backward into the future." We draw this formulation from three frameworks that mean, precisely, to unpack capitalist and colonial logics from different sites around the world that are inspired by radical hope. Each offers tools for what it means to critically approach space, time, and subjectivity, to think about decolonizing each of these. Each, also, sees language as central to this project. They are linked to the Welsh Marxist, Raymond Williams; the Jamaican decolonial thinker, artist and visionary, Sylvia Wynter; and the Anishinaabe philosophies linked to the Great Lakes. We will consider each of these, in due course, in this chapter.

The Marxist literary critic Raymond Williams (1921–88), in his book *Resources of Hope* (1989), has an essay titled "Walking Backwards into the Future." He notes that often the future refers to an idealized past—rehabilitation, rebuilding, recovery—such that a better future is often linked to a return to the past. He writes that we need to face how this is linked with Christian ideals of the fall of man. Instead, he says, we need other ways to imagine a better future, ones with a different understanding of the past. We therefore turn Williams's title to our own purposes. We look for the red threads, in the sense of the key ideas about language that have been turned to the making of social difference and social inequality through the stories that have unfolded over various times and places.

We also look at the red threads in the substantive way in which Engels defines them, although understood somewhat differently. Without understanding economic forces as wholly determinist, we nonetheless note the ways that certain moments in capitalism have global, interconnected, and near simultaneous effects in a range of sites, a clustering that needs to be accounted for (see also Williams 1977, for an approach that has deeply influenced us). These clusterings are often visible in, indeed played out on the terrain of, language. But it is not enough, in our view, to track what people thought and said and did about language. We also need to explain why.

Our assumption is that people have an interest in language because it has value, and it has value because it is tied to how all kinds of resources are produced, circulated, and consumed, including how they are identified as resources at all. We need therefore to look at the nature of the economic and political activities in which language is bound up. In order to understand our present conditions, we need to situate them in the intermeshed histories of capitalism and colonialism. The book is therefore structured to take us loosely, bumpily, unevenly, from the ways in which imperial mercantile capitalism rendered language salient, through industrial capitalism, nationalism, and colonialism, to late capitalism and the globalized new economy, its dislocations and backlashes, and its creative possibilities.

The challenge here is to understand how exactly language gets bound up in more complex circulations and exchanges. We will follow two threads: the first has to do with how language can act as a *resource*, and therefore how it is used to make boundaries that help produce, reproduce, or contest the unequal distribution of other kinds of resources. The second has to do with its role in *legitimation*, that is, helping such inequities not only make sense, but also seem like the only, or the best, way to do things.

Our search for explanations in political economic conditions has led us to the interlocking stories of colonialism and capitalism. To understand how we got to today, we take these as the central formations for the organization of social and material relations of production and distribution of resources, and of people, and of how and by whom they are valued. Embedding language in histories of colonialism and capitalism helps us to illuminate how inequities are constructed, and sometimes deconstructed, on the terrain of, or through, language. It helps illuminate where and how attempts to change these structures have been constrained or obstructed, and where they have succeeded. It helps us understand where our own ideas come from, and what they are connected to, and so what might happen if we follow some threads of the intertwined conditions of our lives, rather than others.

We examine how capitalism and colonialism, working together as an uneven and shifting world system, have made possible and salient particular ways of mobilizing language in the production of inequality and the social differences that legitimize it. We look to discursive struggle, resistance, and change. As we show, the chronology is not linear, and effects on the making of difference and inequality are unevenly spatialized; there are often contradictory and always complex struggles over things that count. Indeed, they often end up being double-edged or ambivalent, as ideas meant to be emancipatory have the unintended consequence of shoring up existing inequalities or making new ones, while ideas meant to be conservative unexpectedly sometimes create openings for resistance and emancipatory social change.

In this chapter we take up each of the points that form the basis of our understanding of how language, colonialism, and capitalism intersect, and lay the foundation for the structure of the book. This backward walk into the future will show us language in many forms. People have different ideas about what language is: a part of our core identity, an attribute of social groups, the working of our brain, and so on. People have notions about what constitutes good or bad, admirable or deficient, polite or aggressive language, whether it is better to speak one language or many. Language has been thought of as a divine gift, as something inherently human and that distinguishes us from animals, or conversely as something shared by all living things. It has been understood as an autonomous system, as a cognitive process, as a technique for mechanical communication, as a social practice. It has been thought of as located in the brain, the soul, nature, and the divine; as a property of the self, of the nation, of humanity, of the universe. But there are reasons why people think these things, in certain places and certain times. Those reasons are connected not just to how we make sense abstractly, but also to how our sense-making allows us to organize ourselves socially, politically, and economically.

Red Flags: Keywords, Hegemonies, Ideologies, and Warty Genealogies

Our approach relies on three main strategies: a focus on *keywords*, on *ideologies* and *hegemonies*, and on *genealogies*. The notion of keyword comes from Raymond Williams ([1976] 1983), who uses the term to identify words that are particularly useful for thinking about how important and social historical processes occur *through* language. Keywords act as red flags, showing where the people with stakes in the game are located, and indeed where the game is taking place. They can therefore also act as red threads, insofar as they link the actors and debates with stakes in the game, helping us uncover what those stakes are, and so what the game is. We follow Williams's ([1976] 1983) lead in tying keywords to "structures of feeling"; feeling is what makes the social and moral orders stick (Eagleton 1991). Williams argues that to understand keywords we need to focus on social rather than personal experience with regard to the institutions, formations, and positions that make experience what it is: part of processes of structuration (see also Giddens 1982).

Let's take one example from debates unfolding as we completed this book: "alt-right," a term that emerged in the United States in 2016 to describe an alliance of right-wing groups largely supportive of the presidential candidacy of Donald Trump. In an article published in the *Globe and Mail* (one of Canada's main English-language newspapers) on November 25, 2016, after Donald Trump was elected to the U.S. presidency, the journalist Sylvia Stead cites the writer Marian Botsford Fraser, who calls "alt-right" a deceptive term:

> "This is not a benign descriptive adjective. It is a euphemism that apparently has been accepted by mainstream media as nothing more than an identifier or description.... To use it as such, without signaling its true meaning, is careless journalism," [Botsford] wrote in an e-mail. "In a very short time, the phrase 'alt-right' has become the new normal, defining the terms for a highly contentious debate, just as the phrase 'pro-life' does." (Stead 2016)

Stead's editorial attracted 32 comments. Some were vitriolic, lambasting Stead as a "Bolshevic" (sic), "raging anarchist," and "socialist," and a believer in "extreme liberalism, feminism, progressive-destructive ideology." Others argued that one couldn't call 50 per cent of Americans White racists: "Assigning derogatory labels for those you disagree with is simply a propaganda effort, a tool designed to suppress critical thought and one that is unfortunately employed just as much by the left as the right." These posters wanted to argue that "alt-right" described extremists, the KKK supporters who tipped the scale for Trump, but weren't the bulk of his support. An interesting minor strand of posters asked what the "alt-left" might designate. Social justice warriors, said some.

As a result, the editor-in-chief of the *Globe and Mail* announced a new policy. While noting that the term "alt-right" had been used numerous times in the paper up until that point, he stipulated that henceforth it should be avoided, and if used, explained. To do otherwise, he said, is to accord legitimacy to White supremacy, to assist it in its own propaganda work. He noted, further, that "the precision of language, married with facts, is the most effective weapon the journalist has to hold people to account. This is never more keenly felt than at times of polarized debate. Adjectives should be used sparingly, and only when the journalist actually knows the subject. It is too easy to slide into caricature at precisely the point the audience is seeking objectivity" (Stead 2016).

Here "alt-right" acts as a red flag, a keyword: its use and its meaning are contested. By tracing the debates around it we can find out why it raises strong feelings, of what kind, and for what kinds of people. It points to a conflict over something profound: a vision of society, a struggle over who makes the rules, and for whom, specifically whether racism is systemic or lodged only in certain individuals. It also involves language in more than one way; not only is it materially a piece of language in and of itself, but also what is contested is its use, its form, and to what other linguistic practices it is tied. Indeed, it helps us understand the fundamental ideas about language that people have, and therefore why language is important to them; for example, to the editor of the *Globe and Mail*, avoiding adjectives is tied to an important understanding of the role of the media in society (providing "objectivity").

Objectivity is sometimes contrasted with *ideology*, as here, with ideology thus constructed as something false. Linguistic anthropologists, too, have used a number of different definitions of ideology (see Woolard 1998 for one review), especially since the 1990s (see Kroskrity 2000; Schieffelin et al. 1998); while some see such multiplicity as a strength, insofar as it makes it possible for many forms of scholarship to meet on this ground, we think it dilutes the concept's analytic utility. We are also concerned that some work in language ideology simply substituted notions of ideology for culture, with little analytic difference. However, a significant strand of this work examined how the *legitimation* of inequity occurs, challenging overly reductionist accounts of the manipulation of people by ruling class interests (Rickford and Rickford 2000; Smitherman 2000; Spears 1999; Zentella 1997). We draw, too, on European work in *critical discourse analysis* emerging at around the same time and focussed on deconstructing the dominant discourses of the state and its agencies (Fairclough 1989, 1992; Fairclough and Wodak 1997; van Dijk 1991; Wodak 1996; Wodak and Richardson 2013).

The conversations engendered at this moment were enabled by a number of converging processes. One was the civil rights and decolonization movements beginning in the 1960s, and the recognition of the limitations of the response of sociolinguistics at the time. Linked to this was the emerging critique of notions of *culture* heretofore dominant in anthropology and linguistics, increasingly seen as overly bounded, as homogenizing difference, and as continuing to place certain groups "outside of time" (Abu Lughod 1993; Fabian 1983; Ortner 2003). Another process was a certain loosening of the strictures of the early Cold War (see Chapter 6) in both the United States and the Soviet Union, which meant that key works by communist linguists became available in English for the most part in the 1970s and 1980s, though they had long been familiar to European communist intellectuals, especially French ones (see Chapter 7).[1] We find ourselves now at another moment of change in relations of power, one in which much of this work remains deeply useful.

Building on this work, we orient to Williams's perspective on ideology, in which the concept needs to be understood as "different formations and distributions of energy and interest" ([1976] 1983, 11) that tie different meanings to the same words. With Williams, Terry Eagleton (1991), and Susan Philips (1998), we agree that the notion of ideology is most useful when used to discuss relations of power; ideologies, in this sense, can be seen as ideas associated with certain groups. Eagleton (1991) ties ideology specifically to the ideas that legitimate dominant political powers; we would extend the notion to the legitimation of any form of power (or attempt at it), and link it necessarily to discourses and practices that constitute their expression and their workings, whether they are explicit or implicit, and whether held by those who benefit most, or, in ways that may be harder to explain, by those who do not benefit much at all.

We will be particularly interested in the recurring intersection of ideologies of language, class, race, gender, sexuality, humanity, and nation. We therefore draw on the insights of work on language ideologies in several ways. One is its focus on *positionality*, *multiplicity*, and *awareness*. The concept of *positionality* is part of the wider approach we mentioned above to thinking about standpoint, and about the provincialization of broad claims to authoritative accounts that were triggered by decolonization and other movements for social justice in the 1960s. By the 1980s, influenced by such critics as Edward Said (1978), anthropologists began looking critically at the role their discipline played in colonialism, and at the effect of their work in the production of colonialism's subjects and subjection. Scientific attempts at producing "neutral" or "universal" or "objective" knowledge became more difficult to sustain, triggering a

---

1 Gramsci's *Prison Notebooks* were smuggled out of prison in the 1930s, but not published until the 1950s and not translated until 1971 (see Gramsci 1971). Valentin Vološinov's *Marxism and the Philosophy of Language*, written in the 1920s, was translated in 1973. Lev Vygotsky's work, much of it written in the 1920s, was translated in the early 1960s, but its impact was felt first in psychology, and had little impact on linguistic anthropology until *Mind in Society* appeared in English in 1978. Mikhail Bakhtin's book, *The Dialogic Imagination*, was a collection of essays written in the 1930s and 1940s that were collected and translated in 1981; his *Speech Genres and Other Late Essays* (a set of essays written across his life span) was published in the late 1970s in Russian, and translated in 1986 (Bakhtin 1992).

broad move to understand where the core ideas of our discipline come from, and what kinds of conflict they might flag.

The concept of *multiplicity* follows from the observation that societies are never homogeneous. Indeed, the discipline of linguistic anthropology stems, as we shall show, from a long-standing concern with linguistic and social diversity as a phenomenon to be described, in order to control it. If societies are heterogeneous, and traversed by relations of power, there are multiple positionalities possible, and multiple ideologies. The question is how some become hegemonic and others marginalized or erased; how at times many frames can coexist even if they may partly overlap or contradict each other, and how others work hard to reduce them to a hegemonic centre.

A linguistic ideological approach also asks questions about *awareness*, including which aspects of language and social life people tend to focus on, and why and how. This includes challenging the distinction between expert and lay analysis, asking analysts to identify their own positions, histories, and ideologies. Such an account needs to ask both why such questions are being asked by those who are asking them, and why those questions are arising at a particular moment, in ways that go beyond intellectual histories, to thinking about political and economic ones.

Most importantly, we aim to understand which assemblages emerge as contested space, and where keywords might instead signal *hegemonies*. We ask how it comes to pass that certain ways of understanding and acting in the world get naturalized, taken for granted, as the best or only way things can unfold, even when they produce conditions that may not be good for everyone. Here we draw on the work of Antonio Gramsci (1891–1937), Sardinian Italian, linguist educator, and journalist. He was also the founder and one-time leader of the Communist Party in Italy, and was imprisoned by the Italian fascist regime from 1926 to 1937. He wrote regularly in prison, with scattered writings smuggled out and later collected as *The Prison Notebooks* (Gramsci 1971).

Gramsci argued that there are two major routes to domination: *coercion* and *consent*, and that ruling classes govern with both. Coercion involves naked force, which usually triggers naked opposition. Consent involves convincing all participants in relations of domination that things are the way they should be; achieving such consent requires shared frames of interpretation, and thus is a profoundly cultural and communicative process. Gramsci's notion of *cultural hegemony* suggests how ruling interests elaborate as "common sense" ideas that support their own position.

As a linguist and a Sardinian living in northern Italy at the crucial juncture of its industrialization, Gramsci was well placed to appreciate the place of language in the elaboration of cultural hegemony. He experienced directly the domination of northern Italy, and of standard Italian, in the making of southern Italians as deficient and as exploitable workers. Under equivalent conditions, others linked (and still link) resistance to centralized state domination to minority nationalism, including linguistic minority nationalism, socialist or otherwise, and to the valuing of the vernacular. Gramsci took the position that, on the contrary, the development of workers and their access to a position of power required investment in dominant language literacy. He argued:

> If it is true that every language contains the elements of a conception of the world and of a culture, it could also be true that from anyone's language one can assess the greater or lesser complexity of his conceptions of the world. Someone who only speaks dialect, or understands the standard language incompletely, necessarily has an intuition of the world which is more or less limited and provincial, which is fossilised and anachronistic in relation to the major currents of thought which dominate world history. His interests will be limited, more or less corporate and economistic, not universal. (1971, 325)

In order to be an actor on the world stage at this particular historical moment, Gramsci was saying, workers and peasants, who are the speakers of the dialects, had to both share a language and own the national language, since it was on national stages that contemporary struggles were being carried out. That language must spread out (diffuse) from urban centres of modern life, he argued, building on a concept of linguistic diffusion characteristic of his professors' positions on language change.

Gramsci's specific ideas about language have to be understood in the context of the prevailing political and economic conditions of his time, as they connect to prevailing debates about language; not surprisingly, those are not necessarily the ones we share for our place and our time. But we do share his notion that language is a key site for the making of consent and for exploring its complex connection to coercion. Indeed, as Susan Gal (1989) notes, a number of Marxist scholars through the twentieth century have discussed the same concerns using different terms (she looks at the work of Gramsci and Williams, but also Valentin Vološinov and Pierre Bourdieu): "Whether the term is *hegemony, symbolic domination, oppositional culture, subjugated discourse*, or *heteroglossia*, the central insight remains: Control of the representations of reality is not only a source of social power but therefore also a likely locus of conflict and struggle" (348).

Attending to keywords, structures of feeling, ideologies, and hegemony requires a detailed attention not only to discursive form and practice, but also to history, politics, and economy (see also Richard and Rudnyckyj 2009). Intellectual histories of ideas often describe *what* happened, with an implicit argument that ideas change because of the way rational scientific debates proceed; instead, we are interested here in understanding *why* and *when* certain ideas happen, with an explicit argument that ideas also change because material and symbolic conditions for making their meaning and value change.

Throughout, we have opted for the telling case over any pretense at exhaustivity. While our account is a loose chronology, we prefer to think of it as taking the form of *genealogies*, which we approach as stories to be told about how and why ideas—in this case about language—become important, contested, circulated, powerful, modified, marginalized, and erased in ways which are far from linear.

While we explicitly eschew the Great Person theory of history, a genealogical approach leads us to be interested in the agency of social actors. As a result, we explore how the biographies of some key figures help us understand why they entered the field at all, and why certain ideas about language make sense to a person with that kind of life experience—as we did above regarding Antonio Gramsci. (This is why we have provided the birth and death dates of the figures we discuss, as a rough way of situating people within political economic formations.)

Since we believe knowledge is socially produced, we need to figure out who is (and is not) doing the producing. This history of social approaches to language may feel unfamiliar to those who have read other accounts. Figures that are central in those accounts may take up a more liminal role, or be more critically understood; figures that are marginal, or erased, from other accounts become more central. Some of the stories we include here may not be familiar, but that does not mean they are new: often, they have been told, but by scholars not widely heard or in places not often frequented by many of us. Sometimes the stories were well known at one moment, but have been forgotten. Sometimes the stories are hard to tell because they reveal warts on major figures in the field; sometimes they are hard to find. Sometimes people are wary of telling the stories because of forms of interrogation, repression, or surveillance that they have been subjected to in the past. Sometimes those who conducted the surveillance do not want to share the stories.

In that respect, we owe a great intellectual debt to the work of Richard Bauman and Charles Briggs (2003). Their book, *Voices of Modernity: Language Ideologies and the Politics of Inequality*, examines how particular features of European ideologies were cast as universal features of the world, in ways that foreclosed new modes of thinking and certain acts of political resistance through the twentieth century. They showed how certain texts, once seen as dusty and remote artifacts of intellectual history, were "in close dialogue with those demons that haunted us in the late twentieth century. Hobbes, Locke, Herder, and their kin seemed to be sitting in the room with us as we read. And their presence did not always seem like that of a trusted ally" (2003, ix).

Bauman and Briggs unpack the ways that scholars of language, especially English, German, and American ones (such as Francis Bacon, John Locke, Hugh Blair, Johann Gottfried Herder, the brothers Wilhelm and Jacob Grimm, Henry Rowe Schoolcraft, and Franz Boas), participated in the hegemonic construction of modernity over and against a constructed pre-modernity linked with labourers, the illiterate, country people, women, and residents of Asia, Africa, and the Americas. Indeed, they show how many such scholars, then and now often construed as progressive, contributed to this binary. Drawing on the work of Dipesh Chakrabarty (2000) and Partha Chatterjee (2010), they work to provincialize the West by showing how the putatively universal ideas about language and tradition were historically produced, and by identifying the work that was invested in constructing them as universal.

Bauman and Briggs, concerned that readings were less productive when they moved too quickly between authors, texts, places, and periods, chose admirably to undertake extended, subversive discussions of a small group of authors. Our work thus complements theirs because we have taken the opposite tack, with the lacunae that accompany that attempt to make linkages across a number of contexts, and to hold the hegemonic and the marginalized in the same frame. Drawing on the work of Hannah Arendt (1906–75), we are interested in exploring how tracing language ideologies helps us discover how imperial and colonial ideologies and practices are intertwined not just with the elaboration of liberal democratic capitalist regimes, but also fascist and communist ones (Arendt [1951] 1968). We aim at understanding not just the elaboration of modernity/pre-modernity, but a finer-grained account.

We also owe an intellectual debt to the European traditions, especially in Catalonia, France, and Britain, which have long used sociolinguistics to engage problems of social inequality and social conflict. The role of the Communist Party in sustaining the postwar anti-fascist movement was crucial in this respect. As we mentioned above, in some cases the concern for social inequality was tied to discourses of decolonization, of particular interest to minoritized peripheries in places like Catalunya and Occitanie (we will discuss the work of Lluis Aracil and Robert Lafont in Chapter 7), and increasingly tied to decolonization-related labour migration and the linking of race, language, and class. In other spheres, the labour struggles at the end of the welfare state drew the attention of French sociolinguists (such as Josiane Boutet, Bernard Gardin, and Jacques Brès), and decolonization itself was a key concern for the former colonies of France that were directly integrated into the French state. These are traditions that explicitly link language to emancipation, and understand sociolinguistics as a necessarily political endeavour. Our effort here is to bring that sensibility into a historicizing frame, one that links nation to empire, over space as well as over time.

Language Out of Place

These critical approaches to Europe show it is impossible to write only local, regional, or national histories (Braudel 1967, 1979a, 1979b; Fabian 1986; Hobsbawm 1987; Tsing 1994; Wallerstein 1974, 1980, 1989, 2011; Wolf [1982] 1997). We have always been global. Those global connections need to be understood as inscribed in relations of power, and imperial centres have a stake in obscuring precisely this. Some people get to tell the stories; other people do not. The stories that get told reflect specific perspectives about who we are, who others are, about who belongs where. We inevitably write from some centres, and account therefore for certain points of view while being inattentive to others. But we try also to write against taking them for granted. In this endeavour we try to take on the call of the literary critic Edward Said (1935–2003) to see how language has played a role in legitimizing empire.

Said's (1978) book, *Orientalism*, catalyzed a new wave of studies of colonialism that considered how imperial domination needed to be understood not just through political and military histories, but also through the role that knowledge and culture played in elaborating ideas of a distinct "us" and "them." He argues that colonialism is implicated in, and indeed drove, the development of such disciplines as history, literary studies, anthropology, medicine, geography, and linguistics. For Said, one of the most developed forms of Orientalism is linked to philology.

Said's insights were enabled by the ways in which he felt *Out of Place* (the title of his 2000 memoir). This is a generative phrase for us. As we will see, many critical linguistic insights are generated from people who are considered out of place or are displaced; the biographies articulate political economic and epistemological insights in complex ways. Said was a Palestinian Arab born in the British Mandate of Jerusalem to Christian parents, and lived in Cairo and Jerusalem until he was sent to the United States for further education. He had an Arab family name, but a British first name (his mother admired Edward VIII, the Prince of Wales) and an American passport (his father also was American, because of military service in World War 1). He was trained at Victoria College, a school in Egypt that was meant to educate an English-speaking elite in the Middle East for rule after decolonization (a classmate became King Hussein of Jordan). He describes his linguistic experience there:

> [T]he school's first rule, emblazoned on the opening page of the handbook, read: "English is the language of the school; students caught speaking any other language will be punished." Yet, there were no native speakers of English among the students. Whereas the masters were all British, we were a motley crew of Arabs of various kinds, Armenians,

Greeks, Italians, Jews, and Turks, each of whom had a native language that the school had explicitly outlawed. Yet all, or nearly all, of us spoke Arabic—many spoke Arabic and French—and so we were able to take refuge in a common language, in defiance of what we perceived as an unjust colonial stricture. (Said 2000, 556-57)

To be colonized, he said, was to be made Other, inferior in ways that legitimized imperial rule over bodies and land, subject to someone else's ways of being. He points out, though, that at the same time colonization usually also unfolded in ways that failed to be completely hegemonic—that forgot or was unable to notice, for instance, that Arabic might be available as a space for alternative modes of being and thinking.

In the chapters that follow, we will see the military enforcement of colonialism, the enslavement of Africans, genocide against colonized populations and Jewish ones, and the interrogation or incarceration of progressive and critical scholars in Italy, the Soviet Union, and the United States. But we will also see revolutionaries overturn the aristocracy in France and new world creoles challenge British, French, Dutch, and American power, we will see working class social movements in Europe attempting to define new linguistic norms, and we will see the civil rights, feminist, and environmental movements in the United States and elsewhere shape new ways of approaching language.

Many scholars have thought about what it takes for spaces to turn into sites for making alternative worlds, radically other and elsewhere, or decolonized and here (see Césaire 2000; Fanon [1952] 1967; Grimshaw 1992). A range of anti-racist, anti- or decolonial, socialist, feminist, and queer scholars are working on the importance of imagining futures, and holding on to hope (Ahmed 2010; Berardi 2011; Berlant 2011; Gibson-Graham 2006; Hage 2002; Harney and Moten 2013; Harvey 2000; Jameson 2005; Muñoz 2009; Narotzky and Besnier 2014; L. Simpson 2011, 2013; Wynter and McKittrick 2015). Many scholars argue in particular that it is necessary to recentre in order to rethink.

Here we return to thinking about walking backward into the future. We draw from decolonial Caribbean thinker Sylvia Wynter (1928–), who is thinking precisely about what it means for those who have been uprooted to become linked to a place, which she calls *becoming Indigenous*. She argues that we need to give humanness a different future by giving it a different past (Wynter and McKittrick 2015, 70). Arguing that the Caribbean is the crucible of modernity— the site where enslaved Africans intermingled with occupying Europeans, Indigenous peoples, and the indentured labourers recruited from Asia—she argues, also, that the ex-slave archipelago is thus a crucial site for thinking what new versions of the human might be (McKittrick 2015, 2). This work introduces a diasporic perspective, too, into thinking about language. Wynter, alongside many others, argues that thinking about and from the perspective of "those cast out as impoverished and colonized and undesirable and lacking reason—can, and do[es], provide a way to think about being human anew" (McKittrick 2015, 3), to move beyond *just existing* to a *just existence*. And she asks what kinds of discursive work need to be done to achieve this (see also Mignolo 2015, 112). Contemporary Indigenous and environmentalist scholars are also deeply involved in rethinking the axes of differentiation (Gal 1991) that legitimized colonialism, calling into question the binaries of human versus nature and reason versus emotion that have led to the destruction of people, places, and indeed all living things (Kohn 2013; McGregor 2015; L. Simpson 2011, 2014; Wohlleben 2015).

Mignolo (2015, 119) notes that for Sylvia Wynter every history is a *history-for*. Throughout this book, we think about what conventional histories of linguistics, sociolinguistics, and linguistic anthropology do. Wynter concludes that we can move beyond *homo economicus* with its focus on distinctive human skills; she calls for a new "Science of the Word," where humans are not confined to their present analytic categories, but are verbs, living relationally. She rethinks being human as praxis, in order not just to describe how people are, but to imagine what they might be.

Let's end this section with an attempt to see what else is going on in the place from which we write, and to which we came in the context of the very genealogies we try to unpack here. This is, also, our third approach to thinking about walking backward into the future. We write from the watershed of the Great Lakes, a series of interconnected freshwater lakes in the centre-east portion of North America, that contain approximately 20 per cent of the world's surface freshwater. As we understand it, Indigenous perspectives on this place ask us to recognize that even as we move around, we are always drinking the water somewhere, living on the land somewhere. They ask us therefore to think about what it means to be in a place, and to acknowledge a wider range of agents and forms of communication than our usual way of placing something called "humans" at the centre. Humans, in this view, are people, but so too are fish, and water (McGregor 2015; Todd 2014).

We learn also that Indigenous perspectives on the place we write from situate us in a long story of movement and migration. Potawatomi biologist Robin Wall Zimmerer (2013) describes a seven-fire prophecy that predicted, as it now describes, the migration history of the Anishinaabe people, up the St. Lawrence and around the Great Lakes.[2] The route prophesied, and taken,

---

2 We draw only on published accounts of this prophecy by Indigenous scholars of the Great Lakes. We recognize there may be further meanings and histories attached to these accounts, to which, as nonindigenous scholars, we are not privy.

goes from the Atlantic Ocean to Montréal (first fire), then to the shores of Lake Huron near what is now Detroit (second fire), then to Manitoulin Island and other places with wild rice (third fire), marks the arrival of the *zaaganaash* (the offshore, or light-skinned people) in what first appeared to be brotherhood (fourth fire), laments the arrival of black robes and books preaching salvation but severing connections with the sacred (fifth fire), and records the attempt to eliminate Anishinaabe people and teachings through separation from homelands, parents, languages, and culture (sixth fire).

In Wall Zimmerer's interpretation, it is now the moment of the seventh fire, and "the people of the Seventh Fire do not yet walk forward; rather, they are told to turn around and retrace the steps of the ones who brought us here. Their sacred purpose is to walk back along the red road of our ancestors' path and to gather up all the fragments that lay scattered along the trail. Fragments of land, tatters of language, bits of songs, stories, sacred teachings— all that was dropped along the way" (368–69). The task of the moment, says Wall Zimmerer, is "to find the tools that allow us to walk into the future," tools that we can find so long as the land and water endure and we try to regenerate people who have humility and the ability to listen and learn (370). Those tools are needed for lighting the eighth fire, according to Anishinaabe scholar, musician, poet, and storyteller Leanne Simpson (2008, 14). That fire is an everlasting fire of peace that can be lit by all humans, but that depends on our actions today. Learning to regenerate people will ultimately mean transforming our ideas about what language is or can do. In accord with this attention to the import of eight, in the following section we offer an overview of the eight chapters of this book, which have helped shape what is possible, and needed, today.

Knotted Histories: Following the Threads through the Book

Our account begins in the fifteenth century because this is the moment when "[t]he several continents would be drawn into one worldwide system of connections" (Wolf [1982] 1997, 129). From that point on, actions in one part of the world would have repercussions for all of the others. Lowe (2015) has called this "the intimacies of four continents" (Lowe counts the Americas as one continent). Mignolo (2015) argues that the year 1492 is a turning point in the history of the world, a bifurcation of history in which what it means to be human is changed, with particularly compelling implications for Africans who were enslaved or killed, Indigenous people who were displaced or changed or killed, and Spanish Jews who were converted, expelled, or killed. We would add that it is a moment at which the meaning of Islam also changes, as Muslims are driven from the Iberian peninsula. 1492 is the date, Mignolo writes,

> that marked the expulsion from paradise, it is the date that prompted the advent and the formation of coloniality or the colonial matrix of power and modern/colonial racism and contemporary articulations of race and racism, and it is the date through which the invention of the modern/colonial Other ascended. (2015, 111)

We will return in Chapter 2 to thinking more about Lowe's notion of "intimacy," as well as a lengthier consideration of why the fifteenth century was the moment at which these connections occurred, since, for a long time, Europe was not of much account in the affairs of the wider world (Wolf [1982] 1997, 71). Here, we will simply sketch how the book unfolds from this moment.

The core of this book is organized in a point/counterpoint structure, with three chapters (2, 4, and 6) laying out the making of difference and inequality in imperial mercantile capitalism, national and colonial industrial capitalism, and the Cold War welfare state, and the chapters that follow each of them showing key critiques of those productions. The notion of reading *contrapuntally* comes from Said's (1993) book *Culture and Imperialism*, in which he argues for an approach that can bring together experiences that have been taken to be discrepant, with separate agendas, internal structures, and external histories as a way of acknowledging "the massively knotted and complex histories of special but nevertheless overlapping and interconnected experiences—of women, of Westerners, of Blacks, of national states and cultures" (32) elaborated in colonial histories, and that need to be understood for decolonial ones. In these chapters, we explore how certain critiques attempt to undo certain kinds of inequities, but others sometimes extend or deepen or transform them. The final chapter is itself contrapuntal: it looks at ideas about language, social difference, and inequality under neoliberalizing finance capitalism, but also key challenges to these.

In the first pair of chapters (2 and 3), we consider *Language, Intimacy, and Empire*. We start with colonial expansion in the sixteenth century and some of the ideologies of hierarchical intimacy and affinity associated with early contacts, ideologies that were challenged as imperial control developed a more formal political structure in the nineteenth century and evolutionary ideologies supported hardened racial boundaries. Chapter 2 offers an insight into how language was dramatically reconceived, and at moments restructured, at two imperial moments shaped by mercantile capitalism (in the sixteenth and seventeenth centuries) and the heyday of formal imperialism (the late nineteenth and early twentieth centuries). It uses the figure and work of Edward Said to frame its attempt to hold the metropole and the periphery—the West and the "other" it created—in the same frame. Both of the imperial moments studied here used structures of feeling—of Christian love or familial relationship—to manage understandings of colonial intimacy and hierarchy.

The first case study focusses mainly on how missionary linguists from sixteenth-century Spain debated whether to use Indigenous languages or not in the New World and in the Philippines to accomplish conversion. The decision to use them required shaping both Spanish and Indigenous languages in ways that would make conversion possible. Since at the core of the issue was the Latin text of the Bible, these discussions were closely linked to debates about how to understand orality and literacy, alphabetic writing and other forms of writing, and debates about the role of Latin in shaping accurate grammars of Indigenous language.

The second case looks at the rise of comparative philology in the context of the relationship between eighteenth- and nineteenth-century India and Britain, in particular the work of British colonial administrators and linguists influenced by the encounter with the linguistic tradition of Pāṇini. It examines the senses of intimacy and hierarchy created through analyses of written languages carried out by such scholars as Sir William Jones, a British colonial administrator, grouping them into what were understood as language families. It shows us the central techniques of linguistic regimentation of the period. These include the makings of comparative word lists, tree diagrams and grammars in a project that was at once one of commensuration and boundary-making. Tree diagrams in particular allowed for a secularization of biblical lines of descent, in parallel with the shift from the divine authority that legitimized royalty to the rise of the bourgeoisie. Languages and peoples needed to be understood in the same frame for governance and conversion to be possible, that is, mappable using the same techniques.

Chapter 3 serves as a counterpoint to Chapter 2 by examining three different kinds of challenges to comparative philology. The first extends from the notion of the family tree, but embeds it in evolutionary theory, a radically different understanding of language change. Evolutionary understandings of language privileged biological difference over and against notions of similarity and affinity, using such differences to hierarchically rank groups of speakers along scales of progress. The hardening of notions about racial difference meant that sites of purported mixture were of particular interest—as a sign of degeneracy to some, as a challenge to evolutionary and genetic ideas for others. The second case, the start of the study of pidgins and creoles, is thus a direct challenge to notions of family trees since these languages were understood as "mixed" languages not legible within genealogical or genetic relationships—and thus inherently threatening to rule legitimized on the basis of racial and linguistic hierarchies of civilization, progress, and modernity. The third challenge is early-twentieth-century critiques of racism and evolutionary accounts by anthropologist Franz Boas and his students. While Boas mounted direct attacks on both, his work nonetheless was based on a notion of time that distinguished the pre-modern from the modern, and on a notion of linguistics that privileged the scientific approach over speakers' understandings. Both resulted in a separation of language from race in ways that inscribed Indigenous peoples in a timeless past destined to disappear, and African Americans in a White, middle-class understanding of civilization. All of these are articulated alongside the rise of industrial capitalism and the intensification, extension, and elaboration of imperial rule. The work of Benjamin Whorf on linguistic relativity elaborates a spiritual, rational, and romantic challenge to some of the forms of alienation experienced under these conditions.

In the second pair of chapters, *The Contradictions of Language in Industrial Capitalism*, we move to the development of nation-states understood as modern in the nineteenth and twentieth centuries, as well as attending to fascist, communist, and universalist responses to the inequities and contradictions such nations created. Chapter 4 examines industrial capitalism and European imperialism from a different angle than Chapter 3, by discussing the rise of bourgeois nationalism and various language technologies for making nations as markets. It describes the tension between two ideologies used to legitimize nation-states: ideologies of the Enlightenment, with a focus on reason, and Romanticism, with a focus on soul and essence. Technologies discussed include the rise of censuses, language standardization, dictionaries, grammars, and literary canons, and conventions of interaction in schooling, as well as the study of linguistic variation across time and space as a problem to be controlled through scientific investigation. It examines the erasures and silencing, especially of women, through the putatively universal notions of fraternal citizenship associated with liberal democracy in nationalism in Europe, as well as the dilemmas of gender in national challenges to colonialism in Asia. It tracks the rise of the construction of "language" as an empirically observable object of scientific investigation, with new foci on spoken language, universal "natural" laws, and linguistic structure. Its major case study is the French Revolution and its aftermath, with consideration of other European nation-states as they emerged mainly in the nineteenth century.

Chapter 5 serves as the counterpoint to Chapter 4 by looking at three kinds of challenges to bourgeois nationalism. The first is a focus on internationalism, linked to the elaboration of international auxiliary languages, a project central to the work of many prominent linguists, though often now dismissed from discussions of their work and marginalized as amateurish. The second is linguistics elaborated in the making of the Soviet Union, in the search for a science of language that would engage with Marxist theory and lay the foundations for international communism within an understanding of modernity as technological progress. Here we will see challenges to comparative philology, understood as bourgeois, but also a complex navigation of nationalism, internationalism, and imperialism. The third challenge to bourgeois nationalism is fascism, as an attempt to purify the equation between language, nation, and race, a move that is understandable as both the nadir and apotheosis of nationalism, and as a sharp reaction to the contradictions of mixing and perceived contamination associated with colonialism.

In the third pair of chapters, *Brave New Worlds: Language as Technology, Language as Technique*, we turn to the effects of World War II and the Cold War that followed it as an explicit battle between capitalist and communist ideologies, continued but also challenged by a shift to decolonization and national and international development in the 1960s, and by complex and frequently contradictory attempts to struggle for equality in the context of liberal democracy, the welfare state, and decolonization. Chapter 6 investigates the elaboration of universalist understandings of language by structuralists and generativists, in part as a challenge to the radical racist relativism of fascism. Such ideologies, however, coincided neatly with post-World War II interests in developing strategies for machine translation, the era's form of artificial language, and helped to fuel the rapid growth of linguistics departments. The chapter considers the silencing of certain scholars who either were, or were seen as, communist, anti-racist, or pro-Indigenous, and the interrogation of others whose affinities were suspect because of their knowledge of languages spoken in communist countries. It considers the rise of new speech technologies for persuasion and propaganda, understood sometimes as tools for democracy-building. As formal colonization was challenged, new ways of dividing up and understanding the world arose under the rubric of area studies, with new ways of understanding language, culture, and society associated with each. This chapter focusses largely on the United States in the late 1940s and 1950s as we see centres of scholarship shifting from Europe (especially Germany) to the United States. It considers the emergence of a focus on syntax and on the tree diagram as a tool for analyzing sentence structure. The separation of language from society depoliticized linguistic study, in some ways that were ironic given that linguistic study of this kind was meant to celebrate universal humanity over and against fascist hierarchies, and because key figures such as Zellig Harris and Noam Chomsky were both astute and active political theorists involved in a number of communist and anarchist movements. The chapter concludes with a study of ideas about language in the work of George Orwell, the British writer whose books *Nineteen Eighty-Four* and *Animal Farm* were used as ideological super-weapons in the battle for minds during the Cold War. His career included colonial service, socialist conversion, a fight against fascists and then communists, and thus traversed all of the key social movements we have studied thus far.

Chapter 7 is a counterpoint to Chapter 6, in that it considers the period generally understood as the "rise" of sociolinguistics in the 1960s and early 1970s in which scholars worked to challenge, in some ways, universalist ideas with more attention to culture, class, race, and gender. Decolonization led to the elaboration of disciplines of language policy and planning for a new group of postcolonial nations. With decolonization, a new set of ideologies of improvement called *development* replaced, and continued, colonial efforts at uplift. The work discussed here also argued for understanding language as social practice and for focussing on spoken interaction in the here-and-now as the proper site for investigation of the workings of power. Here we will look at the experience of a number of key U.S.-based scholars in international development projects, and the ways in which many were shaped by wartime experiences and encounters with gender, racial, and class inequality at home. We will look at the role of foundations, especially the Rockefeller and Ford Foundations, in providing a basis for their work. We will discuss the rise of feminist linguistics. We review the importance of work on African American and Caribbean language, increasingly by African, African American, and Caribbean scholars, for developing a more critical and conflict-based approach to language inequities. This chapter also examines the institutionalization of sociolinguistics in Europe, partly in response to postwar migration and to the mobilization of European "linguistic minorities" in such areas as Catalonia, the Basque country, Brittany, Occitanie, and Wales, partly linked to Marxist concerns for working-class groups in the welfare state.

Chapter 8 is contrapuntal within itself, describing both the capitalist and colonial discourses of the moment, as well as challenges to these. This chapter tracks the period since the 1980s, broadly understood as the end of the welfare state in countries of the Global North and, with the collapse of the Soviet Union in 1989, the end of the Cold War. We follow the ways in which the intensification and extension of the globalized economy, facilitated by neoliberalism, shifted an interest in languages in a number of directions. One theme is the development of debates about how to understand linguistic value and ideology as notions of markets and commodities changed rapidly. Notions of added value and skill are key tropes of neoliberal social organization, pointing to new forms of audit and evaluation, equally discussed as discursive procedures. We see states increasingly concerned about security and the return of Cold War–inspired forms of surveillance and censorship. Eligibility for citizenship is ever more closely tied to labour, and more and more things are commodified. Authenticity is rendered valuable by contrast, though this can quickly shade into nativism, linked in part to feelings of economic precarity. We consider the way increasing disparities of wealth are tied to exactly the forms of difference with which language has long been intertwined, producing pronounced attention to linguistic aspects of problems of race, gender, and sexuality as modes of making inequality. Indeed, in 1951, Hannah Arendt predicted that the unravelling of ravenous capitalism would take place around race:

> If it should prove to be true that we are imprisoned in Hobbes's endless process of power accumulation, then the organization of the mob will inevitably take the form of transformation of nations into races, for there is under the conditions of an accumulating society, no other unifying bond available between individuals who in the very process of power accumulation and expansion are losing all natural connections with their fellow-men. Racism may indeed carry out the doom of the Western world and, for that matter, of the whole of human civilization.... For no matter what learned scientists may say, race is, politically speaking. not the beginning of humanity but its end, not the origin of peoples but their decay, not the natural birth of man but his unnatural death. ([1951] 1968, 157)

This is an apocalyptic view of the future. It orients us to a consideration of how the fractured lives created by late capitalism are linked to the resurgence of White supremacist, nativist, and dictatorial regimes.

However, we also look for sources of hope, movements, ideas, and people who use language to challenge capitalist and colonial logics and imagine different futures. We consider how increased commodification of language and authenticity, often linked to place, is challenged by an eco-linguistics intent to preserve or create an environmental commons. We consider different strategies for challenging racism, including redress, refusal, and reclamation. We consider attempts to redress former harms to minoritized, racialized, or colonized groups as political economic conditions increasingly destabilize the nation-state as a major mode of political and economic organization. These come precisely from former peripheries and the formerly colonized as they seek an alternative to the modes of domination and forms of hegemony from which they have suffered. We also consider refusal (A. Simpson 2007; Tuck and Yang 2014) to respect the heavily policed boundaries among languages that so many missionaries, administrators, teachers, linguists, and anthropologists have devoted so much work to producing; a similar refusal to respect the conventions of standardized language; and above all a refusal to share linguistic resources with those who have failed to treat them with respect in the past and a refusal to permit problematic forms of knowledge production. We also consider new solidarities, new sovereignties, and new social movements.

Chapter 8 thus takes on the ideas of the eighth fire, which note that we are at a crossroads. The approaches we take will shape the future.

The End of the Beginning

In the final paragraph of her book, Arendt writes, "But there remains also the truth that every end in history necessarily contains a new beginning; this beginning is the promise, the only 'message' that the end can ever produce. Beginning, before it becomes a historical event, is the supreme capacity of [humans]; politically, it is identified with [human] freedom" ([1951] 1968, 479).[3] Writing this book has been a challenge and a pleasure. We have, each, been renewed and re-excited about studying language. We have found a range of works we have never read; we have read old texts with new eyes. We mostly agreed; when we didn't, we learned from that. Bonnie may still be more enraptured with the idea of hope than Monica; Monica notes her continuing wariness about the complexities and unintended consequences of social processes. The work is fully collaborative; our names are in alphabetical order.

Many of our conversations about this book were held in the café of the Royal Conservatory of Music at the University of Toronto. It has been an apt setting for the work we do here. It is a place of memory, but also a place of hope. The café opens off a sinuous path called Philosopher's Walk. The Walk starts on Bloor Street, a busy centre for Toronto's cultural institutions and the University of Toronto. There is a heavy stone gate marking the 1901 visit of Prince George, the Duke of Cornwall, and Mary, the Duchess of Cornwall, installed at the instigation of the Imperial Order Daughters of the Empire. The path winds down between the Royal Ontario Museum and the Royal Conservatory of Music. It follows the path of a river, Taddle Creek, which was buried as modern industrial infrastructures shaped the city. You can still see the meandering course of the river in the shape of the path and in the valleys in the landscape; some of the trees growing now existed when the creek still ran. Signs mark the way this river was once the site of fishing weirs built by Indigenous people. There is now a semicircular stone gathering place for outdoor teachings. An artist and student in Women and Gender Studies has buried small fish in bottles at various points along the course of the path; some of the sewer grids are now wrought-iron fish and butterflies.

---

3 We have chosen to replace her 'generic' masculines with forms more legible in our times.

The path goes through a grove of 14 trees. These trees are planted in honour and memory of 14 women, 14 students, killed in Montréal on December 6, 1989, by a gunman spewing hate about women in engineering and in universities. When Bonnie visited on December 6, 2016, others had been there before her. There were roses and rose petals lying at the foot of the trees. Bonnie also left something at each tree, remembering these women, 14 other women she knows, and the hundreds of missing and murdered Indigenous women in Canada. A large boulder in the middle of the grove has a plaque, which reads in part, "May commitment to the eradication of sexism and violence against women be likewise planted in the hearts and minds of you who stand here and all who come after. It is not enough to look back in pain. We must create a new future."

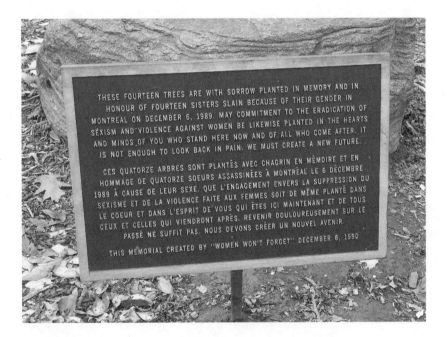

FIGURE 1.2: "We must create a new future." Philosopher's Walk/Taddle Creek, Toronto, 2016 (Photo: Bonnie McElhinny)

PART I

Language, Intimacy, and Empire

CHAPTER 2

LANGUAGE AND IMPERIALISM I: CONVERSION AND KINSHIP

FIGURE 2.1: Canadian Bible Society: Ojibwe Bible and Tagalog Bible. North York, 2017 (Photo: Bonnie McElhinny)

"The First Nations Bible Translation Capacity-Building Initiative"

The Canadian Bible Society is housed on a quiet suburban street in Toronto. You can peer in a window marked "Translate" and see many Bibles on a shelf marked "Other Languages." A key priority of the Society is translation of Bibles into Indigenous languages used in Canada, in both audio and print format. The breaking news on its website in spring 2016 was a revision of its Inuktitut translation (Inuktitut is the language spoken by the Inuit, an Indigenous group in Canada).

The website describes the CBS ministry as including the key task of translation, noting that most languages in the world do not have a translation of the Bible. It argues that "Scripture speaks most powerfully when people have it in their first language," but that the work of translation requires balancing an accurate rendition of the "meaning" of the text while trying to replicate as closely as possible the original text (https://biblesociety.ca/translation). It also notes that languages change over time, and thus the work of biblical translation is never done. The last translation of the Bible into Mohawk was published in 1804, and so a new translation is a priority.

The website includes a rather detailed analysis of various languages or dialects that all go under the name of "Cree," described in various ways ("language continuum," "macrolanguage," "subgroup") and with some speculation about how many language development projects are needed. This language, or language cluster, interests the Canadian Bible Society because it is spoken by so many and is one of the most "viable" First Nations languages (i.e., it has a larger number of speakers than many other Indigenous languages, and is considered more likely to gain, not lose, speakers). Initiatives like the First Nations Bible Translation Capacity-Building Initiative, the website argues, help in the revitalization of languages and provide a foundation for further literary activity. Scriptures translated into these "heart languages" are also said to have healing effects.

What the website does *not* note is the key role that churches in Canada, and elsewhere, played in the attempts to eliminate Indigenous languages. While early missionaries were keen to work in the languages they encountered, for many of the same reasons still articulated on this website, later ideologies suggested that it was necessary to "kill the Indian and save the man" (Pratt [1892] 1973). Many Indigenous children were removed from their families and placed in residential and industrial schools where they were punished for speaking Indigenous languages. Many Protestant churches in Canada, as well as the Canadian government, have recently apologized for their roles in residential schooling (the Catholic Church is a hold-out) as part of a larger Truth and

Reconciliation process for residential school survivors, their families, and their communities (Truth and Reconciliation Commission of Canada 2015). Part of the healing that is mentioned in this website, then, is healing—or attempting to heal—from the effects of racial and colonial violence.

In this chapter, we begin to discuss the roots, causes, and routes of colonialism. We start with an overview of debates over key concepts and an account of what drove European expansion. We then consider two key case studies. The first, in which monarchy and Church collaborate in conditions of mercantile capitalism, concerns missionary linguistics in the Spanish empire in the New World and in the Philippines, especially in the sixteenth and seventeenth centuries. It traces the regulation of language in the interests of the consolidation of centralized metropolitan states and the expansion of their empires. We consider the simultaneous development of strategies for writing grammars and dictionaries for Indigenous languages and vernacular languages in Europe, to fix linguistic forms in the interest of governance and dissemination of Christian beliefs and in the articulation of translation and conversion. *Translation* assumes that one can convert one language into another, without much loss of meaning; Christian *conversion* assumes that differences among humans are not so great that it is impossible to bring all souls into the fold.

The second case study turns to the shift in production of knowledge about language to lay intellectuals; their studies were construed as scientific and secular though they continued to be deeply shaped by spiritual understandings. Starting in the late eighteenth century, *comparative philology* tried to make sense of the relationship of European languages to other languages in the context of increasing global trade, exploration, and military occupation by using notions of kinship borrowed from biblical understandings of genealogy. While comparative philology is often celebrated as a European intellectual achievement, we will see that it actually is enabled by what happens when the close analyses of language developed in powerful religious traditions—Christian, Hindu, and earlier Vedic traditions—came into contact and combined in complex ways during the period in which the British East India Company dominated relationships with India.

Language and religion are thus the two key sites on which understandings of difference are elaborated, before the rise of biological accounts of racial difference in evolutionary thought. The linguistic actions in these two case studies, as they are deeply imbricated in colonial violence, are shot through with a focus on love and kinship. In the first case, the focus is on Christian love and fellowship; in the second, the focus is on elaborating notions of kinship among groups previously taken to be unrelated. Encoded in each are distinct notions not only about social relationships, but about spatiality and temporality, proximity and distance. We will consider, throughout, what the focus on these kinds of intimacy might mean. First, however, we consider some keywords of colonialism, and how, by the fifteenth century, the five continents began to be drawn into a network of global connections.

Colonialism, Imperialism, Postcolonialism, Decolonization

Colonialism, imperialism, postcolonialism, and *decolonization* are keywords, the definition of which vary along three critical dimensions: (1) which countries are treated as colonial; (2) whether the focus is primarily on political or economic systems; and (3) how to describe challenges to colonialism, and how effective these challenges are. We consider each of these dimensions in turn.

Imperialism is understood here as the formal conquest, annexation, and administration of territories to ensure control of raw materials for industry and agricultural products, some of which were not widely available in the metropole (such as rubber, tin, copper, gold, diamonds, sugar, tea, coffee, cocoa, tobacco), and some of which were more cheaply produced elsewhere (such as grain and meat). Imperialism also meant control of markets for goods and control of people, both as labourers and as potential consumers, and even of potential rivals. This definition overlaps in many ways with how we can understand *colonialism*.

Historian Catherine Hall offers a helpful definition of colonialism: the "pattern of exploration and 'discovery,' of settlement, of dominance over geographically separate 'others,' which resulted in the uneven development of forms of capitalism across the world and the destruction and/or transformation of other forms of social organization and life" (2000, 5). This allows us to think about the relationships among European overseas colonialism, settler colonialism, and internal colonialism.[1]

In *overseas colonialism* the focus is on extracting natural resources (e.g., gold, cotton, oil) or human resources (e.g., labour, existing trade networks, convertible souls). In *settler colonialism*, foreign people move into a region, and occupy and claim ownership of the land. They alter the territory's social structure, government, and economy. They often maintain a temporary allegiance to homeland and draw legitimacy from both worlds. This form of colonization leads, by a variety of means, to depopulation, or attempts at depopulation, of the previous inhabitants so that settlers can take over the land (Byrd 2011;

---

[1] We acknowledge that the focus on Europe, common to many definitions of colonialism, sets aside earlier moments of empire, non-European forms of empire, and other relations that can also be understood as empire; see Stoler, McGranahan, and Perdue (2007).

Veracini 2011). *Internal colonialism* (which we will discuss further in Chapter 4) involves similar constructions of peripheries and social difference in the service of legitimating resource extraction and mobilizing labour forces, but within the (often contested) political boundaries of the metropole's state; sometimes these peripheries are also settled from the centre.

Colonialism justifies itself through the construction of selves and others, often defined along racialized/religious lines. However, the distinction is not always binary. Various forms of imperialism share "gradations of sovereignty and sliding scales of differentiation" (Stoler and McGranahan 2007, 9). This means that certain people are seen as capable, to greater or lesser extents, of governing themselves and others are not, and that various ideas are developed to rationalize why some people are seen as more capable than others and to justify domination of some by others.

Apologists for empire tend to obscure or reframe the violence of rule by framing it as benevolent; however, settler colonialism, because it relies on the death and displacement of people already on the land, is particularly prone to erasing its own processes as settlers themselves claim Indigenous status (see Veracini 2011 for a list of discursive and material strategies used to support settler colonialism, and Tuhiwai Smith 1999 for a list of decolonizing research strategies that intervene in them). Many anthropological accounts of imperialism leave settler colonies out of their analyses (cf. Cooper and Stoler 1997, Errington 2008).

A second dimension of contestation is linked to how and whether formal political or economic control is emphasized. Sometimes colonialism is reserved for formal political control while imperialism is used for other forms of domination. We use both terms, sometimes interchangeably, to refer to the relations of domination, the building of hierarchies and differences, and the legitimizing ideologies they share. However, as Williams ([1976] 1983, 159–60) notes, there may be tension between understanding imperialism as a political system, in which colonies are governed from an imperial centre and as an economic system in which outsiders invest in, penetrate, and control markets and raw materials.

Finally, it is difficult to identify what the "end of empire" might look like, since what it means is also necessarily linked to how one defines empire and is thus similarly contested. When people challenge the legitimacy of colonialism and establish their own political sovereignty it is called *decolonization*, though many former colonies also remain tightly tied to each other and to their former metropole through both institutional and informal economic domination. We see their effects in such phenomena as migration patterns, military spheres of influence, trade arrangements, the shape of consumption and artistic achievement, and development discourses (as we will see in Chapters 6 and 7).

Sometimes scholars use *postcolonialism* to refer to what happens after many successful challenges to the political domination of empires and to describe dynamics after the end of formal political control; however, postcolonialism can appear to imply that all forms of colonialism and imperialism have ended. It is especially inappropriate for talking about settler colonies, such as Australia, Canada, New Zealand, or the United States, where colonial occupation continues (Byrd 2011). In such sites, colonialism is best seen as a structure, not an event (Wolfe 2006), a formulation that suggests that colonization is not something that happened at the moment of arrival, but rather is an ongoing elaboration of claims to land and hierarchies of people. For some, decolonization, in either overseas or settler colonies, has to focus on land (Tuck and Yang 2012); for others, it focusses on minds as well (Fanon 1963, [1952] 1967; Memmi 1957). Let's go back, however, to how imperialism begins.

Intimacy and Connection Across Five Continents

For a long time, Europe was not of much account in the affairs of the wider world (Wolf [1982] 1997, 71). To assume that a narration of global history must start with Europe (or the West more broadly) constructed as a natural entity, and with an account of Europe's effect on the rest of the world, is already to adopt an imperial ideology. We are more comfortable with a view that understands colonialism as a moment when new encounters within the world facilitated the formation of categories of metropole and colony, Europe and others, and not a process that began in the colonizing country (understood as already defined) and expanding outward (Dirks 1992, 6).

Metropole and colony therefore need to be treated in the same frame, with consequences for how we understand the idea of nation (see Chapter 4). The formation of something we now call "Europe" or "the West" emerges from encounters and is used to rationalize dominance in them. Such a contrapuntal approach also has consequences for how we write history. As we will see, part of imperial ideology is the celebration of its own achievements as superior, and the simultaneous denigration, without acknowledgement, of the achievements of colonized groups. There is still considerable work for us to do in sociolinguistics and linguistic anthropology in revisiting such histories. The question we consider, in this chapter and throughout, is how such ideologies arose, and what they destroy, co-opt, or integrate without acknowledgement.

The western Mediterranean and Southwest Asia had long-standing connections through trade and state expansion with Greek, and then Roman, empires. The Mediterranean region became divided between Islam and Western Christianity after the decline of the Roman empire, with Muslim armies occupying much of the Iberian peninsula (contemporary Spain and Portugal), as well as much of the Balkans. When Baghdad became the Islamic capital in the mid-eighth century, the most important sites of Islamic trade included Arabia, India, China, Inner Asia, and the Caucasus. There were no major cities in Western Christendom, and European merchants played a relatively minor role in long-distance trade, especially since the Ottoman empire (1299–1922) controlled East-West interactions for centuries, blocking European access to Asia.

In Europe, rural cultivators were tied to particular lords. As regional lords struggled for more control, there was a movement toward consolidation under central kingdoms, legitimized by divine authority and supported by the Church. To get the funds to support these wars, leaders could seize resources from enemies, eke out more from those under their political rule, discover resources to sell or exchange, or try to enlarge their political domain (Wolf [1982] 1997, 105). France and England followed the strategy of trying to consolidate land under their direct control and fought for centuries over land claimed by both, as well as undertaking the Crusades, which understood such actions in Christian terms. War was also the strategy used on the Iberian peninsula by Christian powers to challenge Muslim rulers; these wars continued through 1492. The complex interactions of Europe and "the Orient" are forcibly brought home in accounts of the expulsion of Muslims and Jews from the Iberian peninsula in 1492, in an attempt to spatialize civilization and "civilize" space, which is often understood as the starting point for the elaboration of European imperialism and nationalism.

By around 1300, though, the climate worsened (in the so-called Little Ice Age), epidemics killed large numbers of malnourished people, people began to rebel against the seizure of their means of living, and the only way to deal with the crisis, perhaps in the absence of new technological solutions to improve agriculture, was further expansion (Wolf [1982] 1997, 108). This fuelled the Iberian movement to the "New World," the spread of the fur trade throughout the forests of North America, the intensification of searches for new routes to the Indian Ocean and China and attempts to establish trading outposts there, the establishment of forts and trading posts along the African coasts, and the enslavement of Africans to provide labour for New World agriculture and mining (Wolf [1982] 1997, 105). Each of these movements has distinctive social and linguistic implications that we consider in this chapter and the next.

These activities, extending roughly from the sixteenth through the early nineteenth centuries, are often described as taking place in the age of mercantile capitalism, though of course at any given moment multiple forms of economic exchange prevail (e.g., mercantile capitalism lasted well into the nineteenth century to support the plantation system in the American South). *Mercantile capitalism* is distinguished by the many global interactions that were brokered through private financiers who also served as de facto governments before European states claimed control of certain territories. From Britain, for instance, interactions in what are now known as India and Canada were brokered respectively by the British East India Company and the Hudson's Bay Company; from the Netherlands, that role was played in the area of what is now known as Indonesia by the Dutch East India Company.

This expansion engendered a range of intimate imperial interactions that travellers, colonial administrators, soldiers, and missionaries had to make sense of. There was a range of tools developed and used to imagine these relationships and to develop the knowledge used for imperial administration, from maps to censuses of local populations to early forms of ethnography. As Hall writes:

> For settlers to possess the lands which they fondly constructed as 'vacant' they needed to map them, to name them in their own language, to describe and define them, to anatomize the land and its fruits, for themselves and the mother country, to classify their inhabitants, to differentiate them from other 'natives,' to fictionalize them, to represent them visually, to civilize and cure them. They needed cartographers, botanists, artists and writers as well as soldiers to support their enterprise, and sailors to ensure their traffic across their seas. (2000, 24–25)

To these we add that traders and missionaries, settlers and soldiers also needed tools to "command language" and develop the "language of command" (Cohn 1996). We will see that some of the tools developed to accomplish this suggested forms of affinity and kinship, albeit generally hierarchically understood; others created more marked notions of distance and difference. The distinctions made are not just the binary one between self and other: instead imperialism "operates through precisely spatialized and temporalized processes of both differentiation and connection" (Lowe 2015, 8). Metaphors of family, sexuality, and kinship pervade these accounts, from discussions of sibling relationships to discussions of bastardized tongues, as different forms of racialization are constructed depending on proximities to certain ideas about family (Irvine 2001; Lowe 2015; Stoler 1991). Various forms of classification are meant to regulate forms of interaction in labour, reproduction, and the political sphere (Lowe 2015, 32). The ways various forms of classification were linked to some of the earliest imperial incursions into the New World by Spain are taken up in the next section.

Reduced to and by Christian Love: Missionary Linguistics

The defeat of the last Islamic state on the Iberian Peninsula in 1492 ended nearly 700 years of Muslim-Christian warfare there, though this period also included moments of significant tolerance, cooperation, and intermarriage that were obscured in later accounts. The war, originally a war of conquest, became justified over time as a religious war of liberation, a framing that would be significant for understanding actions in the New World. Jews and Muslims were expelled, or required to convert, though there was a persistent wariness about the peril of "hidden" Jews and Muslims and of "New Christians." The expansion to the New World can be understood as a way of prolonging this strategy of using warfare and seizure of resources, and we will see it used time and time again (including by New World imperialism centred in the United States).

The Spaniards declared themselves victors over the Aztec empire in 1521, the Inka empire in 1572, and the Maya in 1697. Epidemics of European diseases, to which Indigenous peoples in the Americas had little resistance, facilitated these rapid occupations. African gold and American silver fuelled the Spanish economy and many wars in Europe, though ultimately the reliance on resource extraction by Spain led to inflation and a failure to industrialize (except in key regions like Barcelona). These processes in turn led to the decline of the power of the Spanish empire in ways that have lingering effects on the Spanish economy today (and help to explain in part why Catalan nationalism, linked as it is to a strong regional economy, has had such perduring power). The ideology of a wider Spanish empire was, however, resuscitated to support fascist ideologies in the twentieth century.

The Spanish consolidation of power on the Iberian peninsula and its global expansions were simultaneous. The conquest of the Iberian peninsula was accompanied by an attempt to codify the languages central to command of the area. In 1492, the year that Columbus made Europeans aware of peoples and lands previously unknown to them, Antonio Nebrija, a Renaissance scholar who had already produced a grammar of Latin, published a Castilian grammar, one of the first of any modern European language (Mannheim 2011; Mignolo 1992a). The utility of a grammar in a vernacular language was not immediately clear to the queen at the time. Nebrija explained:

> Now, your Majesty ... recall the time when I presented you with a draft of this book earlier this year in Salamanca. At this time, you asked me what end such a grammar could possibly serve. Upon this, the Bishop of Avila interrupted to answer in my stead. What he said was this: "Soon Your

Majesty will have placed her yoke upon many barbarians who speak outlandish tongues. By this, your victory, these people shall stand in a new need; the need of the new laws the victor owes to the vanquished, and the need for the language we shall bring with us." My grammar shall serve to impart them the Castilian tongue, as we have used grammar to teach Latin to our young. (translated by and cited in Mignolo 1995, 38)

Language, Nebrija noted, had always been a tool of empire. Writing a grammar of Castilian, which was understood as a form of corrupted Latin, would standardize its spelling, harmonize its parts, and fix its grammatical laws, like Latin, whose immutability and fixity was seen as a sign of its perfection (Rafael 1988, 24). The vernacular could be spread, too, by the new technology of the printing press, invented around 1440. Literacy rates would soon rise, ideas would diffuse more easily across borders, and Latin would be replaced by vernacular/protonational languages.[2]

Spanish conquest of the New World (related strategies were used in the Philippines) had two intertwined pillars: (1) military subjugation, carried out by a relatively small number of soldiers working with Indigenous allies, and (2) the so-called *conquista pacifica* ('peaceful conquest'), which was carried out by an even smaller number of missionaries who aimed to convert natives to Christianity. It was critical to missionaries to see conversion as something that was not done by force; the conversion would then not be believable. Instead, a reliable conversion was a form of persuasion, of consent, with the person "reduced by love" rather than conquered (Rafael 1988, 156). Conversion, like conquest, is a process of crossing over into the domain of someone else and claiming it as one's own. It implies both a process of annexation and also an attempt to restructure desires and construct certain kinds of affective bonds (Rafael 1988, ix).

As European expansion began in the late fifteenth century, missionaries were some of the earliest travellers to live for sustained periods of time in communities other than their own, studying, recording, and learning to speak these languages in order to convert those they saw as heathen and to engage in what they sometimes saw as quite literally military campaigns against the devil. Witness this quotation from a Jesuit missionary to New France (now part of Canada) in the seventeenth century:

La superstition, l'erreur, la barbarie, et en suite le peché, sont icy comme dans leur empire, nous nous seruons de quatre grandes machines pour

---

2 It was, however, Nebrija's grammar of Latin, not Castilian, that was used as a model by missionaries in the New World and the Philippines, as well as by those writing grammars of other European languages.

les renuerser; Premièrement nous faison des courses pour aller attaquer l'ennemy sur ses terres par ses propres armes, c'est à dire, par la cognoissance des languages Montagnese, Algonquine, et Hurone.

[Hanzeli's translation: "The superstition, the error, the barbarism and following all of that sin are here as in their empire; we will use four grand machines to reverse them. First we will go attack the enemy on its own territory with its own weapons, that is to say, by knowing the Montagnese, Algonquin and Huron languages." (Cited in Hanzeli 1969, 45)]

Christian missionaries often accompanied, or soon followed in the tracks of, European explorers. Missionaries debated a number of linguistic issues, including whether Indigenous languages were suited to the preaching of the gospel, which Indigenous language to use in multilingual areas for missionization, how many speakers a language needed to have to make it worth missionizing, how to change Indigenous languages to make them adequate tools for Christianity, the enormous variability in spoken languages, and how to standardize and simplify them to ease learning and writing (see also Mühlhäusler 1996, 140).

In working through these questions, missionaries deployed language ideologies learned in the study of Latin, Greek, and Hebrew as they constructed civilizational hierarchies associated with written and oral language, and with Christian versus pagan (or 'heathen') cultures and languages (Rafael 1988, 27). A missionary to Micronesia in 1859 wrote that "[w]hile the languages of Micronesia and other heathen nations or tribes are destitute of words and phrases to convey correct ideas of God and moral subjects generally, yet those same languages abound with words and terms respecting disgusting subjects" (cited in Mühlhäusler 1996, 140). Another wrote of Aboriginal languages in Australia that "[a]n acquaintance with the Australian dialects here is of no value as to religious things, just because they have no religion, no worship of any kind, no sacrifices, no prayers, no fears or hopes with references to any other state" (cited in Mühlhäusler 1996, 142). Yet another wrote of Chinese that "[a]lthough the supposition that Satan had a special agency in the formation of the Chinese language cannot be proved ... yet we can hardly conceive of any tongue better adapted than this to promote his evil designs" (cited in Mühlhäusler 1996, 141).

Just the same, conversion was seen as necessary since, in the wake of conquering Muslims and expelling Jews, being a member of Spanish society was seen to entail being Christian. Adopting Christian civility meant a wholesale transformation of the lives of Indigenous people, "from heart, soul, and mind to self-image, bodily practices, lived space, and everyday conduct, including speech" (Hanks 2010, 7). It was language that spread most rapidly. Spain's colonizing project in New Spain and the Philippines was organized by the project of *reducción*, which can mean 'pacification,' 'conversion,' or 'ordering,' depending on context. *Reducción* was meant to transform space, conduct, and language, so that those called "Indios" would live in orderly towns according to the norms of Christian civility, using a new version of their own language that had been transformed to express civility and religion appropriately.

"Reducing" the natives to towns, like "reducing" their language to grammar books and dictionaries, entailed the fixing of names to things and the recording of those names in administrative lists and records. From the perspective of the colonizers, "[t]he process would result … in converting the colonized into arbitrary elements that could be made to fit into a divinely sanctioned order characterized by the hierarchization of all signs and things in the world" (Rafael 1988, 90). While the missionary focus on order critiqued Indios, it also critiqued other Spaniards for the disorderly violence of military conquest and labour extraction, both of which were seen to drive potential converts away from the Catholic Church. Indios were forcibly concentrated into centralized towns built on a rectilinear model; the Spanish destroyed abandoned towns in order to discourage Indios from returning. Many Indios died as a result; others fled. This was not what the missionaries had in mind.

Hierarchies between orality and literacy, and different forms of literacy, were also key to these colonial projects. People without writing systems were seen as less civilized. Alphabetic writing systems were seen as superior to others (such as those extant in the New World, in the Philippines, and in China). How writing systems were used was also assessed by missionaries (cf., e.g., Rafael 1988). Mignolo (1992a, 1992b, 1995) writes about this for the New World; Goody (1986) and Mudimbe (1988) offer some insights into literacy/orality in Africa.

Spanish missionaries and colonial officials disagreed on many other dimensions of colonial rule. Secular colonial officials often argued for the use of Spanish in social interactions, while missionaries argued for the use of native languages. They emphasized mastery of the spoken language in order to be able to preach and to introduce religious texts to people who did not possess writing systems. Missionaries often argued that religious teachings were done in vernacular languages in Europe, so similarly that Indigenous languages needed to be used for full comprehension of the mysteries of the faith; they were a more efficient and rapid route to saving souls. Linguistic ability in native languages was thus highly valued, and carefully assessed, by religious orders.

Still, there were tensions and ambivalences. Requiring the use of European languages could mean ensuring loyalty to the empire; however, denying access could guarantee certain intermediaries the powerful and often lucrative position of brokers between native communities and the state. Those Indios who learned the European languages too well could come to be seen as a threat to the regime, but retaining vernacular languages could be seen as aiding the retention of cultural memories that colonizers wanted Indigenous people to forget (Mannheim 2011, 34, 65, 69). Certain kinds of individuals embodied these tensions: bilingual *mestizos* (people who had a Spanish and an Indigenous parent) could be seen as both useful translators and also dangerous threats if they moved into powerful positions. The tensions can be seen in decrees such as one issued in the late seventeenth century requiring education until the age of 10, and then forbidding it afterwards (Mannheim 2011, 71).

As we saw above, not all vernacular languages were similarly valued by missionaries. They were interested in those with which they could reach the largest number of souls, as seen in the Canadian Bible Society interest in Cree above. Dying languages were of little interest (we'll see the contrast with a keen anthropological interest in documenting such languages, beginning in the late nineteenth century). Missionaries were thus very concerned about "linguistic diversity." This meant that missionization sometimes meant choosing one language (sometimes the colonial language, sometimes an Indigenous language perceived as powerful or widely spoken) and imposing it on others in areas that were linguistically diverse (e.g., Nahuatl in the former Aztec Empire). This could even mean "bringing languages into being" (Mühlhäusler 1996, 145) by developing local contact varieties, that is, naming them, writing a grammar and dictionary for them, and translating a Bible using this grammar and dictionary in ways that ignored a multiplicity of different linguistic entities (not all named) and local speakers' ideas about mutual intelligibility and linguistic differences. Missionaries also sometimes chose languages for use because of their proximity to the mission, rather than their local importance, and then spread them (Mühlhäusler 1996). In general, missionaries were interested in reducing heterogeneity, which was seen as a sign of barbarism and of an overly rudimentary civil society (in Chapter 4 we will see how similar practices were developed in Europe to support nationalism).

Debates about diversity may have been overstated at times in order to construct societies as barbaric. One missionary working in the Belgian-colonized Congo thundered, "Why go only always proclaiming the existence of about 200 different languages in the Congo if one has not yet made their inventory, has not studied them, nor examined the degree to which they are related?" (cited in Fabian 1986, 81). Of course, such enumeration itself runs into problems. How one counts languages depends upon how one classifies them. Nonetheless, citing diversity as a problem justified regulation of language, just as citing other things deemed as problems (hygiene, the treatment of women, and more) justified intervention (Fabian 1986, 82).

Missionary grammars and dictionaries were also a tool of *reducción*, meant to describe and prescribe appropriate norms. Missionaries had to decide when and how to use existing related concepts (like those for god), and when those might feed the idolatry they meant to displace. They had to find ways to express novel concepts such as *baptism, conversion, crucifixion, communion, confession*, and *idolatry*. In *Converting Words: Maya in the Age of the Cross*, William Hanks (2010) analyzes catechisms, dictionaries, and grammars (which drew heavily on Nebrija's Latin grammar) to consider how language itself was both a tool of, and subject to, *reducción*. The use of Nebrija's work gave Catholic missionaries a template, but also caused them to obscure or overlook certain aspects of Mayan grammar, aspects they may have understood in everyday interaction but did not spell out in these texts. In analyzing the dictionaries, Hanks considers a process of *commensuration*, that is, aligning two languages so one can translate between them (2010, 160). He considers which parts of their native language Spanish missionaries translated, and which words they left in Spanish. In the process they produced a new form of Maya, also subject to *reducción*. Hanks (2010, 16) calls the languages that were produced through the processes of linguistic conversion *translanguages*, languages that were not solely European or Mayan, but languages joined through the process of conquest.

What missionaries hoped converts would absorb, of course, is not necessarily what was taken away by Indigenous peoples. Conversions were often seen by Europeans as rapid and as a testament to divine will, but often inadequate in ways that were attributed to the intellectual inadequacy or childishness of the people converted, rather than, say, their resistance to or adaptation of Christian practices (Rafael 1988, 84). Nonetheless, both the colonizers and the colonized were changed by their interactions. The attempt to translate Christianity into native vernaculars changed the vernacular and the consciousness of the speakers; however, Indigenous people's appropriations of Christian and colonial discourse also changed the meaning of that discourse (Rafael 1988, xii, 7). The process of translation meant each group read into the other's language and behaviour possibilities not foreseen by the other. For the Spaniards, translation was a matter of reducing the native language and culture to accessible objects; for Indigenous peoples, it was not so much a matter of internalization as of evading totalization (Rafael 1988, 211).

Though our focus here has been on Spanish empire, such projects of missionization were evident throughout the world. The British and French, blocked from access to other parts of the Americas by the Spanish empire, focussed on the northern peripheries. The goods available there were furs rather than precious metals or spices, and on the whole were seen as less valuable, but nonetheless worth pursuing. The elaborated network of the fur trade followed major waterways, which also served as transport routes for other people, thoughts, and goods, including the Jesuit missionary mentioned above (S. Harvey 2015; Wolf [1982] 1997).

If in many locales one had to be an effective linguist to be an effective missionary, not all effective linguists were effective missionaries. In 1622, the Jesuit missionary Jean de Brébeuf wrote to ask his superiors to send back to France various "superfluous and even dangerous" missionaries who were rendered idle by their inability to use languages and who had become a burden to their peers (Hanzeli 1969, 54). In 1630, Brébeuf produced the first text written in Huron/Wendat, a translation of Jesuit doctrine into *"langage Canadois."* But Christian love eluded his efforts: missionaries were regularly blamed, accurately, by Indigenous people for being accompanied by epidemics, as well as for crop failure, battle defeats, and other trials. It took Brébeuf 10 years in the field to be able to report a grand total of 14 converts.

The Canadian Bible Society is part of this colonial missionary tradition, as is evident by the central and continuing emphasis on Indigenous people and their languages in their mission statement (though immigrants and refugees also come in for some attention). Recording languages for the purposes of missionization is a project that continues in other sites as well. One notable example is the Summer Institute of Linguistics, a U.S.-based, English-speaking organization devoted to the use of linguistics in Protestant evangelization; its goal is to translate the Bible into all of the world's tongues, regardless of the size of the speech community (Mühlhäusler 1996, 144; see also Errington 2008).

In a number of sites, however, the focus on Indigenous languages that was evident in early moments of colonization was often replaced, in later imperial projects and often early national ones, with a focus on one of the colonial languages as ideas about education and nation changed (see also Chapter 4). The Catholic Church promoted the vernacular in Peru for a century or so, but by the early seventeenth century the focus had turned to Hispanization of Native Andeans (Mannheim 2011). In Canada, residential schools run by religious orders from the mid-nineteenth century to the mid-twentieth century forbade the use of Indigenous languages.

While there was an emphasis on the voice over writing in Spanish missionary practice (Rafael 1988, 39), the focus on conversion also had implications for the evaluation and fate of other writing systems that missionaries and other colonial officials encountered. Mayan books and artifacts, which were associated in the missionaries' minds with dangerous pagan beliefs or subversive politics, were confiscated, studied, and disposed of, often in conjunction with practices such as inquisitions using torture to extract testimony and the public humiliation of elites (Hanks 2010). Commentators note the tears streaming down the faces of onlookers as Mayan codexes were tossed onto the pile in one public burning (Mignolo 1995).

A script called *baybayin* was widely used among Tagalog speakers, as well as others in the Filipino archipelago, with one Jesuit commentator even noting that there was scarcely a man or woman who did not read and write among the Tagalogs (Rafael 1988, 44), but it was judged inadequate for the translation of Christian doctrines. For one thing, its function was seen as inappropriate: rather than preserving historical literary texts it was seen as largely used for "barelly intelligible amatory verses written in hyberbolic style" (nineteenth-century commentator, cited in Rafael 1988, 49). Since baybayin did not have a direct and fixed correspondence between script and sounds (it conveyed syllable structures instead), it was assessed as defective when compared to romanized phonetic script. Phonetic writing was seen as perfect because of its closer proximity to the voice, and because the meanings attached to it were not susceptible to as many different interpretations, but could instead be fixed (Rafael 1988, 50). Missionaries focussed, therefore, on rendering Tagalog and other languages in their alphabetic script (while elsewhere, as in northern Canada, other missionaries invented syllabic orthographies for Indigenous languages).

Missionary practices imply that people can enter into a shared community if they engage in similar practices. However, theories of linguistics developed in the late eighteenth century postulated a different kind of kinship, one that tried to imagine kinship in the face of difference. These ways of imagining family were putatively secular, though they had deep roots in the texts and stories shared by "the people of the book" (Christians, Jews, and Muslims), as well as in the practices for linguistic analysis established in Vedic and Hindu religious traditions.

Missionaries, of course, were not the only actors in the colonial process to have something to say about how to understand, through language, the relationship to colonized peoples—as more or less intimate, as more or less other, and as subject, in particular ways, to the power of the colonizer. In the next section, we turn to our second case, and the role of colonial administrators.

Family Trees, Comparative Philology, and Secular Religion

As mercantile capitalism developed, colonial rule increasingly turned to the companies involved (such as the Hudson's Bay Company in northern regions of North America, or the British and Dutch East India Companies), and, eventually, to heightened interest on the part of the state in regulating them. The role of colonial administrators became increasingly important. This section focusses on the particularly influential role of Sir William Jones (1746–94), a British judge on the Bengal Supreme Court from 1783 to 1794. The East

India Company had been founded in 1600 to pursue trade with the East Indies, but ended up trading mainly on the Indian subcontinent, with a focus on India's highly developed textile industry (cotton, silk, indigo dye) as well as salt, tea, and opium. Jones arrived in 1783 as part of an initiative to install British personnel to administer British law.

Jones can perhaps be understood as a kind of bourgeois radical; indeed, though his interests in the "Orient" had long led him to seek an appointment with the British East India Company, this was delayed precisely because of his political views. His modest background may have made him attuned to certain kinds of abuses of political power: he was the grandson of a Welsh farmer and of an English cabinet-maker. (Indeed, India was a source of alternative mobility for a man not born to wealth; Jones eventually earned 10 times as much annually in India as elsewhere, enough to help him save for the political career he wanted at home.) Jones regularly argued that monarchical power should be circumscribed; he was a supporter of the American Revolution and a regular interlocutor of Benjamin Franklin. He decried the institution of slavery. He argued for the extension of suffrage to all with a trade, and supported some of the criticisms of the Irish against their English colonial overlords. Before going to India, he worked as a lawyer on the Welsh circuit, regularly fighting against what he saw as the traces of feudalism by systematically supporting farmers against landlords, villagers against magistrates, and illegally imprisoned tradesmen (Franklin 1995). He arrived in India with an established reputation as a jurist and Orientalist.

Here, *Orientalist* means "a scholar in the field of Orientalism," defined as a field of learned study that started in the Christian West in 1312 with the decision of the Church Council of Vienne to establish a series of academic chairs in Arabic, Greek, Hebrew, and Syriac in various European cities, including Paris, Oxford, Bologna, Avignon, and Salamanca (Said 1978, 50). Until the mid-eighteenth century, Orientalists were biblical scholars studying Semitic languages, specialists in Islam or, once the Jesuits opened up this field of study, on China. From the mid-eighteenth to mid-nineteenth century, an enthusiasm for everything "Oriental" was manifest in the work of every major poet, essayist, and philosopher, with "Asiatic" standing for the exotic, the mysterious, the profound, and the seminal and "Islam" for trauma, danger, peril, and fear (Said 1978, 51, 59). Until late in the nineteenth century, with the consolidation of formal colonial control, academic Orientalists did not usually study contemporary culture but rather the classical period of the language or society they were interested in. Often this was accompanied by an ideology of civilizational decline, with the argument that the highest achievements of the society studied were in the past, and the implication that the European colonial powers were now superior, or justified in their rule, because of this decline.

Indeed, as Edward Said (1978) points out in his book *Orientalism*, it is necessary to understand Orientalism as a mode of discursive construction of "the Orient," as a mode of colonial rule. Said argues that for the European powers, until the nineteenth century the Orient was defined by India and the biblical lands (and thus portrayals of Arabs and Islam), while for the United States the Orient was defined to a greater extent perhaps by Japan, China, and U.S. involvement in southeast Asia. (This has shifted in some important ways in the contemporary period, as "Islam" became the salient condensation of the "Orient.")

Said defines European (and later American) Orientalism as

> a way of coming to terms with the Orient that is based on the Orient's special place in European Western experience. The Orient is not only adjacent to Europe; it is also the place of Europe's greatest and richest and oldest colonies, the source of its civilizations and languages, its cultural contestant, and one of its deepest and most recurring images of the Other. In addition, the Orient has helped to define Europe (or the West) as its contrasting image, idea, personality, experience. Yet none of this Orient is merely imaginative. The Orient is an integral part of European material civilization and culture. Orientalism expresses and represents that part culturally and even ideologically as a mode of discourse with supporting institutions, vocabulary, scholarship, imagery, doctrines, even colonial bureaucracies and colonial styles. (1978, 1-2)

For Said, then, Orientalism is the West's way of "dealing with [the Orient] by making statements about it, settling it, ruling over it: in short Orientalism is a Western style of dominating, restructuring, and having authority over the Orient" (1978, 3).

There are four currents, Said argues, in eighteenth-century thought that led to transformations in the understandings of others, especially the Orient, from a more narrowly religious contrast between the Christian West and others: expansion, historical confrontation, sympathy, and classification. For our purposes, it is important to focus on classification, that is, "reducing vast numbers of objects to a smaller number of orderable and describable types" (Said 1978, 119). These classifications, while putatively secular, are in Said's formulation a form of *secularized religion*; they turn out to be deeply shaped by the forms of faith that the Enlightenment otherwise decried. Thus, Said says, Orientalist knowledge is best understood "not as a sudden access of objective knowledge about the Orient, but as a set of structures inherited from the past, secularized, redisposed, and re-formed by such disciplines as philology, which in turn were naturalized, modernized, and laicizied substitutes for (or versions of) Christian supernaturalism" (1978, 122). The eighteenth-century institutional establishment of the field of "Oriental Studies," especially in the form of comparisons among "Oriental" languages and cultures, is in itself tellingly asymmetrical, with no counterpart in "Occidentalism." Comparison, however, is rarely descriptive, Said notes; typically, it is also evaluative (1978, 149).

In the field of comparative philology of "Oriental languages," Sir William Jones is usually credited with first formulating the idea that languages previously taken as markedly different had, in fact, kinship relations among them. In 1786, in his third annual address to the Asiatic Society of Bengal (a society that he himself founded), Jones said:

> The Sanskrit language, whatever be its antiquity, is of a wonderful structure; more perfect than the Greek, more copious than the Latin, and more exquisitely refined than either, yet bearing to both of them a stronger affinity, both in the roots of verbs and in the forms of grammar, than could possibly have been produced by accident; so strong, indeed, that no philologer could examine them all three, without believing them to have sprung from some common source, which, perhaps, no longer exists: there is a similar reason, though not quite so forcible, for supposing that both the Gothic and the Celtic, though blended with a very different idiom, had the same origin with the Sanskrit; and the old Persian might be added to the same family, if this were the place for discussing any question concerning the antiquities of Persia. (Jones [1786] 1967, 15)

For the first time, then, a number of different languages, spoken in a number of different places and times, were taken to be related. Moreover, Jones eschews the genealogy linking Europe to Greece and Rome that had hitherto legitimized empire in favour of a deeper and more extensive lineage.

The Orientalists, as Trautmann (1997) notes, embraced a rhetoric of love for talking about colonialism. They were interested in how to make Indians love, tolerate, or embrace British rule. They expressed a form of respect for Indian religion and law, knowledge that they wanted to control through knowledge of the language. This form of colonial knowing created a language-based authority that mediated between universalism and claims of national pride and religious difference (1997, 35). Thus intimacy had limits: Jones thought that Indians needed to be ruled with a firm hand until their society could be restored to its former glory. The Royal Society he founded did not include learned natives, something he thought desireable only in some vaguely specified future.

Jones's interest in Sanskrit was fuelled, in the first instance, by needing to rely on native scholars, or *pandits*, for interpretations of law since no British judges were well-versed in that language. Jones mistrusted the pandits, believing they made law as they pleased (Rocher 1995, 74), and argued that the British would remain at the knees of native lawyers until they learned Sanskrit (Franklin 1995, 88). This theme, a wariness of translators and/or those who are multilingual, is one we will see repeatedly in this book.

Jones is given the credit for observing these similarities, but many other scholars were starting to make similar observations (Trautmann 1997). Presumably, however, earlier travellers could also have recorded such similarities, but they largely did not; what made this the moment when noticing and analyzing similarities became possible? In a trilogy of remarkable books, historian Thomas Trautmann (1997, 2005, 2006) has argued that this moment, the British conquest of the Indian subcontinent, brought into conversation, and collision, elite men from two religious traditions with sophisticated strategies for linguistic analysis, which made possible this novel way of imagining the relationship between languages and between nations.

In particular, British Orientalists encountered the tradition of linguistic analysis associated with Pāṇini, who was probably born in the fourth century BCE in Pushkalavati (present-day Charsadda, Pakistan). This body of knowledge was widely considered to be a work of (almost impenetrable) genius. In northern India, six sciences had been elaborated to help support the practice of Vedic ritual (a religion of Indo-Aryans in northern India and a predecessor to Hinduism, though different from it) that have been dated to 1750 to 500 BCE. Four of these sciences focussed on language (the six were ritual, phonetics, prosody, etymology, grammar, and astronomy). Such grammatical study was seen as a key part of the traditional Vedic religion; it helped to preserve the ability to perform key rituals and chants in Sanskrit, without change or corruption even as languages changed (Trautmann 2006, 46).

Pāṇini's grammar comprised close to 4,000 rules for Sanskrit phonology, morphology, and syntax. It was *structural*, spelling out detailed rules for combining various aspects of grammar to produce appropriate Sanskrit, but also analyzing other languages based on how similar they were to Sanskrit (and identifying the changes that needed to be made to them to render them more like Sanskrit). The detailed analyses in Pāṇini's grammar of how to combine and make sounds deeply affected European scholars; indeed, some key European scholars have argued that key innovations in European and British linguistics (such as *phonetics*, the study of the sounds of human speech, and the later discipline of *phonology*, which studies sound patterns) are impossible to imagine without these works (Trautmann 1997, 66). Saussure, Bloomfield, and Jakobson, whom we meet later in the book, were all deeply influenced by Pāṇini.

This account of the production of these forms of Orientalist knowledge as dialogic complicates some aspects of the Saidian account; Said focusses on Europe as a site for Orientalist production in ways that do not challenge European understandings that see India as a site providing data for European theorizing. Trautmann (1997) argues instead that there was a second intellectual renaissance spawned in Europe by the encounter with Sanskrit and its intellectual tradition, akin to the earlier Renaissance linked to encounters with Greek texts.

Ways of understanding language were also deeply shaped on the British side by religion, in this case by biblical accounts of a worldwide flood and the Tower of Babel. In the first biblical tale, found in the traditions of Christians, Muslim, and Jews, the world had become too sinful and humanity ignored calls to change its behaviour. God instructed one devout man, Noah, to build a boat to house his family and two of each species. He then flooded the earth, and drowned all the sinners. The flood was survived only by Noah's family and the animals on the ark, who then repopulated the earth. Accounts of what happened afterwards are a strategy for organizing space, time, and social relationships in the moment of recounting.

In the period immediately after the flood, all people were assumed to speak the same language, until some had the temerity to try to build a tower to reach God; God punished them by imposing multiple languages so they could no longer understand one another. Various expansions of "the people of the book"—the expansion of Islam, and later Christian/European expansion—tried to incorporate new people they encountered into these kinship-genealogical accounts. (In Chapter 5, we will see these distinctions even play a surprisingly central role in the elaboration of communist linguistics.) The names of Noah's sons (Shem, Ham, and Japheth) are often associated with humankind's expansion and dispersion after the flood, with Shem often mapped onto Asia (including the Middle East), Ham onto Africa, and Japheth onto Europe (see Figure 2.2).[3] Christian, Jewish, and Muslim religious traditions understood Ham as the ancestor of all Africans: Ham was understood to have black skin because Noah had cursed him (or Ham's youngest son), after Ham insulted him when he was drunk; this curse was used to justify slavery. It was also used as a way of accounting for migration history. Genealogy, as the study of biological kinship, thus became a tool for geographical, linguistic, and cultural understanding.

---

3 The significance of these distinctions persists until now. Q. Williams (2016) documents decolonizing struggles against stigmatization in South Africa of a nonstandard variety of Afrikaans called Gamtaal (Gam, here is a version of Ham), renamed and reclaimed as AfriKaaps, whose speakers are devalued as stupid, gangsterish, and working class.

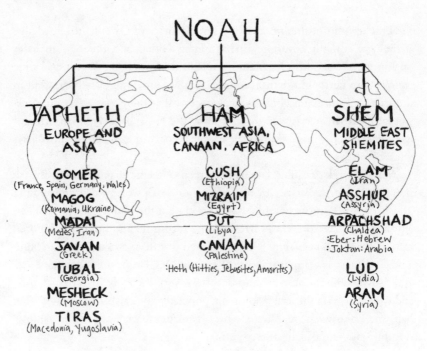

FIGURE 2.2: Biblical genealogy as social and spatial relations: Noah's descendants (Illustration: Andrea Derbecker). Adapted from http://www.foundationsforfreedom.net/References/OT/Pentateuch/Genesis/09TowerofBabel/Genesis10_11Genealogy.html (accessed April 21, 2016)

Note that this way of calculating genealogy only reckons kinship through the patrilineal line. It ignores any linkages through women that could confuse the patrilineage or relationships that could be mapped in other ways, as, for example, a web of life. Illegitimate offspring are not included, either. This form of kinship reckoning was often found in Northern Africa and the Middle East; it is one that anthropologists call *segmentary* (Trautmann 1997).

The story of Noah also has temporal implications. The unfolding of these spatial dispersions was understood to take place within the relatively short time allocated since the Flood. Though there were significant debates about how to calculate this, for British Protestants the matter had been settled by an archbishop in the eighteenth century: God had created the world in 4004 BCE, and the flood had taken place in 2349 BCE (Trautmann 1997, 57). The repeopling of the earth, and the spread of the human race, had to have taken place relatively rapidly, within about 4,000 years.

The encounter between Christian and religious traditions in India had complex implications for this biblical chronology. On the one hand, Hindu traditions also had flood stories, which Jones used to argue that the study of

Hindu scripture fortified and ratified Christian truth (Trautmann 1997, 58). On the other hand, Indian doctrines of immense cycles of time repeating on very long time scales (one figure calculated 4,320,000 years for an entire cycle of four ages) were a significant challenge to biblical notions, attractive to some, but firmly rejected by Jones. One of the most productive effects of this encounter between two different religious traditions was that it made it possible to imagine languages as related. European linguists, schooled in biblical forms of genealogy, encountered Indian structural linguistic analyses and transformed their discussions of similarity into discussions of kinship relations, which they also understood as historical relations.

With these tools for linguistic analysis and temporal orientation in place, all that was needed was a technique for establishing relationships. The strategy used was a deceptively simple one: *word lists*, with which linguists looked for similarities between various languages, as in the following words in a range of languages, from which the proto-Indo-European word for 'mother' is reconstructed (Trautmann 2006, 21).

WORDS for 'mother' (or related) in Indo-European languages

PIE:	*meH₂tér- "mother"
English:	**mother** (Old English: *mōdor*)
Gothic:	**móðir** "mother"
Latin:	**māter** "mother"
Ancient Greek	**mḗtēr** "mother"
Sanskrit	**mātár-** "mother"
Iranian	**mātar-** "mother
Celtic	**māthir** "mother"
Armenian	**mayr** "mother
Albanian	**motër** "sister"

Source: https://en.wikipedia.org/wiki/Indo-European_vocabulary

The use of such word lists is a strategy used by travellers, colonial officials, and missionaries, but developed in a range of imperial settings—in Western European circles (Locke and Leibniz), in the United States (Thomas Jefferson), and in Russia (linguists working for the royal family whose names we have not been able to retrieve). These word lists seem simple, but are not (Trautmann 2006). They focus on words that are assumed to be basic and authentic to the language (numbers, body parts, heavenly bodies, weather), and thus offer a theory of precisely what is seen as essential to basic human survival—and hence a language ideology. They exclude words understood as complex and perhaps foreign, like words linked to arts and science scholarship. They celebrate the "common man" versus the learned man, and assume it is possible to distinguish the "native" from the "foreign." These words are thus abstracted from time, proximity, and communication with neighbouring languages (Trautmann 2006, 37).

The relationships these word lists suggested among languages were debated in genealogical terms; for instance, should Sanskrit be understood as the mother of Indo-European languages, or as their brother? The organization of these relationships into a tree form (modelled on family trees) only occurred in 1853, more than half a century after Jones's initial observations, when August Schleicher, a German linguist, first published two articles using the graphic representation of a tree (in German, *Stammbaum*) (Richards 2008).

The idea of family trees is now so common as a way of understanding linguistic and cultural relationships that it may be difficult to imagine them as a technological innovation for organizing information. We can make three observations about what this new tree technology for representation postulates about the relationships of human languages. First, this structure is distinct from a structure of self-other (a binary, potentially recursive, structure) in that it posits sameness, calculated according to distance (Trautmann 2006). Second, it allows the organization of a large amount of information by calibrating degrees of difference or similarity. Of course, linguists spent a considerable amount of time debating how to draw these trees, and some aspects of all such trees remain contested. Like all informational technologies, trees leave out some information, or set it aside as unimportant. While it suggests all of these languages are related, it also suggests some are more closely related than others (e.g., Indic and Iranian languages are more closely related to each other than to Romance languages and Celtic languages, which are in turn seen as more closely related to each other than to Germanic languages). In this case, to assemble a tree, one assumes similarities are linked to descent structures and not, for example, to mixture or prolonged contact. In addition, a tree structure requires one to postulate a single ancestor. Here, the oldest ancestor of Greek, Latin, and Sanskrit is called *proto-Indo-European* (PIE), from which all these languages are said to be descended. Though there are debates about how to reconstruct PIE, they do not raise questions about whether there is a protolanguage. Note that the structure here is very like the idea of a single language spoken in Eden, and then diversifying.

FIGURE 2.3: Language relationships as family tree (Illustration: Andrea Derbecker). Adapted from http://slideplayer.com/slide/5800822/ (accessed April 21, 2016)

Third, this technology allows the British to answer specific questions that arose for them after their conquest of Bengal in the mid-eighteenth century: who are the Bengalis, how are they related to us, and where are they placed with respect to the nations of the world? For them, Indians posed an enigma: they were a dark-skinned people who were also civilized in ways that challenged prevailing European understandings of White and Black, civilized and primitive. This technology thus allowed scholars to postulate affinities between groups that were seen as potentially physically disparate. The revelation linked to the postulation of this form of kinship is perhaps most powerfully articulated in the words of the German linguist Friedrich Max Müller (1823–1900), who worked for much of his life as a Lutheran outsider in Britain and was a prominent popularizer of linguistic research:

> No authority could have been strong enough to persuade the Grecian army [of Alexander] that their gods and their hero-ancestors were the same as those of [the Indian] King Porus, or to convince the English soldier that the same blood was running in his veins, as in the veins of the dark Bengalese.... Though the historian may shake his head, though the physiologist may doubt, and the poet scorn the idea, all must yield before the facts furnished by language. There was a time when the ancestors of the Celts, the Germans, the Slaves [sic], the Greeks and Italians, the Persians and Hindus, were living together beneath the same roof, separate from the ancestors of the Semitic and Turanian races. (Müller 1855, 29 cited in Trautmann 1997, 177)[4]

In all imperial sites, we see strategies used to establish distinctions between the ruler and the ruled, to justify domination, occupation, and exploitation. We can see this in another aspect of linguistic debates at this time. The languages spoken in southern India were mapped at approximately the same time as proto-Indo-European was being delineated, and were seen as belonging to a separate language family, called Dravidian (Trautmann 2006). The invasion and conquest of this group by the Aryans, presumed to be lighter-skinned and civilizationally superior, was seen as comparable to the British invasion of India. As we saw above, many empires allude to earlier empires to naturalize invasion as part of human history. Later in the century, as the British sought labour for various imperial sites after the abolition of the slave trade, this distinction between northern and southern Indians, Aryans and Dravidians, could also have justified which people were subjected to forms of indentured labour in the Caribbean and various countries of Africa, labour conditions that remained exceedingly harsh. So, the postulation of PIE established a form of kinship between Britain and northern India, as it established differences from groups that were understood as belonging to other language families—especially, and critically, Semitic languages such as Arabic, Amharic, and Hebrew, but also languages from other groups that were postulated at this time, and have since become controversial (Hamitic, Turanian).

Orientalist analysis included, as Said notes, both celebrations of the East and critiques of it. The East is seen as a spiritual site whose religion can be an

---

4 Note that Turanian is no longer used as a linguistic family.

antidote to Western materialism (this is often still part of the allure of yoga, for many practitioners). Easterners are seen as exotic, sensual, promising, sublime, pleasurable, intensely energetic. They are also portrayed as melancholy, fatalistic, rigid, terrifying, indolent. This leads, Trautmann (1997) notes, to both Indophilia and Indophobia. The first was evident in Jones's linguistic work and in his religious analyses when he argued that India offers a benign, and independent, corroboration of biblical history (Trautmann 1997, 80). Encounters with other Indian disciplines, such as astronomy and geography, also evoked enthusiasm for their originality and accuracy.

The enthusiasm for Hindus and Hinduism is also a way of critiquing Muslims, who are styled as "foreigners" and "conquerors," while the Hindus are identified as "native" (Trautmann 1997, 97). The enthusiasm for Sanskrit is significant. Jones enthused, in terms similar to those we saw above, that it was "the most perfect language that is, or, I believe, ever was, on this earth; for it is more perfect than Greek" (cited in Trautmann 1997, 81). Its perfection, in his eyes, lay in that it was understood to be not yet corrupted by change; in addition, ancient writings in Sanskrit were seen as "repositories of the primitive experiences and religions of the human race and, as such, confirmatory of the truth of Christian scripture" (Trautmann 1997, 97). This, too, has a temporal aspect: as in biblical tradition, which focusses on the fall from grace, it is the past that is seen as a source of wisdom, and not the future. However, this form of kinship also firmly places India in Britain's past, a trope that will harden (as we'll see in the next chapter) with the temporal understandings of evolutionary theory.

With comparative philology, then, we see a distinctive form of colonial intimacy. While the tree seems to encode relationships of relatively egalitarian fraternity, in practice the glory of India was taken to have happened in its past. Sanskrit was taken by many to have been a perfected language; Indian civilization in general, including its scientific knowledge, was seen to have declined since then, thus allowing the British to rationalize their rule as a benefit. It is also often linked with other representations of "affection," including close relationships with Indian scholars. India's glory, because no longer extant, was taken to be now available for the taking by Britain; as the saying went, India became the "jewel in the [imperial] crown."

Though the language reconstructed as ancestral for Sanskrit, Latin, and Greek is now often called proto-Indo-European, there was debate in the late eighteenth and early nineteenth centuries about which designation to use. Some used *Japhetic*, after one of Noah's sons. German scholars were particularly inclined to use *Indo-Germanic*. Some also used *Aryan*, from the Sanskrit word *Arya*, used by Sanskrit speakers to refer to "self" versus "others." Aryan was seen as particularly apt, because there were taken to be traces of that word scattered widely across these speakers—in Iran (land of the Aryans) and in Eire (Ireland) (Trautmann 1997). Aryan often implied a civilizational hierarchy, with some linguists (Müller especially) favourably contrasting the Aryans, taken to be people of the plow or agriculturalists, to nomads elsewhere in Asia (he called the speakers of this group *Turanians*); Aryan came, in some usages (including those of the Nazis), to imply a racial hierarchy as well (we will examine this further in Chapter 5).

One notorious instance shows the way the idea of the Aryan was used to establish racial hierarchies intertwined with class hierarchies. Arthur de Gobineau (1816–82), a Frenchman who claimed to be an aristocrat, argued that the aristocracy in France was formed from Germanic blood while the commoners came from inferior Celtic and Latin peoples. Gobineau's work was translated by White supremacist Americans who were advocates of slavery, though they omitted the passages in which he critiqued the United States as an aggregate of Europe's degraded and degenerate racial stock and as contaminated by too much racial mixing (Wright 1999). Understandings of Aryans have also shaped nationalist battles in South Asia, including ongoing debates over whether Sanskrit-speaking Aryans were indigenous to India or immigrants/conquerors from elsewhere (Trautmann 2005). To avoid the connotations of White supremacy and racial hatred that now attach to the word Aryan, the more common name in academic linguistics has become proto-Indo-European.

The Orientalists who advocated learning the languages of India, and whose policies of carefully studying the languages and practices of India were part of colonial policy, were challenged in the early nineteenth century by the Anglicists, who argued for instruction of Indian elites in English. Concern about how to maintain colonial rule deepened in India for both political and economic reasons. It was triggered by a spate of revolutions and wars of independence: the American revolution against the British (1776), the French revolution against the monarchy (1789), the Haitian revolution against France and against slavery (1804), and the establishment of new nations in the former Spanish empire in the Americas between 1810 and 1824.

Instruction in English was seen as promoting assimilation, a healing bond, and active attachment to the empire. Sanskrit was even dismissed by some scholars as too perfect an artificial language, too regular and rich, such that, they said, it must be an invention of priests, a hoax (Trautmann 1997, 124). Fort William, a school that had been set up in Calcutta (now Kolkata) in 1800 for the education of civil servants in any of nine Asian languages, Hindu and Muslim literature, law and customs, world geography, and political economy came to be seen by some as a site that was contaminating young British men with Orientalist thoughts and religions, rather than helping them retain their national character (Franklin 1995, 122).

Challenges to linguistic affinities were paralleled by other challenges to intimacy. Concern about racial mixing between British men and Indian women also accompanied these reforms, with critiques of British men, including some linguists, who married or maintained households with Indian women occurring alongside the promotion of Anglo-only domestic households (Trautmann 1997, 110). For instance, one object of critique was the British Sanskritist Alexander Hamilton (1762–1824), the first professor of Sanskrit in Europe (and a cousin of the well-known American statesman, also named Alexander Hamilton), who had married a Bengali woman (Rocher 2004). Stoler (1991) also notes the sharpening of racial distinctions and the policing of interracial relationships between Dutch colonists and people in what is now Indonesia as colonialism proceeded and questions about colonial authority grew. Indophilia became seen as rather eccentric in Britain, the domain of vegetarians and pacifists, though regularly available even through the twentieth and early twenty-first centuries as a way of challenging mainstream norms—witness the Beatles and their embrace of Indian mysticism.

Jones's contributions, and those of other Orientalists, have often been treated rather generously in the history of linguistics as their knowledge of and interest in Oriental languages are contrasted with the Anglicist colonial administrators who followed, men who often had less knowledge of India or of Indian languages, and who argued for investment in the limited instruction of English rather than in Asian languages. A key Anglicist was the well-known philosopher James Mill, who published his *History of British India* in 1818 without ever visiting India or learning an Indian language. With his portraits of barbarous Indians, he sought to deflate the "exalted, and it may be granted sometimes, exaggerated descriptions of Hindu ... learning, sciences, talents, virtue, which emanated fom the amiable enthusiasm of Sir William Jones" (Mill 1849, cited in Kopf 1995, 146). Thomas Babington Macaulay (then director of public instruction) published a famous "Minute" in 1835, in which he argued for the inferiority of Asian languages, literatures, and knowledge, and for the instruction of select elites in English instead of fostering scholarship in useless native languages.

Anglicist policy was, then, associated more with Indophobia than Indophilia (see Evans 2002; Hall 2009). Anglicists tended to focus on Oriental despotism, depravity, deception, and distrust. If government, laws, and religions were leading to these moral and political problems, they argued (Trautmann 1997, 107), then the cure would be British rule; Indians needed to assimilate (but the British needed to be cautious about assimilating them). Macaulay ([1835] 1972) said that the goal of British rule should be English-medium instruction to form an elite class that was "Indian in blood and colour, but English in taste, in opinions, in morals, and in intellect" (249). English becomes in this missive the site for the repository of modernity, and the science that is worth knowing.

Rather than assessing Orientalists or Anglicists as more or less benevolent, however, it is perhaps most helpful to see changing views in light of the shift from mercantile to industrial capitalism. After the Industrial Revolution of the late eighteenth century in England, a revolution centred primarily around textiles, English industrialists began to seek new markets. If the mercantilists of the British East India Company were interested in fostering, and controlling, the India economy for their own ends, English industrialists were interested in neutralizing competitors in India. The Government of India Act of 1833 further tightened Crown control of the company. After the Indian Rebellion of 1857, the British Government seized control of all administrative functions in India; the East India Company was critiqued for its abuses of power and dissolved, with promises to replace imperial looting with a competent civil administration.

That the Anglicist views largely prevailed after this point helps to explain several important phenomena. One is the spread of English in many English colonies, first among elites and then later through wider forms of public education. The other is one of the oddities of linguistic study, one not fully taken up by Said: though the British were regularly in contact with South Asian languages and scholars, it was continental scholars, especially in France and Germany (such as Bleek, Bopp, Grimm, Renan, Saussure, Schlegel, Schleicher, and Stacey), who came to dominate PIE studies. Germany became a key centre for the study of Sanskrit, in part because the various German states were not unified until the late nineteenth century, and each German statelet had its own specialist at its local university (Trautmann 1997). British knowledge about these languages apparently became less central to imperial rule as English became the key medium for colonial instruction.

By the late nineteenth century, comparative linguistics was challenged in several more fundamental ways. It was challenged by evolutionary thought, which originally drew on and paralleled linguistic models but ultimately departed from them. It was also challenged by scholars who focussed on language mixture, especially in languages forged on plantations in the New World, but also in certain areas of European dialectology. Finally, it was challenged by the elaboration of a focus on cultural relativism and historical particularity in the Boasian tradition in American anthropology.

CHAPTER 3

LANGUAGE AND IMPERIALISM II: EVOLUTION, HYBRIDITY, HISTORY

FIGURE 3.1: Diversity? Unity? Hybridity? Race. (Photo: American Anthropological Association)

"Mixing Things Up"

The image in Figure 3.1 is taken from the website of the American Anthropological Association's project "Race: Are We So Different?," which is where Monica first encountered it (http://www.understandingrace.org). It has been widely used in projects critiquing the idea of race and has also been widely reproduced, including on the website of one American university (Michigan Technological University), advertising a new minor in diversity studies, which is where Bonnie first encountered it (http://www.mtu.edu/humanities/undergraduate/minors/diversity-studies/).

The MTU website cites philosopher Martha Nussbaum (1997) as saying that it is important to understand "the motives and choices of people different from ourselves, seeing them not as forbiddingly alien or other, but as sharing many problems and possibilities with us" (85). But let's take a closer look at this image. To see it as signifying unity in diversity requires us to see it as a three- (perhaps four-) part racial model, with representatives of groups that look, minimally, Black, Asian, and perhaps White. On the American Anthropological Association's website the image changes constantly, with different quarters of the picture being laminated onto a female face. (There is also a male counterpart, though the faces coded as male and female are never intermixed.)

In our view, while the image may blur the distinctions between these groups a bit, it also reinscribes them. It assumes them as central, even natural categories. Where did these naturalized racial models come from? What have been the effects of naturalizing such racial differences, especially for making inequality or for challenging them in the name of emancipation? How are they tied to other differences, especially linguistic ones, or to broader debates about race, nation, civilization in relation to religious versus scientific authority, to nature versus culture, human versus animal?

In the last chapter we discussed the kinship tree models that comparative philologists developed in the context of imperial regimes. In this chapter we will discuss critiques of these models and the debates that surrounded them. We will begin by showing that during the course of the nineteenth and early twentieth centuries, evolutionary theory built on comparative philology but sought to replace divine with scientific authority, just as the emergence of liberal democracy replaced clerical and aristocratic authority with the rise of the national public sphere of the bourgeoisie. Its naturalization of difference as genetic, and as arrayed along a timeline of "progress" from less to more modern and civilized, can be understood as linked to the consolidation and institutionalization of colonial rule, and to its legitimation (the rise of homogeneous and bounded notions of nation is also relevant but will be discussed in Chapter 4). It became important to show how, together, language, culture, and race could allow for the discovery and description of stages of human evolution. The anthropological "comparative method" sought to situate all groups, past and present, somewhere on an evolutionary spectrum from primitive to civilized, making it possible to identify some groups as representative of early stages of evolution and others as exemplars of civilization.

The second part of the chapter addresses a more profound challenge to the tree model of comparative philology, and to the genetic classification that remained central to evolutionary models. This challenge came from isolates, languages not readily linked to others as members of any language "family," and, more importantly, from linguistic forms seen as "mixed." Philologists were concerned with two types. The first were languages in one geographical area that ostensibly ought to belong to different families but that shared important structural features. The example that first caught their attention were the languages of the Balkan area of southeast Europe, which include Slavic languages, Greek, Romance languages, Albanian, and Romany. The second, and perhaps most disturbing, case for comparative philology was that of the pidgin and creole languages forged on plantations in the brutal conditions of enslavement and later of indentured labour. While their existence had long been recognized, they became particularly salient starting in the last half of the nineteenth century, when linguists and anthropologists were attempting to build universal models of language, culture, and race as ranked and interconnected objects.

Both these latter sets of examples challenged the idea that each language had only one ancestor, thereby at the same time challenging ideas of racial and linguistic separation and hierarchy. One solution was to characterize them as simplified or somehow "reduced" (say, because they had fewer case endings or pronoun forms than other languages to which they were related), incorporating them into evolutionary ideologies about the inferior mental and physical capacities of their speakers. However, these languages opened the door to theories of *diffusion* (as opposed to evolution) as an alternative theory of social and linguistic change, and therefore to an alternative valuing of racial, cultural, and linguistic mixture.

Finally, we look at the ideas of the anthropologist Franz Boas and his students in the late nineteenth and early twentieth centuries, ideas that became foundational to the Americanist tradition of anthropology, and with which we still grapple today. Boas (1858–1942), a German Jew who came to the United States in 1887, was centrally interested in challenging the inequities connected to evolutionist thought. He disaggregated language, culture, and race, challenging the comparative method with a method (*historical particularism*) that sought to anchor each race, each culture, and each language in the complex conditions of its own history. At the same time, however, he was committed to modern ideas of progress, seeing some languages (especially Indigenous languages in North America) as windows into the primitive thought that was destined to disappear through the march of progress, and some races (notably African Americans) as requiring better social conditions in order to fully participate in modernity. He shared with scholars of language areas and pidgins and creoles an interest in notions of hybridity, and a preference for privileging diffusion over genealogy to explain difference and change, whether for language, culture, or race. He understood scientific investigation of phenomena observable through fieldwork as a bulwark against discrimination and devaluation, which he understood to be matters of prejudice to be countered through effective education.

His student Edward Sapir (1884–1939) and Sapir's student Benjamin Whorf (1897–1941) disaggregated language, culture, and race even further, facilitating a turn to the study of language as an autonomous domain influential in the development of linguistic thought. Their work can also be seen as attempts to resolve some of the key contradictions of their time, including the way the promises of liberal democracy were both underpinned and undone by imperialism and the way difference as an essential element of humanity could be harnessed both to inequality and to a celebration of possibility.

Imperialism and Industrial Capitalism

We begin by placing these language ideological developments in conversation with other political and economic movements. By the end of the nineteenth century, capitalism in Europe was facing one of its periodic crises (Hobsbawm 1987). Economies had largely shifted from mercantile capitalism to industrial capitalism. The number of industrial producers and industrial economies was growing rapidly (Lenin [1917] 1987). Technological advances improved the output of industry; as a result, ever more goods were produced, but a significant market for consumption had not yet developed. Prices therefore dropped, as did profits. Governments took various measures to protect markets; this is one of the reasons Western European nationalism is often said to have consolidated at this time (see Chapter 4).

There are four key strategies used for this consolidation: protectionism, scientific management, monopoly, and imperialism. *Protectionism* is insulating industries in a nation against competition from imported goods by keeping out foreign goods, and thereby encouraging industries to focus on developing domestic markets. One key way to do this was through unifying linguistic (and therefore communicative) markets (Anderson 1983), whether through education (now extended beyond elites), media, or other institutional means. *Scientific management* describes finely detailed regulation of production processes and of labourers' actions in order to get more work out of them. *Monopoly* means combining potential competitors into one larger unit, making it possible to raise prices without risk of a competitor challenging one's dominance. We will discuss these in greater detail in Chapter 4. The fourth and final strategy, the one central to this chapter, is *imperialism*. Colonies were also sometimes seen as control points for trade or military action, or sites that would enable business penetration elsewhere. While clearly an extension of the forms of empire developed in mercantile capitalism, the word *imperialism* itself actually only entered British politics in the 1870s, and was seen as newly coined (though by 1900 it was widely used; Hobsbawm 1987, 60).

Between 1880 and 1914, one-quarter of the world outside Europe and the Americas was divided into territories formally controlled by a handful of countries: Britain, France, Germany, Italy, the Netherlands, Belgium, the U.S., Russia, and Japan (Hobsbawm 1987, 57–59). The earlier pre-industrial empires of Spain and Portugal had either successfully been broken up by colonial elites seeking to wrest power from a weakening Spain in the early 19th century or were carved up by other imperial powers, though both Spain and Portugal retained some colonies in Africa. By the end of World War 1, 85 per cent of the world was colonized by Europe (Said 1978, 123). The United States also wanted to be seen as a full-fledged power; while wars with Indigenous people continued through the late nineteenth century, the U.S. drew on its experience with settler colonialism to claim new overseas colonies, including those lost by the Spanish in the Spanish-American War (Philippines, Guam, Cuba, Puerto Rico), as well as the independent kingdom of Hawai'i.

By the end of this period there were no independent states left in the Pacific; in Africa, the only remaining independent states were Ethiopia, Liberia, and some parts of Morocco. The Caribbean area was also comprehensively colonized. The traditional empires of Asia (China, Persia, the Ottoman Empire) remained independent, though Western powers carved out zones of influence among them; other zones in Asia remained sites of formal colonial control.

After the emancipation of slaves throughout the nineteenth century, there were increased attempts to differentiate White and Black people on other grounds in order to justify maintaining race as a means of creating labour forces and other forms of economic and political inequality. In many former slave societies, there were also attempts after emancipation or independence to recruit other people, especially from Asia, for the same tasks as indentured labour. Working conditions, however, were little changed.

Some scholars (notably Hobsbawm 1987, 62) see this as the first age of globalization, connected in complex ways to the inequalities also produced by industrial capitalism domestically. Imperialists noted that conquest of other countries helped alleviate tensions produced by industrialization at home, notably those produced by sharp political struggles between classes. The British industrialist Cecil Rhodes argued that if one wanted to avoid civil war, one had to become an imperialist (Hobsbawm 1987, 69). Imperialism was seen as a way of improving economic conditions at home and offering additional sites where dissatisfied Europeans could migrate to find economic opportunities. Ideologies of race and racism inscribed in teleological hierarchies of progress, and legitimized through ideas about nature, language, and culture, rationalized imperialism and allowed even the most disenfranchised and potentially discontented White workers to feel superior to people in (or from) the colonies, whether those white workers were in the colonies or at home.

Race could also be invoked to overcome the class and ethnic diversities of the nations of Europe: "The fiction of common descent enshrined in the metaphor of fatherland and motherland, and applied indiscriminately to the overwhelmingly hybrid populations of Europe, improved the tone of civil and military organization. The racial interpretation of nationhood imparted to the physical, cultural and linguistic hodgepodges known as England, France, Germany, etc., a sense of community based on the illusion of a common origin and the mirage of a common destiny" (M. Harris 1968, 106). At the same time, racism could also be used to ratify class privilege.

The conditions of this period help explain the rise of evolutionary theory and challenges to it in several ways. The idea of the struggle to survive, and of the survival of the fittest, fit neatly with capitalist ideologies promoted by Adam Smith and others, suggesting that the welfare of each individual and society depended upon unlimited competition in the marketplace. This ideology underpinned industrial entrepreneurship and economic competition (M. Harris 1968, 106), and held that groups not able to successfully repel imperial occupation were inferior; they either would or should be eradicated in the path to progress, because they were unfit or needed to be changed, in order to fit into the new societal expectations. Notions of struggle were thus linked with notions of social progress, privileging competition over other ways of imagining social relations and the nation, such as cooperation or altruism.

The violence and inequality involved in fighting for an advantageous position in increased competition for raw materials and labour could be legitimized by constructing social difference as natural (racial), and placing it on a temporal path toward not only civilization, but more importantly, perhaps, a specific idea of modernity and progress linked to scientific reason and technology (we will discuss this idea further in Chapters 4 and 5) in which the aim is not spiritual perfection, but rather ever-increasing improvement. At the same time, scientific reasoning required accounting for all available data, and so the kinds of movements and mixing that evolutionary theory (or comparative philology for that matter) could not account for became a major problem to be resolved. Finally, industrial capitalism had difficulty in reconciling the tension between the promise of progress for all and the inequalities on which it depended, leaving room open for critique and for the kind of universalism that the Americanist approach tried to develop—although, as we shall also see, it too was caught in its own contradictions.

Evolutionary Theory: Language and/as Race

The defining text of this period, Charles Darwin's *The Origin of Species*, was published in 1859. Twelve years later, Darwin published *The Descent of Man* (1871), introducing the concepts of *natural selection* and *human evolution* (he had delayed publishing these ideas earlier because he thought their critiques of divine understandings of human origin would prevent his work from getting a fair hearing). In order to make his case for the evolutionary emergence of humankind, Darwin had to show a fundamental similarity between humanity and higher mammals in mental capacity, including speech (Alter 1999, 97). To do this, he focussed on language, arguing that it owes its origin to the imitation of certain sounds, to animal voices, and to people's own instinctive cries. He thereby opened a debate on whether or not language is what distinguishes humans from nonhumans and, as we shall see in this chapter, different kinds of humans as more or less evolved—that is, closer to or further from other animals. Over time, these works led to a hierarchical understanding of social groupings, rooted not in differences understood as relatively (if not always absolutely) mutable, such as religious or civilizational difference, but in immutable biology.

Darwin drew on geological research that showed that the history of the earth was considerably longer than biblical chronologies would have it. He also drew on the work of Thomas Malthus (1798), who thought that as human populations increased they would have to struggle for survival. However, Darwin departed from Malthus who, in the wake of the violence of the French Revolution, had become pessimistic about the possibility of perfecting human nature; Darwin argued, on the contrary, for the perfectibility of humankind. His work thus reconciled some ideas that might seem irreconcilable: "Following Darwin, one could be both a racist, believing in the hereditary limits of a race or species, and at the same time, one could be an environmentalist, secure in the knowledge that there was no limit to the perfectibility of any species, including man" (M. Harris 1968, 116).

Darwin used evidence from conflicts between various societies to support his argument:

> All that we know about savages ... shows that from the remotest times successful tribes have supplanted other tribes.... At the present day civilized nations are everywhere supplanting barbarous nations, excepting where the climate opposes a deadly barrier.... It is, therefore, highly probable that with mankind the intellectual faculties have been gradually perfected through natural selection. (Darwin [1859] 1871, 154)

Darwin's contemporaries directly and explicitly linked this struggle for survival to arguments in favour of capitalism and colonialism. Herbert Spencer, a key figure in developing the implications of Darwin's work for anthropology, thought that since the time scale for evolutionary change was seen as relatively long and slow, humans simply had the obligation not to interfere with the workings of the laws of nature (e.g., by alleviating poverty, or establishing more developed health care systems), which would eventually eliminate those who were unfit. Soon, this was modified under the name of *eugenics* to favour interference with human reproduction in a variety of ways to ensure that only the "fit" reproduced. It took its extreme form under Nazism, though was scarcely confined to it (see Chapter 5).

The change in understandings of time scale also led to a reassessment of the relative value of biology and comparative philology (Alter 1999, 70). Differences among humans were now seen to have come about on a scale of tens, or hundreds, of thousands of years, a period much longer than that in which Indo-European languages were held to have become differentiated. Biology became seen by many as the critical discipline for understanding human differences, with linguistics as a supplement only for the most recent period (Trautmann 1997, 183). Nonetheless, linguistic evidence remained important, and the relative significance of evidence about language and biology for Darwinian theory, as well as the relative usefulness of comparative philological insights, remained the subject of debate for quite some time.

In Chapter 2, we saw that the taxonomies linked to family trees had a teleological and evaluative bent, and that often (though not always) Indo-European languages were seen as the most civilized. After Darwin, linguistic taxonomies were coupled with the newly developed apparatus of evolutionary theory, though they had also inspired it, such that the forms seen as less "elaborated" were also seen as stuck at earlier moments of evolutionary development. Given the role that trees played in both biology and philology, this did not often require much modification of the data, just changes to the interpretation of it.

The major shift involved providing a scientific, rather than a divine, basis for grouping languages into distinct categories. This new scientific basis posited a natural link between different languages, or types or families of languages, and "races," sometimes understood as "species." The major debates involved whether different language categories represented different stages in the unstoppable evolution toward perfection, in which the fittest survive because they represent different and differently adapted and adaptable species of distinct origins, or in which they could be helped to survive, since, although currently at "earlier" stages of evolution, they were amenable to efforts to move them along the evolutionary scale.

Here we return to Schleicher, whose introduction of the tree as a model for organizing linguistic information we saw in Chapter 2. Schleicher developed his tree diagram before he read Darwin, influenced at least in part by conversations with Ernst Haeckel, a colleague at his university who was a zoologist, naturalist, and talented illustrator, and who likely brought Darwin's work to his attention. Afterward, Schleicher wrote Haeckel an enthusiastic long open letter, which was published in German in 1863 as *Darwinische Theorie und die Sprachwissenschaft*, and translated as *Darwinism Tested by the Science of Language* (1869). Schleicher saw Darwinian theory as ratifying his earlier work, and as offering tools for understanding linguistics as a natural science. In particular, Schleicher left no doubt in this text that he believed that in the struggle for the fittest, Indo-Germanic speakers had already prevailed thus justifying and explaining imperial ventures of the time:

> Not a word of Darwin's need be changed here if we wish to apply this reasoning to the languages. Darwin describes here with striking accuracy the process of the struggle for existence in the field of human speech. In the present period of the life of man the descendants of the Indo-Germanic family are the conquerors in the struggle for existence; they are engaged in continual extension, and have already supplanted or dethroned numerous other idioms. (1869, 64)

He also saw what he described as the "decay" of Indigenous languages in North America and the spread of European tongues as key examples of such a struggle.

Schleicher also postulated that certain languages should be seen as marking earlier stages of languages he saw as more civilized. He described what he saw as the relationship between Indo-Germanic languages and Chinese:

> All the languages of a higher organization—as for instance the Indo-Germanic parent which we are able to examine—show by their construction, in a striking manner, that they have arisen from simpler

forms, through a process of gradual development. The construction of all languages points to this, that the eldest forms were in reality alike or similar; and those less complex forms are preserved in some idioms of the simplest kind, as, for example, Chinese. (1869, 50)

Schleicher argued for congruence between Darwinian perspectives and comparative linguistics, and even argued that the latter had anticipated the former; for him, in fact, linguistics had the advantage of a fuller record for reconstruction than that found for plants and animals (Alter 1999, 74, 76). He differed further with Darwin in his ideas about where humans came from. Darwin espoused *monogenesis*, that is, the idea that all humans were descended from the same ancestors (an idea congruent with Christian ideas about Adam and Eve). However, Schleicher (and others) advocated *polygenesis*, the idea that different groups of humans descended from different ancestors.

The debate marks how linguists were grappling with the problem of how to understand the relationships among languages that were understood as coming from different ones (Alter 1999). *Monogenetic* ideas paralleled biblical accounts that all humans shared a common ancestry, and tended to believe that human nature was modifiable to some degree, perhaps by degeneration or a fall away from the original Edenic perfection, perhaps because of the influence of the environment. *Polygeneticists* tended to be more racially determinist, arguing that races had undeviating physical and moral natures that could perhaps only be altered by interbreeding, although they tended to believe that "miscegenation" led to people who were not "fertile hybrids," or who degenerated from their original racial type (M. Harris 1968). In the late eighteenth and early nineteenth centuries, a number of defenders of slavery were polygeneticists who argued that slavery was a humane form of life because it allowed for an inferior species to be in the care of a superior one (though some Christian monogeneticists made a parallel justificatory argument for "humanitarian enslavement").

Almost all anthropological debates about race in the United States in the first half of the nineteenth century were preoccupied with the controversy between polygeneticists and monogeneticists. Since Darwin was an adherent of monogenesis, his work was seen by some as reconciling the two views: humans had a common ancestor, but it was an ape, not Adam. Some decided to revise portrayals of Adam: instead of being portrayed as white, as he often had been earlier, he was portrayed as black in order to argue that, under the influence of civilization, people had gradually turned white. Others, however, saw Darwin's work as even stronger support for a polygenetic position, one that showed that some races would meet their extinction at the hands of others, the evidence for which was massive European success in the conquest of people in Africa, America, Asia, and the Pacific Islands (M. Harris 1968).

In European linguistics, the debate about monogenesis and polygenesis was waged in part on the terrain of *morphology*, the study of the grammatical shape of languages as expressed through root words and affixes (bits of meaningful linguistic form, that is, *morphemes*, which are not full words and are attached to roots in order to modify their meaning). Grammatical evidence of this kind was seen as more coherent, with fewer elements to explain, and with much more frequently occurring structures than the word-focussed work conducted by most comparative philologists (Errington 2008, 73). It was understood to offer a way of comparing languages systematically, just as comparative studies of anatomy did for bodies.

Earlier scholars, such as the Schlegel brothers, August Wilhelm Schlegel (1767–1845) and Friedrich Schlegel (1772–1829), had already paved the way for such analyses in the early nineteenth century. They had made a distinction between *organic languages*, such as Sanskrit and German, with flexion (roots and suffixes) versus what they saw as more *mechanical languages*, such as Chinese, Basque, and Arabic, which, according to them, had more "primitive" grammatical elements. "Mechanical" languages were seen as passive in the face of external forces (note here the resonance with Orientalist stereotypes of Asian passivity) and were not internally coherent, while organic languages were seen as actively engaged with historical forces, rather than passively submitting to them (see Errington 2008).

Wilhelm von Humboldt (1767–1835), a Prussian linguist and educator, had argued that a language could be understood as more logical the more it rendered grammatical relations explicit, for example, by adding morphological material signalling person, number, position with respect to the speaker, or connections among words (via declensions, conjugations, and prepositions; Joseph 1999). In 1836, he made a four-way distinction between languages representing stages of development, with the earliest being *isolating* (in which morphemes are not tied to each other, as in Chinese), *agglutinating* (in which morphemes are tied together in a string, as in Indigenous languages of North America), *incorporating* (in which one morpheme incorporates another into its form, as in Basque), and what were, in von Humboldt's view, the most developed, fecund, and abundant *inflectional* forms (i.e., which must mark onto root words such meaningful things as number—singular, dual, plural—or gender—masculine, feminine, neutral, as in Greek, Latin, or Sanskrit) (see Errington 2008, 76 for a helpful review).

Schleicher built on this work to distinguish at least three different kinds of languages, understood, in his case, as in some ways parallel to biological species (Lehmann 1967). The first were those that he saw as invariable and monosyllabic, such as Chinese or Burmese. The second were those that he saw as being able to attach affixes before (prefixes), after (suffixes), or in the middle (infixes) of roots, such as Finnish, Basque, most of the Indigenous languages of the New World, and Bantu (an example of a prefix in English is, indeed, "pre," meaning "before"). The third were languages such as all Semitic and Indo-European languages, with obligatory inflections. The difference between Schleicher's views and these earlier understandings lies in how he understood notions of time and race. Schleicher saw those groups that were to be understood as "contemporary primitives" as offering insight into the earliest stages of human evolution.

It was, however, Schleicher's zoologist colleague and friend Haeckel who most fully developed the linkage between language, race, and evolution, arguing that the languages with the most potential were spoken by the races with the most potential. Haeckel became a key proponent of scientific racism and *Social Darwinism* (which argued that the fittest races would prevail). Haeckel postulated the rise of different language groups, linked with each of the major language groups of the world, each of which was a different species. He posited 10 races, hierarchically ranked from Negro to Caucasian (Richards 2008).

Haeckel drew not only on Schleicher, but also on the work of his cousin, Wilhelm Heinrich Immanuel Bleek (1827–75). Bleek was trained in comparative philology at the University of Berlin, where his father was a professor of theology who challenged the historical veracity of the Bible. He became the official linguist for a British expedition to Niger in 1854, and later travelled to Cape Town in 1856 to work as an interpreter and librarian for the Governor of the Cape. His work played a key role in elaborating ideas of racial hierarchy in South Africa (Gilmour 2006). In an essay published in 1853, *On the Origin of Language*, he argued that the purpose of language study was to illuminate human development, understood in evolutionary terms. As Gilmour notes, "Bleek presented a model of language … in which a hierarchical arrangement of *contemporaneous* human groups was mapped differently onto a *sequential* process of evolutionary development" (2006, 175).

To make this argument, Bleek broke with continental philological models that focussed on classical, written languages, not contemporary, spoken ones (as we will see, this will become perhaps the key basis for the development of the autonomous discipline of linguistics). In the first book of his massive *Comparative Grammar of South African Languages* (1862), Bleek argued that comparative philology could allow the reconstruction of history in the absence of written records and insufficient oral histories, giving insight into the earliest and most primitive languages. He was particularly interested in languages that had "stopped" at the lowest levels of development, as indicative of the earliest stages of linguistic development, such as, in his view, the people and languages of southern Africa. For him, this region could serve as a philological laboratory and a window into prehistory.

Bleek's work is notable, too, for the role it gives sex and gender in evolutionary schemata. Bleek divided languages into two categories, prefix pronominal languages (languages such as Zulu, which he argued do not classify nouns by gender) or suffix pronominal ones (languages such as "Hottentot" [Khoi, or San] and all European languages, which he argued do; see Gilmour 2006, 180–81). "Is it, then," Bleek wrote with breathless excitement, "a mere accident that nearly all the nations which have made any progress in scientific acquirement speak sexual languages?" (1869b, xxii–xxiii, cited in Gilmour 2006, 183). This conflation of sex and grammatical gender, of course, reinforces the idea of languages as tied to biological(ly-reproduced) races.

Bleek furthered this connection by articulating his linguistic taxonomy with other forms of science, from anthropometric techniques for bodily measurement being developed in anthropology to climatological research. Discussions of the cranial capacities and anatomical differences of various groups at this time were also used to justify hierarchical discussions about language, with different brain sizes used to suggest different mental capacities, and facial morphology used to justify ability to speak in certain ways. Bleek's work thus participated in a hardening of racial ideas from the mid-nineteenth century on, rationalized through biological thought (whether anthropologists and linguists argued that "primitive" groups were perfectible or not, they all understood them as "primitive").

Anthropologists also drew on linguistic evidence to develop cultural and racial taxonomies. One influential scheme was that of the American lawyer and anthropologist Lewis Henry Morgan (1818–81), who divided human history, and contemporary humans, into three major groups with some subdivisions in each: Savage, Barbaric, and Civilized (1877). He distinguished these groups by their ways of organizing family, other social relations, technologies, and kinship terminologies. Other rankings distinguished, and ranked, the black, brown or red, yellow, and white races, with whites seen in each case as epitomizing civilization and modernity. Morgan (and others) thought that cultures could evolve along the line of progress. The empirical question of the time was taken to be whether all cultures would necessarily go through all stages in the same ways in all hemispheres, rather than any questioning of the divisions.

The key feature that distinguished 'civilized' groups from others were linguistic technologies: a phonetic alphabet and writing. The distinction between orality and literacy was mapped onto the relationship between primitive and civilized (in ways that echo into the 1960s' era of international development discussed in Chapter 7). The example of how different languages and different scripts were understood in the French occupation of Vietnam (1861–1945) can illustrate how these distinctions were used to justify colonial policies. Vietnamese was classified as "monosyllabic" by the linguistic typologies of the time, though inferior even to other monosyllabic languages such as Chinese because it hadn't had time to develop under Chinese imperial rule, and was possibly like a patois (a devalued form of the standardizing languages being developed in Europe; see Chapter 4) or even a pidgin (see the next section of this chapter). Because China had occupied the area now known as Vietnam for a thousand years, those who were literate and elite—aristocrats and civil servants—used a version of the Chinese writing system or a Chinese-style script more fully adapted to Vietnamese.

The monosyllabic nature of Vietnamese was seen by some commentators, including a scholarly French occupier and a missionary, as incompatible with phonetic-style writing or with communicating certain ideas of progress, science, and humanity (DeFrancis 1977, 78–79). Some thought the language would slowly evolve, in light of contact with French, through the stages of being an agglutinative language to an inflectional language; others were wary of this idea (DeFrancis 1977, 142). In any case, however, few colonial administrators wanted to learn Chinese characters, and developing the romanized script was seen as helpful for avoiding untrustworthy (again we see this idea!) translators. However, Jules-Clément Neyret, a late-nineteenth-century French colonial adminstrator in "Annam-Tonkin," as the French called the region, wrote that even if an alphabetic writing system was devised for Vietnamese, it would be of little use, since one could not write a scientific work, or even a simple text on a slightly serious level, in a noninflectional language (DeFrancis 1977, 142–43).

Ultimately, language policy in Vietnam converged on the teaching of French, though debates continued about whether French should be introduced immediately or only in the later years of education. One editor and publisher, Alfred Schreiner, offered what was for the time the most sympathetic European position toward Vietnamese, which was to argue for its use in primary schools and French in secondary schools. Schreiner drew on his own experiences as a bi/trilingual speaker of the patois of Alsace (an area now in France, but which has long alternated between French and Germany control), noting he had done well in school when taught in German, which is related to Alsatian, but not in French. He noted that the dominated will attach themselves all the more to their language to the extent that they are oppressed. Even he, however, drew from this the conclusion not that colonial rule should be ended (though he noted that eventually France would leave, as all other colonial powers had left the areas they occupied), but that it should be more benevolent, while facilitating the necessary evolution that would take place in Vietnam.

In his views, we see how the colonial taxonomies of grammar and hierarchies of writing systems were intertwined:

> The transition from *isolation* [another way of describing monosyllabic languages] to *agglutination* alone will make it possible to modify this

state of things, and this transition depends neither on the will of an academy nor that of a sovereign. In any case, there is lacking in the language and, as a result, in both forms of writing, all the scientific and technical terms of our Western vocabulary. The real defect is there, but this defect has a remedy, for it is entirely possible to give a language all the terms which it lacks.... There is needed in all this only a little money and good will.... And only at this price can all the people of Annam [the word used for Vietnam at the time].... raise themselves to our intellectual level, assimilate our thinking, thus understand us and—who knows?—perhaps esteem us. (emphasis in original; Schreiner 1906, cited in De Francis 1977, 172–73)

In this section, we have seen the incorporation and transformation of certain kinds of comparative linguistics into the evolutionary project, as we have seen the ways that the notions of kinship and blood-relatedness that are linked to Orientalist understandings of comparative philology were elaborated into ideologies of race and species linked to biology. In the next section, we see a more profound epistemological challenge to comparative philology, one that questions the value of a tree structure for understanding relations among languages, races, and cultures, and that equally challenges evolutionary theory's explanations of social, biological, and linguistic difference. Languages that were supposedly "unrelated" but had profound similarities anyway were a major puzzle to be solved. On the basis of their study, scholars suggested that perhaps diffusion and not evolution, proximity and interaction not genetic taxonomy, might be better models for understanding the world.

Slavery, Plantation Labour, Trade, and "Mixed" Languages

Although from the fifteenth century onward travel accounts contain numerous attestation and discussions of the "broken" and "bastardized" languages that linguists eventually called *pidgins* and *creoles*, these languages first started to attract significant scientific interest only in the late nineteenth century, at about the same time that Europe and the rest of the world entered into an era of heightened imperialism, and evolutionary theory eclipsed comparative philology as an adequate theoretical model for colonial expansion. To preserve imperial legitimacy, these languages were often metaphorically understood in terms of illegitimate sexuality, of infantilization, and of primitiveness.

"Bastards" are only threatening under certain conditions. If we understand the family lineages developed in Britain as shaped in part by specific notions of British kinship, "bastards" are threatening because of the challenges they pose to the possibility of the preservation of property by aristocrats or the bourgeoisie. They also challenge notions of racial distinctiveness, raising the spectre of "hybridity" as "the primary metaphor for the dangerous consequences of cross-racial contact" (Lo 2002, 297).

While we have seen that some kinds of languages, such as Chinese and Chippewa, were ranked low on linguistic civilizational and evolutionary hierarchies, other forms of communication were denied the status of languages altogether because they were seen as falling outside the family trees elaborated by comparative linguists. An editorial in a newspaper published in October 1925 describes one such language spoken in Papua New Guinea:

> The pidgin English as spoken in these days is about the most atrocious form of speech perhaps one could find in any corner of the globe. It is neither one thing or the other. Consisting of a mixture of Samoan and Chinese here and there, with an occasional word of Malayan, it is a conglomeration truly worthy of the Tower of Babel. (cited in Mühlhäusler 1986, 16)

The key debates about pidgins and creoles concern the linguistic features considered necessary to meet the criteria for being accorded the status of a "language," as well as about what their existence says about then-dominant theories of language, nation, race, and progress. Many early accounts simply saw creoles as corruptions or impoverished versions of European languages. They were described in many pejorative ways, and were often taken as evidence of the mental inabilities of Black people to learn European languages, or even to learn any languages properly; sometimes accounts attributed the linguistic differences to anatomical differences in the structure of the face or tongue. Some descriptions included "a mutilation without a plan or a rule," "the broken English of the Negroes" or "barbarous, mixed imperfect phrases" (Holm 1988a, 19, 21). Later accounts used once again the measuring stick of grammatical inflection as a key site for assessing hierarchy: the highly inflected grammars of Greek and Latin were held up as the ideals, and the lack of inflections was seen as evidence of a primitive state of development (Holm 1988a, 22). "Mixed" languages also posed challenges to thinking about the fixity of linguistic categories, and about what a "mother tongue" might mean (see Chapter 4). They also served as a terrain for a different, but equally important, kind of debate over the relative influence of universal linguistic principles vs. specific social, political, and economic circumstances in explaining linguistic differences and language change.

We will offer some provisional definitions of the terms *pidgin* and *creole* here, terms that, in keeping with our statement in Chapter 1, we treat as keywords revealing contested political stances and ideologies. The term *pidgin* is often defined in two ways, socially and structurally. A pidgin is sometimes defined as the form of communication that is no one's first language ("mother tongue"), and that springs up in contact situations in which speakers with different language backgrounds need some basic form of communication (Romaine 1988, 2). Sometimes, more controversially, a pidgin is defined in terms of features that are assessed as being "simplifications" of what "normal languages" do (Holm 1988b, xvii); this invites the question, however, of what counts as a "normal" language (and according to whom), and therefore what "simplified" might mean (DeGraff 2001, 2003; Mufwene 2000).

The word *criollo* was first used in the late sixteenth century to describe Spaniards born in the West Indies. The term was later extended to both Whites and Blacks born in the New World, or in other Spanish colonies, and eventually to all their customs, including language, in the late seventeenth century (Holm 1988a, 15). *Creoles* have sometimes been defined as pidgins that are acquired as a first language, in situations where access to other languages is particularly circumscribed (Holm 1988a, 6). This view assumes that all creoles must go through the stage of being pidgins. Some scholars describe creoles as simplified, in ways similar to how that adjective is applied to pidgins and contentious for the same reasons. Such a claim may be understood to imply that creole speakers may be speaking (even, perhaps, only able to speak) something less than a full language (DeGraff 2001, 2003). The linguist Michel DeGraff (2001), a speaker of Haitian creole as well as a scholar of creoles, argues, instead, that creoles should only be defined on social grounds as "a sociohistorical attribute that connotes the results of particular types of (abrupt) language contact marked by exacerbated social distance cum power imbalance" (2001, 228), rather than on "language-internal" grounds.

There were many pidgins and creoles formed under the distinctive conditions of global exchange, including enslavement and trade, after the fourteenth century. One encyclopedic survey documents almost 100, differentiating them according to the language on which they are "based": 15 varieties linked to Portuguese, 2 or 3 to Spanish, 3 Dutch-based ones, 25 French-based ones, around 40 English-based ones, 4 based on African languages, 4 based on Indigenous languages in what is now Canada and the United States, as well as a handful based on other languages (Arabic, Fijian, Japanese, Malay) (Holm 1988b). The overwhelming number of European languages may reflect a bias toward those languages documented in the context of large-scale European mobility, but they also reflect the impact of Western European imperialism and the creation of very particular and inequitable conditions for language exchange. Holm (1988b, 514) argues further that these numbers need to be understood as potentially hiding variation linked to a wide range of economic forms of imperialism, and the varied language ideologies at work in trade and rule.

The sites for creole formation that are most frequently discussed, and often held up as paradigmatic, are plantations in the Americas. One of the practices used to manage enslaved people in order to try to prevent revolt was mixing people with different language backgrounds. On large plantations, there would have been a small number of Europeans speaking English, Spanish, or French, and thus enslaved people would have had limited access to native speakers of those languages of power; the languages they spoke to one another would have drawn on many available linguistic and cultural inputs.

Pidgins and creoles were understood as hybrids, at a time when hybridity was a key concern of social and biological theory. Hybrids can be understood as symbolic terrain for anxieties linked to interracial procreation or other forms of contact that might threaten European domination. They were a key terrain for debates about biological and educational paths for human development, triggered in the mid-nineteenth century by the views of Francis Galton, a half-cousin of Charles Darwin. Galton argued that nature was more important than nurture in human development, and so biological as opposed to educational approaches were most likely to produce satisfactory results. He claimed that people's character and capacities were shaped by heredity, and that therefore humans had the obligation to improve the qualities of succeeding generations with better breeding, a practice he first called *eugenics* in 1883 (Haller 1963, 8–10).

Although his approach focussed on how miscegenation might yield racially beneficial results, often defined as the dilution of non-White traits, most eugenicists, frequently using studies of Caribbean creole speakers, became concerned on the contrary about "mongrelization." Eugenicists such as C.B. Davenport and Morris Steggerda argued that there was significant evidence of "physical, mental and instinct disharmonies in hybrids" (Davenport and Steggerda 1929, 470), and that "hybrids are inferior to either parental stock" (Davenport and Steggerda 1929, 469). They claimed that over many generations the children of interracial unions would "revert" or "degenerate" to one of their parental types, as would, they said, "people transplanted to inappropriate natural environments" (see also discussion in Anderson 2006; Young 1995). The interracial liaisons involved, whether called *amalgamation, intermixture, hybridity*, or *miscegenation*, were seen as threatening and as needing to be prevented (Young 1995, 146–48). In many areas of the United States, so-called miscegenation statutes proscribing such interracial relations and prescribing punishment for them remained in effect through the 1960s.

Discussions about children born of 'mixed race unions' "raised pressing transnational fears concerning the fixity of colonial categories, the immutability of race, and the politics of colonial governance" (Mawani 2009, 167). As biological 'hybrids,' these children were "the physical manifestation of cross-racial desire *and* the source of repulsion and fear" (emphasis in original; Lo 2002, 297). Another point of concern was that White children being cared for by Black women were learning creoles as their first language, languages perceived as more degenerate than the European languages such children should have been learning. Such children symbolized a fear of a form of White degeneracy due to living in the tropics and in proximity to colonized and racialized people. (We will see evidence of this again, in fascist understandings of the form of racial contamination that can occur in colonialism, and in reactions to Jewish speakers and Yiddish in the mid-twentieth century; see Chapter 5.) Pidgins and creoles were understood both as symbols of such miscegenation and as their result.

A key debate, still active today, emerged between *universalists* and *substratists* (Holm 1988a, 27). At stake was the question of whether (or the extent to which) the origin of creoles in the Caribbean stemmed from universal strategies for language simplification or from influence from African languages. Universalist views challenged dismissals of pidgins and creoles and their value for linguistic study; however, in their search for universal explanations, they nonetheless did not challenge the picture of them and their speakers as primitive, since the explanations tended to focus on universal strategies for language learning, or on creoles as "a spontaneous product of the human mind, freed from any kind of intellectual culture" (Saint-Quentin 1872, cited in and translated by DeGraff 2001, 215).

Substratist views, on the contrary, were attentive to the linguistic and historical particularities shaping each creole's formation, and thereby challenged evolutionary views. One example would be the work of Lucien Adam, a linguist from another contact zone (Nancy, France, close to the French/German border), and a magistrate in French Guiana. (He also wrote an essay on the abolition of slavery in the United States before the American Civil War; see Roberge 2006). In *Les idiomes négro-aryen et maléo-aryen: Essai d'hybridologie linguistique* he argued that the creoles he had studied showed retention of grammar and phonology of the mother tongues of those transported from Guinea. Rather than seeing them as simplified forms of European languages, Adam and scholars like him introduced the possibility of taking seriously the role of African languages and of looking for explanations other than evolutionary ones for their existence and their form.

The key European scholar associated with the study of pidgins and creoles in the late nineteenth century is Hugo Schuchardt (1842–1927), a German linguist and student of Schleicher who spent most of his career in Austria. To gather information on the geographical distribution and linguistic characteristics of creoles, Schuchardt wrote to 343(!) colonial administrators, missionaries, journalists, and others in all of the places that he thought likely to have pidgins and creoles (Gilbert 1984). He ended up publishing 700 pages on creoles, favouring cultural, social, and historical explanations over universalist ones.

From 1914 to 1921, Schuchardt and the French linguist Antoine Meillet engaged in an extended and sharp exchange of papers on the nature of creoles. Meillet (whom we will meet again in Chapter 4) argued that linguistic theory depended on the assumption that languages were never so mixed that one could not identify their genetic identity, understood as their European substrate. Schuchardt argued that creoles were truly mixed and belonged to more than one language family. This perspective must be set in the context of Schuchardt's broad interest in linguistic variation, and of his attempts to account for linguistic evidence that did not fit neatly into philological and evolutionary frames. In addition to pidgins and creoles, he was interested in European dialects, in Basque (a well-known isolate, which does not seem to be related to any other language, according to comparative philological and historical linguistic methods of analysis, despite having speakers in a central location in Europe), in Esperanto (see Chapter 5), and in areal phenomena, in which distantly or unrelated languages share features with each other that they do not share with more closely "related" languages (as in the Balkan area, as we mentioned above).

Along with Johannes Schmidt, another student of Schleicher, Schuchardt challenged the genealogical tree model with the idea of *wave theory*. Based on evidence from sound changes (often taken at the time to be the most reliably scientific source of linguistic data), they postulated that a sound change can spread over a given area from dialect to dialect. Instead of a tree, we have the naturalistic metaphor of concentric circles moving out on a surface of water struck by a stone (see Figure 3.2).

Pidgins and creoles, and other "messy" phenomena, thus served as the basis for challenges both to the family tree model of comparative philology and to the ways in which it was taken up and modified and extended by evolutionary theory.

A somewhat different challenge to evolutionary theory, as most influentially formulated by Franz Boas, was aimed at the hierarchical dimension of evolutionary theory, and in particular at racism. In the next section we will take a look at Boas, a German anthropologist who spent most of his career in the United States, and who is understood widely to be the founder of the Americanist tradition in anthropology. Boas's work shows us the difficulty of the search for a critique of the racism embedded in ideas about cultural and linguistic evolution at a time when practicing linguistics and anthropology was necessarily part of colonial enterprises. We will argue that Boas ended up facilitating the separation of the study of language from the study of culture and of race in ways that also allowed for the elision of the colonial conditions

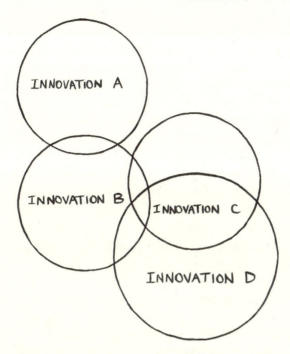

FIGURE 3.2: Wave theory model of linguistic change (Illustration: Andrea Derbecker)

that shaped what he observed. Even as such studies began to challenge evolutionary ideas about race, they contained assumptions about language, culture, history, and civilization that failed to challenge contemporary colonial practices and their impact, and that reinforced modernist, universalist ideas of progress.

Americanist Anthropology: The Limits of Cultural Critiques of Evolutionary Racism

In the United States in the late nineteenth century, industrial capitalism was seen as tearing apart the fabric of rural society, disrupting close-knit communities, and sending workers and their families to impoverished, crime-ridden urban settings. In this post–Civil War era, many African Americans started to migrate north to seek a better life. The inequities of industrial capitalism also brought in much larger numbers of immigrants from outside the United States, notably from southern and eastern Europe, who were seen at the time as "not quite white" (Brodkin 1998). They were also often suspected of anarchist, communist, and socialist subversion of the state. A number had indeed participated in various kinds of political action in Europe. While eventually such immigrants often played central roles in challenges to U.S. capitalism—for example by advocating for pro-labour policies, new income tax legislation, and the elaboration of new health and education policies (M. Harris 1968, 297)—there was resistance to their presence, alongside backlashes against the achievements made by African Americans (Baker 2004; V. Williams 1996). Eugenics movements for racial purification and immigration reform, drawing on evolutionary thought, gained popularity.

This is also a period during which some of the last of the extended military wars between the United States and Indigenous people defending territory and sovereignty were fought. Colonial officials were beginning to move from policies of explicit extermination to neglect, assimilation, and incarceration; reserves and residential schools became two key tools of containment and assimilation. Simultaneously, the United States became involved formally in overseas colonialism in Guam, Hawai'i, Panama, Puerto Rico, the Philippines, and Samoa.

The evolutionary theories we discussed above were as central to American as to European anthropological thought of the time, and for similar reasons. In 1895, William McGee, the first president of the American Anthropological Association, published the following comments in an early issue of *American Anthropologist*:

> Possibly the Anglo-Saxon blood is more potent than that of other races; but it is to be remembered that the Anglo-Saxon language is the simplest, the most perfectly and simply symbolic that the world has ever seen; and that by means of it the Anglo-Saxon saves his vitality for conquest instead of wasting under the Juggernaut of a cumbrous mechanism for conveyance of thought. (McGee 1895, 281)

This was the context into which Franz Boas entered as an immigrant anthropologist, a German Jew with a family history of idealism and political engagement.

Franz Boas was a German-born scholar who studied geography and physics in Heidelberg, Bonn, and Kiel in the 1880s. His father was a successful merchant; his mother founded a Froebel Kindergarten, the pedagogy of which was based on scientific observation and on detailed education in human anatomy and creativity. Boas regularly attributed his life-long idealism to his mother.

His parents were close associates with many leaders of the 1848 revolution in Germany, which challenged aristocratic rule in the name of middle-class political liberalism and working-class radicalism (though the challenge was undone by the difficulty of reconciling those class positions; see Chapter 4 for more on these tensions in Europe). While his grandparents were observant Jews,

Boas's parents, like many others of their generation, embraced Enlightenment rationalism and secularism (V. Williams 1996, 7). This did not, of course, protect them from anti-Semitism; Boas bore a deep scar on his left cheek obtained in a duel he fought to challenge an anti-Semitic slur, a scar he sought to hide in photographs by angling his head to the right (McGee 1895, 281). Boas and his family thus inhabited the contradictions associated with the project of the nation-state: the promise of inclusion and equality, but predicated on the making of a homogeneous population.

Boas's interest in geography and the natural sciences led him to an interest in the life of people and their physical environment, and thus to anthropology. He took his first field trip to Baffin Island to study the ethnology and geography of a group that he called "Eskimos" (now called Inuit). Thus began a life-long interest in Indigenous issues in the Americas, although Boas shifted his focus later to the Northwest Pacific Coast.

Anti-Semitism in Germany not only brought Boas a scarred cheek, it also blocked his access to a teaching position. In 1887, he emigrated to the United States, joining relatives who, along with other activists of the 1848 revolution, had already migrated there, where they played an active role in challenging racism and imperialism and in particular in developing health care and educational structures. In the United States, Boas again faced prejudice as an immigrant and a Jew, making it difficult for him to find a permanent position. However, in 1896 he helped found the first department of anthropology in the United States, at Columbia University.

From this institutional base, Boas played a central role in creating anthropology as a North American professional discipline. He sought to develop research methods and standards of proof akin to the natural sciences, to distinguish professional anthropology from missionary work and from the work of amateurs and armchair anthropologists. He argued for a *four-field approach* including ethnology, physical anthropology, archaeology, and linguistics; this approach remains the signature of North American anthropology today.

Boas also contributed to the professionalization of the field through contributions to the establishment of the American Anthropological Association (1902), as well as journals such as *American Anthropologist*, the *International Journal of American Linguistics*, and the *Folk-Lore Journal* (M. Harris 1968, 9; Hyatt 1990). At Columbia he trained a number of anthropologists, including Ruth Benedict, Melville Herskovits, Zora Neale Hurston, Alfred Kroeber, Robert Lowie, Margaret Mead, and Edward Sapir, who fostered the growth of anthropology at such universities as the University of California at Berkeley, Chicago, and Yale.

Boas's work on racial, cultural, and linguistic difference ranged widely: he wrote extensively on the language and culture of Northwest Coast Indians, on the bodies and cultures of American immigrants, especially those from southern and eastern Europe, on the position of "Negroes" in American society and their cultural achievements in Africa, and on race-mixing. He critiqued eugenics, Nazi science, anti-Semitism, miscegenation statutes, and notions of nationalism. His pamphlets critiquing Aryanism were smuggled into Germany; at one point, they were burned in a public bonfire in one of the German cities where he had studied. He lambasted those who tried to restrict the academic freedom of those who offered such critiques (especially as fellow academics lost their jobs for criticizing U.S. policies during World War 1), criticized fellow anthropologists who worked as spies for the US government, arguing they betrayed the aims of science, and worked with the African American civil rights activist and sociologist W.E.B. Du Bois and the nascent National Association for the Advancement of Colored People (founded in 1910). He published dozens of academic articles, but also wrote widely for popular audiences.

Boas had the clear goal of using anthropology to critique evolutionary theory in ways he intended to be emancipatory. Bauman and Briggs (2003, 256) argue that one goal of Boas's attempts to elaborate a concept of culture distinct from biology was "to help circumvent racism, fascism, and international conflict." We agree, however, with many of the scholars we draw on here that the contradictions in Boas's approach led his work to paradoxically reinscribe notions of racial and linguistic hierarchy. We look here at two of his key ideas, *historical particularism* and the *separation of race, culture, and language*, examining how they were meant as critiques of racism and how their contradictions prevented them for achieving that goal.

We will argue that Boas's commitment to ideas of progress and modernity trapped him in the necessity of nonetheless deciding what was primitive and what was modern. As a result, he ended up locating races, cultures, and languages as separate, whole, bounded products. Even where these were understood as 'hybrid' because of specific historical conditions of diffusion (rather than of the evolution of genetically related organisms), his approach required him to decide which races might be modernizable, and which were, however unfortunately, assigned to the position of disappearing primitives; for example, he understood Black culture, but not Indigenous cultures, as modernizable. Boas's commitment to challenging what he saw as irrational ideas also located race, language, and culture as objects of scientific ('objective,' positivist) study in ways that positioned the anthropologist and linguist as experts whose authority outweighed that of the people they claimed to be representing. Boas's attack, in the end, was on racism as an individually held, socially approved attitude, not the product of the conditions of development of colonialism and expanding capitalism that were key to the ideas of progress and modernity that he held dear.

American Modern: Assimilating Blackness, Disappearing Indigeneity

Since Boas saw evolutionary theory as producing premature generalizations, he tended to shy away from drawing conclusions or making claims that could be seen as making the same error. This extended to all accounts that he saw as deterministic, whether cultural, geographic (e.g., suggestions about how landscape might shape cultural practice), or economic ones (such as those drawn from Marxism) (M. Harris 1968). In the late 1930s, he wrote that "it is no more justifiable to say that social structure is determined by economic forms than to claim the reverse, for a pre-existing social structure will influence economic conditions and vice versa, and no people has ever been observed that has no social structure and that is not subject to economic conditions. ... Cultural life is always economically conditioned and economics are always culturally conditioned" (Boas [1911] 1938, cited in M. Harris 1968, 279–80).

Boas's training in geography led him to see "the spatial distributions of cultural elements as clues to reconstruct the successive temporal contacts of peoples without written history" (Darnell 2001, 41). Like wave theorists (see our discussion of Schuchardt above), he privileged *diffusion* and *migration* as explanations for human differences and similarities, and especially for cultural and linguistic change. He concluded that it would be necessary to understand the particular historical events involved, rather than seeking uniform laws of historical development. In his famous essay on "The Limitations of the Comparative Method of Anthropology," Boas ([1896] 1940) noted that we must "consider all the ingenious attempts at constructions of a grand system of the evolution of society as of very doubtful value ... the presumption is always in favor of a variety of courses which historical growth has undertaken" (276).

He assumed that culture traits clustered at their point of origin, so that a tight cluster would signal recent history. A wide distribution implied greater time depth, though innovations could occur at the peripheries of a distribution of traits. This model is similar to the concentric and overlapping circles of wave theory; it is possible that this is due to the fact that Boas drew on methods developed in European dialectology to describe the diffusion of folklore (Darnell 2001). While Boas argued that for each culture one could trace a variety of traits from diverse sources, which were then all integrated into culture, he refrained from making claims about origins. He thought that notions of origin were not recoverable with ethnological techniques, especially in the absence of concrete traces; indeed, he thought divergence and diffusion could be so marked that any original stock would be impossible to detect. In his 1929 presidential address to the Linguistic Society of America, he argued specifically with regard to American Indian languages, which had no written traces, that they were best understood as *hybrid languages* whose histories would forever remain inaccessible (cited in Darnell 2001, 65).

He wrote, "[I]t is not possible to group American languages rigidly in a genealogical scheme in which each linguistic family is shown to have developed to modern forms, but we have to recognize that many of the languages have multiple roots" (Boas 1929, cited in Herskovits 1953, 84).

Boas's focus on culture and his caution about economic explanations meant he had impoverished tools for talking about colonialism and capitalism. While Boas regularly spoke out against racism, there were a number of questions that a Boasian approach to culture, race, and language did not make visible. His student Melville Herskovits (1895–1963) said, "[M]atters of colonial rule touched him lightly" (Herskovits 1953, 112). The focus on recovering the historic past of Indigenous peoples meant that a Boasian approach described "a culture as it no longer existed rather than analyzing what was often the pathological situation of social demoralization in the midst of which their investigations were actually carried on" (Herskovits 1953, 108). Boas, therefore, commented relatively infrequently on Indian policy, with the exception of a critique of the demoralizing effects of suppressing the potlatch among the Kwakiutl (now known as the Kwakwaka'wakw) (Boas 1888, 636). Thus in Boasian work there was little analysis of "situations where peoples having differing bodies of tradition come into contact, with a view of anticipating and avoiding tension," situations that Herskovits particularly associated with "the practical problems of colonial administration" in Europe and "the Indian problem" in the Americas (Herskovits 1953, 108). Boas's approach, while devoted to critiques of the racist effects, was thus too limited by an idea of historical particularism, and a scientific understanding of culture and language as natural objects, to be able to fully articulate the critiques of what it meant to practice anthropology. In particular, his approach paradoxically reinscribed the reality of different "races," "cultures," and "languages" as distinct, even as it tried to complicate that view.

This is evident in the contrasting and intertwined approaches to Blackness and Indigeneity evident in his work. His very different attention to African Americans and to Native Americans—to race, on the one hand, and to culture and language, on the other—inscribed the first into liberal, modernist ideas about bringing progress to the "underprivileged," and the second into a nostalgia for primitive worldviews understood as disappearing. Perhaps most importantly, it was Boas's commitment to scientific rationality and expertise as a sign of modernity that led to these paradoxical outcomes.

Boas's key tools for addressing discrimination were detailed empiricism and education to remove discrimination and modernize the marginalized, not, as we noted above, accounts of structural inequality or the capitalism and colonialism that produced them. His focus was on making possible the assimilation of immigrants and African Americans, though not Indigenous people, whose languages and cultures he thought unadaptable to modernity, through elaborating a discourse of colour-blindness to counter prejudice (Baker 2010, 217–19), and through achieving "racial uplift" by changing their environment so that it more resembled that of middle-class Whites.

At the same time, historical particularism allowed him to characterize groups in particular ways (for instance, people of colour might still be portrayed as "passionate"), understanding these differences not as determined by inherent capacities, but shaped by (mutable) social environments. Further, despite challenging evolutionary accounts that saw "mixed" offspring as likely to be degenerate or sterile, his interest in "racial mixing" (Boas 1891, [1894] 1940) retains the biological determinism he elsewhere rejected. Indeed, his interest in "half-blood Indians" and "mulattoes" sometimes seemed to shade into suggestions that one could solve the problems of racial distinction by "amalgamation" or "dilution"; he even argued that those people of colour who were the offspring of such "amalgamation" might be best positioned to "lead their race" in a multiracial democracy.

Some of the contradictions in Boas's approach to race and racism may have flowed from his separation of language, culture, and race, and where he studied each. He argued that each pursues a different historical trajectory, rather than seeing all as linked to a single development stage. Some scholars have argued that by mapping race exclusively onto biology, and not language and culture, Boas and his students ended up fuelling the machine of scientific racism (Visweswaran 1998). (This separation made it possible, too, to understand language as an autonomous system and independent field.)

Commentators from the 1940s onward have pointed to some of the more difficult aspects of these contradictions. Herskovits, an anthropologist of African American culture, noted that while Boas was clear in challenging ideas of cultural characteristics as innate, and as the cause of real or supposed social deficiencies and deviations, nonetheless "the consistent contrast he drew in his writing between 'primitive' non-literate, and historic societies, suggests that he never resolved for himself the question of values involved in comparing these types of civilizations, certainly not to any degree approaching the clarity of his resolution of the question of racial differences in endowment" (1953, 114).

More recently, African American scholars have argued that even this account is inadequate (Baker 2004, 2010; V. Williams 1996). Williams (1996) in particular argues that Boas did point to inherent limitations, especially of Blacks. For example, the techniques for cranial measurement Boas learned and used were those developed by the eugenicist Sir Francis Galton. Though Boas argued they could be used for different ends than those Galton intended, his conclusion, after one set of measurements, was that he had demonstrated significant overlap between Blacks and Whites, though the ranges were not identical.

On this basis, he claimed that one therefore should not anticipate "men of high genius" among Blacks, but rather societal change should lead to African Americans participating in all parts of American society in ways proportionate to their numbers, but also proportional to their intellectual capacity (V. Williams 1996, 6).

In 1911, Boas argued that "the North American negroes, [were] a people by descent largely African; in culture and language, however, essentially European. While it is true that certain survivals of African culture and language are found among our American negroes, their culture is essentially that of the uneducated classes of people among whom they live, and their language is on the whole identical with that of their neighbors" (cited in Baker 2010, 24). African American intellectuals resisted this positioning, interested instead in using anthropology to challenge the ideas that "Negroes had no culture." They wanted to elaborate historical and richly particular ideas about African American culture; however, these scholars were marginalized in the academy.

Likely because immigrants and African Americans were understood as being on a path to assimilation in the American melting pot, Boas never studied language in connection with these groups; rather, his study of language was based entirely on his work on Native North America. Baker notes that for every 10 articles in the anthropological literature addressing American Indians, there was one focussing on "American Negroes" or Africans (2010, 11); anthropologists were clear on the fact that American Indians had culture, but debated whether African Americans did. In that sense, it was felt that American Indians were appropriate objects of study for anthropology, while the study of African Americans and immigrants were matters for sociology. This separation also made it difficult to see the intertwined and complementary ways that Blackness and Indigeneity are formed on the context of settler colonialism, with Indigenous people targeted by a logic of elimination in order to access land (Wolfe 2006) and Black people both separated from land and treated as labour (bodies), as well as how immigrants and settlers are understood against each (compare Tuck and Yang 2012).

American Primitive: Extracting Language

In 1911, Boas published an edited volume entitled *The Handbook of American Indian Languages*. He intended this book to illustrate how language could be studied anthropologically. He challenged evolutionary ideas of "primitive" language, such as those we saw in some of the accounts of evolutionary linguistics, by arguing that this was a matter of European observers transferring their own analytic biases onto the perception of cultural material. He regularly noted that the analytic paradigms used for the analysis of Latin and Greek, which we saw being applied by missionaries to Indigenous languages in the Americas during the Spanish empire, were inappropriate and that new methods needed to be developed for the New World (Darnell 2001, 40). As we have said, in the case of "American Indian languages" and of their culture more broadly, Boas nonetheless seems to have simply accepted the prevailing notion that these cultures and languages were destined to disappear. The people in question might benefit from modernity in other ways, he thought, but their linguistic and cultural practices seem to have appeared to him to be too "primitive" for historically situated development.

To carry out a program of understanding differences and change, he proposed very detailed investigations of particular sites through fieldwork rather than armchair speculation. These investigations, he argued, needed to focus on the careful collection of material traces of culture and language. In the absence of material texts, collecting linguistic data for authoritative scientific study required techniques for turning spoken language into bounded objects, which he also called *texts*. Boas saw texts as unassailably objective in their own right (Darnell 2001, 39, 42). He published more than 10,000 pages on the Northwest Coast alone, much of it without commentary (M. Harris 1968, 261); since the material itself was understood to be the kind of collection of natural samples that future generations of linguists and anthropologists could work on, this was considered to be an urgent task given the widespread assumption that Indigenous North American languages were going to disappear.

Thus, Boas's views about language contain the same elements of contradiction as do his views on race, including the effect of constructing anthropology as the objective voice of science in settling social and political debate. Bauman and Briggs (2003) argue that "[l]anguage occupied a pivotal place in Boas's efforts to demonstrate both that human mental processes were fundamentally the same everywhere and that individual languages and cultures shaped thought in unique ways; it thus enabled Boas to present a broad outline of human universals and specificities—a model of culture" (258).

This was even more strongly true of the views of some of Boas's influential students, especially Edward Sapir (1884–1939). Although both Boas and Sapir recognized areal and genetic influences, Sapir emphasized a common historical past more strongly (Darnell 2001, 51). These different ideas about how to study space and history had implications for how language was used as a tool for cultural analysis. For Sapir, language was central, since it was a uniquely rigorous tool for classifying ethnological data and tracing cultural histories (archaeology not yet having developed its own tools for doing so via stratigraphy, the measure of temporal change through examination of observable layers of cultural material; Coupland pers. comm.). It allowed for creating some order among what would otherwise be a confusing mass of descriptive facts (Sapir 1916, cited in Darnell 2001, 55). Indeed, Sapir strongly advocated for a separate science of language ("linguistics"). With Leonard Bloomfield (1887–1949), Sapir helped found the Linguistic Society of America and its journal, *Language*, in 1925 (Darnell 2001, 66).

Language came to be seen less as a part of culture and more as a separate system requiring study on its own terms, an approach that would not be systematically challenged until the 1960s (see Chapter 7). Language, because of its unconscious and habitual nature, was said to provide the clearest insight into native thinking, but anthropologists remained necessary to render the meaning explicit. Language, especially grammar, was seen as a particularly invaluable site for investigating thought because it was least likely to be affected by people's own ideologies. Constructing anthropological authority for anthropologists thus denied it to the subaltern subjects they claimed to represent.

Nonetheless, Boas, as was generally the case for anthropologists at the time, relied on Indigenous subjects and fieldworkers for the collection of the range of artifacts he saw as data, from bodies (and their scientific measurement) to material objects used for subsistence, shelter, and symbolic activities. Indigenous people were not seen as reliable, or even necessary, for understanding the meaning of narratives, but they were understood as crucial to their collection. For his work on Indigenous languages, Boas trained as many Indigenous informants as he could find who knew both Indigenous languages and English, and had sufficient literacy skills to work with him. Some of the most famous include George Hunt (1854–1933), the son of a high-ranking west coast Tlingit woman and an Englishman who worked for the Hudson Bay (fur trading) Company, but whose multiracial background was downplayed when he worked with Boas on Kwakiutl (Kwakwaka'wakw) texts; Henry Tate (circa 1860–1914), who recorded myths with the Tsimshian (see Maud 1985 for critiques of this relationship); and Ella De Loria (1889–1971), an anthropologist of European American and Dakota ancestry. The contributions of some of these contributors were named on the title page of publications (see, for example, Boas and Hunt 1902a, 1902b, 1905), though their contributions are only now being more fully excavated.

Given his understanding of these languages as disappearing, Boas saw the most urgent necessity to be ethnographic salvage work that would make as much information as possible available (Boas [1905] 1974). However, it seems clear that we cannot understand the nature of these texts without understanding the work that Boas's Indigenous collaborators did to transform material into the kinds of objects Boas considered data. For example, there is evidence that Boas asked Hunt to find particularly traditional and authentic forms of speech among the Kwakiutl (Kwakwaka'wakw); Hunt would listen to oral accounts, then go home and reconstruct them (Cannizzo 1983). This evidence indicates that Hunt, understanding what Boas valued, not only transformed speech into textual objects, but also "traditionalized" the "texts." And where English appeared in the texts, Boas himself edited it out, removing evidence of the ways the texts were anchored in colonial contexts (Bauman and Briggs 2003, 279).

Boas's views, then, were most congruent with a left-of-centre political liberalism that believed in maximizing individual freedom, multiracial democracy, advancement by merit, and the importance of the rational mind (M. Harris 1968, 298). He wanted to improve, not repudiate, democracy and nationalism. His thoughts on "Race and Nationality," published in 1915, highlight, in a condensed form, his understandings of race, language, and nation. He critiqued notions of race and toxic notions of nation that rely on the hereditary accounts of race and were inattentive to the diversity within their borders; he refuted explanations of the ongoing war (now called World War I) as due to the inevitable hostility between Teutonic, Slav, and Latin peoples. He challenged the ideas that the "mixed, 'mongrel' races are doomed to permanent inferiority" and decried the "fear of the mongrelization of the American people by intermixtures between the northwest-European and other European types" (65). He asked, if race is a disguise for nationality, can we understand nationalities based upon a community of language? There, too, he noted the counterexamples of states with multiple languages (bilingual Belgium and trilingual Switzerland) as well as adjacent states that share a language (the United States and Canada—he here sets aside French and Indigenous languages!).

He therefore did not see language as the basis of nation. However, he did not set aside the notion of nation. Instead, he argued that the shared community of a nation is that of "emotional life" (Boas 1915, 69); to take on such a notion of nation is to support a new form of national life, the only one that can lead to a free unfolding of human activity. This notion of nation—and here he too entered into an evolutionary teleology—is an inevitable progression of enlarging circles of association, developing increasingly larger political units to facilitate human freedom: from small scattered groups, to the small horde, then to members of the tribe and small states, then to confederation and nations. The next step would be an international federation, where there would no longer be a notion of a foreigner or outsider (see Chapter 5 for other notions of internationalism developed at the same time).

Linguistic Relativity, Colonial Ambivalence, and Modern Alienation

Similar concerns about the importance of navigating a respect for radical difference over and against its potential for creating conflict, for the modern nation and its boundaries over and against universalist ideas about humanity, showed up on a regular basis and in a variety of ways in the late nineteenth and early twentieth centuries. We can see how Boas's own intellectual lineage produced strategies to navigate them, from Sapir's carving off language from race and nation, to the work of Sapir's student, Benjamin Whorf (1897–1941), on *linguistic relativity*, the idea that different languages shape speakers' thoughts differently. In Whorf's work we see perhaps most fully how linguistic anthropologists attempted to neutralize tensions between science and religion, inequality and universalism.

Whorf had a degree in chemical engineering from MIT, and worked for a fire insurance company. Many accounts of his work focus on his scientific background, but his Christian faith is also critical to understanding his work (cf. Hutton and Joseph 1998; Rollins 1980; Schultz 1990). He read widely in contemporary chemistry, physics, and other sciences, particularly with an eye, as a devout Christian, to reconciling scientific findings with his faith. He was critical of evolutionary thought for the ways that it challenged belief in the divine, offering the example of the periodic table in chemistry, as well as from the structure of electricity, light, and energy, as evidence of matter that had been manufactured by a divine source (Rollins 1980, 14). His turn to linguistic analysis was fuelled in part by reading two books on theosophy by Antoine Fabre D'Olivet that had been translated from French by his neighbour.

The Theosophical Society was founded in New York in 1875. Its goal, in a quest for universal brotherhood, was to uncover the spiritual principles that lay behind all religions. Some key thinkers turned to Sanskrit texts of 'Ancient' India as a set of key sources; very quickly, in 1878, the Society moved its headquarters to Madras, India, where it still exists today, with branches in many cities around the world. Though the theosophists argued that they recognized no distinctions of race, creed, sex, caste, or colour, they shared the theory of language development we have seen above, which argued that languages progressed from isolating to inflecting in the movement toward a perfected human race (Blavatsky 1888; Hutton and Joseph 1998, 184, 188). (In Chapter 5 we will see how such ideas had affinities with fascist thought.) Fabre D'Olivet, the author whose works introduced Whorf to theosophy, saw language, including or especially the study of Hebrew, as a medium to link people to the higher realm through the discovery of evidence of human spiritual growth.

Language study became central to Whorf's religious project. In an application (ultimately funded) to the Social Science Research Council, which distributed research funds on behalf of the Rockefeller Foundation (see Chapters 6 and 7), he noted that his linguistic work would help to reveal the underlying basis of all speech behaviour, with "the possible applications of such a science restoring a possible original common language of the human race," and that with this would come the "manifestation of the deeper, psychological, symbolic and philosophical sense contained in the cosmology of the Bible" (cited in Rollins 1980, 49).

At the same time, Whorf's experiences as a fire inspector had led him to see how the ways that people acted were often shaped by words. For instance, people would smoke around gasoline drums that they understood to be "empty," which they interpreted both as "void of contents" and "inert" even when they remained combustible (Whorf 1956a, 35, cited in Lucy 1992, 49). He found a frame for understanding this phenomenon in Boas's and Sapir's suggestions about the historical particularism of language, and Sapir's extension of these suggestions to the idea that language might shape thought. However, Whorf departed from his predecessors in moving beyond a focus on vocabulary and isolated case studies to look at systematic, patterned grammatical differences that worked across a whole linguistic system (he called these *fashions of speaking*; Lucy 1992, 31). He elaborated his argument by contrasting Indo-European language categories with those of Indigenous languages in the Americas. His views thus consolidate an approach to language as an autonomous system.

At times, Whorf seemed to see each language as offering a different angle on a complex universe. At others, perhaps more frequently, he seemed to celebrate Indigenous languages as a better fit for contemporary scientific understandings of the physical world than Indo-European ones. Rossi-Landi (1973) argued that Whorf seemed to want to overcome certain aspects of alienation he felt by revelling in difference, without focussing on exploitation (77). He saw this as both distinctively bourgeois and distinctively colonial in the ways that "the Other" is needed to understand White colonial selves, and make those selves whole (Hutton and Joseph 1998, 198).

Indeed, it is possible to see Whorf's fascination in particular with Hopi as a means to resolve his own ambivalences about how scientific modernity and industrial capitalism had the potential to undermine the spiritual values he found expressed in theosophy—ambivalences that we might argue in fact characterized the entire period, and that were felt, one way or the other, by everyone. Whorf saw Hopi as having transcendental potential, including equally "everything that appears or exists in the mind, or, as the Hopi would prefer to say, in the HEART, not only the heart of man, but the heart of animals, plants, and things, and behind and within all the forms and appearances of nature, in the heart of nature, and by an implication and extension which has been felt by more than one anthropologist, yet would hardly ever be spoken of by a Hopi himself, so charged is the idea with religious and magical awesomeness, in the very heart of the Cosmos itself" (cited in Rollins 1980, 75). These views, in which humans are not sharply distinguished from other aspects of nature, largely disappear from mainstream linguistic thought throughout the twentieth century, though they are resurfacing now as people reconsider what humanity means, in the context of Indigenous resurgence and ecological catastrophe (see Chapter 8). The last article that Whorf published, appearing a few months after he died, was published over two issues in *Theosophist* (1942). In that article he made explicit the way the science of linguistics, as it worked at elucidating how language works, could be key for devising a language of the future that would heighten human consciousness as never before.

We have, over the last two chapters, showed how imperialism lay at the heart of ideas about linguistic and racial difference and inequality, as well as, ultimately, of attempts to challenge those ideas. We have tracked the tension between religious and scientific notions of authority, as the figure of the linguist and anthropologist left the missionary and colonial officer behind. In the next chapter we will investigate more closely the ways that the late nineteenth century period of economic crisis and global expansion was reflected in the growth of discourses and linguistic practices for thinking about the notions of nationalism, especially in Europe, of which Boas was critical. We look at the contemporaneous elaboration of ideas about language as an autonomous system. The time period of Chapter 3 thus overlaps with the time period of the next chapter to some extent, but turns from thinking about the implications of how Europe and the United States were constructing others to more fully focus on how Europe was constructing itself.

PART II
The Contradictions of Language in Industrial Capitalism

CHAPTER 4

LANGUAGE AND EUROPEAN NOTIONS OF NATION AND STATE

FIGURE 4.1: "Le symbole." Morbihan, early twentieth century. Collection Musée de Bretagne-Rennes (France).

"Le Symbole"

What is this strange necklace? It is a "symbole," a symbol here made from the front half of a wooden clog, but which sometimes took the shape of a cow or some other evocation of peasant life. Such objects were used in nineteenth- and early twentieth-century French schools to stop children from speaking Breton, Occitan, or other regional varieties in class. Part of a wider range of disciplinary practices designed, in Eugene Weber's felicitous and well-known phrase, to turn "peasants into Frenchmen" (Weber 1976), symbols were handed to students caught speaking such "patois" instead of French. Sometimes the *symboles* were strung on a cord and hung around the student's neck, or sometimes the students held them. Students were then encouraged to police their peers in order to catch one committing the same infraction, allowing them to pass on the *symbole*. At the end of the day, the last one left holding or wearing it would be punished in some way, through extra homework, a detention, or copying lines in French. Versions of the *symbole* were also used in colonial Algeria for the same purposes. In an interesting twist, similar techniques were used in francophone Canada as late as the 1980s to discourage students from using the dominant language of English.

How can we make sense of this story? Why would it matter what language students spoke in school? What was meant to be accomplished in the punitive practices disciplining body, mind, and tongue? Here we will use this story to follow some threads that lead us to questions having to do with what it meant to turn "peasants into Frenchmen"—or Spaniards, or Italians, or Germans. While we will concentrate mainly on Europe in this chapter, it is important to bear in mind that these threads can be followed elsewhere, allowing us to ask also what it might mean, for example, to turn Arabs into French or British colonial subjects, to "kill the Indian to save the child" (as was said in twentieth-century North America), or to make French Canadians into subjects of an alternative imagined nation.

The Emergence of the Nation-State in Europe

The central knot of this chapter is the emergence of the nation-state as the hegemonic form of the organization of political, economic, social, and cultural life in nineteenth-century Europe. Building on Chapters 2 and 3, we first discuss how empire and nation are inextricably bound up with each other. We go on to talk about how the emergence of the idea of "nations" in nineteenth-century Europe is tied to the development of industrial capitalism and the growth of the bourgeoisie out of the accumulation of the wealth of empire. Though we consider many sites, a large number of our examples are drawn from France, as a leader in the development of the centralized, bourgeois, liberal democratic European nation-state, in the wake of the 1789 French Revolution.

France allows us to examine the relationship between two strong ideas of the nation. The first is associated with the philosophical Enlightenment movement of the eighteenth century, a movement that challenged the legitimacy of the Church and the monarchy on the grounds that they were unjust in the distribution of wealth, and that their authority resided in a religious faith that could be shown to be irrational. "Reason" is the hallmark of this movement. The second is associated with the Romantic movement in art and literature, which focussed on nature as the source of all meaning and authority. These two ideas represent different possibilities of imagining nation, empire, identity, language, and culture, and serve as the grounds for a wide range of political and economic struggles emerging strongly in the nineteenth century and still alive today.

The chapter will then turn more specifically to an examination of the role of language in making European nations, that is, the ways in which language was involved in techniques of construction of the idea of the nation as marked by a convergence of one language, one culture, one history, and one territory. These techniques range from bureaucratic counting procedures that are central to the ability of the state to make its population and govern it, notably in the development of the census, to techniques that discipline tongues, such as the *symbole* with which we began this chapter. They also include modes of making unified languages (standardization, dictionary-making, writing grammars) already developed in the regulation of empire, as we saw in Chapter 2.

We then examine how these techniques helped construct the boundaries between those who would enjoy the full privileges of citizenship, and those who would be understood as always lying outside an ability to master the performances that full citizenship required. We argue that language served here to mask the making of inequality by being constructed as something that could be learned, even if some groups were always positioned as necessarily deficient learners and others as inherently unable to fully learn.

We examine the ways in which the making of the nation is tied to the nature of economic activity, and in particular to the regulation not only of language itself, but of the speaking subject. Finally, we will examine the ways in which the political economy of the liberal democratic, industrial nation-state was tied to a particular idea of science, and so to the development of the science of linguistics, the science of anthropology, and other disciplines that lie at the heart of how we understand sociolinguistics and linguistic anthropology today.

Markets and Liberal Democracy

There are many ways in which European state nationalism built on earlier techniques for making uniform, regulated languages, cultures, and peoples with clear boundaries but of different worth, which served to consolidate centralized power in the metropole and to make colonial subjects. For these reasons, it is certainly possible to think of nationalism as emerging at earlier moments, when political treaties laid the basis for what would become national boundaries in Western Europe (the 1648 Treaty of Westphalia is usually recognized as a key step in this process). In the seventeenth and eighteenth centuries, philosophers such as the Port Royal Grammarians and Descartes in France, Leibniz in Germany, or Locke in England laid the basis of the Enlightenment. The idea that reason, rather than divine right, was central to authority challenged the power of Church and monarchy, and opened the way for the rise to political power of the bourgeoisie. It also centred civil debate within the public sphere as the site and mode of political process.

Bauman and Briggs (2003) suggest that philosophers such as Locke constructed language as the cornerstone of modernity by separating it from society, thus purifying it from the ties to particular social positions, interests, and nature understood to be vulnerable to mysticism, magic, and alchemy, and as a weakness of the *ancien régime* (31, 34). Language was to take a straightforward and clear form, in contrast with the elaborated, elegant, obfuscatory rhetorics of the aristocracy, but also with the plain utterances of working folk. Abstract and general language, write Bauman and Briggs (59), "could thus perfectly embody the liberal ideology that purportedly judges individuals on the basis of their own actions." People would be governed by universal, logical rules, learnable and knowable by anyone, not by the mysterious authority invested in rulers by birth status. These rules themselves were understood as existing in nature, and requiring discovery using principles of rational thought (defined in much the same way). Language then also was understood as rule-governed, with patterns requiring elucidation and codification. Language standardization is thus understood partly as an act of discovery and partly as an act of wrestling potentially unwieldy material into shape.

Gellner (1983) argues that the bourgeoisie-controlled nation-state is an outgrowth of the development of industrial capitalism, a regime that promises better distribution of wealth on the condition of increased unity and uniformity of the market and of economic practices, and premised on continuous growth, though in practice this more equitable distribution is continually deferred. Putting industrial capitalism in place required, he says, the development of shared cultural practices in order to make the unity happen. Among these were languages and linguistic practices, anchored in the soil and in invented histories (see Hobsbawm and Ranger 1983 on the notion of "invented traditions").

Gellner (1983, 1997) and Hobsbawm (1990) suggest that the wealth of empire, based on trade in primary resources, laid the foundations for the development of industrial techniques of transformation of those resources into goods that could then be sold, either to citizens of imperial centres or to colonial elites. The so-called triangle trade, for example, shows us how goods, and therefore ideas, circulated globally: enslaved people, constructed as things, were transported from Africa to America to produce cotton, and cotton went to England to be turned into cloth, which could then be exported to Africa—and to India, and across Europe. Techniques developed in one part of this network could be used for others; indeed, it was often techniques developed for primary resource extraction that were imported to Europe for industrial labour.

The growth of wealth produced from empire also destabilized the political regimes of imperial centres as the rising bourgeoisie sought to wrest power from the aristocracy. Their success triggered a transformation of their territorial base from monarchical centres of empire to national markets as the basis for sustaining, indeed expanding, colonial networks, to the consolidation of industrial capitalism, and the consumption, transformation, and circulation of resources. The bourgeoisie's interests in access to resources came increasingly into conflict with those of the aristocracy, touching off tensions that would take more or less violent forms for decades to come. Using the resources already in place, the bourgeoisie fought for control over the states the monarchies had begun, unevenly and incompletely, to put in place (Hobsbawm 1990; Grillo 1989).

This triggered a struggle over what would count as a national market; Hobsbawm (1990) suggests that a central concern was the facilitation of industrial capitalism through the construction of workable, governable markets, in which there would be access to labour and to consumers. Hobsbawm points to the two main debates that resulted from this approach: the problem of borders, which would trigger conflict throughout the nineteenth and twentieth centuries, and the problem of size, which, he argues, often trumped other concerns in struggles over territory.

The roots of centralized, bureaucratized administrations were in place, as were the technologies for using them to govern populations at a distance. Using examples from colonial areas, Benedict Anderson (1983) argued that the key technique of printing, first used in colonial areas and later imported to metropoles, was foundational to the construction of the "imagined community" participating in capitalist networks. As we will see later, those shared cultural practices—including, and crucially, linguistic ones—were also central to the maintenance of the belief in the claim of industrial capitalism to provide equitable wealth distribution through growth. (Irvine and Gal 2000 and Silverstein 2000 question how hegemonic such communities actually were.) But this also required new forms of authority. Against the divine right of kings, the external source of authority underlying the legitimacy of the aristocracy, the bourgeoisie opposed the secular rights of the people.

This is the basis of *liberal democracy*, the characteristic political formation of nineteenth-century modern nation-states. This formation was oriented to centralized states facilitating the workings of the capitalist market as legitimized through the direct participation of "the people," understood as individuals, toward a generation of profits understood to benefit all "citizens."

But industrial capitalism shares with mercantile capitalism the distinction between centres, the loci of decision-making and the principal beneficiary of capitalism, and peripheries where both labour and resources are to be found. It is uneven, producing struggles over resources and the power to make decisions about their value and their distribution. Under such conditions, the question of how to legitimize liberal democracies and industrial capitalism as principally under the control of bourgeois men was turned into a problem of citizenship (Bauman and Briggs 2003). The main tool for deciding who would count as a citizen was the determination of capacity for the rational thought that allowed the bourgeoisie to challenge the aristocracy and the Church in the first place.

Here we return to Gramsci's ideas about hegemony. The centralized state had both the means of coercion and the means of making consent. While we will not examine all the institutions of coercion and consent here, it is important to remember that the nineteenth century was both the moment when military service was inscribed as a duty of all (male) citizens and the moment when education was understood to be necessary for all. The question, then, became not only how to delimit nations one from the other, or how to decide which nations deserved recognition, but also how to make citizens who would both recognize their membership in the nation and accept its inequalities.

Making Subjects through Language

The "people," then, were largely delimited by concerns over markets and by available technologies for their regulation, but needed nonetheless still to be made. Two reasons have been advanced for this (Higonnet 1980; Grillo 1989; Bauman and Briggs 2003). The first is that for the state to function administratively, it was necessary to further develop the already emergent bureaucracy. For the bureaucracy to function, it was necessary to standardize both mechanisms of regulation and the shape of the citizens it was to regulate. The second is somewhat more complex, and has to do with the problem of legitimizing a fundamentally unequal set of relations.

Language played a key role in these processes. It could be constructed as encoding, even incarnating, the central values of bourgeois capitalism, harnessing both reason and nation to ideas about progress and modernity (DeCerteau, Julia, and Revel [1975] 2002; Balibar [1974] 2007). In this sense, it was in the first instance a fruitful terrain for the legitimization of bourgeois power against aristocratic and divine power. In addition, the standardization of authoritative linguistic forms formed part of this process of building a shared space, in which reading and writing in vernacular languages would facilitate access to participation in political and economic activities, and simultaneously construct the sense of belonging that delimited who could and could not participate. The regional affiliations of feudalism needed to be replaced by national orientations.

The historian Patrice Higonnet (1980) traces some of the early tensions around the limits of democracy at its earliest stages in the French Revolution. He argues that, at the time, political mobilization required the solidarity of bourgeoisie, peasants, and workers. For the first few years of the Revolutionary regime, there was some discussion as to how to do this, including questions about whether it made more sense to bring word of the Revolution to people in their languages, or to create a shared sense of revolutionary commitment through the common use of French (Higonnet 1980; Lüdi 2012). (This, of course, is a version of the dilemma faced by religious missionaries and colonial administrators; see Chapter 2.)

In a famous phrase, the revolutionary Barère articulated the argument for commonality, taking aim first at languages spoken on French territory which he understood to be unrelated to French: "Le fédéralisme et la superstition parlent bas breton; l'émigration et la haine de la République parlent allemand; la contre-révolution parle l'italien et le fanatisme parle basque" [Federalism and superstition speak low Breton; emigration and hatred of the Revolution speak German; counter-revolution speaks Italian and fanaticism speaks Basque] (de Certeau et al. [1975] 2002, 12–13). These were the languages to be suppressed quickly. "Patois," or regional varieties, understood to be closer to French, could be used to instruct their rural (infantilized) speakers in the virtues of the Revolution, in the literacy practices that were central to the administration of the state, and eventually in its language (although it was not until the late nineteenth century that widespread schooling came to accomplish this task across the population).

In addition, we see at this moment the use of survey techniques to describe the population and its characteristics that prefigure the systematic introduction of language questions on national censuses later in the nineteenth century (Gal 1993; Kertzer and Arel 2002). Arguably one of the first sociolinguistic surveys of modern times, such a survey was undertaken for the Revolutionary regime by Abbé Grégoire (Grégoire 1794).

Henri Jean-Baptiste Grégoire (1750–1831) was the son of a tailor in eastern France. He was recruited for Jesuit education as a child, on the grounds of his intelligence, and was deeply influenced by Enlightenment ideas. While he struggled to reconcile them with his faith, he was ultimately able to do so through a commitment to the democratic values of the French Revolution— values evident, for example, in his stance against slavery, a certain support for women's rights, and in favour of universal access to voting. He also argued against the inherent degeneracy of Jews, and for their assimilability into French society if properly educated. The matter of multilingualism was of concern to him for precisely this reason: he felt that the best way to bring the values of the Revolution to all citizens of France was to bring everyone into the discursive space of the state through the language of the Revolution: French. In 1790, he therefore undertook a survey to find out what the distribution of languages actually was in the territory of France, putting an end to a brief period of Revolutionary commitment to multilingualism (Higonnet 1980; Balibar 1985; Lüdi 2012).

A central promise of the Revolution was not only universal suffrage, but also equal, or at least more equitable, distribution of wealth. But, Higonnet shows, the point at which the bourgeoisie realized that this would apply to their property as well as to that of the aristocracy was the point at which practical concerns became symbolic. The problem became less one of mobilizing the population than one of maintaining the legitimacy of a revolution that was not entirely going to keep its promise. From that point, we see the question of citizenship as tied to promises not of actual equal distribution of wealth, but rather of legitimizing differential positioning with respect to that wealth. As we will see shortly, various social categories were mobilized to legitimize different positions of power, including gender, sexuality, religion, ethnicity, race, and a version of class that constructed it as cultural difference.

Here, in a slow process of struggle throughout the nineteenth and twentieth centuries, "democracy" turns out to be differential citizenship as the competitive workings of capitalism organize unequal access to control over the production and distribution of resources. Someone needs to do the work that sustains production; not everyone is going to be able to amass the capital necessary for innovation and expansion. But the promise of democracy must somehow be seen to be kept, solidarities need to be maintained, and the nation-state requires the participation of all its diverse citizens. Of course, there were always forms of resistance that challenged the contradictions of a capitalist democracy— workers' movements, women's movements, anti-racist/anti-colonial protests of different kinds at different moments, movements for international solidarity, and anarchist challenges to state authority, some of which we examine more fully in subsequent chapters. Here, however, we will focus on the first part of the process: the production of commonalities in a shared discursive space.

Making nations and nation-states was accomplished through a variety of techniques and technologies as has been amply described, most influentially by Foucault (1975). As Foucault insisted, it is in modes of making and moulding populations in specific historical conditions that we can see how "*regimes of truth*," or ways of making meaning and moral order, are tied to the interests of differentially positioned parties trying to seize, wield, or resist power, working with (or against) the conditions and resources of their time. The Industrial Revolution and the emergence of the liberal democratic nation-state was an important moment of shift in regimes of truth, and thus in forms of population discipline, that is, in ways of linking social and moral orders. Once the idea of the nation became available, it was also possible to mobilize the idea that protonations already existed, and would achieve their full potential only through organization as a nation-state; this is the "Romantic" or "German" model. It became important to construct shared histories and evidence of shared cultural practices, in specific spaces, with continuity over time (Hobsbawm and Ranger 1983). The idea that nations are natural entities, closely associated with nature, with "roots" in the land, also serves to erase their construction and to legitimize their claims: if they are organic entities, it is not possible to argue about whether or not they exist.

In examining techniques of control, we must first look at the role of national institutions: the military, the state bureaucracy, schooling and higher education, workforce training, religious institutions, the legal and penal system, health care, and the media all can be seen as sites for the construction of national citizens. As government institutions, they bring people into centralized institutional spaces where important resources are distributed; socialize them into the performances expected of them if they are to participate successfully; introduce them to the sanctions on performance; and provide narratives accounting for how what goes on there is meaningful and important, and makes sense. This is true also of these sites as workplaces, and of the other collective and consequential sites of work during the construction of the nation-state, notably industry.

Not surprisingly, most examinations of such institutions and how they produce citizens focus on what the nation, with its insistence on the organic quality of the collective, foregrounds as the most important sites of national production and reproduction: the family and schooling, understood as the key sites of primary socialization of the young, as yet unformed, citizen, or of other newcomers, notably immigrants. While the military obviously also plays a key role, it is also, of course, harder to gain access to it as a space for critical enquiry. Let us note, nonetheless, how important compulsory military service was for bringing together protocitizens, and for making relevant differences, notably between the men who serve and the women who do not or between colonial subjects for whom military service could be a path to citizenship and those denied that access (Cooper 2006).

France, for example, brought together into its military units young men from different parts of the country, and sent them to regions hitherto unknown to them, forcing the use of French on all. In the twentieth century, so-called *coopérants*, who refused military service, were usually sent to the colonies to serve the colonial administration for twice as long as military service (Alisjahbana 1976, 13–14). Many men from the colonies, or from racialized groups, who were pressed into military service also used this as the grounds for claiming more equitable treatment or independence, especially after World War II. (As we will see in Chapter 7, this structure became important in the development of sociolinguistics in France in the 1970s.)

Each institution has its own role, its own part to play, as intertwined as national institutions may otherwise be. They teach you in different ways about what to do with your body, your mind, and your voice—indeed that you have one in the first place. They are sites of standardization, imposing common norms of behaviour that serve as the basis for accomplishing the hegemonic discourse that allows the dominant to not see how they dominate, and the dominated to accept their position as reasonable or logical. That is, they combine the force of coercion through physical violence or threat, for example, of incarceration or other forms of punishment (here we can include being sent to the principal's office, or being handed the *symbole*), with persuasion, building consensus that school learning really is more important than what your parents can teach you on the farm, or that French, German, or Standard Italian is more logical, more beautiful, more refined, or more modern than whatever it was you learned to speak at home—and so producing consent to the practices of regimentation these all involve.

Regimentation: Census, Standardization, Literacy

As we indicated earlier, a major technique of building and regimentation of the state was the *census*, already in use in the eighteenth century. The census foregrounds statistics as a central means of producing knowledge about the state, and provides material on the basis of which the body politic can be described and decisions taken about how to shape it through state action. As Hobsbawm (1990), Arel (2002), and others have described, the question of what the state needed to know about its population was a matter of debate. The central concern was indeed figuring out what constituted the national population, which required determining in advance which characteristics of an individual would be the most relevant to describing the national or cultural homogeneity (or heterogeneity) of a state—and therefore what steps might be necessary to make homogeneity or, at the very least, harmony. (It was also a technique that was being simultaneously developed in the colonies, as the European, and later American, powers took stock of the populations they ruled; Rafael 1988; Cohn 1996.)

In 1873, after much debate at a meeting of the International Statistical Congress, there emerged a consensus that language was certainly a key marker of national belonging, and, most importantly, in the eyes of the delegates, the most likely to provide "objective" assessments and therefore sound data (Arel 2002, 93). Participants at this Congress wanted to get away from having to adjudicate competing claims to nationhood or to national inclusion, and instead aimed at finding ways to provide information that states could both control and use for long-term management. Such data seem to have been of particular concern to the increasingly contested Austro-Hungarian Empire, which was managing burgeoning nationalist movements that threatened its stability, and indeed Austria and Hungary were the first places to include a language question on their census in 1880.

The form of the question or questions reveals a great deal about ideologies connecting language, nationality, and citizenship. Initial formulations referenced what language people spoke or what their native language was. The supposed objectivity of this measure, then, rested on the naturalization of the idea that nations were organic bodies bound by shared history, culture, and language. Each individual constituent would therefore have one culture and one language, which s/he would spontaneously prefer to speak (or which would be the only one s/he would be able to speak). Further refinements in various censuses specify "mother tongue" or "language spoken at home," both of which locate the languaging of the citizen in primary socialization by the mother in her domestic realm. Women and the household become the womb of the nation and emblematic of its language. They also become a terrain for fighting over the management of linguistic diversity, as we discuss further below.

Such language questions remain in wide use around the world (although Belgium stopped using them for purposes of determining policy in 1962, because the tensions between Belgian speakers of Flemish and of French were so high that they threatened to divide the state, and in the eyes of the federal government census results only served to aggravate the conflict; Willemyns 2002). Their foundational ideologies, however, are now sometimes called into question. For example, Canada added a focus on ethnonationalism as the language of race became increasingly critiqued after World War II, but has since added successive questions about knowledge of official languages, and languages used at work, as the Canadian public sphere becomes increasingly uncomfortable with policy based on ethnonationalism (Heller 2011). Very recently, in the

United States adverse reaction caused the government to stop using data about language spoken at home to identify households or communities as "linguistically isolated" (because they were using a language other than English), and therefore in need of remediation, in part because of activism undertaken by linguistic anthropologists committed to social justice (Rosa 2016).[1]

The second major mode of linguistic control was *language standardization*. Already underway in the sixteenth and seventeenth centuries, efforts intensified greatly in the nineteenth and twentieth centuries. The construction of a common, shared, national language was a key tool for ensuring participation in a shared discursive space and a disciplined orientation toward when and how to communicate. Efforts to standardize languages take several forms and have several effects.

First, as we have noted already, standardization allows for the shaping of a nation; by constructing a language to be shared by citizens, it becomes simultaneously possible to draw the nation's borders. Citizens are those who speak the language; noncitizens are those who do not. Language can then also be used to delimit territorial boundaries, that is, to lay claims to territory inhabited by people who supposedly speak (a version of) the national language, and to discipline occupants of the territory who do not. Hence, for example, campaigns in France tried to turn Alsatians into French-speakers at crucial moments when the territory was won from Germany in nineteenth- and twentieth-century border struggles, most especially after Germany's defeat in World War I. This was understood as especially important given that Alsatian could be (and has been) claimed as a version of German and therefore proof that Alsace should belong to Germany (Huck 2015). In addition, as early as the 1790s, the concern that patois-speakers, and Alsatians in particular, could be traitors (Lüdi 2012) reinforced the importance of distinguishing languages from patois, and making sure their boundaries were clean and clear.

We still take speaking the national language as proof of citizenship or potential citizenship. Most countries prefer immigrants who speak the national language to those who do not, and provide language training as a strategy understood to be essential to "integration" (see Chapter 8). More generally, the association between whole, bounded, standardized languages, which allows us

---

[1] For a newsletter item on a letter written to the census bureau on May 27, 2010, on behalf of the American Anthropological Association, by the Society for Linguistic Anthropology Committee on Language and Social Justice, see http://linguisticanthropology.org/blog/tag/linguistically-isolated/. A special issue of the *Journal of Linguistic Anthropology* (volume 25, issue 1, 2015) was also dedicated to an invited forum on "Bridging the 'Language Gap'," with entries from Netta Avineri, Eric Johnson, Shirley Brice-Heath, Teresa McCarty, Elinor Ochs, Susan Blum, Ana Celia Zentella, Jonathan Rosa, Nelson Flores, H. Samy Alim, and Django Paris.

to say things like "I speak French" or "I am learning Arabic," and territorially bounded spaces understood as nation-states produces such banal expressions as the flag seen on websites, bank machines or hotel staff uniforms, and that are meant to iconically represent the languages in which service is available (Billig 1995). The citizenship of the bearer remains inferable, even if possibly problematically so (and officially bilingual or multilingual countries such as Switzerland, Canada, Cameroon, South Africa, or Paraguay are understood to have a problem requiring management).

Indeed, the construction of the ideal of the whole, bounded, fixed language, spoken within the boundaries of a specific territory by prototypically monolingual speakers, creates deviation, which then has to be controlled. Forms of language that are variable and fluctuating become problematic; as we will see below, the (created) problem of linguistic variability has been the object of scientific enquiry ever since. Certainly, one of the things that schools, the media, and literary canons do is try to socialize speakers out of such practices and into standardized ones, or at least into the idea that variability is problematic even if behaviours remain unchanged.

Bilingualism emerged as a particular form of deviance to be patrolled. Andrée Tabouret-Keller (2011) has carefully documented the many ways in which, in France alone, the construction of the nation-state led to institutionalized condemnation of and punishment for bilingualism in the nineteenth century and well into the twentieth—and even today. The *symbole* with which we opened this chapter is one example of schooling's role in constructing speakers and state-sanctioned spaces as monolingual; to that Tabouret-Keller adds the examples of doctors and psychologists condemning the use of nonstate languages in the home lest it lead to confusion, mental and emotional instability, and cognitive development delays in children.

These were not simply deviant and misguided practices of the nineteenth century, which we now know better than to reproduce; while they can be traced as far back as 1840, they are still in circulation today, and have influenced our own lives and emerged in our own work. For example, Monica had relatives worried that her children, brought up bilingual, would be "confused," while others wondered that Monica was not "ashamed" to speak in ways that "mix languages"; in Monica's research in the early 1990s, a Canadian research participant reported that her husband and doctor told her to stop speaking French to a child who began having difficulties in school, and to place the child in an English-language school.

We see here one manifestation of the profound ways in which the linking of "reason" to "progress" and to boundedness ties linguistic practice and proficiency to judgements of cognitive and social competence. We must also, however, link these concerns about bilingualism to fears of contamination not unlike those expressed regarding pidgins and creoles (see Chapter 3), and hence connected to some of the profound ways in which nations have been understood as races to be kept apart, especially when they are arranged hierarchically.

However, the shape of the nation goes beyond the association of bodies and territories through shared bounded languages. The form of the language is also important. The most obvious domain has to do with whether linguistic material is understood to properly belong inside a linguistic boundary or on the outside. Most frequently, attention is paid to lexical material (words) in what is now a long tradition of purism and frequently the subject of debates among interested parties. We can, for example, think of the French accusing Canadian francophones of using too much English because they use discourse markers like "so" and "anyway," while Canadians condemn the French use of English words ending in –ing (le parking, le shopping, and so on). These policing efforts can also extend to prosody, phonology, morphology, and syntax.

Standardization: Grammars, Dictionaries, Canons, Pedagogies

Standardization is not only about what linguistic material properly belongs to what language. It also concerns what shape linguistic material should take and why. Building on older traditions of prescriptive grammar-making and language teaching (notably the teaching of Latin), nation-building standardization projects also undertook to regularize and regulate linguistic form, and in particular syntax. Many vernacular grammars drew on Nebrija's grammar throughout the eighteenth century, which in turn had drawn on Latin and Greek grammatical categories. This allowed both for an inscription in a long and specifically European history of empire as well as a reproduction of widely shared ways of understanding how languages should work. Balibar (1985, 348–50) argues that by the nineteenth century French pedagogical grammars inculcated descriptive categories proper to French, that is, constructed *without* reference to the languages, notably Greek and Latin, which had provided the *ancien régime* with models of grammaticality; word order, conjugation of verbs, and in particular the morphology of the past participle were among the salient zones of difference in grammatical description in these manuals. The first constructed a particularly European tradition; the second further differentiated national and modern (rational) languages, although both use grammar as the tool to accomplish these moves.

Swiggers (1990) has shown how the idea of French as the language of reason (the Enlightenment language par excellence) led to concerns about "clarity" in form. Grammarians worked at making rules that would ensure that the structure of French could be seen as encoding clarity and logic, through, for example, rules determining the placement of clitic pronouns, subject-verb agreement, and gender and number agreement. Speakers of other standardized languages of course dispute the claims to the rational supremacy of French, although France certainly continues to provide a prototypical example of state-led disciplining of linguistic form.

In any case, French is but one example of what, as a result of the standardization project, became a problem of deciding what features should be understood as better or worse manifestations of universal logic. Wilhelm von Humboldt (whom we met in Chapter 2), for example, argued that a language could be understood as more logical the more it rendered grammatical relations explicit, for example, by adding morphological material signalling person, number, position with respect to the speaker, or connections among words (via declensions, conjugations, and prepositions, for instance) (Joseph 1999).

Dictionaries, notably, serve the dual purpose of setting the boundaries of standardized languages, but they also demonstrate the histories of words and how they might be seen to form semantic fields. So do *literary canons* (the list of literary works that are understood as the best and most exemplary in a given nation), arranged chronologically, showing how literary traditions develop in a linear fashion, with continuity both of language and of sensibility. Historical linguistics helped attach linguistic forms to trajectories of nations purified of any forms of internal diversity and not blurred by exchange and contact, and to their supposedly defining characteristics. Language then shapes the discursive space of the nation-state and is imbued with form and content; guides to their interpretation (dictionaries, grammars, textbooks) orient citizens to certain kinds of shared values.

Language is also implicated in the organization of discursive space and the deployment of its meaning-making resources. This is the realm of conventions of selection of which linguistic resources call into play specific communicative practices, who can deploy them, and how. As Bourdieu (1977) pointed out, who the legitimate speaker of the legitimate language at any given moment may be is not a trivial matter: this is how power is produced, reproduced, and potentially contested. Further, this can only happen in the course of the activity of communicating, whether in the moment of face-to-face communication, or through various forms of mediation that render communicative activities more or less ephemeral. Who, then, may be admitted into the circle of citizenship, and who is irrevocably other? Who speaks the language of reason, and who the language of the heart of the nation? Who may speak, and who must be silent? These questions are at the heart of the ways in which the nation-state resolves the paradox of democracy and inequality, and capitalism the problem of unequal distribution of wealth.

Language and Differential Citizenship

The idea of rationality was used in French Revolutionary discourse to construct a moral binary between a revolution characterized by reason, truth, clarity, and virtue, and an *ancien régime* that was constructed as corrupt, decadent, and strangled by its preference for complexity and overdecoration in dress, decor, and discourse (Outram 1987). This binary rested on a profoundly gendered and sexualized ideology of the nation: the *ancien régime* was corrupt because of what was seen as the promiscuous casualness with which the aristocracy approached marriages (marriages were economic arrangements, but romance was something else altogether), because such arrangements allowed women to be hidden powers behind the throne (the mistresses of the king were particular targets of hatred), and because aristocrats adopted what were understood to be feminized cultural practices, such as writing long, flowery sentences in texts too attentive to sentiment. The Revolution, by contrast, adopted "*le langage mâle de la vertu*": the male language of virtue. This language was understood as clean, clear, and to the point.

But if male aristocrats could be disdained as feminized, what of female revolutionaries? Here Outram paints the portrait of Mme. Roland, the wife of an important figure in the Revolution. As engaged intellectually as her husband, there was no obvious role for Mme. Roland to play since women's bodies, by definition, were associated with the corruption of the *ancien régime*. She was able only to open a *salon* where men could gather to talk about the important matters of the day, sitting quietly on the side busying herself with appropriately feminine (and silent) work, and, as Outram quotes her as writing in her memoirs, "biting her lip" to prevent herself from saying anything (1987, 126; our translation).

Bauman and Briggs (2003) argue that this form of gendering became available as a broad strategy of constructing differential citizenship in the bourgeois nation-state. In the interests of privileging male members of the European bourgeoisie (and ratifying a distinctively bourgeois approach to monogamous heterosexuality) within a liberal democracy promising wider distributions of power, the gendered distinction between reason and emotion produced a number of possibilities. The distinction between reason and emotion was also linked to intertwined discourses of class, age, and race (though the examples we provide focus most extensively on class, gender, and sexualization among white Europeans).

First among these possibilities was the relegation of bourgeois women to the margins of power as they could be constructed as not rational enough for full participation in a liberal democratic regime founded on the idea of reason. This justified witholding the right to vote and restricting property rights.

As we have seen, it positioned women as receivers or, at best, as enablers of male authoritative speech. The problem here became how to make women both modern and marginal.

Second, women were associated with the Romantic side of the nation, and hence central to the association of the reproduction of an organic, natural entity. Their role in biological reproduction is assimilable to the reproduction of the nation; the children they produce are protocitizens. Their association with children, indeed, served in part to infantilize them. Similarly, their role in child socialization places them at the heart of the transformation of children into citizens. The home is where the Romantic soul of the nation lies. These remain powerful tropes today: many censuses ask questions about the language spoken at home as a way of grasping the extent of national linguistic unity. And getting pregnant is often understood as a political act, not a personal one. (Monica will never forget once walking into a meeting of minority francophone associations pushing her infant daughter in a baby carriage; the first words anyone addressed to her, or more precisely to her and her child, were "*Ah! La relève!*"—ah! The reinforcements!)

Third, women could be constructed as the guardians of the traditions understood to guarantee the authenticity of the nation, though this could equally trigger a tension among modernity, tradition, and marginality. In internal and colonial peripheries the matter of women's access to newly standardized and imposed languages became a matter of concern both for the centralizing metropolitan state and for local elites seeking either to accommodate it or to resist it but on their own nationalist terms. In some places, such as Brittany, women did much of the work of bilingual brokering; their Breton was both a guarantee of authenticity and devalued as both contaminated by French and insufficiently standardized (McDonald 1989).

In colonial sites, or sites resisting colonization, gender also became salient in constructing new nationalisms. Since colonization was often justified as "rescuing" women from "traditional" or "barbaric" practices (foot-binding, clitoridectomy, child marriages, polygamy), establishing the respected position of women could be a key move in constructing a modern or scientific new nation. Inoue (2006, 2007) discusses how resolving this tension in Japan at the turn of the twentieth century resulted in the invention of a tradition, specifically the construction by male intellectuals of Japanese "women's language." Girls were incorporated into the mandatory state education system in order to be educated as "good wives and wise mothers" who would help raise modern citizens and thus help build a modern Japan, while at the same time remaining guardians of the tradition necessary to the legitimation of the state. Male intellectuals wrote extensively about the verb endings used in the speech of Japanese schoolgirls, thereby institutionalizing a particular form of "women's language" incarnated in the figure of the schoolgirl. "Women's language" quickly became naturalized as an essential and timeless part of culture and tradition, the historical conditions of its emergence erased.

Chandra (2012) shows how gender became a problem in colonial India as people worried about whether Indian women should be educated in English as a way to elevate the national character, or should become guardians of a revalued Marathi. For advocates of English as a national language, languages like Marathi were unchaste and impure, and staking a claim to English would be a way of making it into an *Indian* language. Women who learned English, however, were often criticized by other women for developing (overly) intimate relationships with husbands, at the cost of relationships with other women in their households. Conjugal heterosexuality was seen as a challenge to women's power in more homosocial arenas. Policing language was thus a way to police sexuality, producing as Chandra calls it, a particular tension over the rise of English-related heteronationalism (2012, 26).

In addition to the ways gender and tradition become a terrain for nation building, so too does childhood, which again engenders transformations in how social forms of intimacy are understood and enacted. The nineteenth century is the beginning of a period when the very notion of childhood gets invented, as only working-class children remained important in the labour force (Balibar [1974] 2007). Indeed, feminization, infantilization, and racialization are often intertwined: bourgeois women are not only not rational enough, they are eternally not mature enough for full citizenship, and require the benevolent protection of men. Male colonial subjects are often also understood as feminized, that is, as weak and passive, and colonial subjects more generally are understood as infantilized and needing colonial tutelage (Filipinos were explicitly construed as "little brown brothers" to American colonizers). We will consider this question further when we consider the spread of public education below.

Creating Peripheries

As Raymond Williams (1973) has pointed out, the tension between Enlightenment/revolutionary dimensions of nationalism (associated with "reason") and the Romantic one (associated with "soul," "feeling," "body") was not only gendered, but also spatialized and temporalized. The bourgeoisie were interested in developing industrial capitalism, concentrated in urban areas, not in taking over and reproducing the agricultural production of the aristocracy's landed estates. This shift is understood as linear progress, an urban modernity in rupture with a rural past. The "city" (which did in fact draw more and more people to it from what was fast becoming construed as rural hinterlands) was seen as modern, civilized, progressive, sophisticated, and exciting; it is fully in the present. But it is also dangerous, possibly corrupt, a difficult place for a person to find a mooring. It is where capitalism can eat you up and spit you out, or where you can become the master of your own destiny. The countryside is the repository of the nation's history and of its soul; it is pure, close to nature, rooted, and living in some timeless past. It is romanticized as a site for refreshing oneself from the urban grind. But it is also backward and simple, pre-modern, possibly somewhat stupid (Williams 1973).

The urban bourgeoisie needed to invent the country for its own legitimacy. But note that the country is also the place from which labour comes. We have seen how this process worked to construct regions such as Brittany, Corsica, and the Basque country as places needing to be brought into the republic, but not necessarily ever fully succeeding to be of it. Michael Hechter (1975) lays out a detailed argument regarding the Celtic areas of Great Britain, which we can use here as an example.

Hechter argues that these areas were constructed as a periphery as Wales, Scotland, and Ireland became sources of both labour and raw materials (coal, wool), both necessary for the establishment and growth of the industrial centre of England. The Welsh went down the coal mines at home and in the colonies, as well as into the factories of many large English towns, for example. Their difference—their ethno*linguistic* difference—legitimated this position. In order to move from the Welsh economic and social periphery into the English centre, many things were necessary; some were easier to accomplish, like moving to England, and some harder, like learning to speak English like an English person. The same can be said for the peripheries of France, and of many other countries.

For as long as it is the "French" or the "English" who define what counts as legitimate language, learners from outside can never catch up—the "native speakers" have only to change the rules. For instance, if being literate is the bar for recognition, then when literacy becomes widespread, perhaps small grammatical differences become the shibboleth. If people can command both written language and grammar, then fine-grained phonological differences can be used to create hierarchies (Gal 2012). And, as Bourdieu (1977) pointed out, to the extent that signs of being from the periphery (or other forms of difference) are impossible to entirely eradicate, it is difficult to be accepted as a legitimate speaker however well one masters the legitimate language. (Indeed, as Bonilla and Rosa [2015] point out, some differences are, under some circumstances, functionally "indelible.")

In fact, one is often betrayed by what Bourdieu (1972) calls "hexis," or bodily disposition. Those who make the rules can afford the relaxation of mastery (the informal clothes at an important meeting, the casual slang tossed into a speech), while those who strive to master them are always in a position of tension; those who reject or resist take up oppositional forms, which also allow them to develop forms of solidarity that are crucial to their survival, although they can still be judged by the hegemonic rules. This is where the wearing of the *symbole*, or the slap on the hand, or the cold look turn into bodily dispositions.

The example Bourdieu gives is of the tight, pursed lips of the French middle class striving to maintain linguistic correctness, versus the "*gueule*"—bestial throat—or slack-jawed, low-voiced delivery of working-class men who know they will never be invited to the tables of the elite. These are examples from a moment of mid-twentieth-century stability, when the social and linguistic hierarchy is established and widely known. Rosoff (1994) and Balibar (1985) provide us with a different kind of example, describing the anxiety of French citizens with little mastery of writing as they try as best they can to respond to the attempts of a nascent state bureaucracy to collect information that will determine distribution of state resources; the bureaucracy is figuring out its own rules. In turn, members of the secular and clerical elite construct patois speakers as children to be educated: to be brought into the Enlightenment via the written word, first in their own languages, and then in French (deCerteau et al. [1975] 2002; Balibar [1974] 2007), in practices reminiscent of the work of colonial missionaries.

Centralization, urbanization, standardization—all are part of producing a differential citizenship in which minoritization uses ethnicity, race, and gender to legitimize relations of power that allow for the use of the labour of the deviant, incomplete, or peripheral, and access to the resources they might otherwise control. It also, of course, sets the stage for resistance on those same terms, and so this period also sees the development of minority and colonial nationalisms, promoted by regional elites who see the possibility for transforming their world from periphery to centre, or forms of irredentism, attempts to reclaim and reoccupy territory that can be understood as an attempt on the part of peripheralized minorities to make their own, more comfortable, centre. For example, in the late nineteenth century, priests and bourgeois intellectuals in Occitanie, Provence, the Vallée d'Aoste, and Catalunya (such as the writers Frédéric Mistral or Jaume Verdaguer) responded to the development of centralized French and Spanish literary canons and standardized languages with Romantic nationalist resistance movements. A parallel development is the rise of Zionism, a Jewish nationalist movement, which also invented or renewed a language and claimed a territory.

These so-called renaissances ("rebirths" of nations construed as having had a glorious early modern past, and suppressed by nineteenth-century state nationalisms) involved the mobilization of all the semiotic forms of nationalism (grammars, literary canons, and so on) in the interests of a regional elite. They lay the foundations for later linguistic minority nationalist movements in the 1960s and 1970s, sometimes complicatedly intertwined with Marxist movements, since these were sites constructed as economic peripheries, sources of material resources and human labour (see Chapter 7).

Regulating Relations in Industrial Capitalism

The period of the growth of nationalism is also, as we have said, the period of the growth of state bureaucracies, colonial administrations, state military organizations, and compulsory schooling. It is also the moment of the regimentation of industrial work, in ways that are usually described as "Taylorist," after F.W. Taylor (1856–1915). Taylor, an American, is best known for his early-twentieth-century development of what he saw as rational modes for organizing industrial production; what we know today as the assembly line, in particular. The idea was that workers (or, for that matter, bureaucrats) should be interchangeable parts of a production machine designed to extract the most labour without destroying the workers. Production should not depend on the talent of an individual, or his or her particular whims or circumstances. Indeed, the attempt to establish rigorous procedures for creating language inventories, a trademark of structuralism, has some striking resonance with these efforts.

Control over language is a key dimension of the distribution of power that divides the authority from the governed, since controlling what gets said or written and who can say or write it is one way we exercise control over how we understand our world. Indeed, this includes control even over who gets to speak. As Boutet (2008) has pointed out, a key feature of nineteenth- and early-twentieth-century industrial workplaces was the proscription against speaking while at work (alongside injunctions to control the body by, for example, staying in place and not spitting).

Similarly, if monolingualism is an important dimension of the functioning of the nation, then it becomes important to reward monolingual performances, and to control, suppress, or sanction multilingual ones (as we saw above). This can be done institutionally, of course, as we have pointed out, through monolingual bureaucracies with the state language as the sole language of instruction. It can also organize international relations through carefully compartmentalized multilingualism. For example, multilingualism can be permitted to only those who actually carry out the work of international relations, and only in the form of parallel monolingualisms, that is, keeping the linguistic performances strictly within language boundaries without code-switching, or it can be conducted via the mediation of translation and interpretation, understood as separable communicative acts. (International auxiliary languages offer a third solution, as we will see in Chapter 5.)

The management of any other form of deviant practice, written or spoken (of which multilingualism is only one), can also be done in interpersonal interaction—the relative who asks innocently if we are not ashamed of our bilingual practices; the shopkeeper who refuses to respond to a sanctioned language; the mocking of a classmate's accent. Speakers who are silenced cannot easily offer alternative views of the world, and cannot comfortably play an important role even if they accept the prevailing rules of the game.

Institutional rules regarding turns at talk also allocate speaker roles in ways that make clear who has authority and who does not, though they have changed over time. As Foucault (1975) pointed out, in legal proceedings the accused were not always allowed to speak, and when they have been their access to speech is designed and controlled by someone in authority. The same is true of other state institutions. Schooling was, for much of the nineteenth and early twentieth centuries in Europe, a matter of a master transmitting knowledge into the heads of students. Rote memorization and collective response can be understood as preparations for work in state bureaucracies and industrial workplaces, where individuals were understood to be interchangeable parts of a production machine or bodies for the exercise of the authority of the state, at home or in colonial adminstration.

Increasingly, in the late nineteenth and early twentieth centuries, the industrial, technological economy, and the private and public bureaucracies which administered it, required mass elementary education, or at least literacy, from workers/citizens (Hobsbawm 1987). The focus was no longer on education for the aristocratic elites or the middle class alone. Primary school education massively increased at this time in many different European sites (e.g., the number of students doubled in the Netherlands, tripled in the United Kingdom, and increased by 13-fold in Finland). A national education was seen as requiring a national language of instruction; language thus gained an ever more central role in the definition of nation at this time (Hobsbawm 1987, 146).

But the problem remained of how far to extend such inclusion. The education of African Americans in the United States after the Civil War provides a revealing example. One of the earliest institutions dedicated to the education of African Americans (understood as requiring separate schools), the Hampton Institute, was founded by Samuel Chapman Armstrong, the son of an American missionary in Hawai'i. The Hampton Institute emphasized training in elementary academics and industrial and agricultural labour, coupled with a harsh military discipline, in ways that urged Black students to accept a subordinate role in the New South. The Tuskegee Institute was founded by Booker T. Washington (a Hampton graduate) in 1881 for similar ends. Indeed,

Washington argued that African Americans were ideal industrial workers due to their linguistic adaptability: "In the matter of language he does not cling to his tribal dialect, he does not cling to his African tongue as the Italian and German and Russian Jew do to their languages. He speaks English—or makes a brave attempt to speak it. The same is true of other things" (Washington, cited in Spivey 1978, 48–49). Boas's views on African Americans, as we have seen, echoed Washington's. Armstrong wrote that an English course with reading and elocution and the study of the mother-tongue and literature, as well as classes in political economy and geography and mathematics, would be beyond almost all of those educated by the Institute (cited in Spivey 1978, 26). Thus these groups were being trained to be part of the industrial proletariat.

Such schools were critiqued by W.E.B. Du Bois and other Black leaders as education that aimed to keep Blacks in their place. However, the Hampton Institute was celebrated elsewhere and used as a model. Within the United States it was used as a model for boarding and residential schools for Indigenous students, the first of whom were prisoners of the U.S. Army, as the growing focus on assimilation rather than extermination meant suppressing Indigenous cultures and languages (Engs 1999). These developments, it is worth underlining, were happening at the same as Boas and his students began elaborating critiques of evolutionary and racial hierarchies in anthropology and working to preserve Indigenous languages deemed certain to become extinct.

The model the Hampton Institute provided was later elaborated in Hawai'i, in Liberia along with the plantations run by American rubber corporations, as well as in a number of other African countries subject to British imperialism. Colonial administrators from South Africa studied the industrial and residential school models as they were developing apartheid policy (Engs 1999). Indeed, mass education became a widespread aspect of colonial administration, which had earlier focussed mainly on training Indigenous elites (see, for example, May 1980, 82–83; Makofsky 1989, 33).

When the United States conquered the Philippines in 1898, colonial administrators quickly adapted educational forms from U.S. policy for African American and Indigenous students. In 1900, the Director of the Bureau of Public Instruction wrote to Booker T. Washington, asking for advice on how to organize industrial education in the Philippines along the lines of the Tuskegee Institute; he also visited Tuskegee and the Hampton Institute. He later wrote that "[i]n this system we must beware the possibility of overdoing the matter of higher education and unfitting the Filipino for practical work. We should heed the lesson taught us in our reconstruction period when we started to educate the negro. The education of the masses here must be an agricultural and industrial one, after the pattern of our Tuskegee Institute at home" (cited in May 1980, 93). The brother of W.H. Taft (governor general of the Philippines, and later U.S. president) wrote to him, urging: "Won't you go in for industrial education in the Philippines? Certainly there is no other education for a race like the Negroes that compares with that in its effect upon character and race deficiency" (cited in May 1980, 92).

Industrial education not only required regulating the distribution of languages of power. It also required a harnessing of dominant languages to particular forms of interaction understood to be part of the way in which one socialized students into being the right kind of worker-subject.

This requires us also to take a look at interaction. For example, in a 1913 textbook, *Good Manners and Right Conduct*, intended for the instruction of students in the Philippines (then an American colony), teachers were instructed to "be very particular in every case to have the speaker *look directly into the face* of the one addressed, who in turn should look squarely at the speaker" (Government of the Philippine Islands, Department of Public Instruction, 1913, 20). Dialogues in the book modelled the desired form of direct interaction, a form of interaction contrasted with what was construed as "Oriental" evasiveness, secrecy, or indirectness:

MR. LIRIO: By whom is your father employed, Ambrosio?
AMBROSIO: I do not understand you, sir. [Looking Mr. Lirio squarely in the face] Will you please explain?

Both the teacher and the student were being taught appropriate interactional norms as the teacher was urged to "have the child look up directly at the questioner. He should not hang his head as if ashamed, turn his back, or look off in an opposite direction....Teach the child to look up frankly and speak out truthfully" (Government of the Philippine Islands, Department of Public Instruction, 1913, 42). Dialogues that taught vocabulary and verb conjugations also invoked the norms for modernity, cleanliness, and orderliness promoted by the American public health regime.

TEACHER
(*touching child's ear*): This is your ear, Maria. Show me your ear, Maria.
MARIA
(*pointing to her ear*): This is my ear.
TEACHER: Show me your other ear.
MARIA
(*pointing*): This is my other ear.
TEACHER: *How* many ears have you?
MARIA: I have two ears.
TEACHER: How many ears have I, Pedro?

PEDRO:	You have two ears.
TEACHER:	How many ears have I, Juan?
JUAN:	You have two ears, Miss Reyes. I have two ears. Maria has two ears. Carlos has two ears. Juana has two ears.
TEACHER (*examining Jose's ears*):	Are your ears clean, Jose?
JOSE:	Yes, Miss Reyes, my ears are clean. Mother washed my ears this morning.
TEACHER:	(*Looking at Amparo's ears*). Your ears are dirty, Amparo. Did you wash them this morning?
AMPARO:	No, Miss Reyes, I did not wash my ears this morning.
TEACHER:	You must wash your ears every day. You must not come to school with dirty ears.

(*Civics, Hygiene and Sanitation*, 12–13)

Certain values are here shown to be embedded in the choice of particular languages understood as modern as well as in the interactional techniques associated with them. When one speaks English—or French, or German—one adopts certain modes of bodily discipline, hygiene, and moral codes of conduct, including those that allow for certain classes of people to rule, and others to obey. Such techniques of regimentation (from pedagogies to practices, standardization to surveys), require the making of authoritative knowledge. In the next section, we will turn to the institutionalization of this form of knowledge production in the construction of the idea of a science of language.

Making Scientific Linguistic Expertise

Much of the expertise we have discussed so far involved the disciplining of texts: the making of dictionaries, grammars, and orthographies. These were problems of making whole, bounded languages, fixed in time and space. The question of variability therefore became a key concern; linguistic variability needed to be brought into the realm of order. This was a particular concern not just for texts, but in many ways even more so for spoken language. We saw above how important the regimentation of interaction was; interaction was a key site for organizing social relations, not only in terms of who could speak, but also in terms of how. The problems of variability and spoken langage intersected in nineteenth-century linguistics' understanding of language as a natural scientific object.

Nineteenth-century science more generally was meant to describe (and thereby master and harness progress) features of the natural world. Since language was now understood to be part of that natural world, as we have seen in the ways trees were elaborated for taxonomizing languages and other natural phenomena, nineteenth-century linguists turned their attention increasingly to what they understood to be the most natural dimension of language, and the one most amenable to direct, scientific observation: embodied speech. Established philological approaches, based on analyzing texts, were increasingly critiqued in this endeavour.

Several approaches to the analysis of language-as-speech emerged in the nineteenth century. The first, *dialectology* or *linguistic geography* (Gal 2010; Johnstone 2010; Schrambke 2010), took on the problem of variability and change, for which the dominant models otherwise were the *family tree* and *evolution* (see Chapters 2 and 3). Dialectologists sought to discover the limits of variability in space, tracing the use of specific words, or word forms, or sounds. Given the long-standing problems of language areas such as those that drew Schuchardt's attention (see Chapter 3), dialectologists took on board the argument that this distribution had to take into account *diffusion*, or the transmission of forms through social interaction (see Sandfeld 1930 for a detailed analysis of the Balkan *Sprachbund*). Dialect boundaries were to be drawn through isoglosses, that is, bundles of limits of attestation of forms. It was expected that geographical features (plains, rivers, valleys, mountains) would help explain the shape of isoglosses.

These processes were also linked to the questions of establishing national boundaries and historical continuity, and therefore of claims to territory and to legitimization through incarnation of nationalist modern values (i.e., claims to having both a head and an uninterchangeable sort of heart, as well as a commitment to progress; Bergounioux 2006; Gal 2010). If boundaries looked fuzzy, it became important to untangle the linguistic bits from each other. If claims to territory were disputed, it became important to establish the trajectories of linguistic elements through space and time. If states were in conflict, it was important to be able to show which languages held closest to the central mode of making hierarchy, namely, models of reason.

While initial attempts at dialect geography used random encounters to map out the range of forms, dialectology increasingly turned to speakers understood as most "conservative," that is, least likely to have been "contaminated" either by the standard or by neighbouring linguistic forms. (We see here a version of the investment in the idea of languages as ideal, pure forms, but one that anchors those forms in actual speech, not abstract systems.) The best informant was understood to be an elderly person, as far removed from the modern present as possible (Schrambke 2010).

This contributed to the reconstruction of a pre-modern, rural, national past, where the soul of the nation had not yet encountered the modern processes of change that would inevitably disturb it. It also allowed for explorations of the specific characteristics of national essence as potentially formed by the soil from which it sprung, whether mountain or plain, dry or humid, landlocked or maritime. Ideas of distinctive national landscapes emerge at this same time (Hirsch 1995). By the same token, these forms of dialectology would allow for delimitation of the nation's geographical reach. While most dialectologists came to agree that, despite this framework, actual coherent local "patois" did not exist and the closest one could get might be a bundle of features, nonetheless the scientific rational method applied to their description requires the maintenance of the notion to this day.

We can see this perhaps most clearly in discussions of boundary-making at the end of World War I. Linguists and other scientists (notably geographers and historians; Chevalier 1996) were involved in advising on drawing the boundaries of the new nations to emerge out of the ashes of the Ottoman, Habsburg, and Prussian Empires, as well as settling boundary disputes among combatants. Probably the best-known linguist among them was Antoine Meillet, whom we have already met as a key interlocutor in discussions of pidgins and creoles, and who was among the scholars consulted. Paramount concerns involved the drawing of boundaries between France and Germany, involving precisely those areas (such as Belgium and Alsace) where the German dialect continuum runs into the French one, and which had been areas of political and military contestation for centuries.

Given the difficulty of using dialectological data in this endeavour, Meillet appealed to other criteria familiar in establishing the political status of languages in empires and nation-states, such as whether a language was standardized, used for literary production and education, or in other similar ways could be said to be "civilized" (Meillet 1928; Moret 2009). In a careful consideration of this contradiction in Meillet's position between describing norms and prescribing them, Moret (2011–12) could only conclude that a French linguist in 1919 could act no differently, not because of overt political pressure, but because of the justice of the war effort and the importance of finding a geopolitical solution to European upheaval—a solution that, at the time, could be thought of only in nation-state terms. This is perhaps also not surprising for a linguist who was of bourgeois origins (Meillet's father was a notary), well-versed in descriptive linguistics (he specialized in Armenian), and occupied a post at the Collège de France, a prestigious institution.

While dialectologists argued that their approach was able to account for more of what they observed than the family tree and evolutionary approaches, they remained limited in their ability to account for everything field linguists observed. A key question this raised focussed on how much of linguistic variability could be explained by geographical and social conditions, and how much might be the workings of language itself as a natural object, subject to the laws of nature. Thus one set of problems became the disentangling of "internal" versus "external" sources of variation and change; that is, the relative effect of processes involving the workings of the linguistic system as opposed to those connected to the social practice of communicating.

A key example pitched the so-called *Junggrammatiker* (or Neogrammarians) against linguists who saw language as social. The Neogrammarians were a group of linguists clustered around the Univerity of Leipzig in Germany. Frustrated by philology's inability to explain linguistic change, they followed in the footsteps of such figures as Franz Bopp (1791–1867) and Jakob Grimm (1785–1863) by focussing on sound as the element of language most amenable to scientific analysis. (This is the same Grimm who, with his brother Wilhelm [1786–1859], collected the folktales we still read; indeed, folklore, archaeology, linguistics, and anthropology all emerged together in this period, in the mapping out of the nation in time and space.)

Sound, the Neogrammarians argued, was an element of the natural world because it was directly linked to the articulatory apparatus. As such, it was also amenable to direct observation and measurement; it was, in their eyes, truly empirical, as opposed to reconstructions of protolanguages in historical linguistics, which could only be inferred from texts. In line with other scientific searches of their time, they looked for the laws of nature. They argued that regular sound shifts drove language change.

One of the students of the Leipzig Neogrammarians was the Swiss linguist Ferdinand de Saussure (1857–1913). Saussure is widely credited in Western historiography of linguistics as the father of *structuralism*, sometimes alongside Roman Jakobson, whom we will meet in Chapter 6. Saussure was a Sanskritist, who, like Whorf, also wrote on theosophy. His key work, the *Cours de linguistique général*, was published posthumously in 1916 on the basis of lecture notes taken by a number of students and, it is said, collected by two Swiss linguists, Charles Bally and Albert Sechehaye, leading to some dispute about what Saussure himself might or might not have believed.

Saussure was one of three sons of a well-known Swiss naturalist who specialized in the study of insects (as Protestants, the family had sought refuge from Catholic France in Calvinist Geneva, as did many others). He was, then, brought up in the universe of empirical observation of the natural world. One of his brothers, Léopold, served colonial France as a naval officer in China and Indochina; he became a well-known authority on the Chinese cosmological system. The third, René, became a mathematician and a key figure in the development of Esperanto and the general field of artificial or constructed languages—and so, in his way, also a specialist in linguistic structure. (We will hear more of this story in Chapter 5; Mireille Grosjean says that it was Ferdinand who first received an invitation to an information session about Esperanto in Geneva. Concerned about his reputation as a professor of linguistics if he were to be seen at such a possibly marginal and scientifically doubtful event, he sent his brother René in his stead [pers. comm., La-Chaux-de-Fonds, Switzerland, May 2, 2016].)

Whether or not the *Cours de linguistique général* accurately reflected Ferdinand de Saussure's own thought, the text argued for a rather radical solution to the problem of language change, variability, and linguistic description. It firmly anchored linguistics in the study of the spoken language, but split off the systematic study of language as an abstract system (*langue*) from the study of language as it was actually used by speakers (*parole*). This allowed Saussure also to split off the study of the *synchronic* forms of language (how they manifest themselves in the here and now) from the study of their change over time (*diachronic* analysis). What he privileged as the proper study of language was the description of the linguistic system, or structure—that is, how each element (whether of sound, of meaning form, or of grammar) related to each other according to rules that could be empirically discovered, or in any case deduced, from observation. This move importantly allowed for the construction of language as a properly scientific object in its own right, in all of its dimensions. Neogrammarians had made such an argument for the study of sound (or phonetics) in historical change; Saussure set up the study of all dimensions of language as an empirically and synchronically describable phenomenon, opening the door not only to a host of subspecializations in different aspects of the linguistic system, but also the goal of a holistic description in which it would be necessary to relate each dimension to the other.

The critics of the Neogrammarians agreed that language needed to be understood as a natural phenomenon subject to scientific study. They disagreed over whether the social should be part of that. Meillet, one champion of the "language is social" position, was an avowed follower of the French sociologist Émile Durkheim, who insisted that society is a natural and observable fact like any other. Meillet took Durkheim's emphasis on social facts to the terrain of language, insisting that language needed to be seen as a social fact (Bergounioux 2006). But at the same time, as he put it, "Le langage est un système où tout se tient" [Language is a system in which everything holds together; our translation] (Meillet 1893, 318; but see Koerner 1996/1997 for an argument that Meillet's source for this phrase was the work of Saussure).

Thus the science of linguistics focussed on the object as system, whether radically separated from the social or part of it. This view tended to see language as universal and quintessentially human. Some linguists had ideas about language development as linear, if not teleological, progressing toward better, more effective modes of social organization, cognition and cultural practice, in line with modernity's ideas of progress and the problem of regulating inequality in democracy. This approach overlapped and also stood in tension with other branches of linguistics, in philology and dialectology, centred on a Romantic essentialist linkage of language to the spirit and the soul of the nation, whose claim to political sovereignty is legitimate because of historical continuity of presence and cultural practice on a particular territory—indeed, can be argued to take its shape because of the nature of that soil. This approach also often included evolutionary ideas about progress and perfection.

The progressive inscription of scholarship about language into the institutionalized milieu of scientific scholarship contributed to the naturalization of the idea of the nation, both in the sense that it helped place it within the frame of the natural world, and in the sense that it erased the human actions that constructed it. It also helped sustain the idea of the nation as rational, and thus concordant with liberal democracy, helping to legitimize it over and against other political forms. Finally, as Michael Billig (1995) has argued, it is in the very banality of expressions of nationalism that we can see just how hegemonic the ideological cluster of language, culture, nation, identity, cognition, and territory has become.

The next chapter will take us through three very different forms of response to these ideologies, and to the forms of inequality and difference industrial capitalism and the liberal democratic nation-state constructed and reproduced. Covering in turn Esperanto and two other modes of levelling the international, multilingual, and conflictual European playing field, communism, and fascism, we will examine how language served as a terrain for working out problems of competition over markets and of disparities of wealth.

CHAPTER 5

INTERNATIONALISM, COMMUNISM, AND FASCISM: ALTERNATIVE MODERNITIES

FIGURE 5.1: "Espéranto. La langue équitable." (Courtesy Espéranto France)

"Visions of the Future"

These glasses are part of an awareness campaign conducted by the French association of Esperantists: people who promote the learning and use of Esperanto. The slogan says "Esperanto: The equitable language." Monica first saw it on a sticker on the back of a traffic sign on a Paris street in 2013; the slogan remains current for the organization at the time of writing. Esperanto is usually taken to be an oddity of the past in linguistic circles. Yet here in France in 2017, someone is making a statement about its relevance to contemporary concerns about equity (enough so that in 2013 someone took the trouble to get a sticker on the back of a pretty tall street sign).

In this chapter, we look at sequels to the modernist nationalism explored in the last chapter. Much of what we discuss here, like Esperanto and other so-called International Auxiliary Languages (or IALs), has usually been considered marginal to most accounts of the major ideas about what language is and why it is important. IALs in particular are sometimes treated as amusing efforts by linguists, and are peripheral to mainstream linguistic thought. Our aim here is to show that in fact most responses to the modernist nationalism considered in Chapter 4 are nonetheless intimately tied to those major ideas. Further, while we focus here on the late nineteenth and early twentieth centuries, we believe such responses re-emerge at various key historic moments, or under key historic conditions, when the tensions inherent to nationalism and imperialism become hard to contain.

The more frightening ones we consider—those linked to fascism, and to Nazism in particular—are sometimes bracketed as manifestations of an aberrant historical moment. Following Hutton (1999), we show instead how mainstream linguistic and anthropological theory and practice as it emerged in the 19th century laid the groundwork for those ideas to become thinkable, and indeed attractive to some kinds of social actors under the specific political economic conditions of the time. Indeed, as Arendt ([1951] 1968) shows, fascist regimes draw on and are continuous with the the kinds of race-thinking evident in Orientalist accounts, whether focussed on Jews or Muslims, in Europe or elsewhere, as well as in imperial bureaucracies.

We will examine some of the other consequences of the modern-state, both those that rejected its insistence on bounded difference, and those that took its logic to an extreme. We begin with a discussion of *International Auxiliary Languages*, invented (or constructed) languages designed to facilitate international communication—precisely the communication rendered difficult by the effort to distinguish one national language from another, and rendered important by the political and economic dependence of states whose national markets regulated trade but could not constitute autonomous zones of production and consumption free from outside constraint. Trade and investment required modes of communication across the linguistic boundaries.

We then move on to consider in more detail the problem that nationalism posed for communism, the main challenge to capitalism in the nineteenth and twentieth centuries. We can understand communism as a reaction to the construction of class relations under industrial capitalism, and as a form of insistence that class, not nation, should be understood as the defining line of social difference. In that sense, communism's legitimacy required attention to global class interests, cutting across national divides and breaking ties of national solidarity that could be seen as masking class oppression. As we will see, communist intellectuals, particularly in what became the Soviet Union, struggled with what this meant for the constitution of a communist state and for a communist world movement. A number of alternative solutions were proposed, focussed on the question of how best to spread the Revolution, with debates about the use of one language (Russian or perhaps, at one point, Esperanto) or multiple languages. Such debates were also linked to discussions of the place of language in Marxist social theory.

We will end the chapter with a consideration of what happened to modern theories of language, race, culture and identity in the form they took in European fascism. In many ways, we can consider this process, following Hannah Arendt (1951), to be a logical consequence of the intertwining of modernist nationalism and of imperialism, taking as far as possible the idea that races are incommensurable but also evolutionarily ranked, and that their languages are part and parcel of the organic whole that is the nation.

We will look specifically at some of the ways in which predominant ideas about evolution, hierarchy, and natural differences were available for the development of Nazi race theory (following Hutton 1999), requiring work to be done to establish those differences and those hierarchies. As we will see, just as Bengalis posed a problem for British colonial administrators in the eighteenth century (Are they like us? Are they different? Are they of superior, equal or inferior value?), Yiddish posed a particular problem for German fascist linguistics, as a language close to German but spoken by a race deemed inferior, the Jews. (Both, of course, can be understood as problems of how to understand Orientalized groups.)

We also examine the ways in which language was bound up in fascist modes of discursive control. Today, Nazism in particular is associated with key developments in political discourse and the construction of hegemony through the use of particular forms of mediated communication (notably radio and film), the organization of participant structures and communicative context (for example, leaders' communication to followers in mass, highly scripted, communicative events such as night-time rallies), and the shaping of language itself, notably in prosody and lexicon, oriented to producing the value of fanaticism and the purification of the German language. We will draw heavily on the analysis of a contemporary witness, the German Jewish Romance philologist Victor Klemperer (1995, 2000).

The shape of this chapter points to our view that World War II constitutes a watershed in the political economy of language. The fear of following the Nazi path into genocide discredited much of Romantic nationalist linguistics, helping explain its immediate postwar eclipse by the structuralist dimensions of mainstream linguistic theory.

Peace, Geopolitics, and International Auxiliary Languages

FIGURE 5.2: A Movado watch, La-Chaux-de-Fonds, Switzerland, 2016 (Photo: Mireille Grosjean)

No, this book has not turned into a magazine advertising fancy watches. The reason we want to attract your attention to this image is not so much the watch as its name. Or it might be better to say that we want to talk about the relationship between the design of the watch, its value as an icon of modernity and of the national pride of Switzerland, and the name, which means "movement" in Esperanto. The photo was taken at Monica's request by Mireille Grosjean, a Swiss activist in the Esperanto movement, at Centre de documentation de l'Espéranto et des langues internationales. It shows Monica holding Mireille's watch, against a backdrop of La-Chaux-de-Fonds, which has been for more than 100 years a centre of the Esperantist movement. (Monica also has a Movado watch, but it is harder to see the brand name in the photos of her watch. We tried.)

Note the simple lines, the absence of numbers cluttering up the face. These features are modernism's answer to the accumulation of decorative elements that reached its height with the Baroque end of feudal empire, and reached an apogee in Victorian England and the Qing Dynasty in China (and may be about to return). They connote transparency, strength, and democracy, as opposed to decadence, corruption, and over-accumulation (they are also, it must be said, associated with masculinity, as we noted in Chapter 4's discussion of the gendered aesthetics of the French Revolution).

These features are also associable with industrialism, its strength, and its promise of increased wealth. Industrialism is also tied to the early-twentieth-century ideas about scientific management we discussed in the previous chapter, indeed to the broad notion that objective science guarantees better quality products in every way, leading also to an association with national branding. Link the simple design with the industrial production strengths of Swiss mechanical engineering (the watches are produced in the Swiss canton of Neuchâtel), and you have a semiotically strong product. Add Swiss neutrality and hygiene to the mix. But why Esperanto?

The brief answer is that using Esperanto as a brand name in conjunction with the label "Swiss made" marks a product as both Swiss and universal, an association facilitated perhaps by the traditional Swiss political stance of neutrality, as well as the country's association with finance. Even if the name is not identifiable as Esperanto, it is possible to understand it as vaguely universal. In that sense, it is the opposite strategy from one that plays on national stereotypes and national authentification to add value to a product, as when Volkswagen places ads around the world proclaiming its cars "das Auto" (the car), mobilizing stereotypes about German efficiency and technical competence (Kelly-Holmes 2000, 2005).

Esperanto, first (self-)published in 1887 by its inventor L.L. Zamenhof, was introduced into Switzerland about 10 years later, where it appealed generally to Swiss interests in political neutrality and specifically to the Jewish watchmakers who were building a watch industry in the Jura mountains of northern Switzerland. Achille Ditesheim, from the Alsatian side of the Rhine, had founded a watch company in La-Chaux-de-Fonds in 1881, named L.A.I. Ditesheim et Frères. In 1905, he changed the name to Movado. Other companies, such as the one that became Eterna, also adopted Esperanto brand names. (Mireille Grosjean [pers. comm.], says that the Rado ["wheel"] company came upon its name serendipitously, not deliberately.) A quick look at the Movado website shows that modernity remains part of its brand ("Movado—Modern ahead of its time"), and that its collection includes a large number of Esperanto names (e.g., Amorosa, Bela, Circlo, Luma, Rondiro, and Verto).

As the idea of the nation promoted the constitution of particular forms of difference, so did it emphasize the mobilization of those differences in struggles over resources, and define the many wars of the nineteenth and twentieth centuries. Certainly, IALs were only one manifestation of a general liberal democratic movement of internationalism produced to regulate competition and conflict. In the nineteenth century, these took the form of various congresses and agreements, such as the ones we discussed in Chapter 4 that were responsible for the development of the census.

IALs were developed as a strategy both for international peace and for international commerce, and were also of particular interest to socialist, communist, and anarchist movements that contested the nation-state altogether as the primary means of political organization. They became a focus for a flurry of activity that reached its peak between the 1880s and World War II, involving professional and amateur linguists (often in competition with each other) caught up in the many tensions connected to the building of the liberal democratic nation-state and of imperialism. The principal tension in each was a certain rhetoric of inclusion, in the nation-state or the empire, contradicted by simultaneous practices and policies of exclusion.

IALs remained of interest to socialist, anarchist, and communist movements after that period, notably in China, and have long been harnessed in Asia to issues related to pan-Asianism and to looking for the best basis for Asian—especially Japanese, Chinese, and Korean—engagement with the West. IALs existed before the 1880s and still exist in many forms today (Klingon-speaking fans of *Star Trek*, we're talking to you). Indeed, as we saw at the beginning of this chapter, the best-known IAL, Esperanto, is re-emerging as we write as relevant to contemporary debates about how to fairly manage multilingualism under conditions of globalization (see Garvía 2015; Heller 2017; Sokolovska 2016). Thus, far from being marginal or amusing (no laughing allowed when we get to the part about umlauts in Volapük), IALs are evidence of some of the major tensions produced by the mainstream emphasis on clearly demarcated languages, and by their use to mask the harnessing of social difference to make inequality.

Esperanto's inventor, L.L. Zamenhof, a Jewish optician, was born in 1859 in Bialystok when it was part of the Russian Empire (it is now part of Poland,

and indeed became so during Zamenhof's lifetime). Revealingly, the initials L.L. stand for different things, depending on if you are using the Hebrew, Yiddish, German, Polish, or Russian version of Zamenhof's given names. The story most often told about Zamenhof, who came from a bourgeois family and married into another bourgeois family, is that he was disturbed by the interethnic tensions between Jews, Germans, Russians, and Poles in Bialystok, and more generally by interethnic tensions in Europe at the time; this led him to look for a way for people to talk to each other without one group dominating the other.[1] If one person has to learn the other's language, he felt, that constitutes a communicative disadvantage. Survival in eastern Europe as a Jew meant multilingualism, and it is not difficult to see why Jews at that time and in that place might be interested in means for peaceful integration that would supersede the ethno-national and ethno-religious distinctions that usually worked against them. It is precisely this failure to have a mother tongue, and this cosmopolitan nature, that will lead to some key critiques in Nazi linguistic theory.

Zamenhof's idea was to level the playing field by inventing a language that everyone would learn as a second language and that would be equally easily learned by all Europeans. (While the IAL movement quickly went beyond Europe, its initial conceptualization was based on European problems and European languages.) The IAL project was understood to require making up something as simple as possible, and that would draw as much as possible on a common lexical stock.

Esperanto famously has only 16 rules. One sound corresponds to one letter; word order doesn't matter. Suffixes distinguish nouns (subject and object), adjectives, and adverbs. Verbal suffixes distinguish three tenses (past, present, and future) and three moods (indicative, jussive, and conditional). (Note the repetition here of the ideas of von Humboldt and others that inflection, which happens to be a characteristic of European languages, is a sign of clarity and rationality; see Chapter 3.) Vocabulary is drawn almost exclusively from European languages. For example: *La bruna hundo amas la katon* means *The brown dog loves the cat*. *La* = *The* (invariable); *brun+a* = adjective *brown*; *hund+o* = subject noun *dog*. You can guess the rest. If you speak English or German and any Romance language, you are probably just about ready to make up Esperanto on your own.

The language became known as Esperanto ('hoping') because Zamenhof signed himself Dr. Esperanto when he first published his idea (see Geoghegan 1889

---

[1] Full disclosure: Zamenhof's brother was married to a stepdaughter of Monica's great-great-aunt (her great-grandfather's sister). Family lore has it that Zamenhof used to visit Monica's great-grandfather, an owner of a ribbon factory, in Warsaw. It is not known what they discussed.

for the first English version). It rapidly became clear that the hope in question was not simply for the successful appropriation and wide dissemination of the language, but more so for the international understanding and peaceful relations that it would bring. Zamenhof used a green star to symbolize this hopefulness. He wears a green star pin in most of the photos we have of him, and the star turns up regularly in a wide range of Esperanto-related iconography, for example in posters for Esperantist congresses and in Esperantist publications.

Esperanto was by no means the only IAL invented during that time, nor even the first, and certainly not the last. In addition to those discussed below, consider Occidental, Latino sine flexione, Idiom Neutral, Solresol, or Lingua franca nova, just to name a few; Okrent (2009) offers an exhaustive list. It has perhaps had the broadest and longest dissemination, for reasons we will consider below.

For the moment, we should note that most histories of "invented" or "constructed" languages start from Hildegard of Bingen, who attempted such a project (based on Latin) in the twelfth century, and recount a number of attempts to construct rational languages, on philosophical and mathematical principles, as the Renaissance developed into the Enlightenment. Some attempts were concerned to uncover the core features of language as a means of approaching an understanding of divine creation, as we have seen in missionary language ideologies in Chapter 2 and in Whorf's theosophical speculations in Chapter 3; some aimed instead at uncovering the basis of rational thought, as we explored in Chapter 4 and will explore further in Chapter 6. In this sense, there have been struggles over whether such "invented" languages should be understood as "artificial," as opposed to the "natural" ones we learn to speak as children, or whether human intervention simply makes language better than it would be if left to its (or our) own devices. Since we do not wish to take any of these positions, we will prefer the terminology of "auxiliary," "international auxiliary," or "constructed international auxiliary" languages for this discussion, but we should understand the set of terms as keywords.

The IAL enterprise began intensifying in the late 1870s. The first well-known entry into what became a fraught and complex field was Volapük, published in 1879 by Johannes Schleyer, a Protestant minister from southwestern Germany. While Volapük initially attracted a fair amount of enthusiastic attention, Esperanto, published a mere eight years later, quickly drew away many of Volapük's adherents.

It is largely agreed that the reasons for this were technical. First, Schleyer's aim for simplicity took, among other things, the form of a preference for one-syllable bases for building words (or *morphemes*, the basic unit of meaning in any language). This extreme reduction of linguistic material made it very difficult to retrieve meaning, even when the source language (and source word) was commonly known. The very name of the language shows this: "vol" is derived from "world" ("Welt" in German, with the initial "w" pronounced as English "v"), and "pük" from "speak" or "Sprache."

Second, Schleyer had a fondness for front rounded vowels like /y/ and /œ/, indicated by an umlaut in German as in Volapük (these are the vowels, for example, in French *rue* [street], and German *blöd* [stupid]). Unfortunately, these vowels are not part of the phonetic inventory of many European languages, are difficult to pronounce for people who are not used to them, and add orthographic complexity to what is supposed to be a simple language.

The final problem for Volapük is one that troubles all such auxiliary languages. Since the goal is to make something both universally accessible and as close to simple as possible, stakeholders tend to argue about whether specific technical solutions are the best ones in formal, structural terms (Is this as elegant as it could be?), in didactic terms (Is this easy to teach and learn?), in communicative terms (Can we use this to be understood easily?), and in political terms (Does this give too much of an advantage to speakers of any particular language or language group?). Inventors may have too much invested in their particular creation to respond well to such questions or, even worse, to suggestions for modification, but their passion can also lay the foundation for a charismatic leadership that helps legitimate the language. Schleyer apparently was too possessive of Volapük to allow for reform, or even broader participation in decision-making.

Zamenhof tried to avoid the same trap, but apparently only partly succeeded. Struggles over Esperanto were partly formal and partly ideological; it was the ideological part that was difficult for Zamenhof to concede. The major schism in Esperantist ranks led in 1907 to the regrouping of some followers around a simplified version of Esperanto, called Ido (meaning "offspring," because it is understood to be derived from Esperanto). To some extent, this schism was linked to tensions over whether Esperanto should have primarily a commercial or scientific vocation, or cleave to Zamenhof's initial dream of fostering world peace. The former was counter-attacked as mercenary or elitist. The latter movement was often derided by its critics as attracting too many fuzzy-headed people fond of floating around dressed in green stars. Both sides were derided by speakers of standardized national languages concerned with their own position of power in a politically unstable world (the French in particular had an investment in the status of their language as a *lingua franca* among European elites, and in many ways they still do).

During the years before World War I, and again in the years leading up to World War II, many IALs were constructed, debated, institutionalized, refined, and sometimes abandoned. Baggioni (1997, 322) notes that a high point coincided with the Exposition universelle in Paris in 1900, which became an occasion for celebrating triumphal European capture of world knowledge through empire. This nexus also contained the seeds of the schism between utopian pacifists (usually understood as feminine) and scientists (understood as masculine), who saw in IALs one means for bringing language into the realm of what science could know about the natural world: if you got the rules right, then you were likely onto something about how language as a natural system worked. (As we shall see in the next chapter, this idea laid the foundation for later ideas about machine translation and universal grammar.)

World War I not only led to the death of many participants in IAL endeavours, it also destabilized the movement since it represented exactly the kind of conflict IALs were designed to avoid. In addition, Zamenhof himself died in 1917, though not as a direct result of the war. Nonetheless, the movement picked up again after the war, largely because of the boundary and conflict problems the war had illustrated all too well. This time, the scientific linguists emerged as central authorities. Their work on IALs became oriented, however, perhaps less toward world peace, and more toward grasping universal features of language, in parallel with the development of structural approaches to language in Europe and North America.

We have already seen that René de Saussure (1868–1943), the brother of Ferdinand de Saussure, was a devoted Esperantist (though he had some ideas of his own as to how to perfect it, dubbed Antido and then Nov-esperanto). The Danish linguist (and expert on English) Otto Jespersen (1860–1943), who had played a role in the Ido schism of 1907, was perhaps the most committed of the linguists who were involved in IALs in the early twentieth century; he weighed in with his own IAL, Novial, in 1927. An early proponent of understanding language both as structure and as social fact, Jespersen was the author of one of the major foundational texts of structuralist linguistics (Jespersen 1922). With a central concern to understand linguistic structure in the service of communication, it is perhaps not surprising that the project of building an efficient linguistic structure for international communication would attract Jespersen. One might also hypothesize that as a multilingual Dane on the European periphery, he was also well-placed to understand what was at stake. Many of the other major linguists of the day, including Hugo Schuchardt (see Chapter 3) in Graz and Jan Beaudoin de Courtenay (1845–1929) in St. Petersburg, also weighed in on the matter. These were all linguists who were primarily preoccupied with the problem of linguistic variability and change, and were mainly interested in what IALs could tell them about language as an empirical, scientific object.

This scientific expertise came to dominate the discussion with those "amateurs" still involved. It was harnessed in particular by the Interlingua project begun in 1924 by the American heiress Alice Vanderbilt Morris (1874–1950).

The goal of this project was to construct an *interlingua* that would mainly help people speaking different languages communicate, but unlike most IAL projects, it also aimed at facilitating the learning of other languages (in that sense, it can be seen as an embryonic form of applied linguistics). One of Vanderbilt Morris's first research directors (in the early 1930s) was Edward Sapir, who, in 1925, had already mobilized a group of U.S.-based linguistic anthropologists (including Franz Boas) to sign a manifesto on the desirability of IALs and their ideas about what linguistic criteria should be used to construct them (Sapir 1925). Their main argument was that IALs could "serve as a sort of logical touchstone to all national languages and as the standard medium of translation," though they were clearly also interested in what such languages could tell them about the nature of language as an object of scientific investigation. Along with Jespersen, Sapir was one of the major linguists at the time to remain committed to the project (Baggioni 1997).

World War II destroyed many European adherents of IAL movements (often precisely because they were Jews and/or communists; Tonkin 2011), reinforcing the turn to structural linguistics. After World War II, Vanderbilt Morris recruited the French linguist André Martinet (1908–99), who later became the central figure in French structural linguistics. Both Sapir and Martinet fought with Vanderbilt Morris over the goals of Interlingua research, with both linguists maintaining that basic research into linguistic (and for Sapir, cognitive and cultural) structure should override practical language learning applications. This research was nonetheless understood as emancipatory, insofar as it placed all language forms on an equal basis, equally revelatory of universally shared human capacities for language, whatever the different forms actual practices and worldviews might take. It was thus opposed to the evolutionary teleological model that underlay much of contemporary language policy.

While their concerns were different from those of Europeans, intellectuals in early-twentieth-century Asia often saw in Esperanto an alternative to (other) European languages, as China and Japan in particular became increasingly pulled into European imperialism and a globalizing economy. Esperanto was understood as a way to meet European powers on a more level playing field than would otherwise be possible, as well as protecting national/imperial interests, given the pressures to establish relations with the West. Globalizing science was one important meeting ground (Gordin 2015), exposing Japanese scientists to the problem of international communication and to IALs as a solution through their contacts in a number of fields, from biology to, of course, linguistics (Usui 2008). At the same time, it was the child of a Japanese colonial official in Korea, Tokio Oyama, who introduced Esperanto to that country in 1922, hoping to reduce tensions arising from the colonial imposition of Japanese on Korea (Kim 2006, 141).

In China, Esperanto became of interest in the 1920s and 1930s among Chinese anarchists and communists (Müller and Benton 2006; Lins 2008). After the Chinese Revolution, it was also understood to be linked to the internationalizing interests of communism (at about the same time, as we shall see, as the Soviet Union committed itself to Russification). Today, Esperanto has adherents in South Korea who are looking for a more equitable alternative to "English fever" (fierce competition over learning English; Park 2010) as a means to participate successfully in the globalized new economy (E.Y. Kim, pers. comm.). The emphasis on avoiding English as the language of globalization is of course one of the subjects hotly debated by early stakeholders, especially those from France who feared weakening the status of French as the language of international relations. Plus ça change …

While many of the IALs that saw light in their heyday before World War I no longer have adherents, both Esperanto and Ido still have many, divided mainly by ideological divisions between political and pragmatic goals. In addition to a base in Korea, China, and Japan, other strongholds remain Europe, both east and west (a legacy both of socialism and of Esperanto's original institutionalization), and the Americas. Esperanto in particular has also been taken up by some syncretic, evangelical religious groups in Brazil in search of universal values and a language to go with them, picking up the utopian strain in the Esperantist movement (Pardue 2001).

IALs constructed after World War II have tended to be linked to alternative worlds, in fiction or other forms (Heller 2017). J.R.R. Tolkien invented Elvish in his *Lord of the Rings*. Today, one of the best known IALs is Klingon, the language invented for a group of aliens on the television and film science fiction series *Star Trek*. Other such *constructed languages* (or *conlangs*) have been invented for other Hollywood science fiction films in the early twenty-first century. This turn can be linked to Cold War interests in technology, science fiction, space exploration/colonization, and alternative, often utopian or dystopian, universes, as we will discuss in the next chapter. Today, the Internet is full of *conlang* projects, mainly connected to science fiction or alt-fiction television and film, or to the construction of alternative worlds through popular culture in many ways. They can perhaps be seen as the linguistic equivalent of cosplay. Most material consist of a kind of how-to "build your own language" kit, with little of the grand theory or global vision of earlier efforts.

IALs capture many of the ideological threads of language in modernity, exposing the fault lines created by attempts to delimit the undelimitable. They represent tensions between Romantic ideas about language as the heart and soul of a nation, and therefore languages as incommensurable, and Enlightenment ideas about reason as the source of human perfectibility. They point to the potential for exclusion and conflict inherent in the nation-state model, and count as one attempt among others to mitigate those problems. At the same time, the questions underlying them remain vibrant areas of scientific and political activity, transformed in the post-World War II period into questions of international development, language policy, and language planning, with a publication turned into a research journal (*Language Problems and Language Planning*) and, as we have seen, contemporary involvement in matters of multilingualism, notably its celebration as a dimension of contemporary cosmopolitanism.

In the next section, we turn to a different attempt to overcome nation-state model barriers, represented in various guises by the emergence of socialist and communist movements in the late nineteenth century.

Making Communist Linguistics

One major outcome of the Industrial Revolution was the construction of an urban working class. The collapse of the feudal order and the privatization of formerly common lands left many agricultural labourers with no means to make a living, leading to both urbanization and involvement in settlement of overseas colonies. Working in industrial labour required different forms of temporality (watches, again)—it was less seasonal and cyclical, and more governed by the needs of the work and the employer. The development of class stratification in industrial capitalism was a key feature of the nineteenth and twentieth centuries and of modernity. Here we will turn to the form of resistance represented by socialism and communism, especially as it became institutionalized after the Russian Revolution of 1917.

Socialist concerns about the exploitation of workers included both industrial workers, who were seen as exploited by capitalists, and agricultural workers, who were seen as exploited by feudalists. Their alternative vision was to create a classless society based on collective ownership and collective labour. Socialism is a reaction against the aspects of modernity that created stratified class structures, but not against industrial production itself, nor against modernist concerns with progress toward bright and promising futures (R. Williams 1989).

Nonetheless, as with IAL discourse, the issue remained whether to accept the organization of production via national markets, aiming for international bridges for the advancement of common interests (in the political formation that Soviet policy eventually described as national in form, socialist in content), or more radically break away from the nation-state toward a universal ideology, universally applied. If the workers of the world were to truly unite, the nation-state would have no further function. (Indeed, for these reasons, IALs were attractive to socialist states, especially in the early years of the Soviet Union.) Ultimately the use of national markets with international links prevailed, though not without struggles and debates, many of them on the terrain of language (M. Smith 1993; Slezkine 1994).

We focus here principally on the Soviet Union after the 1917 October Revolution, which overthrew a semifeudal Tsarist regime and established a Soviet regime of an alliance of workers and peasants under the control of the Bolshevik Party. This focus is partly because of the importance of the U.S.S.R in setting policy and practice for the rest of the communist world, and partly because it illustrates well the tensions among empire, nation, and class we are trying to explore (see M. Smith 1998). Nonetheless, we will end this section with a brief look at parallels in China.

We take up three themes. The first has to do with nationalism versus universalism as optimal modes of spreading the Revolution. This takes on a particular form in the Soviet Union (as opposed to other socialist countries), where Russian cultural production struggled with its relationship to Europe and to Asia, and hence in its ability to make claims to both specificity and to the best of both worlds. The second theme has to do with progress toward universal socialism, and what stages of evolution society must go through in order to get there. The third theme has to do with the organization of society, and whether or where language fits Marx's description of the base as economic and the cultural as superstructure—built on, or indeed determined by, the economic base.

Stalin, at Lenin's request, produced a manifesto in 1913 regarding the "national question" (M. Smith 1993). This was important, since the Revolution would bring together the various parts of the former Tsarist Empire, which was not only vast in territorial terms but also comprised a large number of peoples and languages that were understood as distinct from one another. It was in Stalin's text that it was first suggested that while socialism would indeed eventually unite the workers of the globe in a classless society, it was impossible to arrive at that goal in one leap. Rather, Stalin suggested that it made more sense to work with national solidarities to construct socialist states one by one, states that could cooperate and that, through time, would fall away. We can hear echoes of debates among religious missionaries (see Chapter 2) or at the time of the French Revolution (see Chapter 4) over whether it makes the most sense to bring the word of the revelation (whether socioreligious or sociopolitical) to people in their own language, so as to maximize their chances of understanding the message, or whether to introduce them to the language of the movement directly. Thus this story, although shaped by Marxist theory, is also connected to the Soviet Union's complex ties to empire.

The description of Soviet dialect variation and multilingualism was an important first step as a kind of inventory; this can be seen as an extension of previous efforts to map out the boundaries of the Tsarist Empire. However, the

Soviet Union had a different kind of citizen in mind, which led it to focus on not just identifying, but also standardizing, the many languages of the Union. In order to both educate—that is, make the Soviet citizen—and govern, it was as important in the Soviet Union as in capitalist countries to standardize languages, creating orthographies as necessary. As elsewhere, this has been understood as necessary for modernization, but it has often been difficult to rid it of its history as connected to bourgeois nationalism, or to repress its effects in the form of bringing into being specific ideas of specific nations, with their own elites and interests (Slezkine 1994; M. Smith 1993, 1998).

It has also been difficult to balance how specific kinds of standardization might help or hinder communications across groups; Smith (1993) describes Soviet debates about whether to favour latinized or cyrillic orthographies for languages that either lacked a script altogether or had used Arabic orthography, which they wanted to replace in order to resist the influence of Islam. Indeed, in the Soviet Union the relationship to Russian was complex; tensions between understanding Russian as an ethnonational symbol and understanding Russian as a uniter of diverse members of the Soviet Union were never really resolved.

These debates were intertwined with other concerns about language inherited from the Tsarist Empire, notably the question of the union's position with respect to Europe and Asia. As we have seen, the Asian characteristics of the region were devalued by European philology and also later by the Nazi regime; both preferred a genealogy linking Europe to Greece and Rome, and ultimately Aryan areas (from northern India to Nordic countries).

One result was that the Soviet Union invested itself in the construction of linked Soviet republics, each one with a particular linguistic profile, but all of which were expected to teach Russian in school and to communicate in Russian with the political centre. During its early years, the Soviet Union experimented with multilingualism, albeit of a familiar type, made up of whole, bounded, standardized languages. In this sense, the Soviet Union remained squarely within the hegemonic model of language and linguistics, making the same erasures of mixity and boundary processes and, in the end, bringing into being nations of a modern kind, while privileging Russian as the unifying thread.

After the problem of how to bring a multilingual, poorly educated, and highly dispersed population into a socialist state, one that furthermore was undergoing rapid urbanization and industrialization, a second immediate question was that of the construction of a *Marxist linguistics*. This was understood, at least in part, as requiring a theorization of the place of language with respect to the economic base. Should language be considered a "superstructural" phenomenon produced by the economic base? Or is language not relevant to economic production?

This debate grew from the Marxist *base/superstructure* model, which suggests that economic forces shape all else: religion, cultural expression, political life, religious expression, and forms of consciousness. This is the view often associated with Marx's comments published in 1859 in *A Contribution to the Critique of Political Economy*:

> In the social production of their life, men enter into definite relations that are indispensable and independent of their will, relations of production which correspond to a definite stage of development of their material productive forces. The sum total of these relations of production constitutes the economic structure of society, the real foundation, on which rises a legal and political superstructure and to which correspond definite forms of social consciousness. (Marx 1859 [1979], 4)

Engels protested that Marx's comments were often misread, that rather than saying that the economic element was the *only* determinant, he and Marx had argued that law, political theories, and religious views also shaped the course of historical struggles (Engels 1894). Nonetheless, the question remained of how to understand the place of language, within a strong preference for linking it to social, historical, political, and economic processes.

The Russian linguist Valentin Vološinov, writing after the Russian Revolution of 1917, agreed. He critiqued earlier Marxists for ignoring language, but he also critiqued linguists such as Ferdinand de Saussure for studying language as an abstract sign system, rather than as something involved in economic and other social struggles. He argued, instead, that the study of language was a key site for understanding them: "The material of the verbal sign allows one most fully and easily to follow out the continuity of the dialectical process of change, a process which goes from the basis to superstructures" (Vološinov [1929] 1973, 13).

Although the position that language was a superstructural phenomenon produced by the economic base was contested by linguists who remained committed to the idea that there were facts about language that the base-superstructure model could not explain (Slezkine 1996), initial Soviet theories first leaned toward it, continued to debate it, and ultimately removed language altogether from that model in 1951 (see below). Soviet linguistics was thus faced with resolving the tensions between communism's claims to universalism, and both the Soviet Union's recognition of national diversity as well as persistent pan-slavist ideologies privileging Slavs over Asians. It also faced difficulties in resolving communism's commitment to the base-superstructure model and problems that model encountered with accounting for empirical observations. We will examine the attempt to resolve these tensions in the work of Nikolai Marr (1865–1934), whose theories became the official Soviet position on language in the 1920s and 1930s.

Marrism

Like the bourgeois proponents of IALs, Marr was also concerned to address the question of social evolution and language change as part of a Marxist linguistics oriented to the eventual development of the socialist universal state. Marr's critique of Indo-Europeanist historical comparative linguistics was also a critique of European imperialism and racism; he proposed in their stead a view of language origins and development that not only foregrounded class as the relevant distinction, but also emphasized language as common to humanity.

There were three key arguments in Marr's work (see Slezkine 1996; Lähteenmäki 2006). First, Marr argued that dominant European theories of language change, as continuously fragmenting family trees, had things more or less literally upside-down. Marr argued that language had its origins in the sounds accompanying work, though the specific shapes those sounds developed as they became language varied. Thus, he argued that multilingualism was historically the norm, as opposed to positing, as most Indo-Europeanists did, that there were either single origins of mankind or united origins for each different language family, with the language of each core group (race? nation?) subsequently evolving and splitting up over time. Marr argued that language change should be understood as first differentiating from the common labour-related core but then, with diversity, eventually giving way to one common language as the world progressively shifted to universal socialism.

The thesis on how language arose from work was linked to the second argument, his theory of class language, although these ideas sat uncomfortably with Lenin's and Stalin's approaches to Soviet multilingualism, their recognition of national languages, and the efforts put into standardizing them for the purposes of education and modernization. Building on earlier work by his contemporary Lev Iakubinskii, who explored linguistic differences according to position in the class structure (examining, for instance, differences between the language of peasants and of workers), Marr argued that, since language was part of the superstructure, it would reflect quite directly the economic base in which speakers were situated. Thus workers' language should share more features across national boundaries than workers' language would share with the bourgeoisie of their own nation-state. As communism progressed, and class distinctions disappeared, one unified class language would emerge (Lähteenmäki 2006). While Iakubinskii and others in Leningrad, where both Marr and Iakubinskii worked, shared Marr's views about the importance of class, especially given the rapid urbanization and industrialization of the period, they rejected Marr's attempts to closely correlate specific linguistic forms with specific economic structures (Brandist 2015).

Marr's third argument had to do with how he understood language families. As we saw in Chapter 2, existing European linguistic theoretical distinctions among language families focussed on the descendants of Noah's three sons, Japheth, Ham, and Shem, with Japhetic languages understood to cover the area from Europe to present-day Iran. Marr argued for a renewed focus on these languages and offered a new theory of their origin, situating it in the Soviet Caucasus (where both Marr and Stalin were born). (It is not clear why Marr chose to remain within a biblical metaphor, nor why this was considered legitimate. It does show how embedded Soviet linguistics remained within European thought despite its discourse of rupture and revolution.) Situating Japhetic languages in the Caucasus allowed Marr to argue for the specificity of the Soviet space, based on its origins in the Caucasus, astride Europe and Asia but distinct from both. In that sense, he shared with other linguists, as well as with some archaeologists, historians, folklorists, and literary critics, the concern to map out a space for the Soviet Union as distinct, and both prior and superior; at one point Marr argued that Japhetic language was the original one and underlay all of European civilization (Slezkine 1996). This concern with Eurasia had already manifested itself in Tsarist Russia, and led linguist Nikolai Trubetzkoy to explore, along with scholars such as Schuchardt, ideas about diffusion and language areas as alternatives to comparative philology or evolutionary theory (see Chapters 3 and 6).

While Marrism shares a concern to legitimize the limits of political control with both the linguistics of Tsarist Russia and other approaches to language in the Soviet period, certain features specific to it made it vulnerable to criticism: its inability to account for observable linguistic differences, and its investment in some specific claims about the origins of languages (notably that everything reduces to a small set of morphemes). Marr's work was already beginning to be contested before World War II by linguists concerned about how narrow the field was becoming, although the final nail was placed in the coffin with Stalin's statement after World War II that language should be understood as neither in base nor superstructure (Stalin 1951; Slezkine 1996). Since Marr himself died in 1934, and World War II drastically changed the conditions of Soviet existence, it is not surprising that the period from the late 1930s to the late 1940s would be unstable in Soviet linguistics.

Further, much discussion about language took place in fields other than linguistics, as part of a broader discussion across the humanities and social sciences, and often with similar debates and repressions. Still, certain ideas thread through the debates. For example, the idea that language development and its use were closely connected to work was also shared with the major

Soviet contributors to social psychology at the time, notably Alexis Leont'iev (1903–79) and Lev Vygotsky (1896–1934). Their work (still deeply influential in cognitive science globally; see notably Vygotsky 1978) was interested in developing a Marxian approach to psychology by investigating the ways that how we learn about and understand the world are anchored in interpersonal practices, in the activities that tie us every day in interaction with each other and with the material world. The group studied, in particular, how children learn, placing communication at the centre of the process. Interaction and discourse were also of concern to the so-called Bakhtin circle, to which we turn next.

The Bakhtin Circle

The "Bakhtin Circle" had as its central figures the linguist Valentin Vološinov (1895–1936) (mentioned above), and literary critics Pavel Medvedev (1892–1938) and Mikhail Bakhtin (1895–1975). Vološinov died young of tuberculosis; Medvedev, an activist, was arrested during the purges of the late 1930s and killed in 1938; Bakhtin's interest in religion made him suspect and caused him to be exiled to the east. Their work was less widely known than that of the social psychologists, especially in the West, until it was translated in the late 1960s and 1970s.

The Bakhtin Circle was centrally concerned about the relationship between human agency and social reality, about the possibility of action, and about the relationship between the individual and the collective (Bakhtin 1968, 1981; Vološinov [1929] 1973; Medvedev and Bakhtin 1978). It differed with Marr over what constituted relevant linguistic forms (Marr was interested in morphemes, the Bakhtin Circle in discourse) and over what attention to accord to issues of linguistic origins and development. The largely comparative and structural linguistics that dominated the European and American scene had little place in it for speakers, or for interactions. As we saw earlier, linguistic change was largely understood to be a feature of the agentless linguistic system, whether due to "internal" or "external" "forces." This is a problem for socialism, for which the possibility of collective action to produce social, including linguistic, change was a central concern.

At the same time, socialism understood action to be collective, and the social, rather than the cognitive, to be the central locus of activity. In this frame, the Bakhtin Circle's insistence on *dialogism*, *heteroglossia*, and *voice* is a powerful move away from a model that situates language as an autonomous system in the mind of the individual (see Bakhtin 1992). In the first instance, then, the scholars in the Bakhtin Circle argued that language is *dialogic*, rooted in communicative exchange (see Holquist 1990). Further, language was seen as the product and property of the collective, produced, shaped, and reshaped in the course of social relationships. At the same time, because the collective is not fixed and uniform, linguistic forms circulate through multiple contexts of use. Their continued circulation, then, allows them to carry at least the possibility of linkages to other conversations elsewhere, involving other people, and to the meanings and values that mattered there (i.e., they are *heteroglossic*) (Todorov 1984, 68; Vice 1997, 18). In that sense, while utterances may come out of individual mouths, they carry with them traces of their social history and of the experiences of other people (*voices*) (Bakhtin 1968, 68).

In the Bakhtinian approach, all speakers are social actors (in the sense of beings whose existence involves undertaking action in a form that can only be understood as social); none of us is wholly independent of the others. Because we are not all situated in the same place and at the same time, we do not speak with one uniform voice. Nonetheless, we are not situated in radically isolated or different conditions; we do produce shared frames, values, meanings, and modes of expression connected to the conditions of our time (what Bakhtin [1981] called a *chronotope*).

Finally, the Bakhtin Circle was concerned to explain how some voices become dominant and others marginalized. Using the idea of centre and periphery, and of the opposing tendencies of phenomena that can be *centripetal* or *centrifugal* (seeking or fleeing the centre), they sought to account for the often opposing pulls of the centralizing state, particularly strong in urban areas, and those of the village (San Diego Bakhtin Circle 2000). We can read here a version of some of the issues that preoccupied other linguists concerned with language change, but also a thinly veiled critique of a totalitarian state.

From Language as Action to Language as Tool in the Cold War

Socialism is a struggle to make equality under unequal conditions. In the early years of the Soviet Union, scholars worked not only to find ways to legitimate the Soviet Union as a political and cultural entity, but also to find the tools necessary to balance universalism and diversity, centralized control and the possibility of collective action. This period of intellectual creativity in the 1920s began to close down as the crises of the 1930s eventually led to World War II and Stalin turned toward authoritarian centralism.

Russian became more and more important as a key to both communist orthodoxy and political participation. The immediate postwar period was one of widespread Russification. Debates about Marrist linguistics were published in the pages of *Pravda* in the late 1940s, culminating in denunciations under Stalin's own name (though leaning heavily on the work of the linguist Arnold Chikobava; Stalin 1951; Slezkine 1996). Most importantly, Stalin's statement removed language from base-superstructure dialectical dynamics. This move allowed language to be recast as a tool, emphasizing socialist linguistics' long-standing construction of language as a form of social action centrally connected to labour, while freeing it from strictly deterministic relations with the base (as well as serendipitously from arguments about the more doubtful speculations of Japhetology). Finally, it allowed Soviet linguists to distance themselves from the work of certain Russian diasporic scholars, such as Nikolai Trubetzkoy and Roman Jakobson, whose structuralist and functionalist approaches were seen as bourgeois, anti-material, and cosmopolitan, while also making language available as a dimension of Cold War technological competition with the United States (see Chapter 6).

While official policy continued to defend the importance of the languages of the "smaller" nations, Russian also was understood to be a necessary second language for every speaker of any other language, institutionalized as such in the schools of every republic that had another official language. This policy eased up to some extent in the 1960s, as nationality policy put languages other than Russian back into play in their respective republics, albeit as languages associated with local or regional allegiances, and not with the access to higher education or political structures for which Russian remained necessary.

Russian was not officially constructed as a language better suited to socialism than the other languages of the union, but rather as what it was necessary to share in order to remain united. This was clearly crucial during both World War II and the Cold War. At the same time, Russia was the centre of power, and Russian the language through which it would be possible to acquire and help produce advanced technical knowledge as well as socialist theory. Further, the old relations of power dating from the time of the Tsarist Empire left traces in the form of dichotomies between "civilized" Europe (associated with Russian) and "backward" Asia (associated with the languages of the U.S.S.R.'s Central Asian republics), despite Marr's attempts to overcome them.

In that vein, Russia remained understood as the space through which all nations of the Soviet Union would gain access to the civilized world, and Russian as the language in which that process took place. The same was true regarding the USSR's relations with the members of Warsaw Pact countries, which each retained their own national state language and their own minority policies while promoting Russian as the language of international socialism. Russian was supposed to be de-ethnicized and opened as a language that belonged to everyone, no matter their origin (M. Smith 1998). In fact, of course, that de-ethnicization was difficult to accomplish since ethnic Russians were always closer to the centre of decision-making about what counted as Russian and what knowledge Russian would be linked to. Those tensions remain active to this day.

While we have concentrated on the Soviet Union here, we should note that similar problems were approached in similar ways in other parts of the communist world, notably the other major power, post-1949 China.

As we mentioned earlier, Esperanto had already caught the attention of Chinese anarchists in the 1920s. As was the case with the Soviet Union, a high post-Revolution priority was placed on political unification, education, industrialization, and development, with a focus on both the development of minority "nationalities" and ensuring shared communication.

While China is highly linguistically variable, most linguistic varieties spoken within the People's Republic share a writing system: that is, it is possible to communicate in writing even when spoken language is not comprehensible from one variety to another. In that respect, large-scale literacy campaigns were arguably a more effective unifier in China than in the Soviet Union, though there have been frequent debates about whether the writing system should be simplified (DeFrancis [1950] 1975). At the same time, that same writing system is understood as a repository of some of the central values of the Chinese state: its civilization, its sophistication, its reach. This has been one terrain for working out a major tension within Communist China: between China as developed empire and China as incarnation of values associated with peasants and workers. Within the priority accorded to Mandarin as the major linguistic tool for centralized functioning, and a tool that is meant to be de-ethnicized (although achieving that has proved impossible), regions and groups can have subordinate languages linked to their "nationality" status.

Thus in many ways, despite communism's aim to provide a radically alternative path to modernity from liberal democracy and capitalism, its understanding of language as a fundamentally political tool for nation-building retains the shape of how it is understood elsewhere. The making of industrial markets linking nations and empires turned out to look oddly familiar.

Next, we turn to the third response to the inequalities of liberal democracy and nation-building that characterized this period: fascism. As is well known, the totalitarian regimes of Nazi Germany and Stalinist Russia ended up mirroring each other in many ways, offering collective utopia—but only for those willing to follow the path, or selected to do so. Nazism, however, adhered to the idea of the organic nation and its place in evolutionary hierarchies as rationales for inequalities necessary for the betterment of humankind.

Language and Fascism

The previous two parts of this chapter were devoted to reactions to the inequalities produced by industrial capitalism that focussed on egalitarian utopias. Neither bourgeois bridging nor socialist levelling refused modernity; they shared the dream of progress through technology. They also shared a deep ambivalence about the role of the nation in that progress, seeing in it both a fundamental, or at least unavoidable, form of social organization and a potential obstacle to universalism. Like other movements of its time, fascism—and Nazism in particular—sought to use technology to advance progress toward a utopia of wealth and egalitarianism, albeit one confined to members of the (German) nation.

Fascism can also be understood as a reaction to the crises of industrial capitalism, heightened by the destruction of World War I, and notably to problems of inequality. This was also a moment of loss of empire. As Arendt ([1951] 1968) argued in her integration of European histories of anti-Semitism, imperialism, and totalitarianism, fascism in Europe is a product of the second wave of European imperialism that began in the late 19th century. Building on the equation that language = nation = race allowed for a specific form of violent expression (see also McElhinny 2016a), fascism also tried to resolve, in the most isolationist, genocidal, and racist way possible, the contradictions that imperialism raises: the creation of racial proximities and interactions in spheres ranging from families and children to politics and trade, as well as shared languages, in the context of occupation and claims to racial superiority. A focus on imperialist glory and national unity helped redress class antagonisms arising in the wake of industrial capitalism, substituting notions of national/racial superiority for class consciousness and solidarity.

Thomas (2014) argues that Italy, Germany, and Japan did not become fascist because they were not modern, but because they were modern. The lack of a unified German state before 1871 (later than many other Western European countries) meant that the task of unification seemed more urgent for nationalists, especially in light of increasing German migration in the wake of industrialization's economic disruptions and the putative dangers of foreign influence linked to German's imperial presence in Africa and the Pacific (Townson 1992). Germany was hard-hit by World War I, with restrictions placed on its military forces, the surrender of European territory and all of its overseas colonies, and high expenses for reparations. However, as Sheppard (2014) notes, "[W]hat National Socialism promised then was not in the end a revision of the economic system in order to achieve a more equitable re-distribution of the goods of production. ... Class distinctions would not disappear, but they would be reinterpreted ... economic equality would be substituted with social egalitarianism" (16). The Nazi concept of the *Volksgemeinschaft* (people's community) was central to the definition of "Germany" in the interwar years, drawing its boundaries between "races" rather than classes.

With the German empire lost after World War I, the concerns about the purity of Germany were focussed intensively on internal others, European Jews, who were all the more dangerous because their differences were sometimes racially "invisible." The dilemma, as raised even in *Mein Kampf*, was that there was no correspondence between the "racial" boundaries marked out by racial anthropology and linguistics; the task, therefore, was to make them congruent. But which should be prioritized? Hutton (2015) argues that eventually a division of labour emerged between a deterministic race theory based on genetics, and a voluntarist and teleological variety of linguistics.

Fascism constructed itself as strong and pure, and therefore inherently masculine within a clear demarcation of sexes defined by heterosexuality, in which the state has primacy over every other form of social authority (although one of Italian and Spanish fascism's distinctive characteristics was a profound alliance with a strongly patriarchal Catholic Church). The idea of impurity was applied both in prohibitions against biological mixing of races and in deviations from a heteronormative order that by definition not only excluded homosexuals, but constructed them as actively dangerous. Men labelled as homosexuals were also marked out for extermination (this is where the now reclaimed symbol of the pink triangle comes from; it was used by the Nazis as a badge of shame). Fascism has this focus on heterosexual masculinity in common with revolutionary movements, and notably with communism. It sought to be resolutely modern, but through the establishment of rigid forms of hierarchical social order, in which every category had its place and its rank, and remained true to its core "natural" characteristics. In this it was inspired by colonial ideas about racial hierarchy and colonial efforts to avoid racial contamination and to repress or eliminate racial inferiors. Indeed, the Germans first used the technology of the concentration camp in their colony in Southwest Africa (later Namibia; Olusoga and Erichsen 2010).

Here we focus on the ways in which ideas about language resonated with ideas about culture and nation in ways that made a certain kind of sense in the development of fascist theories of society, culture, politics, and economics—a Gramscian sense, in which consent, and not coercion alone, needs to be understood to be at work. While similar arguments can be made about fascist movements elsewhere, as well as contemporary ones, we will focus on German Nazism as the clearest and furthest developed example.

National Socialism in Germany

"Nazi" is a short form of National Socialism, and the term should allow us to hear echoes of both Romantic nationalism and socialism. The socialist dimension is linked to the emphasis on redistribution of wealth under circumstances of major economic destabilization in Germany in particular after World War 1, and more broadly as a result of the stock market crash of 1929 and the resulting widespread depression. The "national" part orients us to asking what the criteria and scope of redistribution might be.

A long tradition of anti-Semitism, especially in the form of political and economic marginalization, facilitated the disenfranchisement of Jews as German citizens (Arendt [1951] 1968). This is one of the ways Orientalism demarcated difference within Europe, as well as between Europe and others, organizing the Christian West's relationships with Islam and Judaism, two other key monotheistic religions (Kalmar and Penslar 2005). This served as a basis for legitimizing the long process begun in 1933 of removing Jews from the economic, as well as the political and social, life of Germany, and of removing Jewish wealth and property from its owners and transferring it to "Aryans" (Vidal 2002). "Aryans" were thus able to take university and professional positions from which Jews were expelled as early as 1933, to buy Jewish-owned property at good rates when Jews were forced to sell, and to receive goods and property later taken from Jews by force.

Vidal (2002) argues that the possibilities of wealth redistribution within the limits of the German state were insufficient. The idea of political expansion, notably in the form of the idea of *Lebensraum* (living space) can also be seen as a problem of wealth redistribution, and legitimized through a realignment of who could count as German on the basis of race rather than residence. This is also linked to a problem of empire. Expansion leads to contact between groups then constructed as incommensurable and hierarchically ranked, but those boundaries are porous (there are a variety of acts of intimacy and "mixing"). One reaction can be to embrace or codify intimacy, another can be fear of contamination, expressed through withdrawing from contact, or purifying the group from within (as with the evolutionary hierarchies we saw in Chapter 3).

Building on the Romantic nationalism that helped construct the nineteenth-century German state, fascism could call on the idea of the German nation to delimit to whom "socialism" and "progress" applied. It also could call on linguistic and anthropological ideas about the specific characteristics of nations, their languages, and their cultures, about their primordial claims to land, and about their place in the development of a hierarchy of value, and therefore of merit and rights. Nazi theory was thus interested in showing how German expressed specific characteristics of the German nation (its strength, its rationality, its ability to capture complex thought), but also where it stood with respect to other languages.

The Nazi chronotope, if we can use that term here, oriented linguists toward a continuation of both the philological tradition, examining the character of German linguistic form as a mode of cultural, indeed national, expression, and the comparative method, seeking to establish the boundaries among languages more or less related to German as well as their place in a hierarchy in which German needed to be shown to be the most civilized, the furthest along the linear path toward human progress and perfection. Debates about the origins ("the homeland") of the Aryans were also claims about Aryan superiority made on linguistic grounds. Nazi linguistics invented very little; rather it combined elements already existing in linguistic and anthropological theory in ways that made sense in Nazi race theoretical terms, and that then also became available for the reproduction of that race theory and the violence it legitimated.

At the same time, it is important to point out that various individual linguists had complex positionings, holding beliefs that might not always sit well together or might even be potentially contradictory. One example might be the Romance philologist Karl Vossler (1872–1949), who was a strong patriot (he had proudly worn the uniform during World War 1 and believed strongly in the Fatherland), holding that language and nation were closely tied, but who apparently never drew the conclusions regarding, for example, anti-Semitism that were available in this line of thinking for others to draw (Vossler 1955; Hutton 1999).

In letters exchanged with the Italian philosopher Benedetto Croce (1866–1952), collected and edited by his son (Vossler 1955), both Vossler and Croce seem to agree on the close alignment of language and nation, although Croce, after early support for the Italian fascist regime, ultimately became an opponent (and a key intellectual influence for Gramsci). For example, in 1919 Vossler writes to Croce: "But it is also good that one is aware that a German eye sees the world differently from a French one, and that no one can climb out of their skin. There are no international eyes, that is, there are already such things, but they mostly see nothing specific, nothing that couldn't be seen by any other" (Vossler 1955, 232). Here we see the kind of radical linguistic relativity sometimes ascribed to Whorf, balancing on the edge of possible linkages with evolutionary and racial hierarchies.

Five years later Croce writes to Vossler about the fascist Italian education minister Gentile's policy of introducing Italian as the language of education in German-speaking South Tyrol, on the Austrian border. Croce disagrees with this policy, saying, "[o]nce we unfortunately have subjects of foreign races and languages within our borders, one must make bearable to them that which they cannot love on the inside and which they must accept under the coercion of politics and the international balance" (1955, 298). Many ideas about race, language, and nation, then, were widely held and widely available. Many people (like Croce) changed their minds about the political conclusions to draw from them, or changed their beliefs about language as they saw the political use made of them. Nonetheless, as we explore in the next section, the idea of whole bounded systems connecting them was central, and, as ever, produced complex anomalies, the most important of which was Yiddish.

Language and Race: Yiddish and Esperanto

A key problem for Nazi linguistic theory was the place and nature of Yiddish. Its ties to German are obvious, and in the 1920s there was some effort to construct it as a possible bridge to the civilizing of Jews (Hutton 1999). As Nazism focussed increasingly on constructing Jews as alien and inferior, however, interest turned to how it was different from German. This was done in two ways.

First, given the appearance of elements in Yiddish traceable to Hebrew and to Slavic languages, it was possible to establish it as an "impure" language, that is, as a language that is inherently contaminated (and contaminating) because it has failed to be true to its pure core, and instead incorporated elements of a variety of (in principle) incompatible languages, languages that were also, importantly, low-ranking on the Nazi scale of development. In that sense, Yiddish could be constructed as not a language at all, but rather as a mixed jargon. (In this, Yiddish is somewhat akin to the way pidgins and creoles were discussed; see Chapter 3.) This helps to explain the categories of groups singled out for exclusion, incarceration, and elimination by the Nazis. The Roma, by virtue of their itinerancy, were also not legible within a nation-state model.

Second, as a non-language in Nazi perspective, Yiddish could not play the important role of "mother tongue," a key element in the ways Nazism linked language to race and nation since the source of the biological nation was necessarily the relationship between mother and child. Worse, in their view, Jews were seen as notoriously multilingual, using Hebrew as a liturgical language, and the other languages of their communities (whether German, Polish, Russian, Greek, Italian, English, French, or anything else) as languages of education, commerce, and other dimensions of everyday life. (Zamenhof, you will recall, spoke at least four languages even before he invented Esperanto.) The structures of Nazi racial ideology thus concluded that Jews could not be said to have any mother tongue at all. And if they did not have a mother tongue, in the terms of Nazi racial science they could not be said to be even a proper race.

Linguistic inventions by Jews were also suspect. Here is what Hitler had to say in *Mein Kampf* about the ways in which "real" (mother tongue) languages could be constructed as being about the truth, and others, such as Esperanto, necessarily as lies:

> Among them is the lie with regard to the language of the Jew. For him it is not a means of expressing his thoughts, but a means for concealing them. When he speaks French, he thinks Jewish, and while he turns out German verses, in his life he only expresses the nature of his nationality. As long as the Jew has not become the master of other peoples, he must speak their language whether he likes it or not, but as soon as they became his slaves, they would all have to learn a universal language

(Esperanto, for instance!) so that by this additional means the Jews could more easily dominate them. (Hitler [1925/6] 1992, cited in Hutton 1999, 300)

Esperanto, we see here, is transformed from a universal language to a Jewish one. Fascist linguistics attended both to the problem of boundaries that is characteristic of nation-state linguistics and to the question of national character as expressed through language, although of course Nazism's focus on reuniting Germans allowed for expanding national boundaries. It entwined a linear dynamic of progress, both in historical-comparative analyses of the relative position of languages and in the mobilization of nations to work toward the triumph of fascism in the world order. And it invested in the idea of language not only as national soul, but also as technology for separating the true from the false, or the pure from the dirt.

It is in this latter sense that we can read some of the discussions of Nazi propaganda, which drew on a thread of linguistic theory linking language to worldview, as well as to national soul. The Nazi regime, partly through its official Ministry of Propaganda, sought to marshal a number of communicative elements in its construction of the spaces where fascist thought and practice were defined and instantiated, as well as in fascist communicative practice itself. These effects were the opposite of heteroglossia.

Race, Propaganda, and Mass Media

Nazi linguistic ideologies did not map only onto space understood in terms of national territory. The Third Reich capitalized on the physical organization of space through architecture, and on the social organization of space (e.g., through mass participation) to create specific conditions of participation in German society. One dimension of these efforts was linguistic, in multiple, and frequently interconnected, senses. The first was the use of the language itself, in time-honoured national tradition. This was important not only for German-speaking spaces, but also for others understood to be satellite nations. The second was the construction of an alternate legitimizing history for German: in order to resist the dominant ideas of European inheritance of classical civilizations from Greece and then Rome, which favoured the Romance languages, German linguists worked at constructing a direct lineage from Greece through Gothic (understood as a proto-German language; Rotsaert 1979). The third was the shaping of the language to incarnate and inculcate the values of vigour, violence, order, and renewal central to fascist values. The fourth was the harnessing of technology to saturate space with the mother tongue and fascist discourse; loudspeakers, film, and radio were central tools in that endeavour, but so were various forms of print.

One example was the introduction of Breton-language radio in Nazi-occupied France (Hutton 1999; Calvez 2000). German philology had long been interested in Celtic languages such as Breton (along with Welsh, Scots and Irish Gaelic, Manx, and Cornish) and their relationship to Germanic ones; it was hypothesized that the two language families were related, and that the Celts may have been the source of Nordic culture shared by Germans. Celtic religious practices and myth were linked to Nazi imaginings of the German past, and to their interest in particular forms of spirituality, tied to nature, the forest, and the north. Celtic languages were thus to be respected; Celtic-speaking areas of Europe were understood as natural allies, and were to be developed as such for the new world order that would emerge from the triumph of fascism after the war.

Radio itself was understood to be a powerful technology and was widely used in Germany itself. Hitler's speeches were regularly broadcast and were meant to be heard by all German citizens. Indeed, Monica's mother remembers being obliged as a child of seven or eight years of age to stand with the entire student body and all their teachers for hours in her Berlin school gymnasium, listening to Hitler. (As a moment in the construction of hegemony this would have been an interesting one to examine, since reportedly the students found the experience very boring, and initially spent time joking about Hitler, walking around making mock salutes. According to Monica's mother, that period lasted only about three weeks.)

Leo Weisgerber (1899–1985), professor of philology at Marburg, was entrusted with the development of a particular experiment in the use of technology for just such a purpose. Given the nonmilitary rank of *Sonderführer* ("special leader"), he was charged with organizing Breton-language broadcasts out of the major centre of Rennes, in northwestern France. We mentioned in the last chapter that Breton had been among the languages of France that the French Republic had tried to suppress in its efforts at building a unified France; stigmatized and marginalized, it was largely understood to be a language of wooden-clog-wearing peasants and fisherfolk. The Breton elite had of course never taken kindly to this construction of things, and they found an ideological home in right-wing resistance to socialist France.

Weisgerber was able to recruit a variety of teachers and writers to the radio broadcast effort, which was led by a former teacher who went by the pseudonym of Roparz Hémon (the son of an abandoned orphan, he rejected the non-name of Nemo [*no one* in Latin] that had been given to his father). The content of the programming was constructed as "purely cultural" and not at all political. Of course, as Calvez (2000) points out, this choice is in and of itself political since it was meant to show Bretons that their language was worthy of being a national language, and that it could be used in public. It was also a way of constructing Breton and Brittany as particular kinds of space: pure, distinct, and devoted to a continuity of history, folklore, and ways of life. It was a form of soft power, a way of building Gramscian consent.

In fact, the signal was weak, the number of hours of programming limited, and Rennes far from the heart of the most western areas where there was a population that actually spoke Breton. It is difficult to say what impact the programming had on its listeners. The project did, however, succeed in mobilizing a class of activists who saw in the support of Germany the best opportunity for the rise of the Celtic peoples, their shift from periphery to centre, and a basis for pan-Celtic and Nordic alliance. And it did lay down the precedent and the infrastructure for minority-language media that the postwar regime built on and that remains relevant for minority language movements from the 1960s to today.

Clearly, such use of technology to create the discursive spaces and conditions necessary for the making of nations does not always have the consequences intended. It also raises a more general question about ideas about language, nation, and identity, in the ways in which it associates saturation of communicative space with the saturation of consciousness, and the construction of unified linguistic spaces with the particular forms of consciousness a given language is understood to incarnate. We will now turn to this final dimension of fascist language ideology and practice through the work of Victor Klemperer (1881–1960), a student of Karl Vossler and a professor of Romance Philology at Dresden, in eastern Germany, in the years leading up to World War II, through his focus on its more banal, everyday manifestation in new ways of speaking.

We will use Victor Klemperer's well-known analysis of the *Lingua Tertii Imperii* for this purpose (Klemperer 2000); usually translated as *The Language of the Third Reich*, this is a distillation of notebooks Klemperer kept from the 1920s to 1945 (published in their entirety as Klemperer 1995). The use of Latin in the title was a deliberate attempt on Klemperer's part to link the Nazi Party's use of the term *Dritte Reich* to the more grandiose aspects of their claim to have founded a new Germany. The term itself legitimates the regime by placing it in a temporal sequence after the Holy Roman Empire and the Wilhelmian Second Empire of the nineteenth and twentieth centuries (France used similar narrative principles in contrasting its successive empires and republics as the monarchy came and went through the nineteenth century, as does the United States through the use of symbols that draw on the architecture and language of Roman empire).

Although Klemperer was a Jew, he was married to a non-Jew (or "Aryan") and had no children. His marriage somewhat (and temporarily) protected him from Nazi persecution, although he immediately lost his university position; he eventually found himself subject to the same racial laws as other Jews—from wearing a yellow star on his clothes to being confined to a "Jewish" residence in which many people were crammed, to having movement in the city restricted, and, finally, at the end of the war, to being summoned for "deportation" (i.e., removal to a concentration camp). He was saved by the fact that Dresden was bombed the day before he was supposed to report for deportation, and he and his wife escaped in the chaos that ensued. At war's end, he returned to Dresden and to his university position. Dresden became part of the German Democratic Republic in 1949; Klemperer remained there until his death in 1960.

His *Lingua Tertii Imperii* was published in 1947 in Leipzig (also in then Soviet-occupied eastern Germany). Translations into French and English occurred only after the collapse of the Soviet Union and of Eastern European socialism more generally (the first translation appeared in French in 1996), followed a few years later by the publication of his diaries, first in German and then in English. In both, Klemperer uses his tools as a philologist to document the discursive changes occurring around him from day to day. What he records is uncannily parallel with the critique of totalitarian regimes produced in novelistic form by George Orwell at approximately the same period (see Chapter 6), though the works were produced on either side of the Iron Curtain.

Klemperer suggests that Nazi officials worked hard at shaping how people thought about things, notably about their place in the world and how to act morally in it, through changing how they talked about things. For him, it was important to link more obvious forms of propaganda (staged parades, long speeches, explicit arguments about why Jews should be considered subhuman or why communism is dangerous, and so on) to banal everyday forms of language, whether spoken or written.

Here is what Klemperer already had to say in his diary on March 27, 1933: "New words keep turning up, or old ones acquire new specialist meanings, or new combinations are formed which rapidly ossify into stereotypes. The SA [*Sturmabteilung*, or "attack division," the paramilitary wing of the Nazi Party] is now known loftily—loftiness is indeed now perpetually de rigueur, for it is the done thing to be fervent—as the 'brown army'" (Klemperer 2000, 26). On April 20 of the same year: "*Volk* [people] is now as customary in spoken and written language as salt at a table, everything is spiced with a soupçon of *Volk*: *Volksfest* [festival of the people], *Volksgenosse* [comrade of the people], *Volksgemeinschaft* [community of the people], *volksnah* [one of the people], *volksfremd* [alien to the people], *volksentstammt* [descended from the people] …" (2000, 30). In addition to these stylistic shifts, Klemperer goes on to analyze such phenomena as "endless repetition" (2000, 15, 31), "the rich sonority of a foreign expression" (9), particular new coinages (e.g., *Strafexpedition*, punitive expedition [43]), "exhaustive use of ironic inverted commas" (e.g., through the use of 'red victories' to refer to gains by Spanish Republicans in the

Spanish Civil War, or 'research scientist' to refer to Einstein [72–73]), the use of contractions (such as *knif—kommt nicht in Frage* [it is out of the question]; or MG—machine-gunner; or HJ—*Hitler Jugend* [88, 92]) and nominalizations for reference, notably referring to individual Jews as "the Jew Klemperer," which of course has the effect of categorizing Jews as other than German (194). He also attends to the nonverbal: pitch of voice, the use of symbols like lightning bolts and Celtic runes. We see here echoes of Vossler's interest in the life of language, as well as a precursor to critical analysis of state and media discourse that would emerge in the 1990s in Europe and elsewhere.

As Klemperer points out, these strategies are effective means of making clear what social categories are legitimate and which are not (German vs. Jew, say, or Nazi vs. Communist), what is valued and what is not (the people and fervour vs. the individual and indifference), as well as of bringing people into the discursive circle (e.g., through the use of acronyms, which only insiders understand). They also make certain actions or actors opaque. Each of these taken alone is neither new nor unique. But taken together, with certain parties able to produce linguistic innovation and others required to follow along, or in the case of some, such as Jews or Roma, prevented from participating, they represent a means of creating a discursive universe and its boundaries. Klemperer says:

> Nazism permeated the flesh and blood of the people through single words, idioms, and sentence structures which were imposed on them in a million repetitions and taken on board mechanically and unconsciously.... [L]anguage does not simply write and think for me, it also increasingly dictates my feelings and governs my entire spiritual being the more unquestioningly and unconsciously I abandon myself to it. ... If someone replaces the words 'heroic' and 'virtuous' with 'fanatical' for long enough, he will come to believe that a fanatic really is a virtuous hero, and that no one can be a hero without fanaticism. The Third Reich did not invent the words 'fanatical' and 'fanaticism', it just changed their value and used them more in one day than other epochs used them in years. ... Making language the servant of its dreadful system it procures it as its most powerful, most public and most surreptitious means of advertising. (2000, 16)

As a philologist, Klemperer had the analytical tools, and as a Jew the marginal position, that allowed him to analyze his own experience as the discursive world around him changed. He shows us homogenizing nationalism taken as far along the road as it can violently go, and the ways in which state action and personal subjectivity can be linked through participation in that uniform discursive world. He shows us fascism as modernist progress taken to the point of destruction and death.

Fault Lines

In this chapter we have seen some of the more dramatic examples recent history has to offer us of what happens when the contradictions of industrial capitalism and modernity catch up with themselves. Here we see the fault lines created by understanding language and society as organic collectives, and the capacity of that understanding to create difference and inequality as well as solidarity and equity. We see the dream of universals up against the social practice of communication. We see technological, rational approaches to language used both to dominate and to emancipate. We see two approaches to friction-free language, one that tries to eliminate barriers to communication by elaborating a universal language to speak across difference, and one that attempts to eliminate such barriers by eliminating difference.

World War II left a deep fear of where evolutionary, naturalized understandings of language could lead us, and a deep desire to never reproduce that destruction of both other and self. The defeat of the Axis eliminated Fascism and Nazism as viable visions of the present and future and, with this, the vision of humanity engaged in a race-based or nation-based struggle for domination. This left in place two contrasting and competitive visions of human universality, sponsored by the major victor powers of World War II, the United States and the Soviet Union.

The former sought to build a liberal international order; the latter promoted a socialist ideal of universality. Both worked within a framework of nation-states. Both victorious powers agreed on the foundation of the United Nations, and on the principles of self-determination of nations and the dismantling of colonial empires, in part because of the access this gave them to sites previously under the jurisdiction of European states. While the two victor powers agreed on the framework of international organization, they profoundly differed on the internal organization of states and on the organization of the international political economy. These differences engendered the Cold War, and the resulting struggle over the allegiance of the newly independent postcolonial polities.

World War II also left a respect for technology, and an orientation to it as a means for foregrounding the potential of human control of social reality. Science and structuralism, language as technology, became the central mode of struggle. The next chapter turns to the Cold War, its fascination with the universal, with structure, with technology—and with ideological control over populations in what was experienced as a war for world domination, and hence for the ultimate truth.

PART III

Brave New Worlds: Language as Technology, Language as Technique

CHAPTER 6

THE COLD WAR: SURVEILLANCE, STRUCTURALISM, AND SECURITY

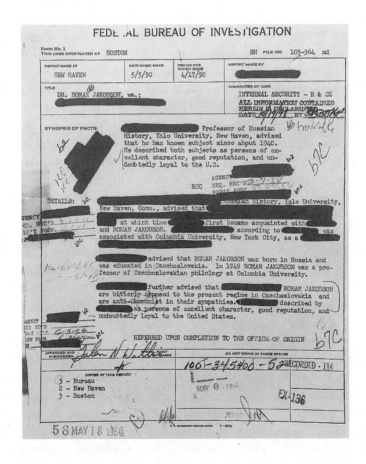

FIGURE 6.1: A page from Roman Jakobson's FBI file (Photo: Bonnie McElhinny)[1]

---

[1] Our thanks to David Price for sharing this file, which he secured through Freedom of Information requests to the U.S. government.

"Black Out"

This image is a page from Roman Jakobson's FBI file. It shows the information gathered, as well as the information that is still not released to the public, putatively because of national security concerns. The text shows there is active discussion about whether Jakobson was anti-communist. Roman Jakobson was scarcely the only scholar to attract the attention of the FBI; during the Cold War, many scholars were publicly critiqued and assailed because of fears of communist subversion, and the currents of work they were undertaking were suppressed. Others engaged in self-censorship.

The House UnAmerican Activities Committee (HUAC), a committee of the United States House of Representatives, was responsible for initiating many of these investigations. Originally established just before World War II to uncover citizens with any political ties understood as potentially subversive, after the war its principal interests were specifically with affiliations of individuals and organizations to the Communist Party or with behaviours (such as homosexual practices or illicit sexual relations) that might make key individuals vulnerable to Soviet blackmail or to entrapment in Soviet espionage.

Anthropologists and linguists were among those whose work attracted HUAC and FBI attention, with lasting effects on their fields. In addition to their own personal vulnerabilities (as evidenced in details about individual sexual histories), the state was interested in what they knew about parts of the world governed by communist regimes, and what work in such sensitive areas as class, race, ethnicity, and gender might say about their loyalty. In *Threatening Anthropology: McCarthyism and the FBI's Surveillance of Activist Anthropologists* (note the double meaning: anthropology as both threatening and threatened), David Price (2004) draws on more than 30,000 pages of FBI and other government documents to show "how the repressive post-war McCarthy era shaped and dulled what might have been a significant and vital anthropological critique of race, class and the inadequacies of global capitalism" (xi).

In this chapter, we will look at a number of dimensions of the conditions of the Cold War that had a long-lasting effect on work on language, in both anthropology and linguistics, particularly in the United States—both as a new global power and as the site for development of what became globally dominant strands of thought about language. We will look first at how the state's understanding of the usefulness of scholarly work on language in aiding the war effort (both hot and cold) turned to its flipside: fear of what scholars could provide to enemies of the state. Here we will examine the explicit targeting of certain kinds of scholars and activists, especially in the 1950s, as a way of investigating which kinds of critical thought were interrupted or forced underground. We will see that the FBI investigated a wide range of scholars, some who were political activists (whether or not that activity was connected to their work on language), some who were not but who were specialists in sensitive geographical areas. The effect was to silence work understood as political.

We will then turn to the ways in which the Cold War actively favoured the harnessing of scientific knowledge to the development of technology, understood as key both to the arms race and to winning the competition between capitalism and communism over which could provide the best modern quality of life domestically and around the decolonizing world. We will see that as Cold War conditions in the United States suppressed work critical of capitalism and of the class, race, gender, and sexuality inequalities it produces, it actively encouraged work that separated language from society and turned it into a technical tool. While there were clearly some marked differences, the suppression of dissenting views and the focus on scientific approaches and on language as a tool thus characterized both Soviet and American approaches during this period.

This linguistic tool was important to security and intelligence in four ways: to influence attitudes, to consolidate loyalty within the United States, to acquire knowledge of the people whose ideas the country needed to understand inside and outside the country, and to control the flow of information (notably through coding and machine translation, as incipient forms of computing). The chapter discusses the growth of the infrastructure for research, development, and training in these areas in the form of Communication Studies, Area Studies, Linguistics, and Applied Linguistics, each focussed on a different aspect of these goals. By developing such fields as separate scientific, apolitical tools it was possible to both implement them with the objective authority of science and contain the political activism of the developers.

This emphasis on the technical also contains some potential for contradiction. We will see in the growth of *generative grammar*, the major school of American linguistics beginning in the 1950s, an attempt to link the decoupling of language and society to the search for human universals, to the human capacity for rational thought, and to the human desire for freedom. In this respect, formalist linguistics can also be understood as a response to the excesses of fascism, and in particular to its racialized essentialization of language, culture, and identity.

The linguistics of this period moves away from the focus on words, sounds, and morphology we have seen in previous chapters to a focus on syntax, that is, on the principles and processes that govern the structure of sentences, understood as foundational to understanding what all languages share, and therefore how to move among them. The focus on syntax was also understood as key to the connection between language and thought and hence, for

Noam Chomsky, the key figure in the search for a Universal Grammar, the pathway to understanding humanity.

The Cold War was not, however, simply a technological competition; it was first and foremost an ideological one. In addition to demonstrating how technology provided evidence for the superiority of capitalism or communism, it was important to convince people of the inherent worth of one or the other regime. Here linguistics was also understood to be both a device for unmasking ideology in order to get to the truth and a means of developing propaganda (domestically called "advertising" in capitalist countries). Both powers took a leaf from the Nazi playbook on propaganda, developing scientific approaches to the study of how to shape people's views in studies of communications, mass media, propaganda, and advertising.

We close with a discussion of the novels of George Orwell, whose portrayals of language and the state became one of the ideological superweapons of the Cold War. Orwell is a complex figure, with a life traversing many of the formations we have seen in the last few chapters: colonialism, industrialization, nationalism, and the struggle against fascism. He became focussed on the power of persuasive language as a means of inhibiting creativity and critique. His novel *Nineteen Eighty-Four* is a dystopic projection of a world in which the state acts against humanity by shaping language so as to prevent individual freedom. Along with Chomsky, Orwell illustrates the ambivalences of the Cold War in the fight for freedom fought through the control of thought.

Battles for Hearts and Minds

The Cold War designates both a space and a time, but also a set of techniques. The Cold War, in the definition of the U.S. army, is "the use of political, economic, technological, sociological, and military measures—short of overt armed conflict involving regular military forces—to achieve national objectives" (1962 document from a U.S. army symposium held in 1962, cited in C. Simpson 1993, 334). It roughly designates the period 1948–89, a period when the Soviet Union and the United States were competing in the development of science and technology, in stockpiling weapons, attempting to explore and dominate outer space, and, throughout all these endeavours, trying to recruit other nations to their side. Since this competition had global implications, for some it wasn't a Cold War at all, but an actual one, especially in the earliest parts of the period on which we focus here; the U.S. and the U.S.S.R. fought proxy wars in and over other sites such as Angola, Cuba, Korea, and Vietnam. While the conflict had clear diplomatic and military dimensions, it also shaped decisions on how to invest in academic work, including work on language, as each side attempted to constrain the power and influence of the other, and win "hearts and minds" (as a Vietnam War slogan had it) around the world. Governments, private foundations, and universities were all connected on the field of academic knowledge production.

In *No Ivory Tower*, the historian Ellen Schrecker (1986) argues that consensus theory, modernization theory, structural functionalism, and a strictly text-based form of literary analysis, New Criticism, all coincide with and are shaped by Cold War dynamics, in which there was sometimes explicit or implicit censorship of alternatives, although sometimes alternate perspectives were just "crowded out" by the prevalence of others. A number of scholars have examined how this played out in different fields, noting that technocratic and social engineering applications were valued while political critiques were not (Chomsky 1997; Cohen-Cole 2003; Isaac 2007; Solovey 2012, 2013; Wax 2008).

Military/industrial interest in mathematical tools that would give a competitive advantage in modern warfare drove the postwar rise of linear programming, operations research, and game theory in American economics. Modernization theory was defined as a liberal, scientific path to progress, over and against dialectical and revolutionary frameworks (and tied to concrete programs of "international development"; see Chapter 7). Socially engaged forms of philosophy were displaced by mathematical logic and linguistic analysis (narrowly defined). A definition of the Cold War as an ideological battle inspired a deeply psychological approach to anthropology, and fuelled research on psychological warfare and propaganda in mass communications and psychology. Area studies was born under the Research and Analysis Branch of the Office of Strategic Services (a forerunner to the Central Intelligence Agency); areas and languages of the world were defined in accordance with their strategic importance and research was funded accordingly. Studies of the Cold War are much less extensive for linguistics; existing accounts of this period tend to focus on the displacement of structuralist linguistics by generative linguistics (see Hymes and Fought 1981). There has been little attention to the way the field was shaped by the political and economic conditions of the time. A major, and recent, exception is the work of Janet Martin-Nielsen (2009, 2010a, 2010b, 2011); we draw heavily on her work in our account.

Therefore, it is in many ways only possible to write a partial and fragmented history of this period because many key documents about the influential relationships between universities, government, and foundations remain classified or extremely difficult to access (and when you get them, as was the case for the image with which we opened this chapter, they are often highly redacted). Further, individuals involved in government-sponsored research in the 1940s and 1950s, when it was considered acceptable, may have become reluctant later to recount their stories in a public environment that became much more critical. As a result of all these factors, this chapter draws on a wider, and different, range of sources than other chapters, including biographies, emerging work in science and technology studies, and the FBI file on Roman Jakobson.

The Investigation of Linguists during the McCarthy Period

In this section we provide profiles of four linguists investigated by the FBI during the McCarthy period. The first two, Melville Jacobs (1902–71) and Morris Swadesh (1909–67), were linguistic anthropologists profiled in Price (2004). We draw on Price's (2004) book for detailed accounts of the ways the work of these two scholars was curtailed. Jacobs did his doctorate with Boas, while Swadesh studied with Sapir. Both worked in a descriptive vein on Indigenous languages; their work, like Boas's, was framed by cultural relativism rather than a decolonial analytic. However, again like Boas, they were politically active on other fronts, especially in the fight against racism. The third, John DeFrancis (1911–2009), was drawn to studies of China and was pulled into the net of the FBI through the defence of a Sinologist colleague. The fourth, Margaret Schlauch (1898–1986), was explicitly socialist, and defected to Poland when she came to the attention of the FBI.

Jacobs published a large number of books, including collections of texts from Native American languages of the Pacific Northwest. Swadesh worked on more than 20 Indigenous languages in Canada, the United States, and Mexico throughout the 1930s. In the late 1930s, under a Depression-era government-funded program at the University of Wisconsin, he employed more than a dozen local Oneida to record and translate Oneida texts; he also worked in Mexico to help establish educational programs in Indigenous languages.

Swadesh was also a consultant with the International Auxiliary Language Association, which standardized Interlingua and in which his supervisor, Sapir, was extensively involved (see Chapter 4). In the process of doing this work on an international language, he developed lists of the 100 and 200 basic vocabulary items most frequently used across languages (Esterhill 2000). These are called *Swadesh lists*, and are still often used in field situations when linguists want to begin developing a grammar of a language. They were also central to his development of lexicostatistics, which used quantitative measures of these items as a way to measure language change (though not necessarily to reconstruct a protolanguage; Hymes 1960). We can see here that the word lists that were used to develop comparative philology (Chapter 2) remain relevant as linguists try to refine scientific methodologies for their application.

Both Jacobs and Swadesh were Jewish and had been involved in activism challenging anti-Semitism and anti-Black racism. Jacobs publicly protested the internment of Japanese Americans during World War II, opposed bills introduced into the Washington state legislature that prevented the intermarriage of people of different races, and regularly spoke on topics such as "Race and the National Situation" to a variety of audiences, from the Young Men's Business Club to the Communist Party. His 1947 textbook with Bernhard Stern, *General Anthropology*, argued, as did many Boasian works, for the plasticity of human behaviour, criticizing racism and the cultural biases of IQ tests.

Swadesh battled anti-Semitism and anti-Black racism in New York, and particularly on the campus of City College of New York. He published articles in Marxist journals such as *Science and Society*. Swadesh's FBI file recorded his participation in a May Day parade and remarked on his letter of protest to the New Jersey governor about the trial of six African Americans accused of a murder. It also recorded his participation in a rally in support of Paul Robeson (1898–1976), a well-known African American singer, actor, civil rights activist, and student of African languages. (Robeson's work had been withdrawn from distribution because his interest in anti-imperialism and anti-racism had led him to an interest in socialism; he is known for having said, upon arriving in Moscow, "Here I am not a Negro but a human being for the first time in my life. ... I walk in full human dignity"; Editors of Freedomways 1998, 76.)

Jacobs came to the attention of the FBI in the early 1940s; in 1941 the FBI had been investigating activities of suspected communists at the University of Washington, where Jacobs worked. In 1947, during hearings on these concerns, Jacobs was called in front of the Washington State Interim Committee on UnAmerican Activities. While three faculty members were fired after these investigations, the university president agreed to retain Jacobs if he signed an oath stating he had not been a member of the Communist Party since 1946, and if he were placed on probation for two years. Jacobs complied, but also sent a statement to the faculty committee on tenure about how his scientific work on racial topics and interracial relations had been challenged by those who were uninformed about questions of race (Price 2004, 49).

Following the 1948 meetings of the American Anthropological Association in Toronto, George Murdock, who had succeeded Sapir as chair of anthropology at Yale, sent a letter (since obtained by Price) to J. Edgar Hoover detailing his suspicions that a communist conspiracy had controlled the AAA's business meeting; Melville Jacobs and Oscar Lewis were two of those charged with converting "the scientific organization into a propaganda tool subserving [sic] their interests" (Price 2004, 72). Murdock had been trained in the evolutionary paradigm that historical particularism challenged. He had been extensively involved as an anthropologist in World War II and as a military government official in Okinawa in its aftermath during the US military occupation. As chair at Yale, he dismantled the interdisciplinary program that Sapir had built and that had placed linguistics, anthropology, and psychology in regular conversation. He saw the range of political causes with which certain Boasians were aligned as threatening to democracy and potentially aligned with communism.

After Murdock's accusations, Jacobs was subjected to two public loyalty trials and years of FBI persecution and surveillance. In 1949, Jacobs and Stern sought a publisher for an edited collection of essays to accompany their successful 1947 textbook. They were unable to find one due to allegations from key figures like Murdock that some aspects of the work were intended to indoctrinate American students in Stalinist beliefs (Price 2004, 91). Jacobs retained severe misgivings about his colleagues and university administration for years afterwards. Throughout the 1950s and 1960s he became more subdued in his academic writings on race, and his public appearances advocating racial equality occurred much less frequently. He concentrated his research on grammars and texts, and during the campus uprisings of the 1960s Jacobs counselled students to be careful when engaging in public protests, quietly referring to his own past troubles (Price 2004, 97).

Although Jacobs retained his tenured job, those like Swadesh, who were in more precarious academic positions, lost theirs. Swadesh was an untenured professor who worked on a year-to-year contract at City College of New York. In 1949 he was suddenly notified that he would not be reappointed, despite a unanimous recommendation of the department appointments committee, ostensibly because he used class time to discuss both campus racism and the recent firing at another university of an anthropologist who was said to be a communist sympathizer. He argued this was a flagrant violation of academic freedom, and also evidence of anti-Semitism. Although Swadesh sought support from professional organizations such as the American Anthropological Association, only a few colleagues were said to have assisted him (Price 2004, 104). Like many targeted anthropologists, he ended up leaving the United States, moving to Mexico in 1956. He taught at the *Escuela Nacional de Antropología e Historia*, living in Mexico City for the rest of his life.

John DeFrancis, with whose work Swadesh was familiar, had a life-long interest in language learning, literacy, writing systems, and social transformation, due to the poverty and family illiteracy with which he grew up as the child of Italian immigrants, and a Depression-era trip to China, where the poverty he saw struck him profoundly. On his return from that trip, he switched from economics to graduate studies in Chinese at Yale and Columbia. His thesis examined issues of how to revise writing systems to support mass literacy in China (DeFrancis [1950] 1975). He began his academic career at Johns Hopkins, where he worked with another scholar of China, Owen Lattimore, who was one of many such area specialists to face charges of being a Soviet spy (despite having been an influential advisor to the U.S. government during World War II). The charges ended Lattimore's academic career in the U.S.; DeFrancis was blackballed for having come to his defence.

After DeFrancis lost his academic position, he worked as a vacuum-cleaner salesman for a while, but returned to academic work when commissioned to write a textbook for first-year students learning Chinese; this evolved into a set of 12 textbooks widely used in the United States in the 1970s and 1980s. During the last decade of his working life, spent at the University of Hawai'i at Mānoa, he began work on the account of Chinese and French colonialism in Vietnam (published in 1977, discussed in Chapter 3), which offers an overview of colonial language policy and ultimately a rather sympathetic account of the rise of Marxist resistance to the colonial state.

Margaret Schlauch was a faculty member (and the first woman to be appointed full professor; Rose 2005) in the English department at New York University, working on literature and linguistics (see Schlauch 1955). Her analyses of Chaucer were seen as innovative feminist work, and they have long been cited in medieval feminist studies. In the 1930s she wrote lengthy critiques of Nazi racial theory, including a pamphlet on *Who Are the Aryans?* written for the Anti-Fascist Literature Committee. She published a lay introduction to linguistics, *The Gift of Language*, in the early 1940s, a book that analyzed the history of English, the nature of grammar, language, and class, and the role of language in propaganda and politics.

Schlauch was also chair of the Greenwich Village Labour Party, and at the centre of a circle of female communists (Wald 2012). She was the founding editor of the Marxist periodical *Science and Society* (in which Swadesh also published). In 1951 she was subpoenaed by the House UnAmerican Activities Committee; she resigned her position and left the United States for Poland, where she lived out the remainder of her days. Her work has been celebrated in Poland, with symposia held in her name as recently as 2002.

In each of these profiles, we see the curtailment of research by scholars, some of whom identified as communist, some of whom defended the rights of communists to articulate their beliefs and decried Cold War scapegoating, and some of whom were suspect for other progressive activism. All of them were involved in multiple, intertwined strands of anti-racist, feminist, and/or anti-capitalist work. Academics who had not been targeted were of course impacted: they learned to avoid those who were stigmatized, as well as to avoid or hide anti-racist or Marxist analyses. Even those criticized by communist regimes were not immune from investigation. The most famous such linguist is Roman Jakobson, whose FBI file opens this chapter.

Suspicious Words, Suspicious Minds

The Prague Linguistics Circle

As we saw above in the case of DeFrancis and Lattimore, specialization in areas of the world tied to communism—especially China, the Soviet Union, and the Warsaw Pact countries—inevitably drew the attention of the FBI. So did knowledge gained from having lived there. The allegiance of those who can translate between two worlds is always suspect (Rafael 2014, 2015, 2016). This is how Jakobson, to his anger and dismay, found himself having to defend himself to the FBI.

Jakobson (1896–1982) was born in Russia into a prominent Jewish industrialist family (though he later converted to Russian Orthodoxy).[2] His work, which drew on Ferdinand de Saussure and Jan Baudouin de Courtenay, focussed on the universal structures and functions of language, and played a central role in the development of structuralism in the 1950s in such fields as anthropology, art criticism, semiotics, and neurobiology.

Before Jakobson turned 20, he was one of the founders of the Moscow Linguistics Circle, a group of linguists who followed other European dialectologists in their focus on what people actually spoke (see Chapter 4). He did two seasons of summer fieldwork in this tradition. Though he himself said little about his life immediately after the Russian revolution in 1917, exercising perhaps the caution required by Cold War contexts, Toman (1995, 36) reveals that he worked for the People's Commission for Education, as Director of Press for a Soviet mission in Estonia, and parsed dialect boundaries to help determine Russian/Ukrainian borders. In 1920, he arrived in Prague, as a translator for the first Soviet Red Cross mission to Czechoslovakia, and in order to continue his doctoral studies away from postrevolutionary turmoil.

Though Jakobson claimed in the context of Cold War suspicions of him that he was anti-communist, Toman argues that in the 1920s his actions read differently (1995, 39–40). The revolution was still associated with a new promising future by him and many others (88–90). The mission was supposed to help transfer Russian prisoners-of-war back to the Soviet Union, but many Czechs resisted the mission as a Bolshevik outfit and one seen as dominated by Jews. Along with other members of the mission, Jakobson was regarded warily as a potential Soviet spy. There were rumors that the real Jakobson had been killed, and that this man was an imposter using Slavic

---

2 These notes come from the biography in the archive of Jakobson's papers at MIT. See Guide to the Papers of Roman Jakobson, MC 0072, MIT, Institute Archives and Special Collections, MIT Libraries (https://libraries.mit.edu/archives/research/collections/collections-mc/mc72.html).

studies as his cover. Ultimately, Jakobson was able to allay Czechoslovakian fears; he eventually became a professor of Russian Philology and Old Czech Literature at Masaryk University, remaining in Czechoslovakia until the Nazi occupation in 1938.

Czechoslovakia had just emerged as a nation-state after the defeat and dismembering of the Austro-Hungarian empire in 1918. It became a multicultural, multinational hub for linguistics research, in part because the new government supported institutions and provided grants for émigrés and refugees (unlike the French and German governments, which were otherwise seen as the scholarly centres of linguistic research at the time; Toman 1995, 103). In 1926, Jakobson, alongside the Czech linguist Vilém Mathesius, the Czech literary scholar Jan Mukařovský, and the Russian émigré and Vienna-based Nikolai Trubetzkoy, founded the famous *Prague Linguistic Circle* (PLC), which drew a diverse group of German, Czech, Ukrainian, and Russian scholars who converged on Prague, seeing it as an island of freedom and democracy in Central Europe after the Russian Revolution, as the Nazi regime became more powerful in Germany (Toman 1995).

The circle was not interested only in linguistics, but also in literary theory, music, and ethnography. They published a journal called *Le mot et l'art du mot* [The Word and the Art of the Word]. For the members of this circle, a key question about language was what it is for; they were interested in how language is linked to tasks and functions (note that there is some resonance here with the Vygotskyan focus on activity theory that we reviewed in Chapter 5) (Toman 1995, 96). Language becomes, in this view, "a domain of human action rather than ... a natural object evolving independent of human will" (Toman 1995, 140). Speakers were seen as modifying their language so as to be better understood. The PLC scholars argued that functionalism and structuralism could unite synchronic and diachronic studies of language, criticizing both historical linguistics, which in their view simply focussed on how language came about, and Saussurean linguistics, which they saw as overly static.

Toman notes that the linguistic traditions critiqued were closely associated with other nations, especially Germany, against which this new nation and its scholars were defining themselves (1995, 132). The PLC also understood its approach as modern and scientific, in keeping with what building the new nation of Czechoslovakia required. The PLC's views explicitly opposed a "spiritual" approach, which saw language as an expression of nation; instead, they argued, tools of communication are materialist. The last collective statement of the PLC (1935) before the Nazi invasion argued for a "planned approach in linguistic economy," which called for linguists to be actively involved in language planning in education, journalism, and translation in order to further develop national and scientific approaches (Toman 1995, 181). At the same time, their focus on optimizing communication also led (here too!) to an interest in international auxiliary languages (Toman 1995, 140–41).

The group applied their approach to two main areas: the sound system and discourse. They argued that it was possible to break sounds into distinctive and opposing features (such as voiced vs. voiceless, nasal vs. oral); these structural features could be clustered by speakers to define phonemes, that is, to use the sound system to make meaningful contrasts. This approach helped found *phonology* as a discipline. A similar approach was applied to discourse: Jakobson's (1960) statement on this issue argues that texts were defined by their dominant communicative function, signalled by key features. Jakobson's model distinguished six universal functions: referential (focussed on context), aesthetic/poetic (focussed on the message), emotive (focussing on the sender's self-expression), conative (features of the text shaped by the receiver), phatic (confirmation that the communicative channel is working), and metalingual (checking that the code is working).

The PLC worked on universalizing, scientific approaches to language, but sought to apply them not only to the modernization of Czechoslovakia but more broadly to an understanding of the Slavic world, in particular to tracing the implications of nationalism and imperialism for eastern and central Europe (Rudy 1985). Jakobson's work elaborated on the cultural heritage of Czechoslovakia, styling it (over and against other prominent claimants) as the cradle of Slavic literary traditions, especially after ninth-century Christian missionary activities. He also studied Jewish language and culture in medieval Prague. Both strands of work (often published under pseudonyms) can be understood as a riposte to Nazi understandings of Czech and Slavic history as mongrelized by interactions with Asia and contaminated by Jews (Rudy 1985, xvi).

Another Russian member of the circle, Nikolai Trubetzkoy (1890–1938), a prince from an aristocratic family, turned his attention to the non-Slavic people of the Russian empire. He argued that Russia was not made up of semi-Asiatic barbarians, as Western reactions critical of the Bolshevik revolution often had it. He felt "those arrogant Europeans ... regard the entire non-European mankind only as [a] source of ethnographic material, as slaves, good enough only for supplying Europe with raw materials and buying European goods" (Trubetzkoy 1921, xv–xvi, cited in Toman 1995, 192). His views, not surprisingly, were popular in Asia and were rapidly translated into languages such as Japanese. He argued against a standard of value that saw Romano-Germanic civilization as the universal measure of all.

Though scarcely a supporter of the Revolution, Trubetzkoy nonetheless challenged prevailing Western European evolutionary models, including those contributing to Nazi racial ideologies. He argued that there was no single proto-Indo-European ancestor, and thus no Nordic homeland for the "original" Indo-European speakers. In contrast with the tree model of language development, Trubetzkoy built on the cases that had intrigued such linguists as Schuchardt (see Chapter 4). He elaborated the notion of *Sprachbund* to account for cases like the Balkans, arguing that geographic proximity and regular contact could allow languages to develop features in common even if they were genetically unrelated or only distantly so. For him, then, language should not be understood as being like a tree, but more like a rainbow. But what he had tried to unite, Nazi racial ideologies separated. Slavs who were seen as having "Mongoloid" racial attributes were targed as undesireable when the Germans invaded Austria (where Trubtezkoy lived and worked) and then Czechoslovakia, with the stated goal of reuniting the German nation. His death in 1938, at the age of 48, is sometimes attributed to the stress linked with being held and interrogated by the Gestapo in Vienna (Battistella 2017).

After the Nazi occupation of Czechoslovakia in 1939, Jakobson fled to Denmark and then Norway. When the Nazis invaded Norway, he fled to Sweden, and then finally to the United States in 1941; there he met many American anthropologists, including Boas and Bloomfield, and the French anthropologist Claude Lévi-Strauss. He first taught at the New School, a hub for many émigré scholars at the time, and then became the Thomas G. Masaryk Chair of Czechoslovak Studies at Columbia University in 1946. While there, he joined the large group of linguists working on international auxiliary languages in general, and Interlingua (see Chapter 5) in particular.

While in New York, Jakobson was a founding member of the Linguistic Circle of New York and of the journal *Word*, and then took a position at Harvard in the late 1940s. In 1957, he was appointed a visiting professor at MIT, and continued in this role until he retired in 1970, publishing key papers on phonological theory with his student, Morris Halle (1923–), a Latvian-born Jewish scholar who worked at MIT from 1951 until his retirement in 1996. Jakobson and Halle's approach to finding universal features governing sound dovetailed with Noam Chomsky's study of syntax to discover the universal features of human language (see more on this, below); Halle also wrote influential works on sound patterns in English with Chomsky in the 1950s and 1960s.

Fear of the Translator

Jakobson came to the attention of the FBI in 1948. As we shall see, he was suspect because of where he was born, where he lived, the languages he knew well and studied, and perhaps because of some of his earlier views, though it is not clear from the released portions of the FBI file that these were known at the time to FBI investigators. The FBI released to David Price 567 of the 618 pages in the file, and many of the pages released are heavily redacted, as the sample page at the beginning of this chapter illustrates. Most of the documents cover the period 1950–53. Price notes that FBI files are often full of mistakes and misinformation (2004, 360), since the FBI often gathered as much gossip as possible but rarely critically evaluated the information, and may even have invented some information and some informants. He notes that these files are a record of the FBI, but not a record one can trust. It is in this spirit, then, that we turn to its contents.

The file offers chilling insight into how comprehensively Jakobson and others were tracked. It includes reports on Jakobson's visit to a Slavistics Congress in Moscow in 1956; reports from calls (labelled as "pretext phone calls") to department secretaries to track Jakobson's movements; a phone log of calls made from his private home phone, with annotations about those that the FBI followed up on; and reports tracking preparations for an extended European trip to various universities in England, Scotland, Denmark, Norway, and France funded by the Rockefeller Foundation to develop European linguistics. It also includes exchanges with Immigration and Naturalization Services about how to evaluate Jakobson's application for citizenship.

There are many reports from agents' interviews with fellow scholars and colleagues from institutions around the United States on Jakobson's character and politics. Views ranged widely. Some argued Jakobson was anti-communist, while others argued that though he was anti-communist upon arrival in the U.S. he had reverted to "Russian beliefs"; some labelled him and his work as pro-communist, and yet others worried that though he was "brilliant in [the] scholastic field, [he was] politically naïve, and might possibly be influenced by enterprising individuals" (report made on May 10, 1950). One person, responding with more subtlety than the FBI could perhaps digest, noted that he was pro-Slav and pro-Russia but anti-Soviet and anti-communist.

After several years of investigation, the FBI found itself perplexed by how to sort through the various contradictory assertions by Jakobson, and Jakobson was becoming increasingly testy. He was subpoenaed to appear before the House UnAmerican Activities Committee in May 1953, though the subpoena was almost immediately revoked. The FBI decided to proceed with a lengthy interview in that month instead. We offer here a detailed account of this extended interview with Jakobson and his wife to give a sense of what such interrogations were like for many scholars.

The agent's report noted that Jakobson and his wife were "decidedly antagonistic," that Jakobson possessed an "explosive temper," and that when answering questions and allegations about his activities in Czechoslovakia and the United States he "frequently used terms such as 'swine, scoundrels and liars' in denying allegations." He is said to have "explosively ranted" and to have exclaimed that he only assented to the interviews because Harvard University authorities ordered him to do so. In an extended discussion of whether he had been instrumental in placing pro-communist or pro-Russian individuals on the faculties of U.S. colleges, he was asked if he had ever attempted to secure an appointment for Morris Swadesh. Jakobson replied that Professor (Ruth) Benedict (a student of Boas's) had solicited his thoughts on Swadesh's linguistic work, but the job (at Columbia) was in anthropology, a department with which he said he had no connection. He assessed Swadesh as a "fairly capable linguist" but that he "disliked him personally"; he said he could furnish no information on Swadesh's outside activities, had no information on his political beliefs or activities, and could not state whether Swadesh favoured principles of communism or was a Communist Party member.

During the course of the interview, Jakobson proposes a bet in which "he would pay a sum of money to any individual who could locate a single line of his writing which could be described as pro-Communist," and made available a bibliography of his works to attach to the report (unfortunately not included in the file). Jakobson himself cites articles that he published in 1922 and 1925 opposing the Soviet Union, and an article for a Catholic publishing house published in 1929 that pointed out the greatness of the Czech Catholic tradition, an implicit challenge to communism's opposition to all aspects of religion. The scholarly works that interested the FBI, *Moudrost starých Čechů* [The Wisdom of Old Czechs] (Jakobson 1943) and *Slavische Sprachfragen in der Sovjetunion* [Slavic Language Questions in the Soviet Union] (1934), are not generally those most widely cited by scholars interested in his work. The first is usually understood by scholars as a detailed defence of Czech and Slavic history, and Jewish contributions to each, against the pseudoscientific attacks promoted by Nazi collaborators (Rudy 1985), though the FBI seemed to read it as evidence of Orientalist, and thus pro-Soviet, leanings.[3] The second seems to be linked to Jakobson's earlier work on Russian dialectology. The extract below, drawn from the agent's notes in Jakobson's FBI file, gives a flavour of these exchanges:

FBI AGENT: Your book "Wisdom of the Old Czechs" has been criticized because it overemphasizes the influence of the East, and the criticism I read stated that the West had a predominating influence.

JAKOBSON: I discussed the Byzantine influence on the Czech culture of the early Middle Ages and I said that this influence is an important supplement to the influence of Rome. This point of view is

---

3 This analysis comes from the Scope and Contents of Collection overview, at the MIT archive (boxes 9 & 10) in the Jakobson papers (https://libraries.mit.edu/archives/research/collections/collections-mc/mc72.html#ref3).

> shared by all the leading Catholic historic students and an
> abstract of my book was published in the "Review of Politics"
> published by the University of Notre Dame. I should like to
> submit this "Review" (Exhibit "B"). All the scholarly reviews of
> my book were most favorable and only the Leftists attacked it.
> (p. 13 of interview)

Five pages of the interview are devoted to summarizing a memorandum that Jakobson gave to the agent, describing criticism of him in print in publications from Russia, satellite nations, and China (the dates in this paragraph refer to those used in the FBI report on the interview; we have not been able to track down all of these references in original sources). A 1923 review in *Pravda*, then the official newspaper of the Communist Party of the Soviet Union, describes Jakobson as a leading representative of formalism, and thus as a bourgeois adversary of Marxist ideology. A 1949 review in another communist publication argued that "[s]tructuralism is one of the most reactionary trends in contemporary bourgeois linguistics.... The theoretical and organizational formulation of structuralism in linguistics is inseparably bound up with the names of men who renounced their fatherland, the typical bourgeois-scholar *cosmoploitans* [sic] Roman Jakobson and Prince Trubetskoy." A 1951 review in yet another Soviet-sphere publication argued that

> [t]he role of Jakobson as the chief pillar of structuralism eloquently
> shows that in its essence linguistic structuralism was one of those trends
> which under cover of progressive phraseology worked as a refined
> ideological weapon to desorientate [sic] the outstanding adherents of
> the Left Intellegenetsia [sic] and to fight against the world views of the
> workers' class, i.e. against dialectical materialism.... Roman Jakobson
> impelled the structuralists to inundate our language with masses of
> superfluous foreign words. He propagated disrespect to the language
> of our classes and to our folk speech.... Jakobson denounced Marxism
> because, according to him, Marxism "doesn't solve the present stage in
> the development of science" ... he has found a last asylum for himself
> and his 'purely scientific' theories in the service of American imperialists.

Though not included in the released portions of this file, similar critiques came from the former members of the Prague Linguistic Circle who had not fled or been executed after the Soviet occupation. Scholars (including Jakobson's son-in-law) who wanted to retain their positions or their lives felt compelled to demonstrate allegiance to and elaborate Soviet linguistic approaches. To protect themselves, some of these scholars argued that the Circle had had a healthy core, but had been penetrated by foreign elements ("the anti-Soviet émigré, cosmopolite and hidden Trotskyite, a veritable monster of our linguistics, Roman Jakobson, who was deceiving a number of our excellent linguists and leading them astray" [Petr Sgall 1951, cited in Toman 1995, 258]). These foreign elements were said to be responsible for the most problematic (because seen as idealistic) advances, like structural phonology. Other scholars argued that the Circle had never been unified, but had been split by class differences. Yet other scholars emphasized that the idea of linguistic convergence was common in both PLC and Soviet Marrist accounts, and so could not be attributed to anti-communist leanings.

In the critiques that Jakobson himself reported, and in those identified by Toman (1995), we can see how the elaboration of Jakobson's kind of structural linguistics came to be seen as opposed to Soviet-style approaches. Jakobson, for his part, argued for a focus on scientific, and thus putatively impartial, approaches. We will see that this focus on putative objectivity is a hallmark of Western approaches during the Cold War, in careful contradistinction to what are seen as the political, and positioned, views of Marxist scientists.

The specific case of Jakobson had fallout far beyond his own life and career. Dell Hymes, often described as one of the founding figures in American linguistic anthropology (see Chapter 7), has noted that in the 1950s it was risky to discuss Marxist thought with people you did not trust, and that as a graduate student he kept Marxist books off his shelves and out of sight (Hymes 1999, vi). Hymes speculates that Cold War politics could have played a role in Harvard's rejection of his own tenure file, given an invitation he arranged for Swadesh to give a talk, as well as subscriptions he had to left-wing journals and his public attendance at meetings on how to revive the left (Price 2004, 343–44). Price notes that concerns and speculations like those of Hymes were widespread, such that "gossip about such decisions spread messages of fear that contributed to an environment that encouraged and even rewarded self-censorship" (344).

The targeting of these individuals shows how particular strands of linguistic scholarship were marginalized, interrupted, and contained. These included Boasian thought, which was linked with anti-racist thought and the description of Indigenous languages (perhaps itself suspect, as an affiliation with groups sometimes described as primitive communists), as well as linguistic scholarship explicitly shaped by Marxist and feminist thought. However, the Boasian focus on cultural variation and plasticity was also criticized by other scholars who were concerned that a focus on human plasticity, especially as evident in certain behaviourist writings, could be used to quell human dissent and creativity.

The new focus was on universalist models of human communication as either structuralist thought or generative linguistics. Such theories found ready sources of funding from the government, including the military, in part because they helped to support projects of machine translation that allowed the automatic and mass translation of texts, especially German and Russian ones, deemed critical to World War II and Cold War security. As linguistic departments mushroomed around the United States, generativist linguistics quickly established itself as the dominant stream. We turn now to the question of why language-related disciplines expanded so markedly in the United States after World War II, and then to a more detailed investigation of such universalist models.

Infrastructure and Institutionalization: Communication Studies, Area Studies, Linguistics, Applied Linguistics

During and after World War II, language expertise came to be seen as strategic for a variety of military, political, and economic ends. In 1941, a partnership between the Linguistic Society of America and the American Council of Learned Societies led to the creation of the Intensive Language Program, which aimed to expand the expertise of American linguists from Amerindian languages to the potentially strategic languages of the world (Martin-Nielsen 2010b, 138). Initially funded by the Rockefeller Foundation, the ILP was expanded by the American military to develop language-learning materials, dictionaries, and phrasebooks for languages seen as crucial for Allied security and intelligence.

After the war, four language-related fields emerged as relevant to Cold War concerns, receiving government support and becoming institutionalized in a variety of sites of research and training, notably as university departments: *Communication Studies, Area Studies, Linguistics,* and *Applied Linguistics.* The first two deployed language in interdisciplinary efforts to achieve Cold War aims, while the last two were more centrally oriented to language. They helped provide the government with content knowledge about people in the United States and around the world, as well as with the tools necessary to ensure the spread of capitalism and liberal democracy, through propaganda and the spread of English.

The new field of *communication studies*, now a key arena for training journalists, public relations personnel, and advertising personnel, arose as a discipline for measuring, and engendering, mass audiences for consumption. Its central question became how to disseminate ideas in ways that influenced people; C. Simpson (1995) calls this the *science of coercion.*

During World War II, Nazi intellectuals such as Josef Goebbels pioneered many modern techniques in communication analysis and social manipulation that were carefully studied by the Allied powers (see also Chapter 5); while some Nazis were hanged for their role in mass genocide, others survived and became key European communication experts after the war. A number of former Nazis were hired by the United States as counterintelligence experts during the Cold War (C. Simpson 1988). The phrase *psychological warfare* first appeared in English in 1941, as a translation of a related Nazi concept, *Weltanschauungskreig* [worldview warfare] (C. Simpson 1993, 319).

After World War II, the field of communications was consolidated; it gained the authority to grant doctorates between 1950 and 1955 (C. Simpson 1993, 315). U.S. military, propaganda, and intelligence agencies provided the bulk of funding for the field. Sociologists who participated in this work during U.S. wartime efforts were, as in linguistics, some of the most respected scholars in the field—people who wrote the textbooks, had the large government grants, edited journals, and had positions at prominent schools where they trained graduate students. Six key centres for the study of communication (including Columbia, Princeton, and MIT) received 75 per cent of their budget from government money that was earmarked for psychological warfare (C. Simpson 1993, 316).

Scholars of communication studied how people could be persuaded to certain beliefs, including and especially American ones, in Cold War pursuits. Communication specialists studied such topics as the impact of Voice of America broadcasts in Iran, Turkey, and Egypt, including during the periods when the CIA supported overthrows of governments in Iran and Egypt; how to engineer public opinion in the Philippines against a communist peasant guerilla uprising; and how to orchestrate communications in counterinsurgency alongside economic development, arms transfers, and police/military training (C. Simpson 1995). Later, the CIA was interested in how to encourage the cooperation of the Vietnamese population in the war between North Vietnam (sponsored by the U.S.S.R., China, and other communist allies) and South Vietnam (supported by the U.S., the Philippines, and other anti-communist allies). It drew on sociological methods and theories of communication popularized at the MIT Center for International Studies (CENIS), one of the most important communication studies research centres in the United States in the 1950s and 1960s (C. Simpson 1995, 84).

In an experiment that was also propaganda in its own right, the U.S. Army dropped millions of leaflets in small towns in Washington, Alabama, and the U.S. far west with the message "Communist bombers might attack your neighborhood," and studied the dispersion of the message. The field became attuned to the politics of its self-presentation, and experimented with different ways of framing its goals so as to make them acceptable. For instance, an extensive annotated bibliography called *International Propaganda and Psychological Warfare*, published in 1952, became *International Communication and Political Opinion* in 1956 (C. Simpson 1995).

These initiatives were thus tied to state interest in areas where communism was perceived to be strongest or to have a strong interest. This concern led to collaborations between universities, foundations—especially the Rockefeller, Ford, and Carnegie Foundations—and the intelligence arm of the state to form *areas studies* programs, which brought social scientific perspectives to bear on various parts of the world. This was a marked departure from before World War II. Up until 1940, the United States had no more than 60 people with PhDs on the non-Western world over all disciplines, many of which were focussed on antiquity (Szanton 2004, 6). During the war, specialists on some regions became intelligence officers and helped train others. After the war, William Donovan, the founder of the CIA, unfolded a plan for the development of area studies, focussing first on an Institute of Slavic Studies and later on other areas where communists were perceived to be threatening the Third World. The key areas were understood to be Africa, China, Japan, Latin America, Middle East, the Soviet Union and Eastern Europe, South Asia, and Southeast Asia.

However, Donovan did not want direct CIA involvement for fear that it would look like intelligence agencies were driving academic research. The CIA therefore coordinated this work with and through foundations established with funding from key American industrialists. The Ford Foundation gave $270 million to 34 universities for FLAS (Foreign Language and Area Studies) from 1953 to 1966 (Cumings 2002, 281) in order to encourage students to engage in intensive language study and to undertake fieldwork studies. Two of the universities Jakobson was connected to (Harvard and Columbia) had area studies programs on Russia and Eastern Europe that were particularly well-funded by foundations (Cumings 2002, 281).

Critiques of these centres have argued that they were closely aligned with, and in regular conversation with, the CIA and FBI, and that the Rockefeller, Carnegie, and Ford Foundations all worked with the state and "laundered" CIA money (Cumings 2002; Diamond 1992). Foreign-born scholars and communist émigrés were often asked to work for the CIA; those who refused were also often investigated, and asked to denounce suspicious others to the FBI. Certain leaders of area studies centres had CIA ties and testified in the McCarthy era. Some scholars were fired if seen as uncooperative or overly radical (for instance, three tenured professors in Korean studies at the University of Washington; Cumings 2002).

The definition of appropriate sites for the centres as major research universities had implications for who did the work. Though historically black colleges in the United States had introduced African studies in the early twentieth century, had developed rich curricula on Africa throughout history—including the slave trade, the Civil War and Reconstruction, the partitioning of

Africa, and transatlantic relationships—and had educated influential African students, they were passed over for large grants for the establishment of area studies in favour of the institutions that were understood as major research institutions; this meant, too, that expertise on Africa was seen as lying less with African American than White scholars (Robinson 2004). Such decisions were often framed in terms of scientific impartiality; there were concerns that African American institutions and scholars would not be sufficiently "objective" (Robinson 2004). This continues to have ramifications for the ways the field has developed, with Black scholars often focussed more on African American and African diaspora issues, while Africanists tend to be White scholars.

Certain disciplines were given more emphasis in ways that also shaped how language study proceeded. Anthropology (which emphasized linguistic analysis more, as part of the four-field model described in Chapter 3) played a large role in South and Southeast Asian Studies, sites where fieldwork was possible; political science (which emphasized linguistic analysis less) was more central to Russian and Eastern European and China studies, areas closed to fieldwork. Anthropologists received more funding in the early days of African studies, but political scientists predominated in later years.

Language was not centred in the same way in all area studies programs. Local philological traditions, as well as the ways that languages had been studied by missionaries and colonial authorities, shaped where and how languages were seen as central. Scholars of South Asia and Japan were often the children of missionaries who had lived and worked in those areas; their rigorous linguistic training led to extensions of the detailed textual studies and certain kinds of ethnography their parents had engaged in or learned from; however, they paid less attention to contemporary developments and societal diversity (Tansman 2004). In South Asian studies this led to the centring of discussions of religion, philosophy, and Hindu practice in ways that perpetuated Oriental stereotypes and made new ones—for instance, casting Muslims as national outsiders in India (Dirks 2004). Language was less central, however, to studies of Southeast Asia (Bowen 2004). In some cases, those who claimed regional expertise had markedly less linguistic expertise than one might expect; Walder (2004) is frank about the low level of literacy in Chinese that many China experts had at the time.

By the early twentieth century, language instruction for Americans, and throughout the American empire, already focussed on English in the context of significant migration and interwar Americanization movements that sought to quickly assimilate new arrivals and colonial subjects. Languages other than English were seen as un-American, unpatriotic, and unsuitable for classroom use; English was seen as carrying ideas of capitalism and democracy to subjects of American colonies and to working-class immigrants, immigrants who were often seen at the time as not quite white, especially if they were from southern Europe or were Jewish, and who were deemed prone to embracing radicalism and Bolshevist thought (Herman 1998, cited in Martin-Nielsen 2010b, 134).

However, there were few resources to meet this challenge. While linguistics was studied in anthropology (in the Boasian and Sapirian tradition of descriptive linguistics for documenting Native North American languages), literature, philosophy, and classics in the early twentieth century, there were no linguistics departments or degrees and few linguistics meetings. The Linguistics Society of America was founded only in 1924. For most of the first years of its existence its leading journal largely published articles on historical analyses of Indo-European languages, Latin and ancient Greek, and Indigenous languages (Martin-Nielsen 2010b, 136). American linguistics, also inspired by Saussure and developed by such scholars as Leonard Bloomfield (1887–1949), increasingly came to focus on structural linguistics in the late 1920s through the early 1950s, though American and Prague School structuralism proceded along different, if often intertwining and mutually inspiring, paths. American structural linguistics was shaped by approaches to linguistic analysis used by missionaries, but also by the need for practical techniques for use in language teaching, whether for immigrants or, sometimes, the army (Velleman 2008). This was also a time when American linguists sought a distinctively American approach, partly to fend off competition for jobs, and likely also as a result of anti-Semitism (see Hall 1969, cited in Hymes and Fought 1981, 15). The structuralist work of Leonard Bloomfield was embraced as such a beacon.

Most linguists worked for the war effort. Eighty of the 96 participants in the Linguistic Society of America's annual meeting were actively engaged in crucial work for the military, and paid through the ILP or U.S. government in 1944 (Martin-Nielsen 2010b, 139). This work included key American scholars in the field at the time or afterwards: Bernard Bloch (1907–65), Mary Haas (1910–96), Einar Haugen (1906–94), Charles Hockett (1916–2000), Robert Hall (1911–97), Morris Swadesh (1909–67), and Leonard Bloomfield (1887–1949).

After the war, linguistics was supported by the army, the navy, the air force, the National Institutes of Health, and private organizations such as the Social Science Research Council of the Rockefeller Foundation. Linguistics was one of the first nontraditional sciences to receive support from the National Science Foundation in the early 1950s. The ILP was taken over by the Department of State, which set up language-training facilities at its new Foreign Service Institute. Here, other illustrious linguists (such as George Trager and Charles Ferguson, whom we will meet in Chapter 7) worked on language teaching materials while also being encouraged to do basic research. Language was seen as critical for diplomatic communications and military intelligence, but also for corporate communications and academic exchange.

Linguistic departments were founded throughout the late 1940s, 1950s, and 1960s, first at the University of Pennsylvania in 1947, then at Berkeley, MIT, Indiana, Illinois, University of Texas at Austin, UCLA, and Ohio State. By 1965 there were close to 30 linguistic departments; by 1970 there were 135. Government funding played a key role in this tremendous growth. Professional societies grew astronomically (the Linguistic Society of America went from just over 800 members to 4,300 between 1950 and 1970; Martin-Nielsen 2010b, 143). Language teaching also was funded after the passage of the National Defence Education Act, designed to remedy the skills of American students in three strategic areas: mathematics, science, and foreign languages. The number of languages taught in high schools and universities jumped markedly.

Thus communication studies, area studies, and foreign or second language learning were fields that developed hand-in-hand, strongly shaped by wartime funding and Cold War intelligence and security concerns. In the next section, we turn to the second thread of Cold War interest in language: the concern for machine translation and how this was linked to the preference for examinations of syntax as central to the analysis of language and humanity.

Machine Translation and the Rise of Syntax

In security and intelligence activities, linguistics research was key to projects ranging from code-breaking to information retrieval, but what Martin-Nielsen calls the defining project of linguistics in the postwar period was *machine translation*, which was meant to enable more rapid access to information written in "the languages of the scientifically creative cultures," as one researcher put it (cited in Martin-Nielsen 2010b, 142). In particular, Western countries wanted access to the scientific and technical knowledge being published in German and Russian. By 1956, the Soviet Union was purported to be markedly ahead in machine translation, and it launched the first space satellite, Sputnik, a year later. The science Cold War was on. Laboratories to study machine translation were established across the United States, at universities such as MIT, Berkeley, and Georgetown, all of which remain key centers for linguistic study, and in nonprofit think tanks.

As Martin-Nielsen writes, "[t]he premise of postwar machine translation was to equip a computer with a set of formal rules which, when applied to an input text in one language (usually Russian or German), would produce an output translation in another language, usually English. These rules worked not by deciphering the meaning of the input text, but by using knowledge of syntactic structure to build an output translation. Here, an understanding of syntax was critical for recognizing the various components of sentences"

(2010b, 142). Many linguists thus turned to the development of formal rule-based syntactic theories and computational applications of these.

Two scholars notable in this regard were Zellig Harris (1909–92) and his star student, Noam Chomsky (1928–). Both were immersed in, and significantly influenced by, socialist forms of Zionism, and were thus thinking through the continuing implications of fascism, communism, and toxic forms of nationalism in Europe as they elaborated their formalist and universalist theories in the scientific, objective languages influenced by mathematics and logic. We will examine the rise of structuralist, formalist linguistics through these two figures.

Not only did they play key roles, they also represent some of the key contradictions entailed by their own attempts to radically separate the study of language from the study of society. While their work in linguistics was facilitated by Cold War interests, both scholars were committed to anti-fascist and anti-capitalist political positions. They sought to tie their work to liberatory positions focussing on human universals, just as that work removed any ability to focus on the concrete dimensions of what emancipation might look like on the terrain of language. While dismissing any attention to actual linguistic practices as falling outside the realm of linguistics and, in Chomsky's case, ensuring that alternative views on linguistics would be silenced (Pavlenko, forthcoming), they also sought to harness the tools of universal grammar to unmasking the effects of state and corporate propaganda.

Rational and Universal Principles for Linguistic Analysis: Late Structuralist Linguistics

Zellig Harris, the founder of the first department of linguistics in the United States at the University of Pennsylvania, was the son of parents who fled Eastern European pogroms for refuge in the United States. The Harris household was culturally Jewish but secular, identifying as left-wing Zionist; they spoke Hebrew at home as part of the effort to revive it as the universal language of Jews and of an eventual homeland.[4] As an undergraduate at the University of Pennsylvania, Harris studied Semitic languages. In 1951, he published *Methods in Structural Linguistics*, a book often taken as the apotheosis of structuralist linguistics, finding markedly economical ways of stating relationships in language, and offering more sophisticated mathematical models than those that had existed earlier (Barsky 2011, 121).

---

4 Zellig and his brother Tzvi became faculty at the University of Pennsylvania. The gendered division of labour between theorizing about language and language instruction is evident in their family. Their sister Enya and Tzvi's wife Shoshana were elementary school teachers who wrote ESL textbooks (with Enya also later getting a PhD in linguistics and teaching English as a Second Language at the University of Pennsylvania).

Harris's commitment to science meant that he thought rational inquiry was the best way to get people to understand the merits of one position over another (Barsky 2011, 58); he was wary of direct action and activism. Barsky notes that "[o]ne way to avoid ... ideological conflict implicit in the study of language and its relationship to race or class or intelligence, as the formalists learned in Russia after the Revolution in 1917, was to work from an objective paradigm such as the physical or natural sciences" (2011, 92). This led Harris to support logical theories of language and information, including structural linguistics and machine translation. His work was funded by the National Science Foundation, the Air Force Psychological Research Division, IBM, and Bell Laboratories, the last of which thought his work could support a communications revolution. Harris's work, in books ranging from *Mathematical Structures of Language* (1968) to *Language and Information* (1988), was seen as providing the key tools for machine translation, decoding, and content analysis.

Like Bloomfield, Harris was interested in developing a science of language, focussed on the relative position of segments of speech utterances. He aimed to reduce discourse to a logical form (Barsky 2011, 41). This had implications for machine translation, and also for politics. One of his students noted that Harris felt that "[i]f you could take some piece of text or discourse which is intended to direct your thoughts in one way or another, then one should be able to be put into a logical form, and demonstrate connections or contradictions that are not obvious" (Barsky 2011, 41). Student work done under Harris's supervision included a master's thesis that used linguistic techniques to consider how influential U.S. magazines slanted discussions of the new Labour government in Great Britain, attempts to rewrite newspaper articles in English into a standard form consistent with formal logic, and translations of chemistry papers into logic-governed statements. Noam Chomsky (also the son of parents who fled the pogroms of Eastern Europe) was assigned the project of doing a linguistic analysis of Jewish American philosopher Sidney Hook's writings from the time when he was a communist to when he became an anti-communist (Barsky 2011, 311).

These studies grew out of work Harris had done with Avukah, a student socialist Zionist group that was active in the 1920s and early 1930s. As part of their quest for a good society, Avukah was interested in how to modify attitudes. Ideology was seen as an attempt to confuse or deceive; hence the goal of literate, educated, articulate radicals was to de-fool themselves, and then help de-fool others (Barsky 2011, 44). This notion became central to both Harris's work in discourse analysis and Chomsky's. It has its Cold War counterpart in attempts to develop scientific approaches to communication and propaganda, as we saw above.

Avukah linked its work to a variety of other liberation struggles, seeing Black struggles against Jim Crow and Jewish struggles against anti-Semitism as analogous, and noting what could be learned from critiques of British colonialism in India for thinking about British colonialism in Palestine (Barsky 2011, 247–48). It fractured over whether its focus should be on support for American involvement in World War II, linked in the mind of many to saving Jews, or a more pacifist, socialist approach that saw the war as a capitalist one, and that wanted to focus on Jewish-Arab workers' cooperation in building a binational, socialist future. Harris belonged to the latter group, and came to spend half of each year on a labour Zionist kibbutz, doing carpentry and other community tasks in an effort to contribute to a new utopian order (Barsky 2011, 55).

Harris also participated in a long-term, wide-ranging, rather nebulous project called the Frame of Reference Project. It was organized like a secret cell; there were many participants, each charged with various pieces of the project, none of whom knew the whole of the project or all of the participants. It ultimately resulted in a book, *The Transformation of Capitalist Society* (1997), published a year after Harris's death, examining the contradictions and cracks in capitalism where the seeds of a postcapitalist society were already evident, and alternatives to capitalism, all of which focussed centrally on reorganizing work, including socialist kibbutzim, workers' councils, producer cooperatives, anarchist collectives, workers' movements, and ESOPs (Employee Share Ownership Plans). It argued that society could move out of capitalism not only by having more equal allocations of resources and more efficient production, but also by eliminating the controlling and controlled behaviour imposed on people by church, family, and education (Barsky 2011, 269). Science and more reliable and rational linguistic communication were seen as keys to achieving this goal.

The book articulates a theory of human nature that suggests it is not fixed, but determined by conditions. It is on this point that Harris and Chomsky most disagreed. Chomsky most famously articulated his critique in a 1959 attack on the work of the behaviourist psychologist B.F. Skinner. Skinner argued that human behaviour could be explained and controlled by the same processes as those used to control animals, such as reinforcing desired behaviours by rewarding them or extinguishing them by ignoring or punishing them. From Chomsky's point of view, it was theories like Skinner's that were being used to control the masses, not point the way to their liberation (Barsky 1997, 99). While he would see a focus on language as central to human liberation, the focus would not be on rational unpacking, but on creative liberation.

Freedom, Creativity, and Human Nature: The Rise of Generative Linguistics

Scholars who are interested in sociolinguistic approaches are often puzzled by what they see as the paradox of Chomsky: a scholar who has generated searing and influential leftist analyses of media and political discourse in books such as *Manufacturing Consent* (Herman and Chomsky 1988) and many later works, while regularly abjuring any social/interactional influence on language form. However, it is possible to see how these are united in the way Chomsky understands human nature, language, and freedom. In the aftermath of the extreme culturally relativist and genocidal policies associated with European fascism in the mid-twentieth century, new versions of linguistic thought emerged that downplayed difference. Such ideas were also articulated within the context of decolonization, critiques of capitalism, and Cold War politics.

The theory of human nature underlying Chomsky-influenced grammatical theory, often called *generative* or *universal grammar*, has strong liberal underpinnings in its assumption that all adult human beings are rational agents; generative grammar rests on the assumption that a key feature of their rational humanity is their capacity for language. The questions for linguistics, then, are what that language capacity looks like and how it works. Chomsky suggested that to answer those questions, it would be necessary to work backward from all the sentences that are grammatical in human languages (and only those sentences) to uncover how the superficial surface differences in human languages (*surface structure*) were linked to a set of transformations of sentences based on *deep structures* that were common to all humans (Chomsky 1957, 1965).

Trees (trees again!) were used to model relationships between surface and deep structures to try to show that sentences were not just strings of words with a flat structure.

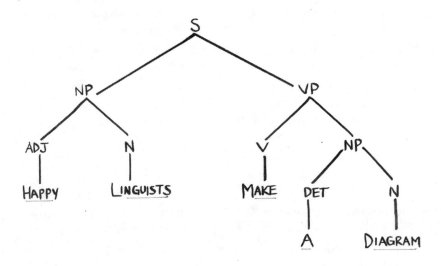

FIGURE 6.2: "Happy linguists make a diagram": Example of a syntactic tree (Illustration: Andrea Derbecker)

The tree in Figure 6.2 shows that *happy* and *linguists* are linked in the structure as constituents of a noun phrase, which is distinctive from the three constituents of the verb phrase. Generative grammar, like liberal theory, suggests that variations among humans are minor and fairly shallow when compared with the overwhelming similarities that unite humans as a species (Otero 1988, 154).

Chomsky has been asked to explain how, if human behaviour and language are heavily guided by universal principles, they differ so much around the world. He explains that these differences are more superficial than deep-seated:

> I think that as human beings we quite naturally take for granted what is similar among human beings and then pay attention to what differentiates us.... But if we could extract ourselves from our point of view and sort of look down at human life the way a biologist looks at other organisms, I think we could see it a different way. Imagine an extrahuman observer looking at us. Such an extrahuman observer would be struck precisely by the uniformity of human languages. (Otero 1988, 402-3)

Chomsky further adduces as evidence the idea that there are many aspects of the linguistic competence of adult speakers that could not have been learned on the basis of the linguistic data available to children during the period of language acquisition. In addition, he argues that language acquisition is remarkably fast, devoid of the sorts of errors we would prima facie expect, and comes in characteristic stages whose order and duration seem independent of environmental factors (Szabó 2004). The linguist thus focusses on grammatical *competence*, but not the kinds of variation one finds in linguistic *performance* (a distinction akin to that between *langue* and *parole* elaborated by Saussure; see Chapter 4). Linguistic competence is a mental construct, a *Universal Grammar* (UG) that is a super-recipe for concocting language-specific grammars. Linguistic theory, for Chomsky, has two goals: (1) to characterize the grammars (and hence the mental states) attained by native speakers, and (2) to explain how grammatical competence is attained (Hornstein 1998).

Chomsky ties this endeavour to showing how the capacity for language shows the existence of the human mind, a basis not simply for rationality alone, but for the human yearning for freedom. Investigations of language are, then, central to investigations of human nature because "[l]anguage ... provides the basic criterion for determining that another organism is a being with a human mind and the human capacity for free thought and self-expression, and with the essential human need for freedom from the external constraints of repressive authority" (Peck 1987, 145). Though Chomsky believes the link between generative linguistics and politics is tenuous, in the sense that it is less scientific fact than moral hope, he argues that political ideas and ideas about ideal social life are always anchored in some idea of human nature. For him, human nature is defined by the capacity and need for creative self-expression and for freedom in control of one's life, with creative use of language as central to free thought, and this suggests the need to find a form of social life that permits the free and full development of each individual's potential, whatever that might be (Otero 1988, 144).

Chomsky's focus on freedom arose in the context of a sprawling activist family influenced by Left Zionist writings (Barsky 1997, 12). Chomsky faced anti-Semitism as a child, particularly from the Irish and German communities living in Philadelphia (Barsky 1997, 15). He became fascinated by the anarcho-syndicalist communes that had been set up during the Spanish Civil War as examples of a working libertarian society (Barsky 1997, 26). He continues to reference the workers' movements in Barcelona as examples of how resistance can spontaneously arise and as examples of what kinds of good society he thinks are possible (Barsky 1997, 17).

With this political and linguistic background in place, Chomsky enrolled in 1945 at the University of Pennsylvania where he soon met Zellig Harris (Barsky 1997). Chomsky was hired as a faculty member at MIT in 1955, and he has been teaching there ever since. When he first arrived he was assigned to a machine translation project conducted at the MIT Research Laboratory of Electronics, which was subsidized by the U.S. military (Barsky 1997, 86), though he did not work on the project itself but on other questions. Nonetheless, in *Aspects of the Theory of Syntax* (Chomsky 1965) he acknowledges that funding was provided by the Joint Services Electronics Programs (U.S. Army, Navy, and Air Force), the Electronics Systems Division of the U.S. Air Force, the National Science Foundation, the National Institutes of Health, and NASA (Barsky 1997, 87).

He has said that because he has been a beneficiary of such funds, he has a particular obligation to interrogate military aims. As linguists became increasingly aware of the impact of disparities in funding, and as some became increasingly uncomfortable with military patronage and its impacts on American domestic and foreign policy, these frustrations were played out in discussions of linguistic data, in debates Randy Harris has called *The Linguistics Wars* (1993). Many critics of Chomsky's linguistics program argued that heavy military investment at MIT gave Chomsky and his colleagues an unfair intellectual advantage in disseminating their ideas (Martin-Nielsen 2010b, 149); Pavlenko (forthcoming) argues that they also used precisely the propaganda techniques they critiqued, such as circulation of draft papers among a select group before subjecting the work to peer review.

Both Harris and Chomsky are, then, emblematic Cold War figures struggling to find ways to critique capitalism while embedded in it and reproducing some of its techniques. We have been tracking the changing understandings of language in the social sciences, but there are other sites where analyses of language were influential in shaping Cold War views. We close with a consideration of another (more obviously) emblematic Cold War figure, the British author George Orwell (1903–50).

Nineteen Eighty-Four as a Weapon of the Cold War

Orwell's life and his iconic anti-totalitarian novels *Animal Farm* (first published in 1945), and *Nineteen Eighty-Four* (published in 1949), show how strong a role language was thought to play in the struggle for freedom, and how the social actors of the time relied on it to help them navigate the contradictions and complexities of the Cold War, with each side claiming to champion freedom and social justice while seeking to control both. These famous novels on the changing dynamics of language and states are bleak books. Orwell was writing, one scholar has noted, at a nadir of hope, at the height of Stalinist excesses and Western reactions, a moment at which "the intellectual stood appalled before the seduction of his own more generous impulses" (Thompson 1974, 86). He was also dying of tuberculosis, succumbing in 1950 at age 46.

In *Nineteen Eighty-Four*, the main character, Winston Smith, is having lunch with Syme, a philologist working on the Newspeak dictionary. They are drinking an oily-tasting gin while spooning up a stew that contains cubes of spongy pinkish meat-like stuff. Someone behind them is speaking in a gabble that sounds like a duck. Winston is asking Syme how the dictionary is coming along. "I'm on the adjectives," says Syme. "It's fascinating."

Syme goes on to describe his work of cutting the language down to the bone, destroying hundreds of words: "After all, what justification is there for a word which is simply the opposite of some other word? A word contains its opposite in itself. Take 'good' for instance. If you have a word like 'good' what need is there for 'bad'?" Winston seems only mildly enthusiastic to Syme, who sadly tells him, "You haven't a real appreciation of Newspeak, Winston.... In your heart, you'd prefer to stick to Oldspeak, with all its vagueness and its useless shades of meaning. You don't grasp the beauty of the destruction of words. Don't you see that the whole aim of Newspeak is to narrow the range of thought? In the end, we shall make thoughtcrime literally impossible, because there will be no words in which to express it.... The Revolution will be complete when the language is perfect" (Orwell [1949] 1986, 53–55).

"Unquestionably Syme will be vaporized," Winston thinks sadly. He venerated Big Brother, but "zeal was not enough. Orthodoxy was unconsciousness" ([1949] 1986, 58). And soon Syme disappears. Winston famously goes on to try to buck the totalitarian regime that constantly monitors everyone's actions, words, and thoughts by having an illicit love affair; he is caught, and tries to hold on to his humanity and his love throughout numerous forms of torture, but finally forswears both when faced with the possibility of having his face strapped into a cage with hungry rats. Rats eat the eyes first, he is told.

The appendix to *Nineteen Eighty-Four* describes "The Principles of Newspeak," a language devised by Ingsoc (English Socialists) to make any critiques of the regime impossible (its resemblance to the strategies Klemperer described in Nazi Germany, though that account would be published later, is startling).[5] The designers of Newspeak intended to diminish the range of thought, not extend it. To do so, some keywords are destroyed (for instance *honour, justice, internationalism, democracy, science*). All such concepts are covered by the vague umbrella word *crimethink*. Ultimately, the goal was *duckspeak*, like that heard by Winston in the lunchroom, so that humans could make articulate speech issue from the larynx without any involvement of the higher brain centres, a portrayal that also rather denigrates ducks.

Orwell regularly argued that speaking with hackneyed phrases made one less like a human and more like a robot or machine. In his essays "Why I Write" ([1946] 1984) and "Politics and the English Language" (1946), Orwell advocated for eliminating murky and stale language as "a necessary first step toward political regeneration" because he believes political speech is often a defence of the indefensible: "Things like the continuance of British rule in India, the Russian purges and deportations, the dropping of the atom bombs on Japan, can indeed be defended, but only by arguments which are too brutal for most people to face, and which do not square with the professed aims of the political parties" (1946, 247).

Ironically, *Nineteen Eighty-Four* became an ideological superweapon of the kind that Orwell deplored (Deutscher 1974, 119). Bonnie remembers reading *Animal Farm*, as many American children did, in junior high school in Western Pennsylvania in the 1970s; the fable about the Soviet Union was explicitly contrasted with the freedom of the West. It was used to reinforce, rather than question, the idea that the United States was all that was good, free, and democratic.

Orwell's critique is enabled by his position as a peripheral and perhaps marginalized member of an elite; he knew privilege well, but did not gain all of its benefits and could see its costs. Orwell's great-great-great-grandfather

---

5 The novelist and fellow speculative fiction writer Margaret Atwood writes that she finds the appendix the most hopeful part of the book (2011, 145–46). It is written in Oldspeak, in the past tense, and thus suggests the regime has fallen and that Orwell may believe more in the resilience of the human spirit than some have thought.

made a fortune in the slave trade and Jamaican sugar plantations (Lucas 2003, 13), though by Orwell's day his family were marginal members in an elite ruling class. His father was an officer in the Opium Office, an office that regulated the production and sale of opium, and was stationed in India; his mother's family were French merchants in Burma.

Orwell had first-hand experience with all of the major totalitarian institutions of the twentieth century. He was educated in the environment that most boys of his class were subjected to, the English public school, which he later described as being locked in a hostile world where rules were impossible to keep and in which one felt a guilt-stricken loyalty to a tyrant (Lucas 2003, 31). His first job was as a colonial police officer tasked with gathering military intelligence in Burma in the 1920s. In his novel *Burmese Days* (Orwell 1934), he explores the guilt, loneliness, and loss of identity of a colonial officer who can neither escape nor accept the social system in which he finds himself (Eagleton 1974); in "Shooting an Elephant," his experience in Burma is the basis for an exposé of the evil of imperialism (Orwell 1950).

When Orwell dropped out of this job, to the despair of his family, he bummed around England and France, living with and writing about people who were working-class and poor (Eagleton 1974, 28; Trilling 1974, 70). He became a socialist, and took up arms in the Spanish Civil War with communists and anarchists against fascism. His book on this experience inspired Chomsky with its picture of anarchic resistance, though Orwell also documented the way media spin hid how the communists ultimately betrayed the anarchists. His life thus engaged with each of the key social movements we have tracked thus far in this book—imperialism, socialism, fascism, communism. His aunt was even married to an Esperantist!

Orwell continues to attract sustained attention perhaps because he speaks to some of the dilemmas and contradictions of the twentieth century as they crystallized in the Cold War. A member of the elite, he is sympathetic to the subaltern but not always clearly convinced by their capacity for social action. He is fearful of betrayal—though by whom is not always clear; by himself, or perhaps by language. Arendt ([1951] 1968) notes that when totalitarian states are successful, they create a sense of terror and a sense of isolation and loneliness, such that people cannot trust each other or perhaps even themselves (477). Organized loneliness, which she sees as characterizing the twentieth century more than any other period, is dangerous because "it threatens to ravage the world as we know it—a world which everywhere seems to have come to an end—before a new beginning rising from this end has had time to assert itself" (478). Orwell, it seems, was a very lonely man.

After years of commitment to socialism, in the last month of Orwell's life he passed the names of 36 people whom he saw as too close to the Soviet

Union or communism to British intelligence for investigation (Lucas 2003, 105–10). While the full list has not been released by the British government or the Orwell archives, it is known to include actor/director Orson Welles, the novelist John Steinbeck (who wrote sympathetically about working-class and immigrant plights), and the singer and activist Paul Robeson, whom we mentioned above. Annotations marked people as "sentimental sympathiser," or "tendency towards homosexuality," or "previously C. P. [communist party]."

The work of George Orwell thus serves as a fitting conclusion to this chapter on the Cold War. Orwell was a complex man whose work was used as a simple symbol of the opposition between communism and capitalism, and used as a slogan though he critiqued such slogans. He believed that language was powerful, but showed the two ways in which friction-free communication could appear: as an attempt to suppress dissent or to express it. He believed in the possibility of clarity and transparency in language. He decried suppression of expression, as he himself participated in it. All these themes have been evident in this chapter as we looked at the surveillance and silencing of linguistic scholars and activists who were communist, socialist, anti-racist, and/or feminist.

Orwell's wariness about human language becoming like that of machines is literalized in this period. Linguistic analysis mushroomed in the context of Cold War oppositions, driven by a need for powerful and accurate translations made by machines, in part because the sympathies of people who could make such translations were always suspect. Such analyses meant positing universals for human interaction, a strategy that also challenged the radical racist relativism of the fascists.

Universalist approaches framing linguistics as objective and impartial served to counter the racist focus on difference in twentieth-century fascist and colonial regimes; however, they also dovetailed with security aims and obscured other ongoing forms of social inequity. In the later part of the Cold War period, modern sociolinguistics emerged to take on some of these questions, though it too was complicatedly shaped by the state-science nexuses, and the growth in foundation support. It is to these questions we turn in the next chapter.

CHAPTER 7

ON THE ORIGINS OF "SOCIOLINGUISTICS": DEMOCRACY, DEVELOPMENT, AND EMANCIPATION

FIGURE 7.1: John Gumperz with two as yet unidentified colleagues, India, 1956 (Source: personal collection, Jenny Cook-Gumperz)

"A Dialectologist in India"

The photo above shows John Gumperz, then a postdoctoral researcher in dialectology, in India in 1956 with two colleagues whom we have not yet been able to identify (please contact us if you recognize these men). How did a U.S.-based German-born Jewish dialectologist, initially trained as a chemist, end up in India in the mid-1950s? How did that experience become a key element in the foundation, especially in the 1960s' United States, of a new discipline called *sociolinguistics*?

This chapter will examine a different side of the postwar period, one that generativist approaches to language were ill-equipped to handle since they entailed active involvement in various forms of social engineering. After World War II, a major concern was to ensure that the world would not again face the economic havoc associated with the Depression and the national rivalries that led to the war; this led to the restructuring of state economies and international relations (Harvey 2005, 9). Two related efforts were joined to achieve this: *development* and *decolonization*. Both were solidly inscribed in modernist notions of linear progress achieved through science and its applications in the service of emancipation from oppression. Political scientists, sociologists, anthropologists, educationists, and economists were all recruited to these efforts, largely through projects funded by private foundations, notably the Rockefeller and Ford Foundations.

Decolonization here refers to the movement to shake off the political control by imperial powers (often violently, as in Algeria and Indochina) and replace it with new nation-states (a political economic form introduced by the imperial powers). *Development* refers to the process of bringing the standard of living of those states up to that enjoyed by the wealthier postwar countries, with refractions internal to welfare states in the West and to communist states devoted to a better distribution of wealth among their own citizens.

Achieving this usually meant investment in industry and in material and institutional infrastructure, notably in agriculture, engineering, medicine, and governance. "Governance" includes development of the strategies of nation-building we are already familiar with: literacy, standard languages, and education. Decolonization and postwar reconstruction also led to labour mobility, with concomitant concerns around language and citizenship.

Linguists were recruited to efforts to understand the facts on the ground well enough to serve as a basis for informed, rational decisions about policies concerning national languages, the regulation of multilingualism, languages of education, language education, and literacy. Their expertise was mobilized in order to solve what were understood as *technical* problems that were amenable to *technical* solutions. This, of course, is what John Gumperz (1922–2013) was doing in India in 1955.

Decolonization internationally triggered similar movements within states. The most notable were movements of national liberation conducted by European linguistic minorities in France, Britain, Spain, and Canada. Decolonizing movements in Africa and Asia were linked to civil rights movements and third world solidarity movements in North America. Indigenous groups in settler countries also launched decolonial movements.

Debates about the causes of and solutions for these inequalities were often held on the terrain of language as the value of standardized languages and literacy was heightened through Global North efforts to democratize access to education at home as well as abroad. These processes brought with them their own sets of concerns around language as a path to full citizenship, with tensions around minoritized vernaculars versus the standardized languages of modern institutions and of global power.

Both decolonization and development were centred within the spheres of the former imperial states, with a focus on facilitating democracy; on the other side of the Cold War, the Soviet Union and its allies also aimed at decolonization and development through communism. Conquest was replaced by a variety of forms of "soft power," from the organization of former imperial spheres into zones of political and economic influence, such as la Francophonie or the Commonwealth, to various kinds of cultural promotion, cultural exchange, and the facilitation of student mobility for higher education from former colonies to the West, to the Soviet Union, or to post-1949 China. While governments were directly involved, they also supported soft power agencies such as the British Council, the Alliance française, or the Japan Foundation. By the end of the 1960s, unemployment and inflation were surging in the Global North despite the efforts of the welfare state. While many different responses were considered, from tightening to loosening state control, most involved forms of intervention bolstered by scientific expertise.

This was the set of conditions that underlay the emergence of the field of *sociolinguistics*, in particular in the United States, the new seat of global capitalist power. The story of that field and this national site will be at the centre of this chapter, since it is there that hegemonic understandings of the relationship between language, culture, and society have developed. At the end of the chapter, we will (too) briefly sketch out some of the ways in which sociolinguistics emerged as a field in the Caribbean and in Western Europe, partly in conversation with American colleagues. While we will not focus on the communist world, we ought to bear in mind Brandist's (2015) argument that many of the concerns taken over by Western sociolinguistics were in fact initially addressed in the Soviet Union (see Chapter 5).

We will show how the field of sociolinguistics emerges in this period as a means to construct engagement with social inequalities in the face of the promises of progress in the postwar period. It is constructed as "new" partly as a means to tie linguistics to sociology, social psychology, and sociocultural anthropology, as part of a broad social science effort to address social problems of development, whether "international" or "domestic" (though we understand those as two sides of the same coin). It is also constructed as "new" as a means to create distance from older traditions tainted with their use by fascism and colonialism; as part of the modernist, progress-oriented spirit of the era, devoted as it was to remaking the world after the war; and in order to engage directly with the influential claims of generativism, widely heralded as nothing short of a revolution.

In keeping with our approach, we will look at how institutional funding arrangements and welfare state and developmentalist ideologies helped shape the field. (This led us to conduct some original research in the archives of the Rockefeller Foundation.) Although many histories of the field are rather relentlessly nationalist, we try to attend to international and transnational exchanges. (Perhaps the fact that Gumperz's Indian colleagues so far remain unknown to North American scholars is symbolic of this lacuna, though Gumperz himself regularly noted it was not just his observations of Indian language and society, but his interaction with Indian linguists that shaped his views.)

We will first consider the set of publications, many of them the result of development-related work, that emerged in the 1960s and 1970s in Canada, the United States, and Europe, and that constitute the canon of the newly named field of sociolinguistics. We turn then to the questions of *literacy*, *standardization*, and the *regulation of multilingualism or linguistic variability* that were central to many development projects, tying them to the construction of the subfield of language planning and language policy. While largely supported by the United States (and notably the Ford Foundation), Britain, and France, this field in particular opened up possibilities for the emergence of expertise among the intellectual elites of the "developing countries," especially in those cases taken to be exemplars of success: India, Indonesia, and the Philippines all stand out. It also led to the institutionalization of research efforts through the establishment of research centres (some tied to universities, some not), and hence to a solid basis for production and reproduction of this subfield.

We will then examine how international development efforts were echoed in the 1960s and 1970s by a concern for similar sets of questions domestically, especially in the United States, and largely by the same set of actors who had been involved in international development projects focussing on multilingualism and standardization, especially under the auspices of the Social Science Research Council.[1]

Here we will see a concern in particular for the ways in which immigration and racial inequality challenged the promise of meritocracy in the welfare state, as evidenced in the work of three scholars often considered the founders of the field: William Labov, John Gumperz, and Dell Hymes. We will examine how their commitment to expert knowledge, in the context of the persistent effects of the McCarthy era, hobbled their emancipatory intentions. At the same time, we will see how the areas of enquiry they opened, with the democratization of access to higher education, allowed the development of for critiques from feminist and anti-racist scholars seeking to better achieve those emancipatory goals. We will then consider the ways in which postwar labour migration, coupled with overseas and domestic decolonization movements, underlay the (somewhat later) emergence of sociolinguistics in Europe, with a stronger focus on political economy. We close with a consideration of the end of the *Trente Glorieuses* and the challenges to sociolinguistics of the end of the welfare state.

Engineering Language: Literacy, Standardization, and Education

The central set of actors in the emergence of sociolinguistics mainly belonged to the generation born between the wars, coming of age in wartime or the postwar period. Many influential scholars were of working-class or regional minority backgrounds; in the United States many were Jews, sensitized to or having directly experienced anti-Semitism in Nazi Europe. Many had been soldiers or occupied other military roles during or after World War II or in the Korean War (for Americans) or the Algerian war (for French sociolinguists). Some grew up in peripheral and colonial contexts (such as Tunisia or Corsica). Some became involved in international or domestic welfare state development projects, working among colonial peripheral groups, in urban working-class neighbourhoods, or, in the long-standing Americanist tradition, on Native American reserves.

---

[1] The Council, incorporated in 1924, was the initiative of a number of professional associations under the leadership of the American Political Science Association. It was funded by a number of private foundations, notably Ford and Rockefeller, but also Carnegie and Russell Sage. It played a key role in counselling the United States government in foreign and domestic policy through the middle part of the twentieth century (Packenham 1973).

The concentration of scholarship they produced began in the 1950s, with reports and scholarly articles built on international development projects or domestic welfare state projects. It culminated in the United States in the period between about 1960 and 1974 in a large number of foundational publications, almost all of them edited and interdisciplinary volumes. Several were the results of conference panels or symposia, some of them supported by private foundations.[2] The Rockefeller Foundation sponsored the Committee on Sociolinguistics from 1963 to 1979; the Committee was the incubator for many publications and for the 1972 founding of *Language in Society*, the first journal in the field (Dell Hymes was its first editor). European publications emerged starting slightly later, and tended to be monographs.[3] Britain, France, and Catalonia were particularly important sites of research. A network of European and North American scholars also met through setting up a Research Commission on Sociolinguistics in 1968 under the auspices of the International Sociological Association.

The U.S.-based publications included many overlapping sets of authors, mostly male. The only regularly contributing woman was the social psychologist Susan Ervin-Tripp, a Berkeley colleague of Gumperz and Hymes interested in child language development (one area relatively accessible to women); others who appeared less frequently included Mary Haas (who had been briefly married to Morris Swadesh) as a representative of an earlier Boasian tradition focussed on Indigenous languages, and Joan Rubin, a member of the earliest group developing the idea of language planning.

The authors in these publications attended to a wide range of sites and situations, but also to a wide range of communicative forms, notably nonverbal ones. Canadian social psychologists formed a strong contingent, highly influenced by the Montréal-based Wallace Lambert and his explorations of social motivations of language choice, and by state and public interest in addressing political tensions around the marginalization of francophone Canadians by increasing

---

2   They include Hymes's 1964 collection of reprinted articles entitled *Language in Culture and Society*; a 1966 special issue of *American Anthropologist* that became Gumperz and Hymes 1972; Hymes 1971, a collection based on a conference on pidgins and creoles held in Jamaica; Lieberson 1966, which gathered the contributions to the first conference sponsored by the Committee on Sociolinguistics in 1964; Bright 1966; Fishman 1972; Labov 1972a, 1972b; Giglioli 1972; Bauman and Sherzer 1974; and Lakoff 1975.

3   They include Basil Bernstein's work published between 1971 and 1977; Dittmar 1973; Trudgill 1974; Marcellesi and Gardin 1974; and Bachmann, Lindenfeld, and Simonin 1981. Two journals were founded in France in the 1970s: the *Cahiers de linguistique sociale*, founded by Jean-Baptiste Marcellesi in 1976, and *Langage et société*, founded in 1977 by Pierre Achard. A 1977 special issue of the generalist journal *Langue française* was also deeply influential (among other texts, it contains the by now well-cited article by Pierre Bourdieu on "the economics of linguistic exchanges"; Bourdieu 1977).

understanding of the personal and community politics of bilingualism. While much of the development of Canadian sociolinguistics lay precisely on the terrain of francophone liberation movements, there were few francophones involved initially, and certainly none are represented in these early volumes.[4]

People working from different disciplinary perspectives had a variety of reasons to converge on the study of language. Sociologists working in the phenomenological tradition were looking at the *social construction of reality* (Berger and Luckmann 1966); they argued that "reality" is *social*, that is, as founded on how we teach each other to interpret the world through interacting with each other—not, as the positivist position held, that reality is natural, and "out there" to be scientifically observed. This line of thought led such sociologists to engage with interaction, and therefore communication, and therefore language, in ways that brought them into contact with linguists exploring situated language use (as we will see below, this approach was particularly important for John Gumperz). Their work intersected with the new field of cognitive science, itself in conversation with, and sometimes critical about, Chomskyan ideas about the innateness of language. Philosophers of language were also interested in exploring language as action and as meaning. The efforts of the 1960s and 1970s are marked by collaborative efforts that stand in marked contrast to the knowledge production of generative linguistics, with its focus on the charismatic figure of Chomsky (see Murray 1998).

Sociolinguists took up two dimensions of what generativist approaches marginalized, developing different definitions of the notion of *performance*, and elaborating a notion of *communicative competence* that moved beyond a focus on cognitive capacity. Different schools of sociolinguistics are defined in no small part by their emphasis on different aspects of this effort, but they shared some fundamental premises.

Notably, sociolinguists argued that performance, or what people observably do with language, had to be a legitimate area of enquiry because it is language too. They also argued that Chomsky's definition of competence was impoverished. Indeed, they took the position, most famously articulated by Dell Hymes, that what mattered is *communicative competence*. Drawing on Roman Jakobson's ideas about the functions of language, they argued that competence was as much about knowing how to use language as it was about knowing how to produce it grammatically (Hymes 1966). For them it was crucial to attend to the real-life relevance of language in the matters of greatest concern

---

[4] Monica has argued that this work was more focussed on either developing consensual models of bilingualism or legitimating Canadian French as a nation-building exercise than on engaging with the inequalities that made language salient at that time (Heller 1996, 1999).

to contemporary society; they wanted to attend to language use because it was in actual practices that questions of difference and inequality play out. As we shall see, these ideas about language and society brought into play a new version of the old tension between understanding language as a structured and autonomous system and understanding it as social action. This tension played itself out not only in sociolinguistics' challenge to generativist linguistics, but also within sociolinguistics itself.

As well, two different approaches emerged for analyzing language. The functionalist view assumed that society was held together by a general consensus of values, and thus focussed on shared norms and values, even where there was heterogeneous practice. The conflict perspective highlighted views that contested the prevailing social order. This latter view was most evident in some European approaches to language study, in areas where Marxist traditions were robust, as well as in anti-colonial sites. In the United States, as we saw, such approaches had been actively suppressed. Conflictual views also became more central as linguistic scholarship moved beyond the purview of white men, and different groups of scholars (white women, racialized scholars) raised new questions about what language was and how to study it.

Language Policy and Planning: Technocratic Solutions

If progress was to be achieved through the modernization of nation-states, a central problem to be resolved was how to make a standard language accessible to all citizens and usable for the purposes of education, as it had been many times before. This is both a problem of standardization and a problem of literacy.

A widely cited statistic in studies of education and development says that a society with a 40 per cent literacy rate is needed for economic "take-off" (Anderson 1966, cited in Street 1984, 2). There was such a cluster of influential books published in the 1950s and 1960s linking literacy to social progress that one commentator described it as a "watershed ... reached" or "a dam starting to burst" (Havelock 1991, cited in Brockmeier and Olson 2009, 9).[5]

The literate/nonliterate distinction was largely mapped onto groups previously understood as racially distinguished according to the evolutionary scales

---

5 Among the best known we find works by Harold Innis (1950), Karl Deutsch (1953), Claude Lévi-Strauss (1962), Marshall McLuhan (1962), Jack Goody and Ian Watt (1963), E. A. Havelock (1963), Walter Ong (1967), and Jacques Derrida (1967). One particularly influential group (including Havelock and McLuhan) at the University of Toronto, supported by the Ford Foundation, is known as the *Toronto School of Communication Theory*. It is perhaps best known for McLuhan's saying, "The medium is the message."

we saw in Chapter 3. While it is less overly evaluative, it nonetheless imports a related cluster of assumptions. First, literacy, like some early accounts of religion (see Chapter 2), allows for "conversion" or "development" into the appropriate form of modern being. It allows for commensurability, that is, for inscription into particular globalizing modes of government and governmentality, as does the inscription into nation-state forms of political organization. Second, it allows for a new mode of evaluation and hierarchization after the evolutionary scales were discredited. If literacy allows people to become empathetic, cosmopolitan, and better at planning change, as one UNESCO document argued (Street 1984), what is supposed about those people beforehand? Street (1984, 3) cites one illustrative example, a study by Patricia Greenfield (1972) on schooled literacy among Wolof-speaking children in Senegal; she concluded that unschooled children lacked the concept of a personal point of view and the cognitive flexibility she found in schooled children. These were new languages for older understandings of African children as radically different and deficient.

In keeping with the largely technicist approach to social and linguistic engineering that often characterized development projects, the dominant "autonomous" approach in scholarship on literacy tended to separate the study of literacy from studies of social context (Street 1984). The focus on literacy as a technical cognitive skill and personal achievement depoliticizes culturally loaded discussions; it holds out the promise that, once acquired, this skill would transform societies and individuals. Further, if illiteracy is diagnosed as a cognitive or social deficit, linked to economic underdevelopment, then the solution to inequity is focussed on individuals and on education, rather than, say, on changing capitalist forms of extraction that are leading to overdevelopment in some sites and underdevelopment in others. Literacy studies were of a piece with the prevailing technocratic or educational 'solutions' that were central to development discourses.

Work on literacy and education tended to assume state-standard monolingualism as the norm, and therefore goal. In many cases, despite decolonization, the language of colonial powers remained the language of education, sometimes alongside newly developed or elevated standard languages. Which languages were used in primary, secondary, and postsecondary education was and remains a lively terrain for debate. In some new states, this was one way to address political struggles among speakers of different varieties with claims to power in the new regime. It was also, of course, a means to retain access to global languages of power, a process supported by former colonial powers equally interested in retaining their spheres of influence.

Existing educational infrastructures had been installed by colonial regimes, and often continued to be staffed by them, as was the case for French *coopération* we discussed earlier.[6] Indigenous elites continued to be trained in the metropole and were expected to learn to act white without actually being able to escape racialization (Fanon ([1952] 1967). In other cases, various forms of bilingual or multilingual education were constructed, or new standard languages were used to replace colonial ones. Some of the standard languages were constructed on the basis of existing linguistic descriptions of Indigenous languages. In others, new "neutral" ones were constructed; a notable example is Bahasa Indonesia, built, in the tradition of International Auxiliary Languages, to be easily learned by a multilingual population (Alisjahbana 1976).

These were the areas of most interest to the new field of *language planning and language policy*, a field that played a major role in building the infrastructure for the new field of sociolinguistics. In the next section we will explore the development of language policy and planning, showing how, while they remain fully inscribed in the technicist modernizing approaches central to development, they nonetheless opened the door to questions about multilingualism more generally, and about its role in the making of inequality.

Domestic Development and American Sociolinguistics

The team in which John Gumperz participated in the 1950s was meant to help India, which gained independence from Great Britain in 1947, begin to look like a proper nation-state. One of the major obstacles to this was said to be the extreme multilingualism and cultural diversity of the Indian population, although some dimensions of the diversity were reduced, violently, by separating off Muslim states in West and East Pakistan (later Pakistan and Bangladesh) from predominantly Hindu India. It was this multilingualism that Gumperz was to study.

The linguistic variability Gumperz and his colleagues encountered led them to enquiries about the relationship among language, society, and culture across and within social landscapes, including cities. Scholars began to ask questions about precisely the ways in which linguistic variability was tied to different forms of social difference, whether based on ethnicity, race, religion, caste, class, or gender. They became interested in how those sociolinguistic differences might matter in people's lives and affect their life chances.

Development and modernization projects laid the basis for the field in a number of ways. In the United States, the Ford Foundation and the Rockefeller Foundation funded development projects with research components, research

---

6 This also happened in Canada; Wade (2016) documents the late 1960s' origins of the sociology department at the new Université de Moncton in the recruitment of three *coopérants*.

centres housed inside universities or independently, and a version of "think tanks" designed to set agendas for research, training, programs, and policies for states, state agencies, and educational institutions. The Rockefeller Foundation's Social Science Research Council Committee on Sociolinguistics brought together just about all of the scholars we now associate with the idea of sociolinguistics in the period from 1963 to 1979; we will discuss the role of the Committee at greater length in the next section, but let us note here that it was a central incubator for the definition of the field at its outset, allowing informally selected participants to meet regularly and to define and carry out agenda-setting research projects that were deliberately designed to link linguistic, anthropological, sociological, and social psychological approaches to the questions they asked.

As the Rockefeller Foundation sent linguists and anthropologists to India in the 1950s, the Ford Foundation also set up projects in India, as well as in the Philippines, Peru, Indonesia, Tunisia, and Egypt (Fox 1975). Several of these had as a major component the development of curricula and teacher training in the area of English as a Foreign Language (EFL). We might interpret this as one attempt on the part of the United States, as a newly emergent world power, to challenge the British Council and the Alliance française in the use of language teaching as soft diplomacy—and hence in laying the groundwork for the role of applied linguistics (in particular as applied to the teaching of English) in spreading English as a global language of democracy and power.

The Ford Foundation also played an important role in the establishment of language policy-related research centres. One such example is the Center for Applied Linguistics, established in 1959 in Washington, DC, with Charles Ferguson (1921–98) as its first director. It had ties to the Columbia-based Interlingua project and other dimensions of the auxiliary language movement, and was devoted to problems of multilingualism and language learning.[7]

Another research centre established at this time was the Centre international de recherche sur le bilinguisme (CIRB) at Laval University in Québec. Its first director, William Mackey (1918–2015), was a key figure in the field of language policy and language planning as related specifically to the issue of bilingualism. The CIRB also benefited from Ford Foundation funds, as well as university support and outside research grants.

---

[7] Ferguson has much in common with many of the other figures discussed in this chapter (cf. Huebner 1999). A working-class Philadelphian, he attended the University of Pennsylvania on scholarship. He studied Arabic linguistics under Zellig Harris, as did Noam Chomsky (see Chapter 6). His early career in the immediate postwar period involved him in the U.S. State Department's Foreign Service Institute language training programs.

The Committee on Sociolinguistics was also involved in organizing conferences in this area, most of them under the intellectual leadership of Joshua Fishman (1926–2015). One of the first, on "Language Problems of Developing Nations," was held in 1966; the Ford Foundation funded continued work on this theme in 1968–69 at the East-West Centre in Hawai'i, bringing together established scholars from the United States and Australia with new scholars from India, Indonesia, and Malaysia. Ferguson organized a similar conference in Ethiopia in the same period.[8]

The field of language policy and language planning, including a focus on developing literacy, took from earlier ideas about language the concept of *typology*: type A situations will require type A solutions, type B situations will require type B solutions, and so on. This approach also characterized the related field of the *sociology of language*, which was concerned to document the social conditions for the maintenance of minority languages, whether those languages were minoritized through immigration or internal colonialism. Typologies also underlay the distinction between *status planning* (changing the social value of a language), susceptible to legal and political engineering, and *corpus planning* (the making of rational linguistic varieties and tools for their use). Both were understood to require the intervention of experts; the latter especially was understood to require the expertise of trained linguists.

These concepts were introduced by Heinz Kloss, whom we discussed in Chapter 4. Kloss's early career in 1920s' and 1930s' Germany focussed on the German "diaspora" in the United States and later, as we saw, on the establishment of hierarchies of language in accordance with Nazi ideologies of language. In the 1960s, Kloss returned to publishing in the area of language planning, based partly at the CIRB, and partly at the reframed and renamed Institut für Deutsche Sprache in Mannheim (Kallmeyer pers. comm.).

His ideas about corpus and status planning were linked to his ideas about language typology, and in particular to his distinction between *Ausbau* and *Abstand* languages. Kloss offered this distinction as a way to draw boundaries among languages, especially as might be relevant to determining political boundaries, a key question in the 1960s' period of decolonization. *Abstand* languages could be described as linguistically different from each other, that is, lacking affinity (principally still understood in "genetic" terms, in the family-tree sense); a country such as India, then, would have a particular set of unification problems because some of its languages are understood as Indo-European and others as Dravidian.

---

8 RF Accession 1, series 1, subseries 19, box 218, folder 1533. These materials come from the materials on the Committee on Sociolinguistics held in the Rockefeller Foundation Archives in Sleepy Hollow, New York. Henceforth, we will abbreviate Rockefeller Foundation as RF.

Ausbau languages were essentially standardized languages deliberately built for social and political purposes to bring together (in his terms, act as a roof over) related (non-*Abstand*) varieties. An example of this might be French as a unifier of patois (see Chapter 4). The state of play between and within them in any given context was understood as relevant to political decisions regarding status or corpus planning. (The distinction has some resonances with Ferguson's work [Ferguson 1959] on Arabic-speaking areas, where different varieties of ostensibly the same language were understood as functionally distributed in what he famously termed *diglossia*—in contradistinction to *bilingualism* as a means to characterize individual repertoires.) Kloss's work provided an expert rationale for state intervention, and was particularly influential in the language planning and language policy undertaken by the Québec government in the 1960s and 1970s, which remains current today. This seemingly depoliticized, typological approach rests, nonetheless, we argue, on Kloss's earlier investigations into the relative development and genetic affinities among languages undertaken on behalf of the development of the language policies of the Nazi state.

In all these distinctions (*status* and *corpus planning*; *Abstand* and *Ausbau* languages; distinctions among various kinds of multilingualism and multilingual political entities—diglossic, contact, bi- or multilingual), we see the influence of both functionalism and structuralism: it matters what (forms of) language are used for what, and by whom. To answer such questions requires understanding language as a system that may not be entirely autonomous (in the sense of being untouchable by human agency), but does have a systematicity of its own that human agency must take into account.

It also brings out as a problem the extent to which both linguistic and social forms can be understood in similar structuralist terms; this marks some of the ways that early sociolinguistics, for all of the pains it took to distance itself from the Chomskyan tradition, still shared some of the assumptions both lines of thought inherited from prewar traditions. These assumptions about the autonomy of language and the usefulness of structural analysis were foundational to sociolinguistic efforts to bring progress to the marginalized and to value stigmatized forms of difference, opening the door to those previously not represented in institutionalized linguistic circles. However, because they were founded on specific ideas of scientific expertise, they demanded adherence to a position often not shared by those others in whose name they aimed to speak, and blunted their own ability to engage in the political dimensions of their work, especially where the linguistic work done assumed that the key site of transformation was increasing access to, or mobility in, the extant social order, rather than markedly changing it.

In the next section we will turn to how U.S.-based sociolinguists began to turn the insights gained from international development to matters of domestic inequality, in the context of the civil rights movements that were linked to international decolonization. We will examine in some detail how the major intellectual threads that were brought to bear on these problems (*variationist sociolinguistics, interactional sociolinguistics*, and the *ethnography of communication*) all tried to turn the tools of their fields to emancipation and progress, but ultimately became subject to the critique that their approach failed to adequately engage with the material dimensions of domination (cf. Chun and Lo 2016).

Challenging 'Deficit': Three Approaches

The Ford Foundation was not only active in international development. As Fox (1975) documents, it also funded within the same Public Education Program one domestic project that was aimed at setting up the teaching of English as a Second Language at the University of California, Los Angeles. It was initially aimed at the regulation of internal diversity by targeting the children of immigrants who spoke languages other than English upon enrollment in school. In Los Angeles, many immigrants were of course from Mexico and Latin America (and a number of American-born children would also have been Spanish speakers), as well as from various sites in Asia. The notions held about these countries' underdevelopment were also attached to the migrants from those countries, or those grouped with such migrants, in ways that showed how language development and education were linked at home and abroad. This program soon added components aimed at the education of Native American schoolchildren and an "English as a Second Dialect" program aimed at African American schoolchildren.

Indeed, just as great attention was being paid to democratization and autonomy in former colonies, similar attention was being paid closer to home. Class, racial, gender, ethnolinguistic, and ethnocultural disparities in income, health, educational attainment, and housing all became of concern to states and to social science. The Committee on Sociolinguistics was very clear about the importance of a focus on domestic concerns. As late as 1975, in a summary of a CoS-sponsored conference at Temple University in Philadelphia entitled "Comparative Ethnographic Analysis of Patterns of Speech in the United States," Dell Hymes commented on the gap in knowledge of the "use of language in our own society." Roger Shuy added "the ethnography of language in our society may be characterized as a vast desert." The conference, invitation-only with 34 precirculated papers, was set up to orient the field in two directions, not always linked: the questions of "ethnic group contact," understood in this case under the rubric "Chicanos in the United States," and institutional settings, particularly educational and medical ones.[9] This focus on institutions is characteristic of the welfare state since it is there that the state is understood to distribute its resources.

---

9 RF Accession 1, series 1, subseries 19, box 215, folder 1301.

In their different ways, the sociolinguists of the 1960s and 1970s largely argued that problems of domestic inequality were related to the gap between communicative competence valued in the institutions of the welfare state, notably in education, and the communicative competence characteristic of marginalized groups, perhaps especially those whose cultural knowledge was largely based on oral practices. They spoke to the persistent claim that if minorities are marginalized, if they do poorly on the increasingly standardized measures of proficiency brought into play in the early twentieth century, it is not because the system is undemocratic; instead, it is because they have some kind of *deficit* in culture, intelligence, or character (see Morgan 1994, 328). A similar logic was applied to international development: a "failure" to modernize was seen as a failure of democracy, or will, or a form of irrationality in those living in countries that were "underdeveloped." They offered instead a view that language practices are culturally variable, and that misunderstandings—and hence unequal appreciation and valuing of diverse language practices—are the result of cultural and linguistic *difference*.

The deficit hypothesis was a strong one in the 1960s. Some (notably the Berkeley psychologist Jensen) argued that this deficit is *genetic* and affects intelligence (Jensen 1969). There is a clear line of continuity between such claims and the theories of racial hierarchies introduced through evolutionary thought and social Darwinism in the nineteenth century. In the 1960s, while such claims still circulated, as indeed they do now, a popular and influential view held that the purported deficit was *cultural* (cf. Bereiter and Engelmann 1966). This notion, which still underlies a wide variety of programs for young children across North America, suggests that children from poor and/or minority homes do not have access to cognitively and linguistically rich environments, and thus lack adequate preparation for school. Cultural deficit theorists argued that this was not the fault of caregivers (although some still chose to interpret things this way), but nonetheless would require state intervention in the form of educational support to fill the "gap."

Some of this work was understood to be bolstered by the influential empirical work of the British sociologist Basil Bernstein (1924–2000), who attributed to differences in communicative style the ways in which educational outcomes reproduced class positions (working-class children do poorly at school and get working-class jobs, middle-class children do better and leverage educational credentials into middle-class jobs; Bernstein 1971–1977). He argued that schools, and the middle class, preferred what he called an *elaborated code*, in which much was made verbally explicit, whether through naming things with words, or by making relations among things or ideas grammatically explicit. The working class, he said, preferred a *restricted code*, in which much was left to shared understanding of context for the successful transmission of ideas.

He located the source of differences in language socialization within the family. This became one central theme in U.S. linguistic anthropology and the anthropology of education in cross-cultural studies of language socialization in childhood and adolescence, and in studies comparing language use at home and school (although results often failed to support Bernstein's position). Indeed, one major facet of work sponsored by the Committee on Sociolinguistics concerned cultural variability and social processes of language acquisition, understood as the "acquisition of communicative competence" in the United States and internationally, with offshoots in bilingual education and teacher training (Slobin 1967). This work also thus became a key avenue of women's access to the field; following Ervin-Tripp, we see work by Shirley Brice Heath (1983), and Elinor Ochs and Bambi Schieffelin (Schieffelin and Ochs 1986; Ochs and Schieffelin 1979) emerging in the late 1970s and early 1980s.

One reading of Bernstein's position was to understand it as a form of *deficit hypothesis*, holding that minoritized and marginalized children do badly in school because they are not equipped with the kind of "developed" language required to grasp the complex concepts transmitted through education (cf. Heller and McLaughlin 2016). Another view located in Bernstein's work is an attempt to seriously engage in the relationship between cultural processes outside and inside school and, in particular, to raise the question of why certain kinds of linguistic practices, notably verbal explicitness, are so valued in our society, but at the same time not widely shared (cf. Heller and McLaughlin 2016). The American sociolinguists of the 1960s and 1970s used their familiarity with culturally variable linguistic practices to argue against the deficit reading, and for a "difference" reading instead—one that both took variability seriously and addressed the differential valuing of it.

We turn now to three major forms of the difference hypothesis, associated with three of the major figures in American sociolinguistics: William Labov, John Gumperz, and Dell Hymes. Along with other colleagues (notably Joshua Fishman and Charles Ferguson), they argued that the analyses produced by the use of their scientific tools showed perfectly rational and complex linguistic processes at play across all languages (whether or not they were linked to writing systems), putting lie to claims that specific linguistic systems were deficient and linked to cognitive deficiency and social marginalization. Linguistic variation, they argued, could be described ethnographically and explained functionally (whether by social function, what Joshua Fishman called *domains*; or by communicative function, in a Jakobsonian vein or an interactional one). They also insisted that marginalized, undervalued linguistic forms often were linked to forms of linguistic creativity and meaning-making that standardized dominant middle-class European languages were incapable of and that institutions failed to recognize.

They all, also, were committed to challenging the idealized homogeneity of the speech community presumed in Chomskyan linguistics. Their focus on heterogeneity, however, centred on variation in linguistic practices, but presumed a relatively unified speech community with unified norms of evaluation (Guy 1988; Morgan 1994; Rickford 1993; G. Williams 1992). This had implications for the kinds of social change their linguistic analyses implied: more often, inclusion into institutions rather than dramatic transformation.

Labov, Gumperz, and Hymes had in common a deep acquaintance with linguistic variability and social inequality. Gumperz's, we have seen, came from his training as a dialectologist and his work in India. He was also a German Jewish refugee from Nazism, who returned to Germany after the war as a translator for the U.S. Army. Dell Hymes (1927–2009), a World War II veteran shocked by what he saw at Hiroshima, was trained as a linguistic anthropologist on Oregon's Warm Springs Indian reservation. The reservation, the product of course of US attacks on Indigenous sovereignty, was occupied and governed by the Confederated Tribes of Warm Springs, which includes three tribes (Wasco, Tenino, and Paiute), speaking Kiksht, Numu, and Ichishkiin languages, as well as being one of the key sites where the trade pidgin Chinook Jargon is spoken.

The early work of William Labov (1927–) was linked to a large project sponsored by Mobilization for Youth, a social service agency focussed on community development, the elimination of poverty, and the prevention and control of juvenile delinquency that had arisen out of an immigrant settlement organization that had operated in Manhattan's Lower East Side for six decades (MFY Legal Services 2013). In the late 1950s and early 1960s, social service workers were concerned about "rampant juvenile delinquency" linked to decades of poverty and discrimination, and enlisted faculty at the Columbia University School of Social Work for assistance. Additional funding came from the Ford Foundation and the National Institute for Mental Health.

Labov's approach, eventually labelled *variationist sociolinguistics*, has been the most strongly linked to a theory of linguistic systems. He has claimed, in opposition to Chomsky, that any theory of language worthy of the name must account for variability observed in linguistic performance; indeed, in a 1972 letter to a colleague, Dell Hymes remarked of Labov that "in a way he'd like to take over TG"[10] (Transformational Grammar, then the common label for Chomsky's generativist approach). The French linguist Pierre Encrevé, in introducing Labov's work to France, argued that it was not antagonistic to linguistics, it *was* linguistics, but "la linguistique mise sur ses pieds" [linguistics put back on its feet] (Encrevé 1976, 9).

---

10 RF Accession 2, subseries 95, box 575, folder 6815.

Labov's approach uses a structuralist/functionalist notion of class, race, gender, and age that saw these principles of social organization as given social "facts," not as terrains of conflict and struggle. His core approach used quantitative, statistical techniques to correlate "sex," "age," "race," and "socioeconomic status" (described as "variables") to empirically describable linguistic forms, specifically to formal units that mean the same thing, such as different pronunciations of the same word or different words for the same object. This approach linked positivist understandings of both language and society in an endeavour to show the systematicity of the relationship, and hence the irrationality of the value judgements that justified the ties between race, class, language, and inequality in public discourse. He sought to remedy social conflict through education about the rationality of language, working toward consensus about this rationality, and laying aside questions about the reasons for devaluing speakers through devaluing their linguistic practices.

Labov focussed on widespread arguments that African American students did not do well in school because of a lack of mastery of what is still usually called "standard English" (although of course one needs to ask "standard" for whom). He argued that the English spoken by African Americans needed to be understood in its own terms. Labov acted as expert witness at a well-known school board trial in 1979, in which the board was accused of failing to provide adequate standards of education through their neglect or devaluing of the linguistic practices of their African American students (Labov 1982). His position has consistently been that more African American English (AAE) should be included in schools as a path toward the appropriation of the forms of language favoured by schools. Labov's position was controversial among members of the Black middle class who argued that the differences were not marked enough to lead to comprehension difficulties, and that the language of instruction should be standard American English (Morgan 1994, 336).

John Gumperz's and Dell Hymes's approaches came to counter deficit hypotheses in ways that placed greater emphasis on the relationship between structural and cultural dimensions of language, and less on the structural dimensions alone. Partly through the influence of ethnomethodologists, interactionist sociologists, and cognitive scientists, Gumperz started looking more closely at the articulation of linguistic and social processes in what he understood to be the places where inequality happened: in actual communicative *interaction* and in what he later called *key situations* (Gumperz 1982a), that is, interactions in institutions responsible for the distribution of resources in the welfare state. These included classrooms, where student performance is judged; job interviews and other petitioner-provider situations; doctor-patient interaction, where communication is key to diagnosis and treatment; the workplace; and courtrooms. (By the late 1990s, Gumperz began using the term *interactional sociolinguistics* to characterize his approach.) In ways similar to Labov, Gumperz sought consensus through the application of rational arguments, and in ways favoured by the institutions of the state responsible for regulating relations with marginalized populations.

His major hypothesis was that language offers multiple channels for doing many things simultaneously, one of them being to call into play the background knowledge interlocutors need in order to be able to understand each other. He pointed to the linguistic forms that did the work of calling these frames into play, referring to them as *contextualization cues*, a term reframed later as *indexes*, following the work of the semiotician Charles Sanders Peirce (1839–1914). How indexes work, according to Gumperz (1982a), is conventional, cooked up over years of face-to-face interaction among people who are organized as a community. They learn how to do that by being socialized into those ways of using language as children, and those ways become deeply rooted and normalized in what Bourdieu (1972) called *habitus*: an enduring orientation to how to make sense of the world and what to value in it.

Gumperz (1982a) argued that it was more and more common for people from different communities to have to interact because people who never had access to education before were going to school, former imperial powers were now recruiting former colonial subjects as labour immigrants, and the welfare state multiplied points of contact between people and the state. He saw the 1960s as a period marked by multiple and novel opportunities for distinct habituses to collide. Misunderstandings, he thought, caused by using one's own frame to interpret someone else's conventions, led to anger, frustration, and stereotyping, triggering prejudice and exclusion.

Like Labov, Gumperz acted as an expert witness, specifically in the case of a Filipino doctor accused of malpractice (1982b). His work also served as the basis for a BBC documentary, *Crosstalk* (1979). Gumperz was invited to collaborate with the London-based National Centre for Industrial Training on a project aimed at solving tensions between workers of South Asian and local origin. Western Europe was experiencing a labour shortage in industrial manufacturing as a result of wartime deaths, a postwar drop in birth rate, increased upward mobility, and an expanding economy. Fundamental shifts in relations with former colonies positioned former colonial subjects as a labour pool, resulting in large-scale migration to Britain, the Netherlands, and France. (Germany, while it had former colonies in Southwest Africa from which there was some migration, recruited most heavily in Turkey.)

The workplace was therefore for Europe the key site for cross-cultural encounter and for racial and ethnic tension. Gumperz and his team used the approach he had developed, examining incompatibilities in culturally conventionalized modes of communication that, they argued, led to misunderstandings and frustration. This was picked up by the BBC as an important intervention in ethnoracial tensions in 1970s' Britain, and to this day remains a reference in the field of cross-cultural communication and anti-racism training, including in our home province of Ontario in Canada (Allan 2005).

Hymes was a major contributor to debates about the importance of reflexivity in anthropological practice, drawing on his own experiences as a white Oregonian working on Native American land not 100 miles from his college town. Trained in linguistic description in the tradition of Boas and Sapir, Hymes encountered a wide variety of forms of oral culture: routinized, structured verbal performances handed down through generations. Moreover, poetry was a major genre practiced by Hymes himself, alongside other anthropology students with whom he trained (one of whom, Gary Snyder, became a Pulitzer-prize winning Beat poet in San Francisco, writing about Indigenous themes).

The contrast between what linguists get when they elicit structures (culturally meaningful only to Euro-American linguists) and when they elicit texts conventionally organized in ways meaningful to their interlocutors was palpable to Hymes. It also ties to Jakobson's ideas about the functions of language, of which one is the poetic. For him, it was necessary to go beyond "referential function" to address "expressive-directive function," linking functions to genres, and finding ways to distinguish them by describing their features. In arguing this position, Hymes drew explictly on Jakobson's accounts, so here, again, we see a convergence of influences on structuralist syntax and a structurally informed sociolinguistics.[11]

At the same time, analytically, Hymes remained committed to an Americanist, and in many ways functionalist, view. He argued that the central issue in understanding language was people's ability to use language in ways that made sense to the people they were interacting with, and that this was a matter of social and cultural knowledge. To describe it, Hymes (1972a) developed a model of S-P-E-A-K-I-N-G as a frame for the *ethnography of communication*. S-P-E-A-K-I-N-G is a mnemonic covering the dimensions of language-in-context to which Hymes thought ethnographers should always attend: *setting and scene, participants, ends, acts sequence, key, instrumentalities, norms,* and *genre*.

Hymes also argued that the world was structured around what he called *narrative inequality* (1996), by which he meant that the institutional agents of dominant society rarely considered the possibility that other people's ways of recounting the world might make just as much sense as their own, using instead, unreflexively, the narrative structures with which they themselves had been socialized. Even though his focus was often more aesthetic than political, his

---

11 RF Accession 1, series 1, subseries 19, box 215, folder 1301.

fieldwork experiences also likely underlay *Reinventing Anthropology* (1972b), a collection he edited that included contributions from a number of anthropologists considering how to reshape the field in the light of, and to participate in, decolonial movements.

The three major scholars whose work we have described, often taken as the founders of the field, shared a concern for legitimizing difference in attempts to remedy inequality, and a scientific approach that removed language and linguistic practice from the conditions in which they were located, thereby weakening possibilities for analyzing how the differences they observed might have arisen or be deployed in ongoing processes of making inequality. In the next section, we will develop this point further through a discussion of explicit concerns raised within the Committee on Sociolinguistics, and its efforts to address some of the more pressing issues of its time.

Fear of the Political

The archives of the Committee on Sociolinguistics show a great deal of ambivalence about what members called the "political" (recall that Hymes was marked by the necessity of hiding Marxist works at Harvard in the 1950s). On the one hand, the members recognized that what they called "ethnolinguistic" diversity was a key dimension of contemporary inequality in the United States, and sought to engage with Native North American, African American, and "Chicano" claims for rights and recognition ("Chicano" was the preferred term at the time for Spanish-speaking residents of the United States). On the other hand, concrete efforts tended to founder.

In one meeting, for example, Allan Grimshaw and John Gumperz worried that too great an emphasis on "Chicano issues" would sideline theoretical issues in favour of applied or activist work. These concerns were expressed with regard to the Committee's efforts between 1972 and 1974 to organize "An Exploratory Conference on the Sociolinguistics of the Chicano Community" in either Texas or New Mexico, which had set out to include nonacademics. However, the Committee withdrew because it felt it had become embroiled in conflicts, in particular seeing some of the outside organizers as "too political" and "too militant."[12] This view was, clearly, not shared by those organizers who saw themselves as quite differently positioned from those who were members of the Committee. For example, one of the Chicano academics remarked that August would be a perfectly fine date for a meeting from a Chicano perspective, because "we don't go off to Europe like Anglos, we have to work").

---

12 RF Accession 2, subseries 95, box 572, folder 6796.

Francophone Canada played a somewhat similar role in the discussion. While francophones organized to resist and redress marginalization, American scholars took on this process as an interesting case study in the modernization of a "folk society" (Handler 1988). Francophone Canada was a possibly safer counterpart for Americans to the intellectual puzzles posed by African Americans and Chicanos, and closer to the United States than other sites. Many early American members of the Committee on Sociolinguistics worked on francophone Canada or Canadian bilingualism; the Canadian sociologist Jacques Brazeau was later invited to join, as was the sociolinguist Gillian Sankoff in the later years of the committee. In all these cases, the activism and militantism of the 1960s and 1970s' Quiet Revolution (the largely successful struggle for access to education and upward social mobility undertaken by the Québécois francophone elite) was largely kept off the table as a matter for intellectual enquiry.

The dominant strains of U.S.-based sociolinguistics, then, tried to balance two objectives. The first objective was to develop a truly interdisciplinary theoretical approach to understanding language as a cognitive and social process at the same time, in strong contradistinction to the Chomskyan approach (though, as we have said, it shared rational approaches and structural influences). It tried to push forward a Sapirian agenda, increasingly linking linguistic structure to social and cultural structure, bridging the disciplines devoted to understanding language, society, culture, and cognition. The new field of sociolinguistics took empirical data and systematic analysis as its core; one of its early (1968) conferences examined what it called "language as an obstacle to social science research"—by which it meant the ways in which the materiality and variability of communication impeded commensurability among disciplines and needed to be reflexively taken into account in analyses of what constituted data and what that data might mean.[13]

Later, the Committee undertook, under the leadership of Allan Grimshaw, the simultaneous analysis of a single piece of data not only by members of the Committee but also by outsiders, in an effort that can perhaps be understood as a last attempt to fulfill the Boasian notion of autonomous, objective texts. If the exercise failed, it was, interestingly, partly because of disagreement among scholars from different disciplinary areas about what the data should look like; that is, far from agreeing on the objective "fact" of the interaction, scholars disagreed profoundly on what it was they were analyzing.

The second objective was to find a way to engage in some of the major public debates about inequality of the time, in terms of both international and

---

13   RF Accession 1, series 1, subseries 19, box 217, folder 1309.

domestic development, in particular and constrained ways. Indeed, the focus on race, and increasingly on gender, could be seen as linked to the distinctive American dilemma of grappling with its histories of settler colonialism and slavery, but doing so on the ground of what were construed as identities linked to individuals rather than larger axes of inequality; this helps to explain why class is so infrequently invoked in American anthropology, including linguistic anthropology, at this time (Ortner 2003). We will see that class (but not always race) is more centred in the European traditions (discussed below).

The contradictions in the approach explain some of the ways the door was opened for the consideration of a range of forms of inequality, and the beginnings of access to the conversation on the part of white women and racialized women and men (either as groups often problematically labelled as 'minorities' or as citizens of new countries in former colonies), a question to which we next turn.

In the next section, we consider first the major critiques that the "difference hypothesis" approach of Americanist sociolinguistics triggered, which came mainly from the kinds of people whose marginalization had been the central area of their concern. As we will see, these critiques focussed on the ways in which the rational, scientific approach of the mainstream failed to account for the structures of inequality that explained why the forms of speech they analyzed were devalued in American society. We will see that the attention to "ethnolinguistic difference" was recast as requiring attention to racism and reframed as one of many forms of structural inequality, including, notably, sexism to which sociolinguistics now also turned its attention.[14]

Challenging Consensus

Liberal sociolinguistics triggered a variety of social critiques from a growing diversity of participants. By the 1980s and 1990s critics had moved the conversation from *deficit* and *difference* to a third approach, *dominance*, which centred problems of power and inequality as objects of analysis, and which can be understood as a form of conflict analysis. Here we will treat two significant conversations: the rise of feminist critiques, and anti-racist critiques centred on how to analyze African American English. (The next section will look at related debates about pidgins and creoles and new nationalisms.) We note that an intersectional analysis would now call for attention to entwined understandings of how gender, race, class, and sexuality unfold; if we treat them separately

---

14 Discussions of homophobia largely appear later; see Kulick (2000) for a review.

here it is because this approach was not fully evident in this early work, just as the separation of studies of African American English from pidgins and creoles instantiated one position in an ongoing debate. In this section, then, we are also considering how some of this early, critical work assumed divisions that scholars are still in many ways trying to overcome.

Feminist Linguistics

In an essay reflecting on her own experiences as a graduate student as compared with the graduate students she mentors, Susan Philips (2010) reminds us that during the 1960s and 1970s, the period in which she was being trained, the position of women in academia was still precarious. The expectation remained that women would marry, have children, and leave the field. And while Hymes (Philips's supervisor) clearly used his position as Dean of the Graduate School of Education at the University of Pennsylvania and as chair of the Committee of Sociolinguistics to open up possibilities for a range of scholars and types of scholarship, it has been alleged that he was responsible for sexually harassing a number of women, which had a major impact on the careers of more than one female scholar (this information comes from personal communication with a number of scholars).

By our count, the Committee on Sociolinguistics, a centre of power in the field, had 23 male members over the course of its life (1963–79), including one member of a racialized minority, Eduardo Hernandez-Chavez (a former student of Gumperz, he replied to the invitation to join that he had stopped working on language after his dissertation; Hymes, then chair, insisted that that was not a problem). It had two female members, Susan Ervin-Tripp and Gillian Sankoff (their terms did not overlap). There was some discussion of recruiting another former student of Gumperz, Claudia Mitchell-Kernan, an African American woman known for her work on African American youth language practices; she does not seem to have become a member.

When women were present, it was often as observers, though many were invited to present papers at committee-sponsored conferences, especially those on acquisition and education. We see evidence in the Rockefeller Foundation Archives of women, especially Susan Philips, who was invited in such a capacity, frequently reminding the group that attention to women in the data discussed is minimal or entirely absent, or suggesting that perhaps a session might be chaired by the woman whose work was being discussed. Virginia Hymes, Dell Hymes's wife, once acted as secretary, taking notes at the 1975 meeting on patterns of speech in the United States mentioned above. Correspondence among members regularly features the use of the term "man" to refer to a generic colleague.

Interestingly, it was a woman trained as a syntactician, Robin Lakoff, who produced one of the most influential early works noting the need to take gender more seriously as a category of analysis. Her influential 1975 book, *Language and Woman's Place*, had a memorable cover image of a white woman with a Band-Aid over her mouth. Reflecting on her book nearly 30 years later, Lakoff (2004) notes that as a student of Chomsky's at MIT she could not help but be aware of his active stance in the anti-war movements, and it was hard as a student there to remain neutral about events in the larger world: the youth revolution against the Vietnam War and women's liberation born out of the civil rights and anti-war movements. However, she felt that the study of transformational linguistics did not offer enough information about mental states, desires, and personal identities to provide tools for such engagement. For her and others, the question was what parts of psychological and social reality required linguistic encoding.

Her book was also inspired by generative semantics, a critique of Chomskyan linguistics' marginalization of meaning as a legitimate area of enquiry. Lakoff wrote the book as a linguistics professor at the University of California, Berkeley. She had been recruited to share a joint position with her then-husband, George, as many early women academics were.

Lakoff's book drew largely on her linguistic intuitions (in Chomskyan tradition) and anecdotal observations to describe women's language as having three characteristics: a lack of resources for women to express themselves strongly, an encouragement of women to talk about trivial subjects, and a requirement that they speak tentatively. Lakoff argued that a female speaker faces a double bind. If she does not learn to speak like a lady, she will be criticized or ostracized. If she does learn to speak like a lady, she will be systematically denied access to power on the grounds that she is not capable of holding it (see McElhinny 2004 for a summary). Women's language was thus seen through the lens of deficit.

A number of Lakoff's students at Berkeley instituted a regularly recurring conference in the 1980s on Women and Language (later retitled Gender and Language) at which many young scholars, especially from the San Francisco Bay Area, first presented their work, and then published them in conference proceedings and later in edited collections (see, for example, Hall et al. 1992). Indeed, Bonnie's first academic publication was in such a proceeding. This institutionalization thus gave Lakoff's work a central place in defining a feminist linguistics agenda. However, Lakoff's work did not analyze the ways that ideologies of whiteness, heterosexuality, and class might be specifically linked to the linguistic behaviours she was describing.

Deborah Tannen, a student of both Lakoff and Gumperz, took up the difference hypothesis to address some of Lakoff's concerns in a 1990 best-seller entitled *You Just Don't Understand*. To do this she built on early work published in a book edited by Gumperz (Maltz and Borker 1982) explaining why, in her view, men and women, still implicitly heterosexual and overwhelmingly still white, so often seem to have problems communicating, arguing that men and women's communicative styles are like two different cultures.

Other feminist sociolinguists argued that a focus on cultural differences served to neutralize and mask relations of domination and resistance (Uchida 1992; we discuss below how a similar critique was addressed to Gumperz by anti-racist scholars). This strand of work was partly energized by the work of Judith Butler (1990), who, drawing on speech act theory, saw gender and sexuality as *performative*; it developed in the 1990s and 2000s into a robust field examining gender and sexuality as categories related to the harnessing of social difference to the making of social inequality, as well as to explorations of forms of gender and sexuality that critique the rigid binaries emerging from structural approaches (see Chapter 8). These critiques converged with others making similar arguments on the field of race.

Difference and Domination: Anti-Racist Critiques

In the late 1970s, the Nigerian-born, Berkeley-based anthropologist of education John Ogbu argued forcefully that cultural differences need to be understood as products, not causes, of inequality, and that educational success needed to be understood in the context of experience-based expectations that it will lead to employment—an experience not shared by African Americans and other structurally marginalized groups (Ogbu 1978). In addition, three critiques published in the late 1980s and early 1990s (Singh et al. 1988; Sarangi 1994; Kandiah 1991) re-analyzed some of the British data Gumperz had analyzed as miscommunication.

These critiques noted that the difference hypothesis abstracted out any sociological, structural dimensions of racism or sexism or class prejudice, placing too much emphasis on agency and on a notion of language as a neutrally structured system, rather than as a form of social action. They saw, in the increasing silence of failed job-seekers or frustrated welfare applicants in the key situations Gumperz analyzed, not the victims of innocent misunderstanding but the all-too-aware responses of racialized speakers recognizing that once again they would be denied access to resources by White (and almost always male) gatekeepers unwilling to see their petitioners as full human beings. Where Gumperz saw the remedy in education, his critics sought more systemic intervention into social, racial, and linguistic hierarchies, in the form of institutional incorporation of minoritized practices.

In the realm of variationist sociolinguistics, critiques emerged of the history and politics of the study of African American English. In a critical overview, Morgan (1994) notes a series of recurring debates—about what to call it; about whether AAE is a language or a dialect; who speaks it; what its linguistic origins are, including its relationship to other varieties of English, African languages, and other linguistic varieties in the African diaspora; the political conditions from which it arose; its features; the implications of its continued existence; and the role of African American activism in the scholarly representation of culture and language.

Morgan further argues that Labov's work, while key in challenging ideas that AAE represented impaired cognitive development and marked social pathology, also perpetuated both gender and racial stereotypes since he saw young men who participated in the street culture of inner cities as being the most "authentic" speakers of AAE (Morgan 1994, 328). All other members of the community were constructed as outsiders, or cultural misfits in some way, to the core speech community. African American women, in particular, were often characterized in negative ways—as linguistically conservative, aggressive, or domineering (Morgan 1994, 335). (Clearly, these speech practices were markedly different from those characterized by Lakoff.) Morgan points to the counterargument presented by the sociolinguist Claudia Mitchell-Kernan, whose earliest work in a Black community in California showed that gender differences did not exist there (Mitchell-Kernan 1971).[15] Morgan's own work pointed out that how to define class and status remains a challenging question for African American communities, since members have been denied access to the traditional indicators of housing, occupation, and employment (1994, 337).

Other African American and Afro-diasporic scholars trained at the University of Pennsylvania also extended but critiqued Labov's work (see Baugh 2000; Rickford 1999). Rickford (1993), for example, argued that understanding the unequal conditions of postplantation social relations was necessary for explaining linguistic variation in the Caribbean, thereby influentially extending the kinds of information about social context considered important to take into account.

In the 1980s and early 1990s a number of other African American, African, and Afro-diasporic scholars (e.g., Salikoko Mufwene 2000; Geneva Smitherman 2000; Arthur Spears 1999; Don Winford 2003; Kwesi Yankah 1998) took on problems of the relative position of African American English in both the U.S. English landscape and the international African diasporic one, shifting

---

15 Mitchell-Kernan's work was sharply criticized in a prominent journal by Thomas Kochman (1973); Kochman's review was full of innuendos about Mitchell-Kernan's class and gender, including dismissive comments about why an "attractive young Black woman" found men in the community willing to talk to her (Morgan 1994, 335). As a result, Mitchell-Kernan's work subsequently found less of an audience in both studies of African American English and in the feminist linguistic work around Berkeley than such ground-breaking and detailed work deserved, until Morgan and prominent literary scholars wrote her work back into the canon.

focus from difference to participation in global processes linked to imperialism and slavery. Thus the emergence of Afro-diasporic and African American scholars is linked to scholarship with an explicit interest in how the language spoken by African Americans should best be understood, and who is best placed to define it. The locus of expertise begins to shift, and the ground was laid for a wider apprehension of how language figures into the making of social difference and social inequality. Many African American writers and scholars believe that a number of (especially White) sociolinguists inscribe racist stereotypes of African American English by not considering, or underplaying, African language influences in ways that resonate with the late-nineteenth-century debates we saw in Chapter 3 (Morgan 1994, 33).

Pidgins, Creoles, and New Nationalisms

The broader frame used by these scholars linked interest in African American English to decolonization more broadly, notably through the resurgent interest in pidgin and creole studies, especially in the Caribbean, where they served as a field of struggle for new nationalist movements seeking to replace former languages of colonial power (English and French) with creoles. This process opened the way for contributions by scholars from former colonies, such as Beryl Loftman (later Bailey) in Jamaica, Richard Allsopp in Guyana (Holm 1988a, 45), and Lambert-Félix Prudent and Georges Mérida (1984) in Martinique.

The major conferences on creole languages were convened in sites that had had plantation economies. The first conference was convened in Jamaica in 1959 by Robert LePage (1961), an English linguist teaching at the University College of the West Indies, a site that he made the first centre for creole studies (see also Tabouret-Keller and LePage 1985). Debate continued to centre around whether to privilege European or African languages as sources, and whether to focus on social conditions or linguistic ones. Further influential conferences were held in Hawai'i and in Jamaica in the 1960s and 1970s. Holm (1988a, 60) notes that even as leadership for regular conferences on English Caribbean linguistics shifted from North American and British linguists to Anglophone West Indians, tensions remained within the organization between First and Third World scholars on questions about funding and access to publications and publishing.

We see the study of pidgins and creoles as making three key contributions to mainstream sociolinguistics. First, these studies moved sociolinguistics toward the legitimization of knowledge production from what were initially thought of as "developing countries." Second, these studies fostered a recognition that forms of language other than the standard languages that development theory assumed must be desirable might be taken seriously as authenticating national languages. National movements around them, and more generally movements for their recognition (e.g., as languages of literature and education), emerged, for example, in the Caribbean and the Indian Ocean (cf. Glissant 1990; Eisenlohr 2007; St-Hilaire 2009), although many such movements may also be fraught with struggle over who decides what counts as legitimate language.

Third, these languages, and scholarship on them, moved beyond the new nationalisms to which they were initially linked, and served as a means for critiquing class inequities and colonialism and for building solidarities among creole-speaking areas otherwise still oriented to their former metropoles, as well as potentially among other minoritized groups with stigmatized languages. For example, Rickford's (1993) analysis of the ideologies and practices of different members of a village on a former sugar plantation found that the ideas individuals had about the role of language in achieving occupational status were linked to their position within the community. Relatively more privileged community members saw the use of English as *contributing* to more prestigious status; they didn't call for any change in the social order, but just wanted to increase their access to the material and symbolic resources that guaranteed progress. Those less privileged, some of whom were explicitly Marxist, saw it as *reflecting* status, with the prestigious value of English being just another aspect of ruling-class ideology; for them, improvement of social conditions meant rebellion against the dominant social order. One community member articulates this perspective succinctly (note Rickford's choices in orthographic representation):

> Abee na waan dem Englishman teaching and ting da no mo, man. Dem ting da mus done. Yuh see, dem a write dem own book fuh suit dem own self, an awee mus larn from dem and *subdue* under dem! "We don't want the Englishman's teaching and so on any more, man. Those things must end. You see, they write their books to suit themselves, and we must learn from them and be *subdued* under them!" (emphasis in original; Rickford 1993, 14-150)

Taken together, feminist, anti-racist, and anti-colonial critiques of what rapidly became mainstream sociolinguistics in the United States of the 1970s point toward an opening up of the field, and a shift not only to theories of difference (over and against deficit theories) but into theories of dominance. In the next section we will turn to the complex relations of this field with the emergence of sociolinguistics in Europe, about a decade later than it took form in the United States. We will see that the different conditions there led to a greater focus on class and labour than on race, gender, and institutions, allowing—partly under the influence of the Communist Party among intellectuals in France and Catalunya—for another approach to problems of conflict and inequality.

The Rise of Sociolinguistics in Europe: Class and Conflict

If the United States dominated the development of sociolinguistics, there were also scholars in Western Europe equally interested in approaches that better addressed the issues of linguistic minority nationalism, reconstruction, labour migration and, perhaps to a lesser extent, decolonization that those countries were experiencing. While they shared with the U.S. the values of the welfare state, they drew on somewhat different intellectual traditions in which dialectology, philology, and text analysis played a major role. They experienced class as the major fault line in social organization, and class conflict as the major threat to a postwar social order; in some cases, especially in France, the left and its Marxist alliances were central, rather than marginalized or scapegoated, approaches.

The institutional bases of European dialectology and philology were preserved in the German- and Spanish-speaking areas, not incidentally the sites of key fascist regimes, where departments largely remained organized as philological faculties. This was not the case in France or in Britain, where linguistics (or the "language sciences" in France) emerged as a separate structure. Within those separate structures, the ground was laid for struggles with generative grammar that remain active today, although structuralism generally became the dominant mode of doing linguistics.

One major issue was the rise of linguistic minority movements, as had been the case in Québec and Acadie. In Britain, these issues tended to focus in particular on Wales; in France on Breton, Corsican, and Occitan; in Spain on Catalan and Basque. As we have seen, most work by francophone scholars in francophone Canada had been devoted to language planning and policy, followed by variationist students of Gillian Sankoff at the Université de Montréal working on linguistic description; the first were explicit, the second implicit, efforts to change the status of the language, standardize it, and legitimize its authentic vernacular. There were certainly parallels in Europe and, in fact, an active intellectual exchange among minority sociolinguists, especially between Catalunya and Québec. For instance, the Catalan sociolinguist Lluis Aracil (1941–) developed the notions of *normalization* (the spread of use of a minority language to all spheres of social life, along the lines of dominant nationalist ideas of uniformity) and *normativization* (development of a legitimate linguistic norm, or standard), which were to guide status and corpus planning in many areas, and strongly so in Québec (Aracil 1965, 1982).

Virtually all the attendees at the earliest meetings of sociolinguists in France in the late 1960s were Marxists (Duchene, Boutet pers. comm.), drawing on a Marxist tradition of attention to language as praxis, and language as work, as well as on the role of language in class struggles to challenge assimilatory approaches. As early as 1956, Marcel Cohen (1884–1974), a student of Antoine Meillet and a member of the Communist Party, had published a pioneering effort to conceptualize what he called "language work," combining Soviet activity theory's understanding of language as work with a typological approach to the social organization of professions. This produced a first approximation of what *language work*—that is, in which language is both the product and process of work—itself might look like (say, in translation, creative writing, or stenography), though it took another generation of scholars to pick up that thread.

The communist Robert Lafont (1923–2009), who had spent World War II in the French Resistance, together with Catalan colleagues developed the notion of a *sociolinguistics of conflict* (1971, 1997), daring to name and emphasize as central to sociolinguistic thinking the relations of power that sociolinguists in North America approached only indirectly. Lafont was an Occitanist, that is, a student of Occitan language and culture, as well as a political advocate for Occitan autonomy. The Corsican and communist Jean-Baptiste Marcellesi took a different tack, arguing that to adopt such standardizing procedures was to fall into the trap of the oppressive techniques of the centralized nation-state that linguistic minority movements were resisting (his work was mainly published in the 1970s and early 1980s, then collected in a 1989 publication). He offered instead the idea of *polynomia*, in which different variants (of Corsican in this case) would be recognized as legitimate. Of course, in many ways this simply multiplies the problem of which variant belongs to whom and under what circumstances, but the concept makes its point.

Lafont also founded the École de praxématique in Montpellier, which focussed on how speakers drew on linguistic resources to engage in social action. Marcellesi launched the journal *Cahiers de linguistique sociale* in 1976 and, with his colleague Bernard Gardin, coauthored the earliest monograph on sociolinguistics in French (1974). Their work, which laid the foundation for the École de Rouen, extensively explored the discourse of labour struggles and other sites of social conflict. This set of publications was followed a few years later by a volume written by three sociolinguists, including one who was based in the United States, which provided a summary of American thinking in the field (Bachmann, Lindenfeld, and Simonin 1981); this work introduced a more ethnographic and interactionist approach to French sociolinguistics, which was also influenced by ethnomethodology.

In the 1980s and 1990s, an interdisciplinary group of scholars launched a network on *Langage et travail*; among the work produced we can include

Gardin's attention to the language practices of union members and union meetings; Jacques Brès and Françoise Gardès-Madray's work on miners; and Josiane Boutet and colleagues' work on Électricité de France, the national electricity company, some of it collected in Lefèvre and Tournier (1987).

British sociolinguistics was also concerned with class as the central organizing principle of British society and of key concern in labour struggles as industrial capitalism came into crisis. In Britain, the dominant approach linked dialectology and variationist sociolinguistics. Peter Trudgill was a central figure in this process through his studies of the region of Norwich and the publication of a textbook in 1974. Addressing the problem of why working-class people keep talking the way they do, even if it is stigmatized, Trudgill hypothesized that there are two forms of *prestige*: *overt* and *covert*. Overt prestige, he argued, accrued to official, standard languages, but members of marginalized groups had their own investment in solidarity, so that even if they might recognize what the language of power was in the dominant areas of life, they accorded covert prestige to the varieties that were important in their lives in working-class communities. Lesley Milroy did parallel work on working-class communities in Northern Ireland, developing new methods for analyzing networks of communication, understood as an observable structural underpinning for solidarity (Milroy 1980).

While this distinction could be incorporated into liberal ideologies that saw certain behaviours as suitable for public and others for private space, a more radical interpretation would see covert prestige as a challenge to the more competitive, less accessible, and hierarchically oriented overly prestigious varieties. This approach to class thus suggests more attention to the dynamics and subjectivity of class-based inequality than work done following Labov in the United States.

Pierre Bourdieu (1930–2002) was also an influential contributor to European and international thinking about language as practice. He was the child of a postman who grew up in a dialect-speaking village in the Béarn region of France (Béarnais, a version of Gascon, is a Basque-influenced version of Occitan) (Wacquant 2006). He trained at the prestigious École normale supérieure before being conscripted into the French army to serve in Algeria. He chose not to enter the reserve officers' training corps, purportedly to stay with people of his own modest social background. He worked as a clerk and then stayed on as a lecturer in Algiers, conducting ethnographic research during the Algerian war on the Kabyle peoples.

Working in the area of education with his colleague Jean-Claude Passeron, Bourdieu took up the problem of class within a broader consideration of the role of higher education in France in reproducing not only class relations, but also gender difference (for instance, they ask why women tend to be found in the social sciences and the humanities, while men are found in the natural sciences), as well as inequalities between Paris and the provinces (Bourdieu and Passeron 1977). Their work more explicitly attached the shared linguistic preferences of middle-class (urban) families and educational institutions to what they called the role of schooling in masking, or mystifying, the processes of reproduction of class- and gender-based inequalities.

Bourdieu and Passeron argued that language was central precisely because it could be constructed as something anyone could learn, and so if a student failed to master valued practices it could be construed as a failure of the individual (or of his or her family or community), rather than a failure of the school. They understood this to index the function of the school as both social selection and its mystification, or masking, both centrally communicative processes. In this, they joined the burgeoning work on interactional sociolinguistics in Britain and the United States, though they had a greater interest in providing a structural account of why there was unequal distribution of access to institutional resources.

At the same time, American sociolinguists were invited to France, and Labov in particular set off a cycle of work in France on the language of youth as a site for understanding language change (Laks 1984). In the face of the domination of a variety of forms of structuralism, Bourdieu (1977) published a response to both Labov and Chomsky arguing that language needed to be understood not only as social practice; its forms could only be explained within a theory of symbolic and material exchange as it operates in concrete, historically contingent market conditions. Like the sociolinguistics of conflict, Bourdieu placed social relations of power at the centre of his concept of language, although Lafont attended more to political relations and Bourdieu to economic ones.

Most of these efforts, of course, had to imagine methods of enquiry adapted to urban milieux (see our discussion in Chapter 5 of how much of this work was prefigured by early Soviet sociolinguistics). For some, the answer lay in a focus on specific sites (such as workplaces) or activities (such as union meetings). Others focussed on the development of *urban sociolinguistics*, somewhat along the lines of Labov's notion of urban dialectology, and certainly within the same idea that the problems of the welfare state were urban problems. In many ways we have complementary myopias in an uncoupling of race and class: if in the United States "urban sociolinguistics" was linked to "race" (Chicanos and African Americans), in France and elsewhere in Europe it was approached as a conflation of class and new forms of labour migration, mainly from former colonies.

Indeed, labour migration and urban multilingualism became a key focus across Europe. The issue of management of multilingual workplaces formed the context for one of Germany's first large-scale sociolinguistic projects (Klein and Dittmar 1979). Another large-scale project, for which Gumperz acted as an advisor, was conducted in the 1980s in Mannheim (Kallmeyer 1994). Framed as urban dialectology, it included close attention to the local Turkish population. Such projects led to explorations of urban multilingual practices across Europe, especially among youth in working-class neighbourhoods (Pfaff 2010; Jørgensen 2008; Dirim and Auer 2004).

At the same time, French linguists in particular, perhaps more so than British, Spanish, Portuguese or Italian, continued to circulate widely in former colonies (less often, sociolinguists from the former colonies began to circulate in France). Calvet (1974) examined the workings of French colonialism on African multilingualism; Chaudenson (1979) examined the creoles of the Indian Ocean. Others took the description of multilingualism in former colonies as a way to contest the rigid monolingualism of the French state (Manessy and Wald 1979), joining the linguistic minority movements in that effort, albeit largely in vain. Further, the teaching of French both in former colonies and to the increasing numbers of non-French-speaking migrant children arriving in French schools formed a zone of encounter and of enquiry around what it meant to promote a dominant national language under these new postcolonial conditions.

Broadly, the particular issues that formed the nuclei of sociolinguistic work, though manifested somewhat differently in each major language area, nonetheless all sprang from the same general sets of welfare state, (post-)colonial concerns: the relationship between social, political, and economic inequality, and cultural and linguistic difference, in an era when democracy was supposed to fulfill its promises of emancipation and access to wealth.

The End of the *Trente Glorieuses*

The 30 years after the end of World War II (1945–75) are sometimes referred to in French as the *Trente Glorieuses*, the 30 glorious years when all seemed within reach, even the moon. The history of the "rise" of sociolinguistics is very much a history of the *Trente Glorieuses*, although we can see in them the beginnings of a crisis of failed promises of the welfare state and decolonization.

We have seen in this chapter how sociolinguistics developed in a context shaped by postwar efforts at development and reconstruction organized by major foundations. These foundations organized scholars on development projects in postcolonial states and then worked with them to apply their experience in domestic projects of social renewal and combatting discrimination and inequality. The focus on social improvement and social engineering, especially in the context of decolonization and self-determination, inevitably led to a backlash aimed at reaffirming the agency of those who were the objects of the social engineering projects. In the next chapter, we will explore the ways in which economic liberalization affected discussions of linguistic value and language work, as well as shaped questions about how to understand inequity in more intersectional terms.

CHAPTER 8

LANGUAGE IN LATE CAPITALISM: INTENSIFICATIONS, UNRULY DESIRES, AND ALTERNATIVE WORLDS

FIGURE 8.1: Nayaano-nibiimaang Gichigamiin (the Great Lakes) in Anishnaabewomin (Ojibwe). Version 2. Source: Charles Lippert and Jordan Engel. 2015. *The Decolonial Atlas: Re-imagining the World* (https://decolonialatlas.wordpress.com) (accessed 6 January 2017).

"Nayaano-nibiimaang Gichigamiin"

In Chapter 1, we pointed out that we write from a particular place, the watershed of what are called in English "the Great Lakes." This region has figured in the imperial and national histories we have described and has been called by a number of names, in a number of languages, both indigenous and imperial. How it is pictured, labelled, and talked about tells us a great deal about the interests that lie behind constructing the region, and water, trees, rocks, and settlements, as having particular meanings and values, which are organized in particular ways. Maps like this one orient how we understand the world. Recently, critical geographers have begun to ask how we might understand the world differently if we make new maps. The figure we open this chapter with is the work of two such mapmakers, Charles Lippert and Jordan Engel, contributors to *The Decolonial Atlas: Re-imagining the World* (https://decolonialatlas.wordpress.com). Published in 2015, this map does several things. First, as Lippert and Engel point out,

> A note on the compass—The Anishinaabe traditionally orient themselves to the East, which is why East appears at the top of this map. Because the standard orientation is different in European and Anishinaabe cultures, we've included the English word "North" and the Anishinaabemowin word "Waabang," meaning East, on the compass. The compass rose itself is in the form of a medicine wheel, an indigenous symbol used across the continent to denote the four directions.

The map thus physically reorients us from the map we are used to, in which north is up and west is centred.

Second, the map centres the lakes ("The Five Freshwater Seas") as physical geographical features; it allows the lakes an integrity currently broken by the political border between the United States and Canada. Finally, it uses Ojibwe names for places meaningful to the Ojibwe people whose territories include these lakes. Some of these names index key plants and animals (beaver, blueberries, caribou). Some describe recognizable features (long rapids, four lakes, waterfalls) or how people use them (harbour, portage). Still others link them to collective names for groups of people (Iroquois, Ojibwe).

This map asks us, then, to think about this place in different frames, to, as the site says, "re-imagine" the world. It requires new ways of thinking about time, about place, and about personhood. This map evokes a time when Europeans were not present, or a form of Indigenous futurity when European modes of social organization no longer prevail. It invites us to gather up inherited knowledge resources to rethink the present and the future, reorienting us physically, politically, economically, and cognitively, in order to help us inhabit the world differently. It allows us to think about who and what is erased in the worlds we inhabit and seek to create. It makes no claims to represent a better world and, of course, this map itself is a representational choice as a map and makes choices among other available map representations.[1]

Why are such alternative worlds appearing now? Why are the very languages that were disciplined and punished not long ago being reclaimed and remapped? How are people responding to these and other initiatives? This chapter considers the political economic changes at the moment that help account for the kinds of phenomena the map represent, and that situate us at a moment of intense social change in which language plays a particularly important role.

We argue that the conditions of late capitalism intensify and extend the ways in which capitalism operates to produce profit around the globe, especially as the alternative regimes of communism faltered and shifted in the 1990s. These processes move certain legitimizing discourses that were previously on the terrains of the cultural and political to the economic. They destabilize national and neocolonial regimes, with their bounded, separated, and ranked hierarchies of language, culture, race, gender, and class, opening up possibilities for the cosmopolitan elites who profit from them; conservative responses from those who fear losing out (or have already lost out) from political economic change; and cracks that permit reimaginings intended to reduce the increased wealth gaps that late capitalism produces.

In many cases, the processes that draw our attention come in the form of boundary-crossing, as people compete over newly valuable linguistic resources and make solidarities across new structures of power (both for and against). At the same time, that boundary-crossing triggers a pushback in the form of renewed insistence on old boundaries and old relations of inequality. The blurring of gendered, racialized, and linguistic boundaries sits in tension with a long series of heightened forms of violence, still racialized and gendered.

---

1 When they gave us permission to use the image, the mapmakers asked us to share their comments describing some of the choices they made in making this map. They relied on written as well as oral sources, drawing on phonetic transcriptions in old journals, maps, and books, as well as on contacts familiar with names used earlier in the twentieth century. As their area's Anishinaabe population was mainly Potawatomi and Odawa, the words reflected on the map are sourced from those groups' vocabulary, but the map uses Fiero-Nichols orthography, which does not reflect vowel syncope. The website page accompanying the map includes four types of names: pre–BlackHawk Wars names, post–BlackHawk Wars names, general naming patterns (independent of time), and pun-based names. Finally, the map shows only about half of Chicagoland's Anishinaabemowin toponyms; the accompanying page also contains a note mentioning plans for future maps that will cover the toponyms left off this version (Charles Lippert, pers. comm., January 22, 2017). Other Ojibwe speakers call the same lake chi'niblish (Simpson 2015:126).

In the next section we briefly review the conditions of late capitalism that we want to attend to, focussing on the intensification and extension of capitalism that we began experiencing, arguably, in the 1970s and 1980s, in order for us to consider how language is connected to changing understandings of space, time, and humanity. We then examine the ways in which changing regimes of value in late capitalism are linked to discussions of value in linguistic anthropology, especially in critical discourse analysis and studies of language ideology. We consider some of the ways in which eligibility for citizenship, ever more closely linked to labour, is linked to forms of language that are rendered measurable and to selves that are constructed as bundles of skills or as performances. We will discuss how authenticity and real emotion, or affect, become more and more valuable, as more and more things are understood as commodities (manifested, for example, in debates around who is a native speaker, in service industries like call centres, and in discussions of branding). "Authenticity," however, can shade into nativism, nationalism, and racism as ways of speaking are inalienably attached to certain kinds of bodies, and as certain kinds of bodies are always seen as speaking in a deficient way, measured against an ever-retreating measure of appropriateness. As always throughout history, dystopias, utopias, and pragmatic approaches jostle for position.

We will end with the role of language in contemporary social actions that inspire us to imagine alternative worlds. We consider how ideas of the commons challenge notions of commodities. We consider strategies for redress for racialized and colonial harms, as well as strategies for reclamation and refusal. Finally, we consider new forms of sovereignty, solidarity, and social movements.

Late Capitalism: The Expanding Reach of the Market and the Neoliberal State

In the last chapter, we described the institutionalization of Western sociolinguistics in the era of the Cold War welfare state, ending with the economic and political shifts in the 1970s and 1980s. The Fordist regime of mass production of standardized products in Western economies had become so successful and efficient that it began to overproduce, leading to the layoff of workers and a reduced demand for products (Harvey 1989); rising unemployment was accompanied by accelerating inflation (Harvey 2005, 14). Both liberal democratic nation-states and communist ones were unable to successfully distribute resources and regulate capitalism. These are the conditions underlying what we think of as *late capitalism*, although "late" implies an imminent shift to something other than capitalism. We accept it as a way of talking about a number of phenomena.

One is the growth of finance capitalism, that is, an increasing decoupling of money from direct exchange for material goods or services that characterizes industrial capitalism, and a move to speculative forms of assessing value, with the concomitant growth of communication-heavy financial industries. Speculative forms of capitalism are generally seen as emerging regularly in world history as markets become saturated and profits level off. The key techniques for dealing with these problems can be understood as both extension and intensification (Harvey 1989, 2000). Companies engage in

- searches for new markets for products;
- trying to sell products at a lower price than competitors, which usually means finding cheaper sources of materials and labour;
- creating new kinds of customers and new kinds of desires;
- specializing in specific products for specific groups (*niche* products for *niche* markets); and
- justifying higher prices through *adding value* in some way to products.

These processes required liberation from the constraints of nation-state markets, triggering what is usually thought of as *globalization* and *neoliberalism* (Allan and McElhinny 2017). *Globalization* marks the international flows of people, products, information, services, and capital that embody the extension and specialization of networks of production, circulation, and consumption. There is some debate about whether global flows have in fact increased in recent years—certainly, we have seen significant global flows since the late fifteenth century in this book—but it is likely that the *scale*, *velocity*, and *penetration* of global capital have grown significantly (Appadurai 2001, 18), in ways that may change our experiences of space and time as compressed and accelerated (Harvey 1989).

Neoliberalism captures the legitimizing discourses connected to the dismantling of the welfare state, as well as the regulation of national markets required for such forms of globalization. In the Global North, governments privatized public enterprises, reduced taxes, broke labour unions, encouraged entrepreneurial initiative, and induced a strong inflow of foreign investment. At the same time, socialism was also "rolled back." In China, economic reforms described as "socialism with Chinese characteristics" (Harvey 2005; Yang 2007) wedded neoliberal and Keynesian economic policies, centralized state planning, and authoritarian rule. Countries in the former Soviet bloc undertook market reforms. In the Global South, international bodies such as the International Monetary Fund and the World Bank enforced free market fundamentalism in return for loans in a process called *structural adjustment*.

Many companies from the Global North, encouraged by deregulation and tax breaks for investment, went "offshore" or got "delocalized" or "outsourced," meaning that they closed down workplaces in the Global North, especially those involved in industrial manufacturing, and opened them in Asia, Africa, and Latin America. A post-Fordist regime of flexible accumulation has emerged in place of industrial mass production, allowing companies to respond rapidly to intensified cycles of competition and shifts in conditions of production and consumption through developing flexible labour processes and production arrangements, as well as consumption focussed on niche markets, all of which have transnational implications.

While rapidly increasing the wealth accumulation of a small minority, 'flexibility' resulted in increased uncertainty for most people, as a result of lower wages, job insecurity, increased labour migration, and disappearance of support services. It also led to poverty and crime. All these combined to heighten fear and anxiety: Italian anarchist and critical communication scholar "Bifo" Berardi (2011) argues that this is a moment of exceptionally deep despair. Scholars writing from or about a few key sites hit by the 2008 economic crisis note an extraordinary rise in sentiments of linguistic anxiety in particular, in a scramble for access to any or all linguistic resources available in a world that experiences scattered hegemonies (Grewal and Kaplan 1994) and where it is not clear which skills will allow one to succeed (Park 2011; Park and Lo 2012; Wee 2008).

Means of measuring productivity and efficiency also intensified in the form of new accounting and audit procedures extended from industrial practices (Strathern 2000; Urciuoli and LaDousa 2013). Audit cultures focus on "economic efficiency" as well as "good practice." External control and loss of local autonomy are also associated with responsibility, transparency, and increasing access. *Audit* and *accountability* thus tie financial processes to moral claims (Strathern 2000, 1). These technical approaches, like others we have seen, deflect critique, leading to debates on how to refine the measurement of linguistic skills rather than debates on whether measurement, or the focus on linguistic skills, is the most appropriate site for addressing questions about equitable access to work or citizenship (Bell 2013; McNamara 2009). We can see evidence of hegemony in that even those who may be placed at a disadvantage by these forms of measurement see them as fair (Shohamy 2009).

Proponents of neoliberalism not only had to transform divisions of labour, welfare provisions, and reproductive and audit activities, they also had to change what Harvey calls "habits of the heart" (2005, 3). Neoliberalism thus is also a set of legitimizing discourses that allows late capitalism to make sense to people and that helps orient their habitus in ways better suited to the new conditions. Harvey argues that neoliberalism also responds to these feelings by building on the liberal premise of individual freedom, interpellating individuals as entrepreneurial actors in every sphere of life (2005, 2).

This is at odds with other changes at the structural level, including increases in state attention to incarceration, surveillance, and a range of microregulatory interventions, both within states and across borders, some of them involving appeals to the expertise of linguists and anthropologists (Wacquant 2012). Certain categories of people are generally singled out for particular surveillance; in Canada and the United States, Black and Indigenous people are disproportionately incarcerated and are much more regularly portrayed as prone to violent or terrorist action, in ways that help legitimatize state violence (Crenshaw and Ritchie 2015; Nichols 2014; Taylor 2016). Immigrants and refugees are often also targeted. Thus one way in which language is involved in contemporary shifts lies in the making of new hegemonic discourses to rationalize these practices.

Language is involved in still more ways in what Gee, Hull, and Lankshear (1996) call "the new work order." Indeed, since work is the central target of late capitalist reorganization, more linguistic anthropologists are investigating work than at any time since the Marxist European sociolinguistics earlier in the twentieth century. The extended and intensified extraction of primary resources, still key to the world economy, receive significant pushback from wide-ranging coalitions of people, often built through social media, which leads to public relations spin by companies and governments (Klein 2014). In both the primary and the secondary sector (industry), manual labour is increasingly mediated by computers, requiring greater language skills on the part of (fewer) workers linked into more extended networks of production, requiring new, linguistically mediated forms of management—some of them involving the management of multilingualism or other forms of linguistic variability (Heller and Duchêne 2012).

The tertiary sector of work in knowledge, communication, and service has become increasingly important, especially in the Global North, involving language as both process and product of work. In contrast to the suppression of communication in industrial workplaces (Boutet 2012), contemporary workplaces are built on communication; the *workforce* has become the *wordforce* (Heller 2010b). Language is involved as information and knowledge; it is also involved as a means of making and addressing niche markets defined by linguistic difference, and making niche products in which language adds symbolic, and therefore monetary, value. Language becomes inscribed as a potentially commodifiable, ideally flexible resource, increasing the importance of a wide range of linguistic forms and practices across multiple markets. It underlies what we can think of as the *language industries* (Heller 2010b), where language becomes a product. Even interactions that might once have been understood as leisure, or work-breaks, are seen as having an economic potential that has yet to be be tapped; McElhinny (2012, 230) cites a business publication in which two analysts encouraged managers to find ways to mine the grapevine and water-cooler conversations for the productive insights they might yield, since "conversations are as much a core business process as marketing, distribution, or product-development."

In addition, multilingualism in important market languages, understood as the standardized forms of former imperial nation-state languages, is a signature of the cosmopolitan elite whose members compete for access (especially for their children) to Mandarin, English, Spanish, and French (and perhaps also Russian and Portuguese). Language education becomes an important language industry, as do new attempts at making translation more efficient. Here the old tension between language as skill and language as soul takes on new dimensions, as we argue about what constitutes a good translation or language lesson, and whether you need a 'native speaker' to provide one. The same is true at the other end of the class hierarchy, as service workers are expected to provide multilingual (or other linguistically variable) services for little pay and no security (for instance, Duchêne 2011 documents the ways baggage handlers in a Swiss airport are called up to service counters to provide linguistic assistance). Similarly, while some educators focus on providing ever more individualized educational experiences for those who can afford them, those who cannot find themselves in educational regimes that are ever more regimented by fixed curricula and forms of audit.

People react in a variety of ways to the changes they experience. One way is a renewed attachment to the structures (and structures of feeling) of empire and nation. In the Global North, we see intensified anti-immigrant and nativist sentiments, explicit calls for White nationalism/supremacy, and a return to the glory days of nation (as in Britain's 2016 vote to leave the European Union) or of empire (as is evident in Donald Trump's election slogan "Make America Great Again"). However, we also see states subject to structural adjustment seek alternatives (as in Greece, for example; see Canale 2015; Theodossopoulos 2014), and new (or renewed) attempts to reimagine economic modes of existence that reduce, rather than enhance, precarity and inequality (Gibson Graham 2006). Language is used to navigate the boundaries that are made even stronger by conservative pushback, embracing the possibilities of a democratic cosmopolitanism, of a plural, polycentric world. It is possibly this phenomenon that has captured the most attention in linguistic anthropology and sociolinguistics as the discipline tries to build on its commitment to social justice, but also, crucially, because the explanation of linguistic variability lies at the heart of the discipline's very existence.

Such searches are also evident among grassroots movements seeking alternative forms of solidarity independent of state boundaries, such as those underlying environmentalist movements, as well as the (often connected) global movements for Indigenous rights. Alternative visions manifest themselves through debates over keywords, as in the debate about the meaning of "alt-right" we discussed in Chapter 1, the use of the term "terror" (Hodges and Nilep 2007), or as in struggles over whether to understand Indigenous people protecting their land against extraction as *water protectors* or *terrorists*. These are all debates about value, and about how what we know is linked to where we stand.

Language, Inequality, and Ideology

Building on the call in the late 1970s and 1980s to further understand how *legitimation* of inequity occurs, critical discourse analysis and postcolonial sociolinguistics through the 1990s built on work by Foucault, Gramsci, Said, Vološinov, and Williams to understand the role that discourse and ideology play. *Critical discourse analysis* (CDA), building on European philological traditions of text analysis, emerged in Western Europe; scholars in the United States developed the idea of *linguistic ideologies*. We will discuss these in turn.

Slembrouck (2001) notes that the British strand of work in CDA (notably by Norman Fairclough, 1989, 1992) arose during the Thatcher years in the UK, as the role of unions was challenged, citizens were increasingly understood as consumers, and the forms of health, education, and social welfare elaborated under the Keynesian welfare state were being reconfigured and cut. Work in the Netherlands, notably by Teun van Dijk (1991), and in Austria, notably by Ruth Wodak (1996), arose out of a context in which the destabilizations of late capitalism were also expressed in the form of racism, including a resurgence of what many had hoped were largely discredited expressions of fascism. As a Jewish survivor of the Holocaust (her family fled to Britain and returned to Vienna after the war) and a student of the German political philosopher Jürgen Habermas, Wodak has been especially attuned to discursive manifestations of racism and to seeking modes of democratic existence (see, for example, Wodak and Richardson 2013).

These scholars combined techniques from the Frankfurt school of critical media analysis, the anti-Chomskyan systemic-functional and social-semiotic approach of Michael Halliday (1973), 1970s' work in critical linguistics at the University of East Anglia (Kress and Hodge 1979; Fowler 1979), and the Birmingham School of Cultural Studies, especially the anti-racist critiques of media and analyses of hegemony of Jamaican-born, British-based Stuart Hall (1971), to develop an approach that would reveal the processes of legitimation of neoliberalism in the discourses of various arms of the state and media. The approach was institutionalized through journals (the flagship journal, *Discourse & Society*, was founded in 1990; other journals were founded later, notably *Language and Politics* in 2001).

As in the analyses of Harris and Chomsky that we saw earlier, this body of work tends to assume that discourse obscures power, and that rational analysis, especially from experts, can help illuminate how power works and thus challenge it. CDA sought to go beyond formalist or descriptive analysis to show how social arrangements are historically conditioned outcomes that are the result of struggle (Slembrouck 2001, 36). This approach also openly and explicitly argued that linguistic analyses should be coupled to challenges to inequitable practices; the work aimed to be both explanatory and emancipatory (Slembrouck 2001, 35).

The critical assessments of CDA note that the approach requires a closely focussed analysis of texts and their circulation, without attention to the material, institutional contexts in which they are produced; history and social context are assumed, or sketched in rather broad terms (Blommaert and Bulcaen 2000; Blommaert et al. 2001; Heller and Pujolar 2009). This work has also been critized for collapsing signification and significance, that is, assuming that the expert's analysis of the text is shared by other readers or viewers (Widdowson 1995). However, at that time CDA also offered a well-formed body of social critique, whereas work in interactional sociolinguistics, conversation analysis, and ethnography of communication often did not adopt such a lens (Bucholtz 2001; Rampton 2001).

At the same time, but with little in the way of dialogue, U.S.-based linguistic anthropologists began producing a significant body of work on *language ideologies*, defined as "beliefs, feelings, and conceptions about language, structure and use, which often index the political economic interests of individual speakers, ethnic and other interest groups, and nation-states" (Kroskrity 2010, 192). It is possible to understand the U.S. interest in ideology as shaped by a Reagan administration that was undertaking reforms similar to, and in concert with, those introduced in Thatcher's Britain; many American linguistic anthropologists were working in sites affected by welfare state reforms and structural adjustment. However, the approach is most often framed in terms of intellectual history despite the fact that it challenges a distinction between expert and lay analysis, and asks analysts to identify their own positions, histories, and ideologies.

Certain authoritative accounts (cf. Kroskrity 2010) also focus on U.S.-based scholars, including the key figures of Roman Jakobson, Dell Hymes, William Labov, and Michael Silverstein (we have met the first three; Silverstein [1945–] is a professor at the University of Chicago who studied at Harvard under Jakobson). The European work we have described was largely set aside, although by the turn of the millennium U.S.-based scholars began to attend to European scholarship that seemed to offer tools for engagement with social theory and politics (e.g., Collins 2001), while European-based scholars began to attend to the ways in which linguistic anthropology offered richer tools for analyses of process and context (Rampton 2001; Slembrouck 2001), leading, among other developments, to Rampton's delimitation of a UK-based approach that he called *linguistic ethnography*—a term first evoked by the scholars we met in Chapter 7, meeting under the auspices of the Committee on Sociolinguistics (Rampton et al. 2007).

Virtually all the scholars who published in the volumes often seen as central to U.S. discussions on language ideologies were White (the single exception is Rachelle Doucet, a Haitian scholar who is second author on a paper with Bambi Schieffelin, her graduate supervisor; Schieffelin and Doucet 1998), though there were key questions about race and racialization in these volumes (Collins 1999 on Ebonics; Kroskrity 1998, 2000 on Tewa, a Native American nation; Hill 1998 on Mexicano; Briggs 1998 on Warao). At the same time, in parallel venues, scholars of colour were producing key works on ideologies and linguistic racism. These include Ana Celia Zentella's (1997) repeated calls for a sociopolitical linguistics (for a profile see Figueroa 2016), as well as the analysis of Ebonics debates, discourse, and discrimination by John Baugh (2000), John Rickford and Russell Rickford (2000), Geneva Smitherman (2000), and Arthur Spears (1999). Only a very few of these works focussed on gender and sexuality (see Briggs 1998; Hill 1998); that work took place, instead, in other key volumes published at about the same time (cf. Cameron 1992; Hall and Bucholtz 1995; Hendricks and Oliver 1999; Mills 1995; Morgan 2002). These feminist and anti-racist works are thus positioned to the side of this genealogy of work on linguistic ideologies.

Several recent works have noted the need to go beyond a focus on language ideologies. This includes work by Marxist sociolinguists, many of them based in areas of the Western European periphery (such as Ireland and Spain) that were particularly hard hit by the 2008 economic crisis, who argue for a more markedly economically determinist account than what we offer here (Block, Gray, and Holborow 2012; Holborow 2015; McGill 2013). Scholars working in areas affected by the 2008 Asian financial crisis have turned their attention to the meaning of precarity and anxiety (Bae 2014; Gao and Park 2015; Hiramoto and Park 2014; Jang 2015b). In the United States, a cluster of works argues that we need to re-examine what we mean by "materiality" (Shankar and Cavanaugh 2012), though the frequent continued erasure of problems of power, and specifically of earlier Marxist works on that theme, may provide evidence of the intellectual legacies of the Cold War in the U.S.

At the same time, ethnographic explorations of the shifting value of language are increasingly leading to renewed attempts to link sociolinguistic theory to political economy. We see this in explorations of the role of language in a number of domains, from citizenship and labour migration to commodification and popular culture. We turn to these explorations in the following sections.

Managing Your Assets: Language Quality, Linguistic Diversity, and Citizenship

The multilingual and multicultural policies that were developed in part to support postwar labour migration have given way to an increased focus in the Global North on *integration* (Hogan-Brun et al. 2009). This can be seen as a reaction to economic precarity as well as to increased claims to citizenship of family members of workers recruited earlier, to continuing migration from sites of European colonization, to migration from Eastern Europe with the fall of the Iron Curtain and the expansion of the European Union, to migration away from war and poverty in the Middle East, the Near East, and Africa, and to anti-Islamic sentiment engendered by acts of terrorism and the War on Terror. Immigrants and prospective citizens are increasingly asked to take language tests as well as tests of knowledge about the country they want to enter.

Language testing is not a new strategy for maintaining borders. In 1897, the Colonial Office in the UK convened premiers of its many dominions (from Canada to Tasmania to Natal) to discuss "certain Imperial questions." Some of the leaders represented areas then considering restriction of movement of those they called the "coloured races." The Colonial Office was concerned such legislation might provoke nationalist anger in other parts of the Empire, especially in India. Thus, while supporting the colonies' rights to protect labour and White society, they suggested they "arrange a form of words which will avoid hurting the feelings of any of Her Majesty's subjects" (cited in Buck and Frew 2010, 27).

It was thus that language became the grounds for exclusion. Some regions of what are now Australia and New Zealand adopted legislation that required people to be able to write, upon dictation, 50 words of a European language. The language and the passage were at the officer's discretion; occasionally Welsh was used, or particularly difficult English passages, to ensure it would be possible to bar Asian polyglots from entrance.[2] Such legislation shaped migration policy in a number of polities for another 70 years.

In many ways, less overt, but related, practices only increased after World War II; after European and North American inaction in the face of Jews requesting asylum from Nazi persecution, it was no longer possible to simply say, as Canadian officials once did, "none is too many" (Abella and Troper 1982). Instead, 'neutral' language testing provides a seemingly objective way to

---

2 One customs officer administering the test as late as 1950 used the following text: "the harassed pedlar met the embarrassed cobbler in the cemetery gauging the symmetry of a lady's ankle in unparalleled ecstasy" (Dutton 2002, cited in Buck and Frew 2010, 28).

ensure state control over citizenship; language-based forms of measurement, and the language ideologies that underlie them, are now widely used to judge new claimants to citizenship, elementary school students, and all workers in some sectors (see, for example, Jang 2015a; Park 2011), as well as refugee claims (Maryns 2006; Patrick 2016).

More broadly, we see a greater state focus on linking language to employment as the key to citizens' and migrants' integration (Piller and Takahashi 2011; Harris et al. 2002), as well as to ensuring loyalty. This results in policies aimed at compulsory language instruction, whether provided directly by the state or more often contracted out to NGOs or charitable institutions (Allan 2014; Codó and Garrido 2014; Pujolar 2007). Increasingly, states that previously subsidized language learning now require immigrants to pay for these tests, or require demonstration of proficiency prior to immigration, feeding the transnational language education industry as well as the domestic one (Yeung and Flubacher 2016). The tests chosen, and the immigrants who are required to take them, create zones of exception that often construct racialized hierarchies of citizenship.

The legitimacy of language testing regimes for immigrants and labour migrants is signalled through the professionalization of language testing and concomitant institutionalization of quality control. For instance, the Association of Language Testers in Europe (ALTE) was established in 1989 by the Universities of Cambridge and Salamanca. On their website, they present their quality control procedure:

> The ALTE Q-mark is a new *quality indicator* which member organisations can use to show that their exams have passed a *rigorous audit* and meet all 17 of ALTE's *quality standards*. The Q-mark allows test users to be confident that an exam is backed by appropriate processes, criteria and standard. (http://www.alte.org/setting_standards, accessed May 5, 2015; emphasis added)

Professionalization also facilitates the imbrication of standardized language testing more broadly into neoliberal audit culture: the words in italics index elements of that discourse.

Such testing regimes have an impact not only on countries that receive large numbers of immigrants, but also on countries that send migrants, especially those for whom export of labour is a key economic element. In the Philippines, the implementation of structural adjustment policies in the 1980s led to labour-exportation policies that capitalized on the English language and health-related skills developed during the American colonial period and after. The state focussed on nurses, midwives, and live-in caregivers (England

and Stiell 1997; Lorente 2007). Increasingly, however, as caregivers from other countries learn English, Filipinas are also required to both provide evidence of their English proficiency and learn other languages. Lorente (2012) describes how, in 2007, a government agency in the Philippines founded a new Language Skills Institute to train Filipino workers in such languages as English, Spanish, Mandarin, Japanese, Korean, Italian, and Russian. Overseas workers would henceforth be known as Pinoy Workers of the World (Pinoy WOW).

At the same time, seemingly paradoxically, governments, universities, corporations, and NGOs all tout the value of diversity. Diversity often invokes a discourse of benign variation that bypasses power, history, and economy to suggest a harmonious pluralism, an invocation of difference without a commitment to action or social justice (Ahmed 2012). Diversity tends to focus on "colour" (popular images are boxes with crayons of every colour or many-coloured hands in a circle) as a way of flagging cultural/racialized difference, but it also includes linguistic diversity. Some sociolinguistic theories adopt diversity as an analytic, highlighting, or branding, its salience by hailing it as a new phenomenon, and pointing in particular to linguistic diversity as a challenge to prevailing ideas about language as a whole, bounded object. These works use a variety of terms, including *metrolingual*, *translingual*, *transidiomatic*, *superdiverse*, *hyperdiverse*, *post-multilingual*, *post-national*, *polycentric*, *pluricentric*, *polylingual*, and *polynomic* (see Pennycook 2016 for a review). Much of this work sees this approach as emancipatory, revaluing linguistic practices that a nation-state frame has tended to label deviant and deficient, though occasionally it is overly celebratory in ways that are inattentive to material inequities.

However, the three key strategies used to manage diversity in organizations or polities tend to retain the idea of language as bounded object. These strategies are (1) multilingualism, (2) use of a lingua franca, or (3) linguistic translation (either with people or with technology). The first depends on either including a range of people each speaking a different language or requiring individuals to speak many languages. However, not all languages are equally valued: for example, citizens of the European Union are expected to build repertoires consisting of European standardized national languages, not Wolof, not Arabic, not Punjabi, and probably not Basque or Franco-Provençal either (van Avermaet 2009). Indeed, it is often expected that immigrants should learn a national language first and should be "protected" from the expectations of acquiring the elite forms of multilingualism for which middle-class citizens compete.

A second strategy for the management of diversity is, conversely, the adoption of a single lingua franca. While in some quarters this has led to a renewal of interest in Esperanto, the most frequently debated question in the literature on language and globalization is how to understand the effects of cultural and linguistic imperialism, especially of English (Canagarajah 1999; Phillipson

2008), which is increasingly promoted as natural, neutral, and technical (Singh and Han 2008). Many countries report education in English at ever younger levels (Lin and Martin 2005). So-called first circle countries (Kachru 1991; these are Britain, Canada, Australia, New Zealand, and the United States) have developed a wide variety of forms of English teaching, both bringing learners (and spenders) to their countries and exporting the product around the world. "Second tier" purveyors of English-as-capital (Jang 2016), notably Singapore, Hong Kong, and the Philippines, are also important sites for the development of the English-teaching industry.

Thus, transnational *educational migration* has also "become an important strategy for acquiring valuable linguistic resources in the globalized neoliberal economy" (Hiramoto and Park 2014, 146). Middle-class Korean families in particular aim to advantageously position their children through *jogi yuhak* [early study abroad] (Bae 2014). Another strategy for learning English is recruiting domestics who are fluent in English to provide early childhood socialization (cf. employers of Filipinas in Taiwan and Singapore; Lan 2003; Lorente 2007).

However, it is not enough for people to speak or write what their teachers argue is "good English"; the evaluation of their competence must be turned into convertible currency, recognized as valuable in the markets that use it. This is another site where standardized proficiency tests, the most widely used of which are produced, not coincidentally, in England and the United States, are important. Such certification (often expensive to obtain) both supports the language industry and helps make learners' linguistic capital convertible, while at the same time allowing for regulation of access to the English-language market and to the resource of English. What counts as good English keeps changing, however. So many now do well on standardized written tests in South Korea that students need to seek other markers of distinction in spoken language (Jang 2015a, 2015b). Even where speakers command the same varieties, different speakers will be assessed differently (Bonilla and Rosa 2015).

A third major strategy for the management of diversity offers the promise of transparent transformation of one language into another through seamless technology. Google Translate is a well-known attempt to provide machine-mediated translations (so much cheaper than paying interpreters!), although there are also increasing numbers of translation "hotline" services that aim to centralize translation and interpretation, allowing employers to avoid the need for hiring multilingual speakers. The City of Toronto, for example, relies on a phone service based in Monterey, California, which is not coincidentally linked to the military language learning facility there, and which translates more than 100 languages to any caller who has questions about city services (Good 2009).

All these strategies not only produce specific forms of work, they also produce specific forms of workers, and shift language increasingly into the economic realm. In the next section, we will examine the consequences of the idea of flexibility in late capitalism and changing notions of language for notions of personhood.

Brave New Selves: "I Am a Business, Man!"

Neoliberalism requires changes in personhood from a version where your work is a portion of your life to understanding your entire being as a business—a Me, Inc. (Gershon 2011). The artist Jay Z was recently quoted as saying, "I am not a businessman, I am a business, man!" (see Allan and McElhinny 2017). Jay Z clearly has successfully made the change.

"Skills and Selves in the New Workplace" is the title of an influential paper by Bonnie Urciuoli (2008), which argues that language socialization, and socialization through language, increasingly aims at producing the *flexible worker*, imagined as "a bundle of skills" valued on the labour market. Two kinds of skills are involved. *Hard skills* are the skills (like engineering, or accounting, or knowledge of anatomy) that are seen as critical to the job. Certified knowledge of standard languages is sometimes seen as a hard skill, viewed as enhancing one's competitiveness and economic value in the global economy (Wee 2008). *Soft skills* can be understood as an ability to fit in, dismissing Bourdieu's idea of habitus as a durable orientation deeply internalized through socialization, and replacing it with the idea of a teachable, learnable, flexible technique of the self.

This skilling of the self is linked to the expansion of the tertiary sector, in which communicative skills in particular play a central role. Flexible workers deal with a wide range of clients, and so must have not only broadened spoken repertoires, but also a wide variety of forms of literacy. The language skills that once were the province of the elite are now understood to be basic requirements for employment (Duchêne 2011; Gee et al. 1996). But both hard and soft skills are class-differentiated, soft skills especially so: for middle-class workers skills may lie in the styles of interaction they use to fit into corporate culture (Martin 1994); for the under- or unemployed they may lie in the interaction styles necessary to proving they merit the benefits of the "workfare" regimes that have often replaced welfare. Putative lack of skills, rather than structural conditions for their marginalization, can then be used to blame workers.

Of course, in many ways this phenomenon is not entirely new. Secretaries and stenographers provided language skills related to both literacy and multilingualism for their employers, and telephone and telegraph operators built the foundations for the later call-centre industry (Heller 2011; Hughes 1943; Inoue 2011). Translators, interpreters, and scribes have been providing crucial services for millennia. What is new, we argue, is that these processes are not only intensified by competition, but the elements of linguistic form and linguistic practice that compose them are increasingly amenable to being treated as commodities, that is, as resources available for exchange and measurable (perhaps with difficulty) in terms of money. Certified knowledge of a language may be worth the same annual bonus or hourly wage component as other forms of certified skill acquisition (Roy 2003). They may be increasingly detachable from certain bodies or more easily circulated. This reorients our understanding of what and who we understand ourselves to be.

This process is manifested equally in shifts in discourses regarding the identities of collectivities. From organic bodies with political rights, they may be reconstructed as collective "bundles of skills" and therefore as "added value." Monica witnessed this transformation in her fieldwork in the 1990s. Canadian federal language policy changed programs aimed at the "preservation of minority language and culture" into programs aimed at helping official language minority communities (anglophones in Québec, francophones elsewhere) undertake "economic development" (Silva and Heller 2009). This had immediate repercussions on the ground. To give one concrete example, the community newspaper in one francophone community in Ontario had long published pieces focussing on ethnolinguistic pride and minority political rights. One day in 1996, it published an article by a community leader arguing instead that local francophones should be pointing out to county officials that their bilingualism ought to be understood as "added value." This notion of French-English bilingualism as "added value" indeed began to emerge in a number of sites across Canada. For example, a few years later, the lobbying organization for francophones in Manitoba (one of Canada's prairie provinces), adopted "C'est si bon" [It's so good] as a slogan and brand, providing their representatives with boxes of mints with that label to give away at events. One such agent marveled at how much easier it was to get anglophones' attention through this strategy than it had been before, when efforts were concentrated on discourses of political rights.

Linguistic skills are indeed recognized as a potential asset by both states and, increasingly, corporations. For example, the Canadian government developed an economic plan in the early twenty-first century that explicitly mentioned language industries as an area in which Canada has developed now-exportable human and technical resources of potential interest to consumers globally. In addition, language has caught the attention of business schools and management studies, with an increasing number of papers on the topic of language.

To understand language as a skill is to understand it as an activity rather than an attribute. In that sense, the disembodied understandings of skill in neoliberal discourse converge in interesting ways with views developed in the 1980s and 1990s, focussing on language use as a site for performance, or practice, or act of identity, as an activity or an accomplishment of ethnicity, race, and gender (for reviews see Chun and Lo 2016; McElhinny 2014). This practice-based approach participates in a wider move within linguistic and sociocultural anthropology since the mid-1970s (Hanks 1990; Ochs and Capps 1996; Ortner 1996) as a reaction against structural-determinist social theories that did not incorporate a sufficient sense of human agency. This work also challenges the liberal (or humanist) ideologies of personhood that we saw in Chapter 4, which located attributes as inalienable dimensions of specific kinds of bodies (Butler 1990, 10). However, to focus on practices and activities alone may be to focus on agency, but it loses sight of systemic and structural inequities in institutions. Gender and race are not personal characteristics, but structural principles organizing social institutions, and shaping recruitment, allocation, treatment, and mobility of people within these (see Chun and Lo 2016; Gal 1991).

Thus it is striking to note that a focus on elaborating these discourses of social construction, performance, and activity in feminist sociolinguistics emerged as emancipatory in many works in the late 1980s and early 1990s, in such critical and influential books in the United States and Western Europe as Goodwin (1990), Hall and Bucholtz (1995), Livia and Hall (1997), McIlvenny (2002), and Litosseliti and Sunderland (2002). Many of us—and Bonnie decidedly includes herself (see McElhinny 1995, 1998)—were implicated in the elaboration of these ideas. A more political economic approach allows us to ask when and how representing the self as performed in sociolinguistic accounts contributed to the formation of an ideology of a flexible subject in a flexible workforce more adequate to a globally dispersed, multinational corporate culture (Hennessey 1993).

Treating language as a technical skill or as a performance are only two ways that language is made meaningful in late capitalism. They remain in tension with the idea that language has a soul. A focus on authenticity continues to provide an alternative source of value in the globalized new economy; although presented as positive, authenticity can quickly shade into nativist and exclusive understandings of identity as well. Authenticity also poses distinctive dilemmas for racialized subjects. In the next section we will turn to the ways in which persistent Romantic notions of language, nation, and personhood intersect with new conditions, producing struggles over which values should prevail and hence whose capital will be recognized.

Affect, Authenticity, and Embodiment

As we saw above, even when language teaching is 'skilled' it can draw on ideologies of authentic languages and authentic speakers; English, notably, is most valued when delivered by 'native' speakers understood as White bodies from imperial centres. Further, authentic language adds value to experiences otherwise sold as being about something else Romantic, whether natural or cultural or both. The consumption of such experiences in the form of eco-tourism and cultural tourism has greatly increased as niche marketing comes to leisure. Of course, the consumption of experience often takes the form of consumption of authentic objects, most often in the form of food, drink, or souvenirs. The authentic value of all of these can be intensified by being presented in authentic language, whether as part of the activity or as part of the branding. This authenticity is powerful because it situates communication in the realm of affect.

Indeed, communication and affect are increasingly central in service jobs in health care, education, finance, entertainment, and advertising, where the production of feelings of well-being and even passion are key for the workers and their clients (Hardt 1999).

Consider this example:

FIGURE 8.2: Workers in a call centre

The picture in Figure 8.2 is a stock photo from a databank of a smiling call centre representative, whose labour is largely *communicative*. (Originally, we had contacted an outsourcing consultant website for permission to reprint a similar photo, but we were quickly referred to a standard website with more than 10,000 images of call centre representatives, from which we drew this image.) This woman dispenses information, always with a smile; her work is therefore not just technical, it is also *affective*. It links reason and emotion in one warm, and usually female or at least feminized, voice; often enough these are women of colour. Feminization is constructed partly through the minoritized, marginalized status of service providers, sometimes described as *temporal migrants*, living lives out of sync with their families and friends, and with whole clusters of services arising to meet the needs of their unusual schedules (Mirchandani 2012; Salonga 2010). They can be located in the Global South or in peripheral regions of the Global North, populated by "already" bilingual or multilingual workers displaced by deindustrialization. They also draw on underemployed ("already" bilingual) immigrant workers in the Global North, and on educated, underemployed nomadic youth in such places as Barcelona or London.

In many ways communicative labour can be just as tailorized as manual labour (Cameron 2000; Boutet 2012); both talk and bodies are regulated, the first through scripts ("Hello, Monica, how may I help you today?") and the second through work stations to which workers are physically attached through wires (see Heller 2010a for an overview). In this sense, language is understood as a skill, just as simultaneously the "human touch" is also understood as key. The tension sometimes surfaces in interesting ways: some workplaces are now explicitly branding themselves as *not* using a script. A bank with headquarters in Toronto launched an advertising campaign in 2016 that shows customers who are surprised when they do not encounter a scripted greeting or are not contacted by call robot.

Sectors such as call centres, in which workers and clients are often in or from different regions, classes, and nations, get particular attention because they are constructed as symbols of the transition from industrial, white, masculine, working-class, First World work to feminized, racialized, "offshore" production (Heller 2010a). However, they can have other meanings as well: in the Philippines, call centres are seen as a way of creating work in the Philippines, so fewer workers need to leave the country to find lucrative positions, or so those who have had to leave can come back. Call centres are also sites that are seen as relatively welcoming of gender-nonconformity or sexual diversity (Salonga 2010), just as they are seen as threatening to heteronormative ideas of masculinity (Heller et al. 2015).

Studies of paid caregiving, another key area where affect and communication are central, have received particular attention because of the ways they highlight the interaction of the negative impact of structural adjustment policies in the Global South with the privatization of health, elder care, and child care in the Global North. That interaction produces the tragic irony of Third World women supporting their own families by leaving them to care for wealthier households, which themselves become more multicultural and cross-class as a result (see, for example, England and Stiell 1997; Lorente 2007).

The provision of other forms of reproductive labour, such as kinship work, sexual talk, and food preparation, often previously understood in many feminist analyses in the 1980s as unpaid labour done by women, has also become significantly more commodified (see McElhinny 2010 for a review). While socialist feminists in the 1970s and 1980s called for wages for housework to challenge the devaluation of women's work in homes, this form of stratified reproductive labour reinforces rather than challenges gender, class, racial, and national hierarchies. The call for wages can now be seen as furthering the commodification of interactions in a realm previously governed by "love." Indeed, as affect becomes commodified, authenticity becomes prized. This ironically leads to workshops and sites for learning, from Canada to Fiji to Russia, to express emotion effectively in a range of areas, (Wilce and Fenigsen 2016).

In many parts of the Global North, consuming authenticity has a long history, as part of varied forms of colonialism and the early days of tourism. As leisure itself was industrialized and democratized in the postwar period, elites began to compete for ever more authentic experiences. As industrialized tourism and mass production of authentic products themselves started to become a saturated field, it became necessary to find new ways to distinguish one product from another. One way to do this was language.

FIGURE 8.3: "cé faitte icitte/not made in china": mugs made in Québec by Hugo Didier (courtesy of Hugh Didier)

Consider the example in Figure 8.3. Monica frequently sees them at an exhibit and sale of ceramics held every summer since the 1990s in a small tourist town in rural Québec. They are made by a second-generation potter in his Montréal workshop. The French text on the mugs can be translated as "This is made here," but the orthography marks the text as a transcription of spoken language bearing shibboleth-like features of regional, Canadian French, as opposed to standard or European French (the vowel quality of "est" [is], the pronunciation of the /t/ in "fait" [made], the epenthetic /t/ of "ici/icitte" [here]). The text is playful, but the sentiment is serious: these mugs were made in Québec and not in China (that part of the text is probably in English because that is the language in which items are usually marked "Made in China"). The text is also the only thing that distinguishes these mugs from plain, store-bought, white mugs; that and the fact that they are exhibited at a ceramicists' show and identified as the artistic work of a particular named potter.

Tourism has emerged as a major way for peripheries suffering the dislocations of deindustrialization to remake their economies. While Canada scarcely qualifies as a poor country, nonetheless it has peripheries, such as the one where the ceramics exposition takes place. In another example, there may be no cod fishing left in the Gulf of the St. Lawrence, but that does not stop the Atlantic provinces of Canada from selling their identity as a fishery-based culture, with distinctive cultural mores and ways of talking (e.g., the tourism bureau of Newfoundland and Labrador launched an ad campaign in 2014 that highlights local ways of speaking as one of the things to be consumed there; at the time of writing, the video was still available on their website).

Here we have the development of niche products (from experiences to material things) in which nation-state forms of authenticity serve to add value to products that otherwise are hard to distinguish from others. We look for products so niche that you can only get them in one place, ideally with the smell of the earth or the plants or the animals that were part of their making. We like products even better if we can meet the people who make them, though not imagining the hands. We are rarely interested in the seeing the hands that touched those products; instead their pictures and their stories help anchor the product in place and time and in social and cultural practice. Language figures in the process in the form of *narration*, in the use of place *names*, the names and images of iconically local figures, and in the use in both labelling and narration of distinctive linguistic *forms*. Hence advertising has turned more and more to finding ways of orthographically representing nonstandard language varieties, mobilizing its oral forms, and linking them to specific places and either to culturally significant specific moments or to the past in a claim to historical continuity. Distinctive linguistic forms are now also well recognized as elements of consumable artistic products, from theatre to song to film. They can circulate on global circuits of production and consumption, as well as attracting consumers to specific places (see Heller 2010a for a review).

The commodification of language as authenticity raises a number of questions. If what is being commodified is by definition variable, it is hard to know exactly how to understand its nature as a commodity, which, in order to be exchanged, and in particular monetized, must be constructed in some way as an object. Its value in a market that also values language as skill is hard to calibrate. It requires shifting forms of subjectivity since people have to draw on their authentic capital in ways that are recognizable as authentic by consumers; in some cases, this might mean ceding control of authenticity to those better at marketing it. People have to find ways to understand the relationship among different kinds of performances, for different kinds of audiences, some of them commodified, some not, some perhaps somewhere in-between.

This means marketing has changed. One of the sharpest changes in corporate worlds in the last 15 years is that many successful corporations now produce brands rather than products. Naomi Klein (2000) argues that branding is not the same as advertising. Ads inform people about the existence of a product, and argue that their lives will be better if they use it. But now, Klein argues, companies are advertising brands—a lifestyle, an experience—and penetrating into domains previously untouched by commercialism (see Gaudio 2003). A review of a recent book by a branding consultant quotes him as saying "most organizations hire me on as an itinerant sleuth whose mission is to smoke out that foggiest, most abstract of words: desire. Desire is always linked to a story, and a gap that needs to be filled" (Schacter 2016, B14). Now both marketing consultants and linguistic anthropologists are trying to figure out stories.

We also note that, while much work focusses on the effects of neoliberalism in terms of market productivity, the market also requires consumers. The disciplined self, required for work, may be at odds with the indulgent self required for consumption; however, the enterprising self also seeks to achieve freedom and fulfill the self through lifestyle consumption (Rose 1999) in ways that trouble the separation between production and consumption (see Yang 2015). For example, Gray's (2012) analysis of textbooks for teaching English in the global market shows a dramatic increase in the use of celebrities since the 1970s to market the cosmopolitan and successful lifestyles to which learners are told they can aspire with the use of English. A focus on consumer-based identities obscures structural barriers to achievement, but also eclipses class-based forms of solidarity by creating consumer-based ones.

The relatively recent rise of queer linguistics can be understood as shaped by, as it studies, the way desire works in these new social formations (Cameron and Kulick 2003b; Leap 1995; Livia and Hall 1997; and the *Journal of Language and Sexuality*, founded in 2012). Gramsci (whose work we saw in Chapter 1) argued that Fordist forms of work attempted to enforce heterosexual unions. Workers (presumptively male) were seen as more stable, and likely to buy more, if married. But it is less clear that contemporary capitalism, with its focus on flexibility, mobility, individuation, and desire, requires heteronormativity. Roger Lancaster (1993) argues that late capitalism is instead "foremost about harnessing desires and marketing them to disparate populations, thereby soliciting new needs, new wants, new identities, and new experiments in lifestyle" (319). Social movements focussed on gender and sexuality, he argues, are agents and beneficiaries of this transition from Fordism to post-Fordism in ways that have created new forms of life, families, and desire, including "flexible relationships, temporary unions, negotiable role expectations, recombinant families, gay families, open relationships" (Lancaster 1993, 319). Naisargi Dave (2010) takes these questions a step further by considering how queer identities are complexly imbricated in political and economic contexts in her consideration of the politics of becoming "Indian and lesbian" within India's structural adjustments in the 1990s, the resultant transnationalization of social service provision and increase in foreign funds for NGOs, and postcolonial debates about what is considered "authentic" tradition and nation. The rise of queer linguistics and anthropology alongside these economic and political changes suggests that the effects of such changes cannot be overly rapidly or simply assessed as negative or positive. Queer linguistics has been a key site for theorizing desire not as a psychoanalytic field or solely confined to sexuality; instead, desire, after the formulations of Deleuze and Guattari (1987), Deleuze (2000), and Deleuze and Parnet (1987), can be something linked to sleep, walking, music, spring, and old age. It becomes something that one charts geographically, like the map we saw above, to see what is possible and the way desire moves, acts, and makes connections (Cameron and Kulick 2003a, 97).

Indeed, the intertwining of desire, authenticity, and language is often complex and difficult to navigate. These tensions are marked in a short story by Anishinaabe writer Leanne Simpson (2013, 107–8). In "gezhizhwah" [to cut], an older Indigenous person is telling a younger one a story. The young one is a bit cheeky. When the auntie starts talking about a sexy protagonist, the young one interrupts, not wanting to hear old people talk about sex, and to say that surely it is more decolonized to use a rez (reservation) accent rather than big English words. The older one has the final word: "what do you know about decolonize? you think sexy is pornographic. you think i can't use five dollar words. you think i'm only authentic if i'm talking rez. you the one suppose to be listening anyway. how can you be doing any listening when you're all critical about my authentici-ty?"

Who is listening and who is talking is a pivotal point. The tension between skill and soul also emerges in debates about multilingualism and education. We saw above how the conditions of late capitalism have resulted in a proliferation of policies and programs aimed at increasing the standard-languages repertoires of cosmopolitan elites; these sit uncomfortably alongside programs aimed at recognizing stigmatized forms of multilingualism and multidialectalism, and which support the development of standard language skills while maintaining (rather than suppressing) minoritized practices that students bring to the classroom. However, these approaches fail to capture the very different value attached not only to language varieties but also to embodied speakers (Bourdieu 1977). It is not enough to speak the legitimate language; you must also be a legitimate speaker. Indeed, "raciolinguistic ideologies produce racialized speaking subjects who are constructed as linguistically deviant even when engaging in linguistic practices positioned as normative or innovative when produced by privileged white subjects" (Flores and Rosa 2015, 150). So language ideologies not only rank speaking subjects as racialized and gendered (and classed), they also produce those subjects as racialized, gendered, and classed, and locate authenticity of different values and kinds among them. This is the central point made by Frantz Fanon, in *Black Skin, White Masks* ([1952] 1967): social perceptions are deeply shaped by imperial categories, such that who "I" am is developed in relation to how others see us, and "in a society structured by racial categories, becoming black is bound up with being perceived as black by a white person" (Mignolo 2015, 116).

Thus the effects of late capitalism are complex, with intensified tensions between the frames of reason and emotion (here constructed as 'skill' and 'affect' or 'authenticity') that we have tracked throughout this book. Established categories of class, race, gender, and sexuality can be reproduced as structuring principles of inequality within capitalism, just as their repressive effects can be disturbed and challenged. In the last sections of this chapter, we turn to a set of alternative explorations of ways in which language is reclaimed from capitalism and used to push back against repression, in favour of redress, reconciliation, and possible reimaginings.

Recapturing the Commons

David Harvey argues that one of the distinctive features of contemporary capitalism is *accumulation by dispossession* (2005, 159). This can include accumulating or privatizing land and assets, suppressing the right of the commons, further commodifying labour power, and forms of debt and credit. All these are seen as the penetration of the market into areas previously uncommodified, or untouched by capitalism, or perhaps areas that others would argue should *not* be commodified or marketized, or should be decommodified.

Scholarship in the 1980s and 1990s on language and landscape, and language and environment, sometimes called *ecolinguistics*, explicitly addresses the impact of increasingly environmentally destructive practices of the primary and secondary sectors, though it often only implicitly articulates these within political economic frameworks (Myerson and Rydin 1996; Mühlhäusler and Peace 2006). Drawing on all the naturalizing forms of language ideologies we saw in previous chapters, it takes a number of forms.

One is the extension of critical discourse analysis to the ways in which environmental issues are covered in the mass media and discussed in legislatures, or how corporations and nonprofits have seized upon "green" advertising strategies to promote their products (see McElhinny 2006). These studies all critique the assessment of value understood only in terms of financial profit for corporations. Some explore the uses of language, especially narration, as a mode of suggesting alternatives, including the value of the commons, Indigenous sovereignty, spirituality, or collective forms of sociability (see, for example, Carbaugh 1996; Feld 1996a, 1996b; Strang 2004).

Recent ethnographic studies in political ecology, Indigenous studies, and linguistic anthropology have argued that stories are key to constructing a sense of place and creating effective attachments to environmental aims. Margaret Somerville (2013) argues that changing our relations with water means "creating new stories of water" (7) in order to construct water as a *commons*, thus counteracting the strategies that made water into a commodity and constructing a different sense of who can and should participate in decisions about it. A number of organizations around the Great Lakes (e.g., the Freshwater Lab, Great Lake Commons, Lake Ontario Waterkeeper, Lost Rivers, Ryerson Urban Water) have launched storytelling projects. The stories change the notions of place and time and personhood around water. Rather than deterritorialized, dematerialized, and dehistoricized accounts of water, the stories reconnect people to the watersheds they live in, the times they have experienced the water, and the people they were and were with.

Language is understood, too, as part of the natural world to be preserved as a commons, as having an ecology (Mühlhäusler 1996) with explicit links made between environmental devastation and language "endangerment" or "death." This metaphor seeks to reclaim language from an overly technical and hubristically progress-oriented frame, and resituate it as one among many other elements of a natural environment whose balance we ignore at our peril. It therefore situates languages as one dimension of environmentalist critiques of the effects of industrial and finance capitalism—albeit at the price of potential essentialization (Duchêne and Heller 2007). In some cases, *language revitalization* is understood as parallel to land claims or claims for restitution of cultural artifacts and human remains, that is, as an attempt to restore Indigenous control of material and immaterial culture stolen, repressed, devalued, and destroyed by colonial powers. Here language can be used to construct globalizing strategies of solidarity, in particular among Indigenous groups resisting the assumption that the nation-state is the proper frame for struggle.

Although some ideas about language revitalization are linked to ideas about elaborating new forms of polity and new forms of sovereignty, they may reproduce an understanding of language as a whole, bounded object that is the collective property of a whole, bounded group, causing revitalization efforts to run into old problems related to standardization: who gets to decide what counts as language, and whether language should be understood as fixable through such tools as dictionary-making, grammar-making, and linguistic analysis (as well as transmissible through mainstream modes of schooling). They also raise questions about legitimacy of speakers: while some Indigenous scholars are arguing that if First Nations want international recognition of their sovereignty they should start setting criteria for outsiders to learn language (Lyons 2010), others may be concerned specifically about White scholars learning the Indigenous languages of these territories, since to do so was becoming a sign of White privilege while so many Indigenous people did not have access to these languages. It is also important to recognize that the discourse of endangerment is also adopted by speakers of such languages as French, Swedish, and English, in the service of nativist backlashes against immigration, Indigenous claims, and other forms of diversity.

Finally, the turn toward imagining power differently, in less hierarchical ways, has also led scholars to seek alternative models for describing language (Heller 2008; Pujolar 2001; Tsitsipis 2007). Some scholars have been inspired by the concept of *rhizome*, introduced by Gilles Deleuze and Félix Guattari (1987) in order to find a democratic analytic (see Hagood 2004; Leander and Rowe 2006; Muehlmann 2012; Pietikäinen 2014). Trees, they argue, are not tools for "the people," because they are the tools for mapping lineage in order to decide who inherits. In their view, the use of trees by Chomsky enforces and requires grammaticality while claiming to map it.

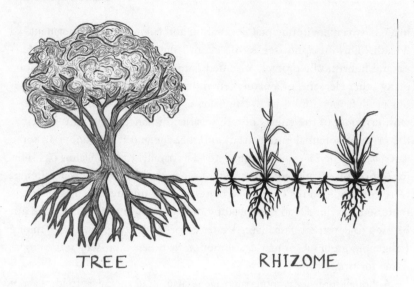

FIGURE 8.4: Trees versus rhizomes (Illustration: Andrea Derbecker). Adapted from http://www.lookfordiagnosis.com/mesh_info.php?term=Rhizome&lang=1

Rhizomes, by contrast, are portrayed as less directional. They can be connected to multiple other things. Deleuze and Guattari (1987, 7) cite Uriel Weinreich, a student of Yiddish, as understanding language as heterogeneous, in ways they apply to rhizomes: There is no mother tongue; no ideal speaker-hearer; no language; no linguistic universals; no structure, no generative model. Rhizomes, they argue, analyze language by decentring. Rhizomes, they argue, are discontinuous, deterritorialized. Unruly.

Is this, then, where we end up? We're not so sure. The rhizome offers a spatial metaphor for globalization. It is, perhaps, less temporally ordered than a tree. It might be too decentred. Understanding trees and rhizomes metaphorically might not get at how trees and rhizomes interact (it turns out that certain trees require the work of mushrooms in order to grow, and the mushrooms also require the trees) or how they communicate (more on this below). This might further objectify and control 'nature' in ways that we need to further unpack. It obscures the persistence of regimentation and the intensification of surveillance. What the metaphor of rhizome does capture is a restless search for new, nonhierarchical strategies for understanding how time and space feel.

Reclamation, Redress, Refusal, and Reimagining

In this section, we further consider the strategies undertaken on the terrain of language to repair past harms and, on that basis, to move forward to more equitable and more peaceful futures. We opened this chapter with *renaming* and have also discussed language *revitalization*, both understandable as acts of *reclamation*—of control over representations, and hence over resources. We will now discuss two speech acts: *redress* from states directed toward those they have harmed; and *refusals* from the oppressed to continue to collaborate in political economic structures, including those involved in knowledge production, that harm them. We will close with a consideration of the kinds of *reimaginings* enabled by these acts of reclamation and redress.

Here we come back to the ways that hands are erased from accounts of authenticity. Hands ask people to think about labour, about racialization, about working conditions, about housing conditions, about cleanliness, about sanitation. The erasure of hands from accounts of authenticity is the erasure of these issues. A number of U.S.-based scholars of color, many living transnational lives, argue that instead we need to pay attention to language as embodiment, and in particular to how embodiment is about racialization (Baugh 2016; Chun and Lo 2016; Flores and Rosa 2015; Rosa and Burdick forthcoming; Lo and Rosa 2014; Reyes and Lo 2009). We pointed out above how this work allows us to link the racialized making of difference and inequality to the workings of legitimacy and authority; in the same text Flores and Rosa (2015, 151) argue for "[a] framework of raciolinguistic ideologies" in order to "examin[e] not only the 'eye' of whiteness but also its 'mouth' and 'ears'." This perspective can of course be easily extended to an intersectional analysis linking race to all other structuring principles of difference and inequality.

This means also understanding how communication is implicated in constructions of racialized power (Alim, Rickford, and Ball 2016; Dick and Wirtz 2011; Trechter and Bucholtz 2001). Hall et al. (2016) explore this question through an analysis of the hand gestures of Donald Trump. Part of his brand, the gestures devalue whole categories of people in ways that continue to reproduce the biological reductions of evolutionary theory. Trump caricatured a reporter with disabilities with flailing wrists, Mexican migrants with derogatory border-crossing gestures, a governor as a (read "working-class") sloppy eater. He reinforces his right to impose these readings through a "pistol hand" gesture to shoot down opponents, "convey[ing] arrogance, sovereign power, and community force" (2016, 80).

One strategy for challenging these processes is through seeking redress. One form in which such redress has been offered is the speech act of apologies, in particular apologies for past harms accomplished through racialization. Political scientists have recently noted that we live in an "age of apologies" for certain kinds of historical wrongs (Howard-Hassman and Gibney 2008; Nobles 2008). Political scientist Melissa Nobles lists 72 apologies from heads of state, governments, and religious institutions since 1965, most of which—66—have occurred since the mid-1980s between states (2008, 155). Apologies have not only been made between nation-states, but also within them. For instance, since 1985, Canadian governments have made about 10 major apologies, or quasi-apologies, or "statements of reconciliation" (McElhinny 2016b), all of them for various forms of racialized harm. There are apologies to Indigenous people for relocation or incarceration in the course of Canadian settler colonialism, apologies to those interned during wartime because they shared the ethnic or national identity of enemies, and apologies for racialized barriers to migration. While they can be understood as attempts on the part of states to redress and include, they often have other, more complicated effects. In particular, they need to be assessed with an eye to precisely how they intervene in or, on the contrary, enable White supremacy, and how they are framed by the White gaze.

This frame is important when we consider why such apologies are happening now. Most analysts have offered explanations couched in *political* and *temporal* terms, arguing that 50 or so years after a significant event (World War II, or the end of colonial rule) is a natural period in which commemoration occurs, perhaps because at least some of those adversely affected still survive at that point. However, to single out certain kinds of actions as requiring redress also suggests that other kinds of harms (for instance, those linked to economic inequities) do not fall within the category of those requiring apologies (Henderson and Wakeham 2013). A focus on wartime actions allows states to suggest that such exclusions are unusual and limited, and that the nations now are different. But settler colonialism continues, as do continuing political and economic influences from former colonizers and international regimes on their colonies. Redress is most controversial for Indigenous nations, who are asserting their own sovereignty, and arguing a focus on resurgence rather than reconciliation and state recognition (cf. Alfred 2009; Coulthard 2011; Million 2013).

It is possible to understand apologies in neoliberal terms as well. It is not accidental that apologies occured at the same moment as policies of trade liberalization, economic deregulation, and state retrenchment in the 1980s and early 1990s. James (2013) argues that *neoliberal multiculturalism* is the state's way of distinguishing between legitimate and illegitimate forms of diversity, and that focussing on the business or trade advantages of diversity marginalizes claims by anti-racist and anti-colonial activists. Though many apologies have been accompanied by modest forms of financial compensation, it is here that we might see them as "cheap talk"—the forms of compensation still cost the state less than the regular funding of ongoing initiatives.

In this context we can perhaps also understand the emergent politics of *refusal*. As articulated by Indigenous social scientists and their allies, refusal signals an intent to engage directly with the consequences of knowledge production and to think carefully about what it harms and what it enables, in whose hands—and refusing to engage with the harmful. The Mohawk anthropologist Audra Simpson notes that anthropology has often imagined itself as the voice of the colonized. She argues that cultural analysis needs to be disaggregated into a variety of narratives in which *voice* is linked with sovereignty "at the level of enunciation, at the level of method, and at the level of textualization" (A. Simpson 2014, 97). This too requires different notions of time, place, and personhood. It challenges the timeless portraits, or portraits of Indigenous people as caught in the past, replacing them with notions of the future.

Studies of language revitalization are still linked with tradition and ceremony, Simpson notes, but also other practices of nationhood, citizenship, rights, justice, political recognition, and proper ways of being in the world (A. Simpson 2014, 98). This focusses linguistic analysis on sovereignty and struggle, not cultural difference, where sovereignty is not generally understood as adopting the same forms as the Westphalian nation-states described in Chapter 4. For Simpson, this means the studies she is willing to undertake are those that contribute to sovereignty or complicate simplified representations of Indigenous people (2014, 113). She refuses to undertake other forms of work; she asks that anthropology centre such struggles in its work. She firmly states that some studies should not be done, and she firmly states that some studies should not be done by some people.

This Is How We Hope

The logic of late capitalism is a logic of anticipation (Adams, Murphy, and Clarke 2009), of trading in commodity futures, sometimes of building certain kinds of individual desiring selves (Ahearn 2003). We want to end in a different place and time, reimagining futures differently, as we have seen so many others do across the stories we have recounted in this book. In *Cruising Utopia: The There and Then of Queer Futurity*, José Esteban Muñoz argues that "[w]e must strive, in the face of the here and now's totalizing rendering of reality, to think and feel a *then and there* … we must dream and enact new and better pleasures, other ways of being in the world, and ultimately new worlds" (2009, 1). It is this form of longing that he calls *queerness*. Queerness is not yet here; we are not yet queer: "[q]ueerness is that thing that lets us feel that this world is not enough, that indeed something is missing…. Queerness is about the rejection of a here and now and an insistence on potentiality or concrete possibility for another world" (1).

We can find parallel insights in early-twenty-first-century works that seek to build from reclamation, redress, and refusal into reimaginings; these include Indigenous futurities, Afro-futurities, feminist and Marxist and other decolonial and anti-racist futurities (Ahmed 2010; Berardi 2011; Berlant 2011; Gibson-Graham 2006; Harney and Moten 2013; Hage 2002; Harvey 2000; Jameson 2005; Narotzky and Besnier 2014; L. Simpson 2011, 2013; Wynter and McKittrick 2015). Early work in sociolinguistics on sexuality (Cameron and Kulick 2003a) argued that one way to do queering was to start from desire; this notion is now taken up more broadly as a basis for making futures. Tuck (2009) argues for moving beyond a focus on damage to desire, without denial of structural inequity.

We close here with a few examples that speak to us, that show us new ways of imagining worlds we might want to at least try to make. This necessarily draws on work close to our hearts as we map emergent structures of feeling we come across. As we indicated in the preface, Bonnie is looking for what might sustain activist scholars through the tough moments; Monica remains mindful of the ways in which most efforts have perverse and unintended consequences to which attend. Bonnie's attention has been drawn to social movements, Monica's to more perhaps pragmatic, interstitial modes of navigating the mess of struggle, work, and contradiction in everyday life.

In some ways the two come together in the use of social media. They offer tools for inventing new forms of literacy, new forms of reading, new ideas about the appropriate sites and forms of knowledge production, new spaces for that to happen. They make new networks and new hubs (Ramirez 2007). For social movements, they provide, for example, "new tools for documenting incidents of state-sanctioned violence and contesting media representations of racialized bodies and marginalized communities" (Bonilla and Rosa 2015, 4). They provide sites for "collectively constructing counter-narratives and reimagining group identities" in part because of the ways they construct shared feelings of temporality during protests and confrontations with police, and in part because they create new days of import and days of protest (Bonilla and Rosa 2015, 6). At the same time, of course, they also offer new tools for state surveillance, resulting in shifting grounds of engagement, and new kinds of violence.

When the police moved in on protestors contesting a pipeline in South Dakota in 2016, invitations quickly went out to watch and witness. Bonnie received a prompt from a Toronto-based Indigenous activist while sitting in a car on the way from Pittsburgh to Toronto, and watched thousands of people put up supportive posts. Bonnie wrote, "Toronto is watching," and watched it flicker by, seeing Kansas, Boston, Miami, Copenhagen, Honolulu, and many others watching too. Social media has played a key role in a range of protests, from #waterislife and #idlenomore reactions to Canadian state infringements on Indigenous sovereignty and environmental protection (Coates 2015; Kinonda-niimi Collective 2014) to #occupy's critique of capitalist inequities (Martin Rojo 2016; Flowerdew and Jones 2016), to #blacklivesmatter (Bonilla and Rosa 2015) and the Arab Spring (Dole 2012).

Sometimes the possibilities are more local and use other, older technologies. Renzi (2008) documents the activities of Telestreet, an Italian collective that realized it was possible to plug into street-level zones falling just outside the control of Italian state television to organize neighbourhood broadcasting. In less explicitly theorized ways, small groups of people are plugging into electricity grids to create an alternative neighbourhood on the edges of Yellowknife (the capital of Canada's Northwest Territories), also using the infrastructure of the employment market generated by Canada's language policies to support explorations of alternative modes of living closer to the land (Heller and Bell 2012).

Aiming to live closer to the land has also shifted ideas about personhood. For increasing numbers of people, the extensive work put into dividing the human from the nonhuman (and then ranking both) now needs to be undone. "Life" has been a crucial axis of differentiation, and "language" has been a key dimension of elaborating an anthropocentric approach. This moves us beyond thinking about trees and rhizomes as metaphors for organizing knowledge, and beyond the asymmetries of thinking about them in terms of protection; such connections move us onto the terrain of reciprocal relations, with new narratives, new narrators, and new ways of telling stories. We see trees considered in this way in such books as *The Hidden Life of Trees: What They Feel, How They Communicate* (Wohlleben 2015) and *How Forests Think* (Kohn 2013). The same considerations have been extended to water, dogs, birds, deer, moss (McGregor 2015; L. Simpson 2011; Wall Zimmerer 2003), and what the Potawatomi biologist Robin Wall Zimmerer calls "other non-human persons" (2003, 12).

However, the formulation is not merely one of cultural difference, as Whorf had it, but a political one: if fish and others are understood as persons (as corporations currently are), then *sovereignty* must be understood differently (Todd 2016). If the language of 'nation' is still used, what is meant is not the Westphalian, territorial notion we saw earlier. Leanne Simpson (2016) offers one vision: the nation as *Kina Gchi Nishnaabeg ogamig* [the place where we all live and work together], as described by Doug Williams, a Mississauga Nishnaabeg elder from Curve Lake First Nation. This idea of nation is a hub of networks, rather than exclusive territorial claims, including "connections to each other, to the plant nations, the animal nations, the rivers and lakes, the cosmos, and our neighbouring Indigenous nations" (L. Simpson 2016).

Barlow (2009) focusses on water as a basis for the development of the commons, moving "towards a new freshwater narrative." She documents dozens of different kinds of such efforts; for example, Anishinaabe women initiated water walks that, like the map that began this chapter, offer walkers an opportunity to become intimately associated with the Great Lakes in an Indigenous frame and with each other, as people take turns carrying the copper vessel of water and the eagle staff that lead the group. The water, on these walks, is often referred to as "she" (see also McGregor 2015). People learn the Ojibwe word *nibi* for water, and other words for objects and greetings. Elders offer speeches entirely in Ojibwe, even if only a few understand, calling into being a new kind of audience. In the summer of 2017, Grandmother Josephine Mandamin will lead a reverse migration walk, the For the Earth and Water Walk 2017, starting in Minnesota, tracing around Lake Superior, Lake Huron, Lake Erie, and Lake Ontario, and then walking along the St. Lawrence River to the eastern Atlantic shore. This, perhaps, echoes the seventh fire journey.

We began with Junot Diaz's thoughts on radical hope, and we end with his thoughts on decolonial love. Diaz writes that "the kind of love that i was interested in, that my characters long for intuitively, is the only kind of love that could liberate them from that horrible legacy of colonial violence. i am speaking about decolonial love ... is it possible to love one's broken-by-the-coloniality-of-power self in another broken-by-the-coloniality-of-power person?" (Diaz 2012). We are all broken by colonialism. Leanne Simpson (2013) draws on this phrase, builds on it, to imagine many kinds of decolonial love. We close with the one she describes in her story "gwekaanimad," which means 'shifting wind' in Ojibwe. She imagines a parade where there are no watchers, but only doers, and the doers include the ones with wings and hooves and paws:

> they felt good those ones. no one forgot them that day. they looked us in the eye that day. you know when that one, maybe a special one, looks you in the eye, and maybe for just a second you don't look away. maybe for a second you just let yourself look back, and then maybe you feel something, something good. something that maybe you think you aren't supposed to feel, maybe something you didn't feel for a long time. and for that second you get all filled up with that special one. that one that makes you stay when you should go. full of potential. full of hope. full of love. and you fill yourself up with as much of that special as you can. and then you just keep walking, you just hold your head up high and you keep walking. walking instead of floating. (139)

So we end, as we began, by walking. Walking backward into the future, that we will all create together, as we reimagine language, land, love, and much more.

REFERENCES

Abella, Irving, and Harold Troper. 1982. *None Is Too Many: Canada and the Jews of Europe 1933–1948*. Toronto: University of Toronto Press.
Abu Lughod, Lila. 1993. *Writing Women's Worlds: Bedouin Stories*. Berkeley: University of California Press.
Adams, Vincanne, Michelle Murphy, and Adele Clarke. 2009. "Anticipation: Technoscience, Life, Affect, Temporality." *Subjectivities* 28 (1): 246–65. https://doi.org/10.1057/sub.2009.18.
Ahearn, Laura. 2003. "Writing Desire in Nepali Love Letters." *Language & Communication* 23 (2): 107–22. https://doi.org/10.1016/S0271-5309(02)00046-0.
Ahmed, Sara. 2010. "Happy Futures." In *The Promise of Happiness*, 160–98. Durham: Duke University Press. https://doi.org/10.1215/9780822392781-006.
Ahmed, Sara. 2012. *On Being Included: Racism and Diversity in Institutional Life*. Durham: Duke University Press. https://doi.org/10.1215/9780822395324.
Alfred, Taiaiake. 2009. "Restitution Is the Real Pathway to Injustice for Indigenous Peoples." In *Response, Responsibility and Renewal: Canada's Truth and Reconciliation Journey*, edited by Gregory Younging, Jonathan Dewar, and Mike DeGagné, 163–72. Ottawa: Aboriginal Healing Foundation.
Alim, H. Samy, John R. Rickford, and Arnetha F. Ball, eds. 2016. *Raciolinguistics: How Language Shapes Our Ideas about Race*. New York: Oxford University Press. https://doi.org/10.1093/acprof:oso/9780190625696.001.0001.
Alisjahbana, Sutan Takdir. 1976. *Language Planning for Modernization: The Case of Indonesian and Malaysian*. Berlin: Walter de Gruyter.
Allan, Kori. 2005. "Colonizing 'Access, Participation, and Equality': Selling 'Active' Citizenship, Neo-liberalism and the Governing of Ontario's Diverse Workforce in 'the New Global Economy'." Master's Research Paper, Department of Anthropology, University of Toronto.
Allan, Kori. 2014. "Learning How to 'Skill' the Self: Citizenship and Immigrant Integration in Toronto, Canada." PhD diss., University of Toronto.
Allan, Kori, and Bonnie McElhinny. 2017. "Neoliberalism, Language and Migration." In *The Routledge Handbook on Language and Migration*, edited by Suresh Canagarajah. New York: Routledge.
Alter, Stephen. 1999. *Darwinism and the Linguistic Image: Language, Race and Natural Theology in the 19th Century*. Baltimore: Johns Hopkins Press.

Anderson, Benedict. 1983. *Imagined Communities*. London: Verso.
Anderson, Warwick. 2006. *Colonial Pathologies: American Tropical Medicine, Race, and Hygiene in the Philippines*. Durham: Duke University Press. https://doi.org/10.1215/9780822388081.
Appadurai, Arjun. 2001. "Grassroots Globalization and the Research Imagination." In *Globalization*, edited by Arjun Appadurai, 1–21. Durham: Duke University Press. https://doi.org/10.1215/9780822383215-001.
Aracil, Lluis. 1965. "Conflit linguistique et normalisation linguistique dans l'Europe nouvelle." In *Cahiers de l'IRSCE*. Perpignan: Institut de recherche en sémiotique, communication et éducation, Université de Perpignan.
Aracil, Lluis. 1982. *Papers de Sociolingüística*. Barcelona: Edicions de la Magrana.
Arel, Dominique. 2002. "Language Categories in Censuses." In *Census and Identity: The Politics of Race, Ethnicity and Language in National Censuses*, edited by Daniel Kertzer and Dominique Arel, 92–120. Cambridge: Cambridge University Press.
Arendt, Hannah. (1951) 1968. *The Origins of Totalitarianism*, new ed. Orlando: Harcourt Press.
Atwood, Margaret. 2011. "George Orwell. Some Personal Connections." In *Other Worlds: SF and the Human Imagination*, 141–49. Toronto: McClelland and Stewart.
Bachmann, Christian, Jacqueline Lindenfeld, and Jacky Simonin. 1981. *Langage et communications sociales*. Paris: Hatier.
Bae, Sohee. 2014. "Anxiety, Insecurity and Complexity of Transnational Educational Migration among Korean Middle Class Families." *Journal of Asian Pacific Communication* 24 (2): 152–72.
Baggioni, Daniel. 1997. *Langues et nations en Europe*. Paris: Payot.
Baker, Lee D. 2004. "Franz Boas Out of the Ivory Tower." *Anthropological Theory* 4 (1): 29–51. https://doi.org/10.1177/1463499604040846.
Baker, Lee D. 2010. *Anthropology and the Racial Politics of Culture*. Durham: Duke University Press. https://doi.org/10.1215/9780822392699.
Bakhtin, Mikhail. 1968. *Rabelais and His World*, translated by H. Iswolsky. Cambridge, MA: MIT Press.
Bakhtin, Mikhail. 1981. *The Dialogic Imagination*, translated by C. Emerson and M. Holquist. Austin: University of Texas Press.
Bakhtin, Mikhail M. 1992. *Speech Genres and Other Late Essays*, edited by Caryl Emerson and Michael Holquist, translated by Vern W. McGee. Reprint, Austin: University of Texas Press.
Balibar, Renée. 1985. *L'institution du français. Essai sur le colinguisme des Carolingiens à la République*. Paris: Presses universitaires de France.
Balibar, Renée. (1974) 2007. *Les français fictifs*. Reprint, Fernelmont, Belgium: E.M.E.
Barlow, Maude. 2009. *Our Water Commons: Toward a New Freshwater Narrative*. Ottawa: Council of Canadians.
Barsky, Robert F. 1997. *Noam Chomsky: A Life of Dissent*. Cambridge, MA: MIT Press.
Barsky, Robert. 2011. *Zellig Harris: From American Linguistics to Socialist Zionism*. Cambridge, MA: MIT Press.
Battistella, Edwin. 2017. "Nikolai Trubetzkoy." In *Oxford Research Encyclopedia of Linguistics*. https://doi.org/10.1093/acrefore/9780199384655.013.355.
Baugh, John. 2000. *Beyond Ebonics: Linguistic Pride and Racial Prejudice*. Oxford: Oxford University Press.

Baugh, John. 2016. "Discursive Practices, Linguistic Repertoire and Racial Identities." In *The Routledge Handbook of Linguistic Anthropology*, edited by Nancy Bonvillain, 206–19. New York: Routledge.

Bauman, Richard, and Charles L. Briggs. 2003. *Voices of Modernity: Language Ideologies and the Politics of Inequality*. Cambridge: Cambridge University Press. https://doi.org/10.1017/CBO9780511486647.

Bauman, Richard, and Joel Sherzer, eds. 1974. *Explorations in the Ethnography of Speaking*. Cambridge: Cambridge University Press.

Bell, Lindsay. 2013. "Diamonds as Development: Why Natural Resource Exploitation Fails to Improve the Human Condition." PhD diss., University of Toronto.

Berardi, Franco. 2011. *After the Future*, edited by Gary Genosko and Nicholas Thoburn, translated by Arianna Bove, Melinda Cooper, Erik Empson, Giuseppina Mecchia Enrico, and Tiziana Terranova. Edinburgh: AK Press.

Bereiter, Carl, and Siegfried Engelmann. 1966. *Teaching Disadvantaged Children in the Pre-School*. Englewood Cliffs: Prentice Hall.

Berger, Peter, and Thomas Luckmann. 1966. *The Social Construction of Reality*. Garden City: Doubleday.

Bergounioux, Gabriel. 2006. "Entre épistémologie de la grammaire comparée et figure de l'intellectuel: la situation d'Antoine Meillet." In *Meillet Aujourd'hui*, edited by Gabriel Bergounioux and Charles de Lamberterie, 109–36. Paris: Peeters.

Berlant, Lauren. 2011. "Introduction: Affect in the Present." In *Cruel Optimism*, 1–21. Durham: Duke University Press. https://doi.org/10.1215/9780822394716-001.

Bernstein, Basil. 1971–77. *Class, Codes and Control*. Vols. 1–3 of *Towards a Theory of Educational Transmissions*. London: Routledge and Kegan Paul.

Billig, Michael. 1995. *Banal Nationalism*. London: Sage.

Blavatsky, Helena P. 1888. *The Secret Doctrine: The Synthesis of Science, Religion and Philosophy*. London: Theosophical Publishing.

Bleek, Wilhelm Heinrich Emanuel. 1862. *Comparative Grammar of South African Languages*. London: Trübner and Co.

Block, David, John Gray, and Marnie Holborow. 2012. *Neoliberalism and Applied Linguistics*. London: Routledge.

Blommaert, Jan, and Chris Bulcaen. 2000. "Critical Discourse Analysis." *Annual Review of Anthropology* 29 (1): 447–66. https://doi.org/10.1146/annurev.anthro.29.1.447.

Blommaert, Jan, James Collins, Monica Heller, Stef Slembrouck, Ben Rampton, and Jef Verschueren. 2001. "Discourse and Critique: Part One: Introduction." *Critique of Anthropology* 21 (1): 5–12. https://doi.org/10.1177/0308275X0102100101.

Boas, Franz. 1888. "The Indians of British Columbia." *Popular Science Monthly* 32: 636.

Boas, Franz. 1891. "Mixed Races." *Science* (n.s.) 17 (425): 179. https://doi.org/10.1126/science.ns-17.425.179.

Boas, Franz. (1894) 1940. "The Half-Blood Indian." In *Race, Language and Culture*, 138–48. Reprint, Chicago: University of Chicago Press.

Boas, Franz. (1896) 1940. "The Limitations of the Comparative Method of Anthropology." In *Race, Language and Culture*, 270–80. Reprint, Chicago: University of Chicago Press, 1940.

Boas, Franz. (1905) 1974. "The Documentary Function of the Text"; Letter to Professor Holmes, July 24, 1905. In *A Franz Boas Reader: The Shaping of American Anthropology*,

1883–1911, edited by George W. Stocking, 122–23. Reprint, Chicago: University of Chicago Press.

Boas, Franz. 1911. *The Handbook of American Indian Languages.* Washington: Government Printing Office.

Boas, Franz. (1911) 1938. *The Mind of Primitive Man.* Reprint, New York: Macmillan.

Boas, Franz. 1915. "Race and Nationality." *International Conciliation* 3: 63–76.

Boas, Franz. (1920) 1940. "The Classification of American Languages." In *Race, Language and Culture*, 211–18. Reprint, Chicago: University of Chicago Press, 1940.

Boas, Franz. (1929) 1940. "Classification of American Indian Languages." In *Race, Language and Culture*, 219–25. Reprint, Chicago: University of Chicago Press, 1940.

Boas, Franz, and George Hunt. 1902a. *Kwakiutl Texts I.* Vol. IV of *Publications of the Jesup North Pacific Expedition* in *Memoirs of the American Museum of Natural History*, vol. V. Leiden: E.J. Brill.

Boas, Franz, and George Hunt. 1902b. *Kwakiutl Texts II.* Vol. III of *Publications of the Jesup North Pacific Expedition* in *Memoirs of the American Museum of Natural History*. Leiden: E.J. Brill.

Boas, Franz, and George Hunt. 1905. *Kwakiutl Texts III.* Vol. V of *Publications of the Jesup North Pacific Expedition* in *Memoirs of the American Museum of Natural History*. Leiden: E.J. Brill.

Bonilla, Yarimar, and Jonathan Rosa. 2015. "#Ferguson: Digital Protest, Hashtag Ethnography, and the Racial Politics of Social Media in the United States." *American Ethnologist* 42 (1): 4–17. https://doi.org/10.1111/amet.12112.

Bourdieu, Pierre. 1972. *Esquisse d'une théorie de la pratique.* Geneva: Droz. https://doi.org/10.3917/droz.bourd.1972.01.

Bourdieu, Pierre. 1977. "The Economics of Linguistic Exchanges." *Social Sciences Information. Information Sur les Sciences Sociales* 16 (6): 645–68. https://doi.org/10.1177/053901847701600601.

Bourdieu, Pierre, and Jean-Claude Passeron. 1977. *Reproduction in Education, Society and Culture.* London: Sage.

Boutet, Josiane. 2008. *La vie verbale au travail. Des manufactures aux centres d'appels.* Toulouse: Octares.

Boutet, Josiane. 2012. "Language Workers: Emblematic Figures of Late Capitalism." In *Language in Late Capitalism: Pride and Profit*, edited by Alexandre Duchêne and Monica Heller, 207–30. New York: Routledge.

Bowen, John. 2004. "The Development of Southeast Asian Studies in the United States." In *The Politics of Knowledge: Area Studies and the Disciplines*, edited by David Szanton, 386–425. Berkeley: University of California Press.

Brandist, Craig. 2015. *The Dimensions of Hegemony: Language, Culture and Politics in Revolutionary Russia.* Leiden: Brill.

Braudel, Fernand. 1967. *Les structures du quotidien.* Vol. 1 of *Civilisation matérielle, économie et capitalisme, XVe–XVIIIe siècle.* Paris: Armand Colin.

Braudel, Fernand. 1979a. *Les jeux de l'échange.* Vol. 2 of *Civilisation matérielle, économie et capitalisme, XVe–XVIIIe siècle.* Paris: Armand Colin.

Braudel, Fernand. 1979b. *Le temps du monde.* Vol. 3 of *Civilisation matérielle, économie et capitalisme, XVe–XVIIIe siècle.* Paris: Armand Colin.

Briggs, Charles. 1998. "'You're a Liar, You're Just like a Woman': Constructing Dominant Ideologies of Language in Warao Men's Gossip." In *Language Ideologies: Practice and Theory*, edited by Bambi Schieffelin, Kathryn Woolard, and Paul Kroskrity, 229–55. Oxford: Oxford University Press.

Bright, William, ed. 1966. *Proceedings of the UCLA Sociolinguistics Conference*. The Hague: Mouton.

Brockmeier, Jens, and David Olson. 2009. "The Literacy Episteme from Innis to Derrida." In *The Cambridge Handbook of Literacy*, edited by David Olson and Nancy Torrance, 3–22. New York: Cambridge University Press. https://doi.org/10.1017/CBO9780511609664.002.

Brodkin, Karen. 1998. *How Jews Became White Folks and What That Says about Race in America*. New Brunswick, NJ: Rutgers University Press.

Bucholtz, Mary. 2001. "Reflexivity and Critique in Discourse Analysis." *Critique of Anthropology* 21 (2): 165–83. https://doi.org/10.1177/0308275X0102100203.

Buck, Andrew R., and Charlotte Frew. 2010. "Citizenship and Language Tests in Australia: Issues of Law and History." In *From Migrant to Citizen: Testing Language, Testing Culture*, edited by Christina Slade and Martina Möllering, 24–39. Basingstoke: Palgrave Macmillan.

Butler, Judith. 1990. *Gender Trouble: Feminism and the Subversion of Identity*. New York: Routledge.

Byrd, Jodi. 2011. *The Transit of Empire: Indigenous Critiques of Colonialism*. Minneapolis: University of Minnesota. https://doi.org/10.5749/minnesota/9780816676408.001.0001.

Calvet, Louis-Jean. 1974. *Linguistique et colonialisme. Petit traité de glottophagie*. Paris: Payot.

Calvez, Ronan. 2000. *La radio en langue bretonne. Roparz Hémon et Pierre-Jakez Hélias: deux rêves de la Bretagne*. Rennes: Les Presses de l'Université de Rennes. https://doi.org/10.4000/books.pur.8814.

Cameron, Deborah. 1992. *Feminism and Linguistic Theory*. New York: St. Martin's Press. https://doi.org/10.1007/978-1-349-22334-3.

Cameron, Deborah. 2000. *Good to Talk? Living and Working in a Communication Culture*. London: Sage.

Cameron, Deborah, and Don Kulick. 2003a. "Introduction: Language and Desire in Theory and Practice." *Language & Communication* 23 (2): 93–105. https://doi.org/10.1016/S0271-5309(02)00047-2.

Cameron, Deborah, and Don Kulick. 2003b. *Language and Sexuality*. Cambridge: Cambridge University Press. https://doi.org/10.1017/CBO9780511791178.

Canagarajah, Suresh. 1999. *Resisting Linguistic Imperialism in English Teaching*. Oxford: Oxford University Press.

Canale, German. 2015. "Mapping Conceptual Change: The Ideological Struggle for the Meaning of EFL in Uruguayan Education." *Journal of Linguistics and Language Teaching* 7 (3): 15–39.

Cannizzo, Jeanne. 1983. "George Hunt and the Invention of Kwakiutl Culture." *Canadian Review of Sociology and Anthropology/La revue canadienne de sociologie et d'anthropologie* 20 (1): 44–58. https://doi.org/10.1111/j.1755-618X.1983.tb00888.x.

Carbaugh, Donal. 1996. *Situating Selves: The Communication of Social Identities in American Scenes*. Albany: State University of New York Press.

Césaire, Aimé. 2000. *Discourse on Colonialism*, translated by Joan Pinkham. New York: Monthly Review Press.

Chakrabarty, Dipesh. 2000. *Provincializing Europe: Postcolonial Thought and Historical Difference*. Princeton: Princeton University Press.

Chandra, Shefali. 2012. *The Sexual Life of English: Languages of Caste and Desire in Colonial India*. Durham: Duke University Press. https://doi.org/10.1215/9780822395294.

Chatterjee, Partha. 2010. *Empire and Nation: Selected Essays*. New York: Columbia University Press. https://doi.org/10.7312/chat15220.

Chaudenson, Robert. 1979. *Les Créoles français*. Paris: Nathan.

Chevalier, Jean-Claude. 1996. "Les linguistes français et les pays d'Europe de l'Est de 1918 à 1931." *Cahiers de l'ILSL* 8: 57–74.

Chomsky, Noam. 1957. *Syntactic Structures*. The Hague: Mouton.

Chomsky, Noam. 1965. *Aspects of the Theory of Syntax*. Cambridge, MA: MIT Press.

Chomsky, Noam. 1997. *The Cold War and the University: Toward an Intellectual History of the Postwar Years*. New York: New Press.

Chun, Elaine, and Adrienne Lo. 2016. "Language and Racialization." In *The Routledge Handbook of Linguistic Anthropology*, edited by Nancy Bonvillain, 220–33. New York: Routledge.

Coates, Ken. 2015. *Idle No More and the Remaking of Canada*. Regina: University of Regina Press.

Codó, Eva, and Maria Rosa Garrido. 2014. "Shifting Discourses of Migrant Incorporation at a Time of Crisis: Understanding the Articulation of Language and Labour in the Catalan Non-Governmental Sector." *International Journal of Multilingualism* 11 (4): 389–408. https://doi.org/10.1080/14790718.2014.944529.

Cohen, Marcel. 1956. *Pour une sociologie du langage*. Paris: Albin Michel.

Cohen-Cole, Jamie. 2003. "Thinking about Thinking in Cold War America." PhD diss., Princeton University, Princeton, NJ.

Cohn, Bernard S. 1996. *Colonialism and Its Forms of Knowledge: The British in India*. Princeton, NJ: Princeton University Press.

Collins, James. 1999. "The Ebonics Controversy in Context: Literacies, Subjectivities and Language Ideologies in the United States." In *Language Ideological Debates*, edited by Jan Blommaert, 201–34. Berlin: Mouton de Gruyter. https://doi.org/10.1515/9783110808049.201.

Collins, James. 2001. "Selling the Market: Educational Standards, Discourse and Social Inequality." *Critique of Anthropology* 21 (2): 143–63. https://doi.org/10.1177/0308275X0102100202.

Cooper, Frederick. 2006. "Modernizing Colonialism and the Limits of Empire." In *Lessons of Empire: Imperial Histories and American Power*, edited by Craig Calhoun, Frederick Cooper, and Kevin Moore, 63–72. New York: New Press.

Cooper, Frederick, and Ann Laura Stoler, eds. 1997. *Tensions of Empire: Colonial Cultures in a Bourgeois World*. Berkeley: University of California Press. https://doi.org/10.1525/california/9780520205406.001.0001.

Coulthard, Glen. 2011. "Subjects of Empire: Indigenous Peoples and the 'Politics of Recognition.'" In *Home and Native Land: Unsettling Multiculturalism in Canada*, edited by May Chazan, Lisa Helps, Anna Stanley, and Sonali Thakkar, 31–50. Toronto: Between the Lines Press.

Crenshaw, Kimberlé Williams, and Andrea J. Ritchie, with Rachel Anspach, Rachel Gilmer, and Luke Harris. 2015. *Say Her Name: Resisting Police Brutality against Black Women*. New York: African American Policy Forum and Centre for Intersectionality and Social Policy Studies.

Cumings, Bruce. 2002. "Boundary Displacement: The State, the Foundations, and Area Studies during and after the Cold War." In *Learning Places: The Afterlives of Area Studies*, edited by Masao Miyoshi and Harry Harootunian, 261–315. Durham: Duke University Press. https://doi.org/10.1215/9780822383598-012.

Darnell, Regna. 2001. *Invisible Genealogies: A History of Americanist Anthropology*. Lincoln: University of Nebraska Press.

Darwin, Charles. (1859) 1909. *The Origin of Species*. New York: P.F. Collier.

Darwin, Charles. 1871. *The Descent of Man and Selection in Relation to Sex*. New York: D. Appleton.

Dave, Naisargi. 2010. "To Render Real the Imagined: An Ethnographic History of Lesbian Community in India." *Signs (Chicago, Ill.)* 35 (3): 595–619. https://doi.org/10.1086/648514.

Davenport, Charles Benedict, and Morris Steggerda. 1929. *Race Crossing in Jamaica*. Baltimore: Lord Baltimore Press.

De Certeau, Michel, Dominique Julia, and Jacques Revel. (1975) 2002. *Une politique de la langue. La Révolution française et les patois: l'enquête de Grégoire*. Paris: Gallimard.

DeFrancis, John. (1950) 1975. *Nationalism and Language Reform in China*. Princeton: Princeton University Press. Reprint, Octagon Books.

DeFrancis, John. 1977. *Colonialism and Language Policy in Viet Nam*. The Hague: Mouton.

DeGraff, Michel. 2001. "On the Origin of Creoles: A Cartesian Critique of Neo-Darwinian Linguistics." *Linguistic Typology* 5 (2–3): 213–310.

DeGraff, Michel. 2003. "Against Creole Exceptionalism." *Language* 79 (2): 391–410. https://doi.org/10.1353/lan.2003.0114.

Deleuze, Gilles. 2000. "Desire and Pleasure." In *More or Less*, edited by S. Lotringer, 248–57. Los Angeles: Semiotext(e).

Deleuze, Gilles, and Félix Guattari. 1987. *A Thousand Plateaus: Capitalism and Schizophrenia*, translated by B. Massumi. Minneapolis: University of Minnesota Press.

Deleuze, Gilles, and Claire Parnet. 1987. *Dialogues*. New York: Columbia University Press.

Derrida, Jacques. 1967. *De la Grammatologie*. Paris: Édition de Minuit.

Deutsch, Karl. 1953. *Nationalism and Social Communication: An Inquiry into the Foundations of Nationality*. Cambridge: Springer.

Deutscher, Isaac. 1974. "The Mysticism of Cruelty." In *George Orwell: A Collection of Critical Essays*, edited by Raymond Williams, 119–32. Englewood Cliffs, NJ: Prentice-Hall.

Diamond, Sigmund. 1992. *Compromised Campus: The Collaboration of Universities with the Intelligence Community, 1945–1955*. New York: Oxford University Press.

Díaz, Junot. 2016. "Radical Hope." *New Yorker*, November 21. http://www.newyorker.com/magazine/2016/11/21/aftermath-sixteen-writers-on-trumps-america.

Dick, Hilary, and Christina Wirtz. 2011. "Racializing Discourses: A Special Issue of the Journal of Linguistic Anthropology." *Journal of Linguistic Anthropology* 21 (S1): E2–10. https://doi.org/10.1111/j.1548-1395.2011.01094.x.

Dirim, İnci, and Peter Auer. 2004. *Türkisch Sprechen Nicht nur die Türken: über die Unschärfebeziehung Zwischen Sprache und Ethnie in Deutschland*. Berlin: Walter de Gruyter. https://doi.org/10.1515/9783110919790.

Dirks, Nicholas, ed. 1992. *Colonialism and Culture*. Ann Arbor: University of Michigan Press. https://doi.org/10.3998/mpub.9302.

Dirks, Nicholas. 2004. "South Asian Studies: Futures Past." In *The Politics of Knowledge: Area Studies and the Disciplines*, edited by David Szanton, 341–85. Berkeley: University of California Press.

Dittmar, Norbert. 1973. *Soziolinguistik. Exemplarische und Kritische Darstellung ihrer Theorie, Empirie und Anwendung. Mit Kommentierter Bibliographie Schwerpunkte Linguistik und Kommunikationswissenschaft*. Frankfurt: Athenäum-Verlag.

Dole, Christopher. 2012. "Revolution, Occupation and Love: The 2011 Year in Cultural Anthropology." *American Anthropologist* 114 (2): 227–39. https://doi.org/10.1111/j.1548-1433.2012.01421.x.

Duchêne, Alexandre. 2011. "Néolibéralisme, inégalités sociales et plurilinguisme: l'exploitation des ressources langagières et des locuteurs." *Langage & Société* 136 (2): 81–108. https://doi.org/10.3917/ls.136.0081.

Duchêne, Alexandre, and Monica Heller, eds. 2007. *Discourses of Endangerment*. London: Continuum.

Eagleton, Terry. 1974. "Orwell and the Lower-Middle-Class Novel." In *George Orwell: A Collection of Critical Essays*, edited by Raymond Williams, 10–33. Englewood Cliffs, NJ: Prentice-Hall.

Eagleton, Terry. 1991. *Ideology: An Introduction*. London: Verso.

Editors of Freedomways. 1998. *Paul Robeson: The Great Forerunner*. New York: International Publishers.

Eisenlohr, Patrick. 2007. "Creole Publics: Language, Cultural Citizenship, and the Spread of the Nation in Mauritius." *Comparative Studies in Society and History* 49 (4): 968–96. https://doi.org/10.1017/S0010417507000825.

Encrevé, Pierre. 1976. "Preface: Labov, linguistique, sociolinguistique." In *Sociolinguistique*, by William Labov, 9–35. Paris: Minuit.

Engels, Friedrich. (1894) 1968. "Letter to Borgius, January 25, 1894." In *Marx and Engels Correspondence*, translated by Donna Torr. New York: International Publishers. https://www.marxists.org/archive/marx/works/1894/letters/94_01_25.htm.

England, Kim, and Bernadette Stiell. 1997. "'They Think You're as Stupid as Your English Is': Constructing Foreign Domestic Workers in Toronto." *Environment & Planning* 29 (2): 195–215. https://doi.org/10.1068/a290195.

Engs, Robert. 1999. *Educating the Disenfranchised and Disinherited: Samuel Chapman Armstrong and Hampton Institute, 1839–1893*. Knoxville: University of Tennessee Press.

Errington, Joseph. 2008. *Linguistics in a Colonial World: A Story of Language, Meaning and Power*. Oxford: Blackwell.

Esterhill, Frank. 2000. *Interlingua Institute: A History*. New York: Interlingua Institute.

Evans, Stephen. 2002. "Macaulay's Minute Revisited: Colonial Language Policy in Nineteenth-Century India." *Journal of Multilingual and Multicultural Development* 23 (4): 260–81. https://doi.org/10.1080/01434630208666469.

Fabian, Johannes. 1983. *Time and the Other: How Anthropology Makes Its Object*. New York: Columbia University Press.

Fabian, Johannes. 1986. *Language and Colonial Power*. Berkeley: University of California Press.
Fairclough, Norman. 1989. *Language and Power*. London: Longman.
Fairclough, Norman. 1992. *Discourse and Social Change*. Cambridge: Polity.
Fairclough, Norman, and Ruth Wodak. 1997. "Critical Discourse Analysis." In *Discourse and Social Interaction*, edited by T. Van Dijk, 258–84. London: Sage.
Fanon, Frantz. 1963. *The Wretched of the Earth*, translated by Constance Farrington. New York: Grove Press. Originally published as *Les damnés de la terre* (1952).
Fanon, Frantz. 1967. *Black Skin, White Masks*. New York: Grove Press. Originally published as *Peau noire, masques blancs* (1952).
Feld, Stephen. 1996a. "A Poetics of Place: Ecological and Aesthetic Co-Evolution in a Papua New Guinea Rainforest Community." In *Redefining Nature: Ecology, Culture and Domestication*, edited by R. Ellen and K. Fukui, 61–88. Oxford: Berg Press.
Feld, Stephen. 1996b. "Waterfalls of Song: An Acoustemology of Place Resounding in Bosavi, Papua New Guinea." In *Senses of Place*, edited by Stephen Feld and Keith Basso, 92–135. Santa Fe: School of American Research.
Ferguson, Charles. 1959. "Diglossia." *Word* 15 (2): 325–40. https://doi.org/10.1080/00437956.1959.11659702.
Figueroa, Yomaira C. 2016. "The Life Work of Ana Celia Zentella: Anthropolitical Linguistics, Bilingualism and Linguistic Communities at a Crossroad." *Centro Journal* 28 (1): 176–95.
Fishman, Joshua, ed. 1972. *Readings in the Sociology of Language*. The Hague: Mouton.
Flores, Nelson, and Jonathan Rosa. 2015. "Undoing Appropriateness: Raciolinguistic Ideologies and Language Diversity in Education." *Harvard Educational Review* 85 (2): 149–71. https://doi.org/10.17763/0017-8055.85.2.149.
Flowerdew, John, and Rodney Jones, eds. 2016. "Occupy Hong Kong." *Language and Politics* 15 (5): 519–642. https://doi.org/10.1075/jlp.15.5.01flo.
Foucault, Michel. 1975. *Surveiller et punir*. Paris: Gallimard.
Fowler, Roger. 1979. *Language and Control*. London: Routledge and Kegan Paul.
Fox, Melvin. 1975. *Language and Development: A Retrospective Survey of Ford Foundation Language Projects, 1952–1974*. New York: Ford Foundation.
Franklin, Michael. 1995. *Sir William Jones*. Cardiff: University of Wales Press.
Gal, Susan. 1989. "Language and Political Economy." *Annual Review of Anthropology* 18 (1): 345–67. https://doi.org/10.1146/annurev.an.18.100189.002021.
Gal, Susan. 1991. "Between Speech and Silence: The Problematics of Research on Language and Gender." In *Gender at the Crossroads of Knowledge: Feminist Anthropology in the Postmodern Era*, edited by Micaela di Leonardo, 175–203. Berkeley: University of California Press.
Gal, Susan. 1993. "Diversity and Contestation in Linguistic Ideologies: German Speakers in Hungary." *Language in Society* 22 (3): 337–60. https://doi.org/10.1017/S0047404500017279.
Gal, Susan. 2010. "Language and Political Spaces." In *Language and Space*, edited by Peter Auer and Jürgen Schmidt, 33–49. Berlin: Mouton de Gruyter.
Gal, Susan. 2012. "Sociolinguistic Regimes and the Management of 'Diversity'." In *Language in Late Capitalism: Pride and Profit*, edited by Alexandre Duchêne and Monica Heller, 230–61. New York: Routledge.

Gao, Shuang, and Joseph Sung-Yul Park. 2015. "Space and Language: Learning under the Neoliberal Economy." *Journal of Linguistics and Language Teaching* 7 (3): 78–96.

Garvía, Roberto. 2015. *Esperanto and Its Rivals*. Philadelphia: University of Pennsylvania Press. https://doi.org/10.9783/9780812291278.

Gaudio, Rudolf. 2003. "Coffeetalk: Starbucks™ and the Commercialization of Casual Conversation." *Language in Society* 32: 659–91.

Gee, James Paul, Glynda Hull, and Colin Lankshear. 1996. *The New Work Order: Behind the Language of the New Capitalism*. Sydney: Allen and Unwin.

Gellner, Ernest. 1983. *Nations and Nationalism*. Oxford: Blackwell.

Gellner, Ernest. 1997. *Nationalism*. London: Weidenfeld and Nicolson.

Geoghegan, Richard. 1889. *Dr. Esperanto's International Language, Introduction and Complete Grammar*. Warsaw: Ch. Kelter.

Gershon, Ilana. 2011. "Neoliberal Agency." *Current Anthropology* 52 (4): 537–55. https://doi.org/10.1086/660866.

Gibson-Graham, J.K. 2006. *A Postcapitalist Politics*. Minneapolis: University of Minnesota Press.

Giddens, Anthony. 1982. *The Constitution of Society*. Berkeley: University of California Press.

Giglioli, Pier Paolo, ed. 1972. *Language in Social Context*. Harmondsworth: Penguin.

Gilbert, Glenn. 1984. "The First Systematic Survey of the World's Pidgins and Creoles: Hugo Schuchardt, 1882–1885." In *Papers from the York Creole Conference, September 24–27, 1983. York Papers in Linguistics* 11: 131–40. Department of Language, University of York.

Gilmour, Rachel. 2006. *Grammars of Colonialism: Representing Languages in Colonial South Africa*. New York: Palgrave Macmillan. https://doi.org/10.1057/9780230286856.

Glissant, Édouard. 1990. *Poétique de la relation*. Paris: Gallimard.

Good, Kristin. 2009. *Municipalities and Multiculturalism: The Politics of Immigration in Toronto and Vancouver*. Toronto: University of Toronto Press. https://doi.org/10.3138/9781442690417.

Goodwin, Marjorie Harness. 1990. *He-Said-She-Said: Talk as Social Organization among Black Children*. Bloomington: Indiana University Press.

Goody, Jack. 1986. *The Logic of Writing and the Organization of Society*. Cambridge: Cambridge University Press. https://doi.org/10.1017/CBO9780511621598.

Goody, Jack, and Ian Watt. 1963. *The Consequences of Literacy*. Indianapolis: Bobbs-Merrill.

Gordin, Michael. 2015. *Scientific Babel: How Science Was Done before and after Global English*. Chicago: University of Chicago Press. https://doi.org/10.7208/chicago/9780226000329.001.0001.

Government of the Philippine Islands, Department of Public Instruction. 1913. *Good Manners and Right Conduct*. Manila: Government Printing Office.

Gramsci, Antonio. 1971. *Selections from the Prison Notebooks of Antonio Gramsci*, edited and translated by Quintin Hoare and Geoffrey Nowell Smith. Reprint, New York: International Publishers.

Gray, John. 2012. "Neoliberalism, Celebrity and 'Aspirational Content' in English Language Teaching Textbooks for the Global Market." In *Neoliberalism and Applied Linguistics*, edited by David Block, John Gray, and Marnie Holborow, 86–113. London: Routledge.

Greenfield, Patricia. 1972. "Oral or Written Language: The Consequences for Cognitive Development in Africa, the United States and England." *Language and Speech* 15 (2): 169–78.

Grégoire, Abbé Henri. 1794. *Rapport sur la nécessité et les moyens d'anéantir les patois et universaliser l'usage de la langue française du 16 prairial an II*. Paris.

Grewal, Inderpal, and Caren Kaplan. 1994. "Transnational Feminist Practices and Questions of Postmodernity." In *Scattered Hegemonies: Postmodernity and Transnational Feminist Practices*, edited by Inderpal Grewal and Caren Kaplan, 1–36. Minneapolis: University of Minnesota Press.

Grillo, Ralph. 1989. *Dominant Languages*. Cambridge: Cambridge University Press.

Grimshaw, Anna, ed. 1992. *The C.L.R. James Reader*. Oxford: Blackwell.

Gumperz, John. 1979. *Crosstalk*. London: British Broadcasting Corporation.

Gumperz, John. 1982a. *Discourse Strategies*. Cambridge: Cambridge University Press. https://doi.org/10.1017/CBO9780511611834.

Gumperz, John, ed. 1982b. *Language and Social Identity*. Cambridge: Cambridge University Press.

Gumperz, John, and Dell Hymes, eds. 1972. *Directions in Sociolinguistics: The Ethnography of Communication*. New York: Holt, Rinehart and Winston.

Guy, Gregory. 1988. "Language and Social Class." In *The Sociocultural Context*, vol. IV of *Linguistics: The Cambridge Survey*, edited by Frederick Newmeyer, 37–63. Cambridge: Cambridge University Press.

Hage, Ghassan. 2002. "On the Side of Life: Joy and the Capacity of Being. Interview with Ghassan Hage." In *Hope: New Philosophies for Change*, edited by Mary Zournazi, 150–71. New York: Routledge.

Hagood, Margaret C. 2004. "A Rhizomatic Cartography of Adolescents, Popular Culture, and Constructions of Self." In *Spatializing Literacy Research and Practice*, edited by K.M. Leander and M. Sheehy, 143–60. New York: Peter Lang.

Hall, Catherine. 2000. "Introduction: Thinking the Postcolonial, Thinking the Empire." In *Cultures of Empire: A Reader. Colonizers in Britain and the Empire in the Nineteenth and Twentieth Centuries*, edited by Catherine Hall, 1–37. Manchester: Manchester University Press.

Hall, Catherine. 2009. "Macaulay's Nation." *Victorian Studies* 51 (3): 505–23. https://doi.org/10.2979/VIC.2009.51.3.505.

Hall, Kira, and Mary Bucholtz, eds. 1995. *Gender Articulated: Language and the Socially Constructed Self*. New York: Routledge.

Hall, Kira, Mary Bucholtz, and Birch Moonwomon, eds. 1992. *Locating Power: Proceedings of the Second Berkeley Women and Language Conference*. Berkeley: Women and Language Group.

Hall, Kira, Donna Goldstein, and Matthew Bruce Ingram. 2016. "The Hands of Donald Trump: Entertainment, Gesture, Spectacle." *HAU* 6 (2): 71–100. https://doi.org/10.14318/hau6.2.009.

Hall, Stuart. 1971. *Deviancy, Politics and the Media*. Birmingham, UK: Centre for Contemporary Cultural Studies.

Haller, Mark. 1963. *Eugenics: Hereditarian Attitudes in American Thought*. New Brunswick, NJ: Rutgers University Press.

Halliday, Michael. 1973. *Explorations in the Functions of Language*. London: Edward Arnold.

Handler, Richard. 1988. *Nationalism and the Politics of Culture in Quebec*. Madison: University of Wisconsin Press.

Hanks, William. 1990. *Referential Practice: Language and Lived Space among the Maya*. Chicago: University of Chicago Press.

Hanks, William. 2010. *Converting Words: Maya in the Age of the Cross*. Berkeley: University of California Press. https://doi.org/10.1525/california/9780520257702.001.0001.

Hanzeli, Victor Egon. 1969. *Missionary Linguistics in New France; A Study of Seventeenth- and Eighteenth-Century Descriptions of American Indian Languages*. The Hague: Mouton.

Hardt, Michael. 1999. "Affective Labor." *Boundary 2* 26 (2): 89–100.

Harney, Stefano, and Fred Moten. 2013. *The Undercommons: Fugitive Planning and Black Study*. Wivenhoe, NY: Minor Compositions.

Harris, Melvin. 1968. *The Rise of Anthropological Theory: A History of Theories of Culture*. New York: Columbia University Press.

Harris, Randy Allen. 1993. *The Linguistics Wars*. New York: Oxford University Press.

Harris, Roxy, Constant Leung, and Ben Rampton. 2002. "Globalization, Diaspora and Language Education in England." In *Globalization and Language Teaching*, edited by David Block and Deborah Cameron, 29–46. London: Routledge.

Harris, Zellig S. 1951. *Methods in Structural Linguistics*. Chicago: University of Chicago Press.

Harris, Zellig S. 1968. *Mathematical Structures of Language*. New York: Interscience.

Harris, Zellig S. 1988. *Language and Information*. New York: Columbia University Press.

Harris, Zellig S. 1997. *The Transformation of Capitalist Society*. Lanham, MD: Rowman and Littlefield.

Harvey, David. 1989. *The Condition of Postmodernity: An Inquiry into the Origins of Cultural Change*. Oxford: Wiley-Blackwell.

Harvey, David. 2000. *Spaces of Hope*. Berkeley: University of California Press.

Harvey, David. 2005. *A Brief History of Neoliberalism*. Oxford: Oxford University Press.

Harvey, Sean. 2015. *Native Tongues: Colonialism and Race from Encounter to the Reservation*. Cambridge, MA: Harvard University Press. https://doi.org/10.4159/harvard.9780674735798.

Havelock, Eric A. 1963. *Preface to Plato*. Oxford: Basil Blackwell.

Heath, Shirley Brice. 1983. *Ways With Words: Language, Life and Work in Communities and Classrooms*. New York: Cambridge University Press.

Hechter, Michael. 1975. *Internal Colonialism: The Celtic Fringe in British National Development*. Berkeley: University of California Press.

Heller, Monica. 1996. "Langue et identité: l'analyse anthropologique du français canadien." In *De la polyphonie à la symphonie: méthodes, théories et faits de la recherche pluridisciplinaire sur le français au Canada*, edited by Jürgen Erfurt, 19–26. Leipzig: Leipziger Universitätsverlag GmbH.

Heller, Monica. 1999. "Heated Language in a Cold Climate." In *Language Ideological Debates*, edited by Jan Blommaert, 143–70. Berlin: Mouton de Gruyter. https://doi.org/10.1515/9783110808049.143.

Heller, Monica. 2008. "Language and Nation-State: Challenges to Sociolinguistic Theory and Practice." *Journal of Sociolinguistics* 12 (4): 504–24. https://doi.org/10.1111/j.1467-9841.2008.00373.x.

Heller, Monica. 2010a. "The Commodification of Language." *Annual Review of Anthropology* 39 (1): 101–14. https://doi.org/10.1146/annurev.anthro.012809.104951.

Heller, Monica. 2010b. "Language as Resource in the Globalized New Economy." In *The Handbook of Language and Globalization*, edited by Nik Coupland, 347–65. Oxford: Wiley Blackwell. https://doi.org/10.1002/9781444324068.ch15.

Heller, Monica. 2011. *Paths to Postnationalism: A Critical Ethnography of Language and Identity*. Oxford: Oxford University Press. https://doi.org/10.1093/acprof:oso/9780199746866.001.0001.

Heller, Monica. 2017. "Dr. Esperanto, or, Anthropology and Alternative Worlds." *American Anthropologist* 119 (1): 12–22. https://doi.org/10.1111/aman.12824.

Heller, Monica, and Lindsay Bell. 2012. "Frontiers and Frenchness." In *Language in Late Capitalism: Pride and Profit*, edited by Alexandre Duchêne and Monica Heller, 161–82. London: Routledge.

Heller, Monica, Lindsay Bell, Michelle Daveluy, Mireille McLaughlin, and Hubert Noël. 2015. *Sustaining the Nation: The Making and Moving of Language and Nation*. Oxford: Oxford University Press.

Heller, Monica, and Alexandre Duchêne. 2012. "Pride and Profit: Changing Discourses of Language, Capital and Nation-State." In *Language in Late Capitalism: Pride and Profit*, edited by Alexandre Duchêne and Monica Heller, 1–21. New York: Routledge.

Heller, Monica, and Mireille McLaughlin. 2016. "Language Choice and Symbolic Domination." In *Discourse and Education. Encyclopedia of Language and Education*, 3rd ed., edited by Stanton Wortham, Deoksoon Kim, and Stephen May, 1–9. Switzerland: Springer International. https://doi.org/10.1007/978-3-319-02322-9_19-1.

Heller, Monica, and Joan Pujolar. 2009. "From CultureActe to CultureBiz: The Political Economy of Tourist Texts." *Sociolinguistic Studies* 3 (2): 177–202.

Henderson, Jennifer, and Pauline Wakeham. 2013. "Introduction." In *Reconciling Canada: Critical Perspectives on the Culture of Redress*, edited by Jennifer Henderson and Pauline Wakeham, 3–31. Toronto: University of Toronto Press.

Hendricks, Christina, and Kelly Oliver, eds. 1999. *Language and Liberation: Feminism, Philosophy and Language*. Albany: SUNY Press.

Hennessey, Rosemary. 1993. *Materialist Feminism and the Politics of Discourse*. London: Routledge.

Herman, Edward S., and Noam Chomsky. 1988. *Manufacturing Consent*. New York: Pantheon Books.

Herman, Ellen. 1998. "Project Camelot and the Career of Cold War Psychology." In *University and Empire: Money and Politics in the Social Sciences during the Cold War*, edited by C. Simpson, 97–133. New York: New York Press.

Herskovits, Melville J. 1953. *Franz Boas*. New York: Charles Scribner's Sons.

Higonnet, Patrice. 1980. "The Politics of Linguistic Terrorism and Grammatical Hegemony during the French Revolution." *Social History* 5: 41–69.

Hill, Jane. 1998. "'Today There is No Respect': Nostalgia, 'Respect', and Oppositional Discourse in Mexicano (Nahuatl) Language Ideology." In *Language Ideologies:*

Practice and Theory, edited by Bambi Schieffelin, Kathryn Woolard, and Paul Kroskrity, 68–86. Oxford: Oxford University Press.

Hiramoto, Mie, and Joseph Sung-Yul Park. 2014. "Anxiety, Insecurity, and Border Crossing: Language Contact in a Globalizing World." *Journal of Asian Pacific Communication* 24 (2): 141–51.

Hirsch, Eric. 1995. "Introduction. Landscape: Between Place and Space." In *The Anthropology of Landscape: Perspectives on Place and Space*, edited by Eric Hirsch and Michael O'Hanlon, 1–30. Oxford: Clarendon Press.

Hobsbawm, Eric. 1987. *The Age of Empire 1875–1914*. London: Abacus.

Hobsbawm, Eric. 1990. *Nations and Nationalism since 1760*. Cambridge: Cambridge University Press.

Hobsbawm, Eric, and Terence Ranger, eds. 1983. *The Invention of Tradition*. Cambridge: Cambridge University Press.

Hodges, Adam, and Chad Nilep, eds. 2007. *Discourse, War and Terrorism*. Amsterdam: John Benjamins. https://doi.org/10.1075/dapsac.24.

Hogan-Brun, Gabrielle, Clare Mar-Molinero, and Patrick Stevenson, eds. 2009. *Discourses on Language and Integration: Critical Perspectives on Language Testing Regimes in Europe*. Amsterdam: John Benjamins. https://doi.org/10.1075/dapsac.33.

Holborow, Marnie. 2015. *Language and Neoliberalism*. London: Routledge.

Holm, John. 1988a. *Theory and Structure*, vol. I of *Pidgins and Creoles*. Cambridge: Cambridge University Press.

Holm, John. 1988b. *Reference Survey*, vol. II of *Pidgins and Creoles*. Cambridge: Cambridge University Press.

Holquist, Michael. 1990. *Dialogism: Bakhtin and His World*. London: Routledge.

Hornstein, Norbert. 1998. "Noam Chomsky." In *Routledge Encyclopedia of Philosophy*, vol. 2, edited by Edward Craig, 335–41. London: Routledge.

Howard-Hassman, Rhoda, and Mark Gibney. 2008. "Introduction: Apologies and the West." In *The Age of Apologies: Facing Up to the Past*, edited by Mark Gibney, Rhonda Howard-Hassman, Jean-Marc Coicaud, and Niklaus Steiner, 1–12. Philadelphia: University of Pennsylvania Press.

Huck, Dominique. 2015. *Une histoire des langues d'Alsace*. Strasbourg: La Nuée Bleue.

Huebner, Thom. 1999. "Obituary: Charles Albert Ferguson July 6, 1921– September 2, 1998." *Language in Society* 28 (3): 431–37. https://doi.org/10.1017/S004740459900305X.

Hughes, Everett. 1943. *French Canada in Transition*. Chicago: University of Chicago Press.

Hutton, Christopher. 1999. *Linguistics and the Third Reich: Mother-Tongue Fascism, Race and the Science of Language*. London: Routledge.

Hutton, Christopher. 2015. "Sociolinguistics and Its Metalinguistic Paradox." Paper presented at The Sociolinguistics of Globalization: (De)centring and (De)standardization, University of Hong Kong, Hong Kong, June 3–5.

Hutton, Christopher, and John Joseph. 1998. "Back to Blavatsky: The Impact of Theosophy on Modern Linguistics." *Language & Communication* 18 (3): 181–204. https://doi.org/10.1016/S0271-5309(97)00031-1.

Hyatt, Marshall. 1990. *Franz Boas, Social Activist: The Dynamics of Ethnicity*. Westport, CT: Greenwood Press.

Hymes, Dell. 1960. "Lexicostatistics so Far." *Current Anthropology* 1 (1): 3–44. https://doi.org/10.1086/200074.
Hymes, Dell, ed. 1964. *Language in Culture and Society*. New York: Harper and Row.
Hymes, Dell. 1966. "Two Types of Linguistic Relativity." In *Sociolinguistics*, edited by William Bright, 114–58. The Hague: Mouton.
Hymes, Dell, ed. 1971. *Pidginization and Creolization of Languages*. Cambridge: Cambridge University Press.
Hymes, Dell. 1972a. "Models of the Interaction of Language and Social Life." In *Directions in Sociolinguistics: The Ethnography of Communication*, edited by John Gumperz and Dell Hymes, 35–71. New York: Holt, Rinehart and Winston.
Hymes, Dell, ed. 1972b. *Reinventing Anthropology*. Ann Arbor: University of Michigan Press.
Hymes, Dell. 1996. *Ethnography, Linguistics and Narrative Inequality: Towards an Understanding of Voice*. London: Taylor and Francis.
Hymes, Dell. 1999. "Introduction." In *Reinventing Anthropology*, edited by Dell Hymes, v–xlix. Ann Arbor: University of Michigan Press.
Hymes, Dell, and John Fought. 1981. *American Structuralism*. New York: Mouton.
Innis, Harold. 1950. *Empire and Communications*. Oxford: Clarendon Press.
Inoue, Miyako. 2006. *Vicarious Language: Gender and Linguistic Modernity in Japan*. Berkeley: University of California Press.
Inoue, Miyako. 2007. "Language and Gender in an Age of Neoliberalism." *Gender and Language* 1 (1): 79–91. https://doi.org/10.1558/genl.2007.1.1.79.
Inoue, Miyako. 2011. "Stenography and Ventriloquism in Late Nineteenth Century Japan." *Language & Communication* 31 (3): 181–90. https://doi.org/10.1016/j.langcom.2011.03.001.
Irvine, Judith. 2001. "The Family Romance of Colonial Linguistics: Gender and Family in Nineteenth-Century Representations of African Languages." In *Languages and Publics: The Making of Authority*, edited by S. Gal and K. Woolard, 13–29. Manchester: St. Jerome.
Irvine, Judith, and Susan Gal. 2000. "Language Ideology and Linguistic Differentiation." In *Regimes of Language: Ideologies, Polities, Identities*, edited by Paul Kroskrity, 35–84. Santa Fe: School of American Research Press.
Isaac, Joel. 2007. "The Human Sciences in Cold War America." *Historical Journal (Cambridge, England)* 50 (03): 725–46. https://doi.org/10.1017/S0018246X07006334.
Jakobson, Roman. 1934. "Slavische Sprachfragen in der Sovjet-union [Slavic Language Questions in the Soviet Union]." *Slavische Rundschau* 6 (5): 324–43.
Jakobson, Roman. 1943. *Moudrost Starých Čechů: Odvěké Základy Národního Odboje, Napsal* [The Wisdom of Old Czechs: The Old Foundations of the New Resistance]. New York: Československý kulturní kroužek.
Jakobson, Roman. 1960. "Closing Statement: Linguistics and Poetics." In *Style in Language*, edited by Thomas Sebeok, 350–77. New York: Wiley.
James, Matthew. 2013. "Neoliberal Heritage Redress." In *Reconciling Canada: Critical Perspectives on the Culture of Redress*, edited by Jennifer Henderson and Pauline Wakeham, 31–46. Toronto: University of Toronto Press.
Jameson, Frederic. 2005. *Archaeologies of the Future: The Desire Called Utopia and Other Science Fictions*. London: Verso.

Jang, In Chull. 2015a. "Language Learning as a Struggle for Distinction in Today's Corporate Recruitment Culture: An Ethnographic Study of English Study Abroad Practices among South Korean Undergraduates." In "Critical Perspectives on Neoliberalism in Second/Foreign Language Education," special issue, *Journal of Linguistics and Language Teaching* 7 (3): 57–77.

Jang, In Chull. 2015b. "Stratification of English-speaking Interlocutors in Educational Migration: A Discursive Strategy of South Korean Undergraduates Studying English Overseas." Paper presented at The Sociolinguistics of Globalization: (De)centring and (De)standardization, University of Hong Kong, Hong Kong, June 3–5.

Jang, In Chull. 2016. "Consuming Global Language and Culture: South Korean Youth in English Study Abroad." PhD diss., University of Toronto.

Jensen, Arthur. 1969. "How Much Can We Boost IQ and Scholastic Achievement?" *Harvard Educational Review* 39 (1): 1–23. https://doi.org/10.17763/haer.39.1.l3u15956627424k7.

Jespersen, Otto. 1922. *Language: Its Nature Development and Origin*. London: George Allen and Unwin.

Johnstone, Barbara. 2010. "Language and Geographical Space." In *Language and Space*, edited by Peter Auer and Jürgen Schmidt, 1–17. Berlin: Mouton de Gruyter.

Jones, Sir William. (1786) 1967. "The Third Anniversary Discourse, on the Hindus." In *A Reader in Nineteenth-Century Historical Indo-European Linguistics*, edited and translated by Winifred P. Lehmann, 7–20. Reprint, Bloomington: Indiana University Press.

Jørgensen, J. Normann. 2008. "Polylingual Languaging around and among Children and Adolescents." *International Journal of Multilingualism* 5 (3): 161–76. https://doi.org/10.1080/14790710802387562.

Joseph, John. 1999. "'A Matter of Consequenz': Humboldt, Race and the Genius of the Chinese Language." *Historiographia Linguistica* 26 (1–2): 89–148. https://doi.org/10.1075/hl.26.1-2.06jos.

Kachru, Braj. 1991. "World Englishes and Applied Linguistics." In *Languages and Standards: Issues, Attitudes, Case Studies*, edited by M.L. Tickoo, 359–83. Singapore: SEAMEO Regional Language Centre.

Kallmeyer, Werner. 1994. *Kommunikation in der Stadt*. Berlin: Walter de Gruyter.

Kalmar, Ivan, and Derek J. Penslar, eds. 2005. *Orientalism and the Jews*. Hanover, NH: University Press of New England.

Kandiah, Thiru. 1991. "Extenuatory Sociolinguistics: Diverting Attention from Issues to Symptoms in Cross-Cultural Communication Studies." *Multilingua* 10 (4): 345–80. https://doi.org/10.1515/mult.1991.10.4.345.

Kelly-Holmes, Helen. 2000. "Bier, Parfum, Kaas: Language Fetish in European Advertising." *Cultural Studies* 3 (1): 67–82.

Kelly-Holmes, Helen. 2005. *Advertising as Multilingual Communication*. London: Palgrave Macmillan. https://doi.org/10.1057/9780230503014.

Kertzer, Daniel, and Dominique Arel, eds. 2002. *Census and Identity: The Politics of Race, Ethnicity and Language in National Census*. Cambridge: Cambridge University Press.

Kim, K.M. 2006. "1920's Esperanto Spread Movement and the Perceptions of National Movements Activists." *Historical Studies (Melbourne, Vic.)* 16: 133–63.

Kino-nda-niimi Collective. 2014. *The Winter We Danced. Voices from the Past, the Future and the Idle No More Movement.* Winnipeg: ARP Books.

Klein, Naomi. 2000. *No Logo: Taking Aim at the Brand Bullies.* Toronto: Vintage Canada.

Klein, Naomi. 2014. *This Changes Everything.* Toronto: Knopf.

Klein, Wolfgang, and Norbert Dittmar. 1979. *Developing Grammars: The Acquisition of German Syntax by Foreign Workers.* Berlin: Springer Verlag. https://doi.org/10.1007/978-3-642-67385-6.

Klemperer, Victor. 1995. *Ich Will Zeugnis Ablegen Bis Zum Letzten.* Berlin: Aufbau-Verlag.

Klemperer, Victor. 2000. *The Language of the Third Reich: LTI Lingua Tertii Imperii, a Philologist's Notebook.* London: Athlone.

Kochman, Thomas. 1973. "Review of *Language Behavior in a Black Urban Community* by Claudia Mitchell-Kernan." *Language* 49 (4): 967–83. https://doi.org/10.2307/412076.

Koerner, Konrad. 1996/1997. "Notes on the History of the Concept of Language as a System 'où tout se tient'." *Linguistica Atlantica* 18/19: 1–20.

Kohn, Eduardo. 2013. *How Forests Think: Toward an Anthropology beyond the Human.* Berkeley: University of California Press. https://doi.org/10.1525/california/9780520276109.001.0001.

Kopf, David. 1995. "The Historiography of British Orientalism, 1772–1992." In *Objects of Enquiry: The Life, Contributions, and Influences of Sir William Jones (1746–1794)*, edited by Garland Cannon and Kevin Brine, 141–60. New York: New York University Press.

Kress, Gunter, and Robert Hodge. 1979. *Language as Ideology.* London: Routledge and Kegan Paul.

Kroskrity, Paul. 1998. "Arizona Tewa Speech as a Manifestation of a Dominant Language Ideology." In *Language Ideologies: Practice and Theory*, edited by Bambi Schieffelin, Kathryn Woolard, and Paul Kroskrity, 103–22. Oxford: Oxford University Press.

Kroskrity, Paul, ed. 2000. *Regimes of Language: Ideologies, Polities, and Identities.* Santa Fe: School of American Research Press.

Kroskrity, Paul. 2010. "Language Ideologies—Evolving Perspective." In *Language Use and Society (Handbook of Pragmatics Highlights)*, edited by Jürgen Jaspers, 192–211. Amsterdam: John Benjamins.

Kulick, Don. 2000. "Gay and Lesbian Language." *Annual Review of Anthropology* 29 (1): 243–85. https://doi.org/10.1146/annurev.anthro.29.1.243.

Labov, William. 1972a. *Language in the Inner City: Studies in the Black English Vernacular.* Philadelphia: University of Pennsylvania Press.

Labov, William. 1972b. *Sociolinguistic Patterns.* Philadelphia: University of Pennsylvania Press.

Labov, William. 1982. "Objectivity and Commitment in Linguistic Science: The Case of the Black English Trial in Ann Arbor." *Language in Society* 11 (2): 165–202. https://doi.org/10.1017/S0047404500009192.

Lafont, Robert. 1971. *Décoloniser la France.* Paris: Gallimard.

Lafont, Robert. 1997. *Quarante ans de sociolinguistique à la périphérie.* Paris: l'Harmattan.

Lähteenmäki, Mika. 2006. "Nikolai Marr and the Idea of a Unified Language." *Language & Communication* 26 (3–4): 285–95. https://doi.org/10.1016/j.langcom.2006.02.006.

Lakoff, Robin Tolmach. 1975. *Language and Woman's Place*. New York: Harper and Row.
Lakoff, Robin Tolmach. 2004. "Author's Introduction: Language and Woman's Place Revisited." In *Language and Woman's Place: Text and Commentaries*, edited by Mary Bucholtz, 15–28. Oxford: Oxford University Press.
Laks, Bernard. 1984. "Le champ de la sociolinguistique française, de 1968 à 1983, production et fonctionnement." *Langue Française* 63 (1): 103–28. https://doi.org/10.3406/lfr.1984.5198.
Lan, P.C. 2003. "'They Have More Money but I Speak Better English!': Transnational Encounters between Filipina Domestics and Taiwanese Employers." *Identities (Yverdon)* 10 (2): 133–61. https://doi.org/10.1080/10702890304325.
Lancaster, Roger. 1993. *The Trouble with Nature: Sex in Science and Popular Culture*. Berkeley: University of California Press.
Leander, Kevin M., and Deborah W. Rowe. 2006. "Mapping Literacy Spaces in Motion: A Rhizomatic Analysis of a Classroom Literacy Performance." *Reading Research Quarterly* 41 (4): 428–60. https://doi.org/10.1598/RRQ.41.4.2.
Leap, William. 1995. *Beyond the Lavender Lexicon: Authenticity, Imagination and Appropriation in Lesbian and Gay Languages*. Amsterdam: Gordan and Breach.
Lefèvre, Josette, and Maurice Tournier, eds. 1987. "Discours syndical ouvrier en France." *Mots* 14 (1): 5–198.
Lehmann, Winifred. 1967. "August Schleicher: Introduction to a Compendium of the Comparative Grammar of Indo-European, Sanskrit, Greek and Latin Languages." In *A Reader in Nineteenth-Century Historical Indo-European Linguistics*, edited and translated by Winifred P. Lehmann, 87–97. Bloomington: Indiana University Press.
Lenin, V.I. (1917) 1987. "Imperialism: The Highest Stage of Capitalism." In *The Essential Works of Lenin: What Is to Be Done? and Other Writings*, edited by Henry M. Christman, 177–364. Reprint, New York: Dover.
LePage, Robert, ed. 1961. *Creole Language Studies II: Proceedings of the Conference on Creole Language Studies, University of the West Indies, Mona, 1959*. London: Macmillan.
Lévi-Strauss, Claude. 1962. *La pensée sauvage*. Paris: Plon.
Lieberson, Stanley, ed. 1966. *Explorations in Sociolinguistics*. Bloomington: Indiana University Press.
Lin, Angel, and Peter Martin, eds. 2005. *Decolonisation, Globalization: Language-in-Education Policy and Practice*. Bristol: Multilingua Matters.
Lins, Ulrich. 2008. "Esperanto as Language and Idea in China and Japan." *Language Problems and Language Planning* 32 (1): 47–60. https://doi.org/10.1075/lplp.32.1.05lin.
Litosseliti, Lia, and Jane Sunderland, eds. 2002. *Gender Identity and Discourse Analysis*. Amsterdam: John Benjamins. https://doi.org/10.1075/dapsac.2.
Livia, Anna, and Kira Hall, eds. 1997. *Queerly Phrased: Language, Gender, Sexuality*. New York: Oxford University Press.
Lo, Adrienne, and Jonathan Rosa. 2014. "Racial and Linguistic Ontologies. Society for Linguistic Anthropology Presidential Conversation." American Anthropological Association Annual Meeting. Washington, DC, December.
Lo, Jacqueline. 2002. "Miscegenation's 'Dusky Human Consequences'." *Postcolonial Studies* 5 (3): 297–307. https://doi.org/10.1080/1368879022000032801.
Lorente, Beatriz. 2007. "Mapping English Linguistic Capital: The Case of Filipino Domestic Workers in Singapore." PhD diss., National University of Singapore.

Lorente, Beatriz. 2012. "The Making of 'Workers of the World': Language and the Labor Brokerage State." In *Language in Late Capitalism: Pride and Profit*, edited by Alexandre Duchêne and Monica Heller, 183–206. New York: Routledge.

Lowe, Lisa. 2015. *The Intimacies of Four Continents*. Durham: Duke University Press. https://doi.org/10.1215/9780822375647.

Lucas, Scott. 2003. *Orwell*. London: Haus Publishing.

Lucy, John. 1992. *Language, Diversity and Thought: A Reformulation of the Linguistic Relativity Hypothesis*. Cambridge: Cambridge University Press.

Lüdi, Georges. 2012. "Traces of Monolingual and Plurilingual Ideologies in the History of Language Policies in France." In *Multilingualism in European History*, edited by M. Hüning, U. Vogl, and O. Moliner, 205–30. Amsterdam: John Benjamins. https://doi.org/10.1075/mdm.1.11lud.

Lyons, Scott. 2010. *X-Marks: Native Signatures of Assent*. Minneapolis: University of Minnesota Press. https://doi.org/10.5749/minnesota/9780816666768.001.0001.

Macaulay, Thomas Babington. (1835) 1972. "Minute on Indian Education." In *Selected Writings*, edited by John Clive and Thomas Pinney, 237–51. Reprint, Chicago: University of Chicago Press.

Makofsky, Abraham. 1989. "Experience of Native Americans at a Black College: Indian Students at Hampton Institute, 1878–1923." *Journal of Ethnic Studies* 17 (3): 31–46.

Malthus, Thomas. 1798. *An Essay on the Principle of Population, as It Affects the Future Improvement of Society with Remarks on the Speculations of Mr. Godwin, M. Condorcet, and Other Writers*. Anonymously published.

Maltz, Daniel, and Ruth Borker. 1982. "A Cultural Approach to Male-Female Miscommunication." In *Language and Social Identity*, edited by John Gumperz, 196–216. Cambridge: Cambridge University Press.

Manessy, Gabriel, and Paul Wald, eds. 1979. *Plurilinguisme: normes, situations, stratégies: études sociolinguistiques*. Paris: L'Harmattan.

Mannheim, Bruce. 2011. *The Language of the Inka since the European Invasion*. Austin: University of Texas Press.

Marcellesi, Jean-Baptiste. 1989. "Corse et Théorie Sociolinguistique: Reflets Croisés." In *L'Île Miroir*, edited by G. Ravis-Giordani, 165–74. Ajaccio: La marge.

Marcellesi, Jean-Baptiste, and Bernard Gardin. 1974. *Introduction à la sociolinguistique: La linguistique sociale*. Paris: Larousse.

Martin, Emily. 1994. *Flexible Bodies: Tracking Immunity in American Culture from the Days of Polio to the Age of Aids*. Boston: Beacon Press.

Martin-Nielsen, Janet. 2009. "Private Knowledge, Public Tensions. Theory Commitment in Post War American Linguistics." PhD diss., University of Toronto.

Martin-Nielsen, Janet. 2010a. "Redefining What Matters: Syntactic Explanations in American Linguistics 1955–1970." *Canadian Journal of Linguistics/Revue canadienne de linguistique* 55 (3): 331–58. https://doi.org/10.1353/cjl.2010.0009.

Martin-Nielsen, Janet. 2010b. "'This War for Men's Minds': The Birth of a Human Science in Cold War America." *History of the Human Sciences* 23 (5): 131–55. https://doi.org/10.1177/0952695110378952.

Martin-Nielsen, Janet. 2011. "A Forgotten Social Science? Creating a Place for Linguistics in Historical Dialogue." *Journal of the History of the Behavioral Sciences* 47 (2): 147–72. https://doi.org/10.1002/jhbs.20493.

Martin Rojo, Luisa. 2016. *Occupy: The Spatial Dynamics of Discourse in Global Protest Movements*. Amsterdam: John Benjamins.

Maryns, Katrijn. 2006. *The Asylum Speaker: Language in the Belgian Asylum Procedure*. London: Routledge.

Marx, Karl. (1859) 1979. *A Contribution to the Critique of Political Economy*, edited by Maurice Dobb. Reprint, London: Lawrence and Wishart.

Maud, Ralph. 1985. "The Henry Tate-Franz Boas Collaboration on Tsimshan Mythology." *American Ethnologist* 16: 156–62.

Mawani, Renisa. 2009. *Colonial Proximities: Cross-Racial Encounters and Juridical Truths in British Columbia, 1871–1921*. Vancouver: UBC Press.

May, Glenn. 1980. *Social Engineering in the Philippines: The Aims, Execution, and Impact of American Colonial Policy, 1900–1913*. Westport, CT: Greenwood Press.

McDonald, Sharon. 1989. *We Are Not French: Language, Culture and Identity in Brittany*. London: Routledge.

McElhinny, Bonnie. 1995. "Challenging Hegemonic Masculinities: Female and Male Police Officers Handling Domestic Violence." In *Gender Articulated*, edited by Kira Hall and Mary Bucholtz, 217–43. New York: Routledge.

McElhinny, Bonnie. 1998. "Genealogies of Gender Theory: Practice Theory and Feminism in Sociocultural and Linguistic Anthropology." *Social Analysis* 42 (3): 164–89.

McElhinny, Bonnie. 2004. "'Radical Feminist' as Label, Libel and Laudatory Chant: The Politics of Theoretical Taxonomies in Feminist Linguistics." In *Language and Woman's Place: Text and Commentaries*, edited by Mary Bucholtz, 129–35. Oxford: Oxford University Press.

McElhinny, Bonnie. 2006. "Written in Sand: Language and Landscape in an Environmental Dispute in Southern Ontario." *Critical Discourse Studies* 3 (2): 123–52. https://doi.org/10.1080/17405900600908087.

McElhinny, Bonnie. 2010. "The Audacity of Affect: Gender, Race and History in Linguistic Accounts of Legitimacy and Belonging." *Annual Review of Anthropology* 39 (1): 309–28. https://doi.org/10.1146/annurev-anthro-091908-164358.

McElhinny, Bonnie. 2012. "Silicon Valley Sociolinguistics? Analyzing Language, Gender and 'Communities of Practice' in the New Knowledge Economy." In *Language in Late Capitalism: Pride and Profit*, edited by Alexandre Duchêne and Monica Heller, 230–61. New York: Taylor & Francis.

McElhinny, Bonnie. 2014. "Theorizing Gender in Sociolinguistics and Linguistic Anthropology: Towards Effective Interventions in Gender Inequity." In *The Handbook of Language, Gender and Sexuality*, 2nd ed., edited by Janet Holmes, Miriam Meyerhoff, and Susan Ehrlich, 48–67. Oxford: Basil Blackwell. https://doi.org/10.1002/9781118584248.ch2.

McElhinny, Bonnie. 2016a. "Language and Political Economy." In *The Routledge Handbook of Linguistic Anthropology*, edited by Nancy Bonvillain, 279–300. New York: Routledge.

McElhinny, Bonnie. 2016b. "Reparations and Racism, Discourse and Diversity: Neoliberal Multiculturalism and the Canadian Age of Apologies." *Language & Communication* 51: 50–68. https://doi.org/10.1016/j.langcom.2016.07.003.

McGee, W.J. 1895. "Some Principles of Nomenclature." *American Anthropologist* 8 (3): 279–86. https://doi.org/10.1525/aa.1895.8.3.02a00060.

McGill, Kenneth. 2013. "Political Economy and Language: A Review of Some Recent Literature." *Journal of Linguistic Anthropology* 23 (2): 84–101. https://doi.org/10.1111/jola.12015.

McGregor, Deborah. 2015. "Indigenous Women, Water Justice and Zaagidowin (Love)." *Canadian Women's Studies* 30 (2–3): 71–78.

McIlvenny, Paul, ed. 2002. *Talking Gender and Sexuality.* Amsterdam: John Benjamins. https://doi.org/10.1075/pbns.94.

McKittrick, Katherine. 2015. "Yours in the Intellectual Struggle: Sylvia Wynter and the Realization of the Living." In *Sylvia Wynter: On Being Human as Praxis*, edited by Katherine McKittrick, 1–8. Durham: Duke University Press.

McLuhan, Marshall. 1962. *The Gutenberg Galaxy: The Making of Typographic Man.* Toronto: University of Toronto Press.

McNamara, Tim. 2009. "Language Tests and Social Policy: A Commentary." In *Discourses on Language and Integration: Critical Perspectives on Language Testing Regimes in Europe*, edited by Gabrielle Hogan-Brun, Clare Mar-Molinero, and Patrick Stevenson, 153–64. Amsterdam: John Benjamins. https://doi.org/10.1075/dapsac.33.12nam.

Medvedev, Pavel N., and Mikhail M. Bakhtin. 1978. *The Formal Method in Literary Scholarship: A Critical Introduction to Sociological Poetics*, translated by Albert J. Wehrle. Baltimore: Johns Hopkins University Press. Originally published as *Formalńyĭ metod v literaturovedeni*.

Meillet, Antoine. 1893. "Les lois du langage I: les lois phonétiques." *Revue internationale de sociologie* 1: 311–21.

Meillet, Antoine. 1928. *Les langues dans l'Europe nouvelle*. Paris: Payot.

Memmi, Albert. 1957. *Portrait du colonisé, précédé du portrait du colonisateur*. Paris: Buchet/Chastel.

MFY Legal Services, 2013. *MFY Legal Services, Inc.: Mobilizing for Justice since 1963*. New York: MFY Legal Services.

Mignolo, Walter. 1992a. "Nebrija in the New World: The Question of the Letter, the Colonization of Amerindian Languages, and the Discontinuity of the Classical Tradition." *L'Homme* 32 (122/124): 185–207. https://doi.org/10.3406/hom.1992.369532.

Mignolo, Walter. 1992b. "On the Colonization of Amerindian Languages and Memories: Renaissance Theories of Writing and the Discontinuity of the Classical Tradition." *Comparative Studies in Society and History* 34 (2): 301–30. https://doi.org/10.1017/S0010417500017709.

Mignolo, Walter. 1995. *The Darker Side of the Renaissance: Literacy, Territory, and Colonization*. Ann Arbor: University of Michigan Press.

Mignolo, Walter. 2015. "Sylvia Wynter: What Does It Mean to Be Human?" In *Sylvia Wynter: On Being Human as Praxis*, edited by Katherine McKittrick, 106–23. Durham: Duke University Press.

Million, Dian. 2013. *Therapeutic Nations: Healing in an Age of Indigenous Human Rights*. Tucson: University of Arizona Press.

Mills, Sara. 1995. *Feminist Stylistics*. London: Routledge.

Milroy, Lesley. 1980. *Language and Social Networks*. Oxford: Wiley.

Mirchandani, Kiran. 2012. *Phone Clones: Authenticity Work in the Transnational Service Economy*. Ithaca: Cornell University Press. https://doi.org/10.7591/cornell/9780801450648.001.0001.

Mitchell-Kernan, Claudia. 1971. *Language Behavior in a Black Community*. Monograph Language Behavior Lab, No. 2. Berkeley: University of California Berkeley.

Moret, Sébastien. 2009. "Linguistique et nouvel ordre européen autour de la Grande Guerre." In *Discours sur les langues et rêves identitaires, Cahiers de l'ILSL 26*, edited by Ekaterina Velmezova and Patrick Sériot, 129–44. Lausanne: Université de Lausanne.

Moret, Sébastien. 2011–2012. "Antoine Meillet et le futur des empires après la Première guerre mondiale." *Langages* 182 (2): 11–24. https://doi.org/10.3917/lang.182.0011.

Morgan, Lewis Henry. 1877. *Ancient Society*. New York: Holt.

Morgan, Marcyliena. 1994. "Theories and Politics in African American English." *Annual Review of Anthropology* 23 (1): 325–45. https://doi.org/10.1146/annurev.an.23.100194.001545.

Morgan, Marcyliena. 2002. *Language, Discourse and Power in African American Culture*. Cambridge: Cambridge University Press. https://doi.org/10.1017/CBO9780511613616.

Mudimbe, V.Y. 1988. "The Power of Speech." In *The Invention of Africa: Gnosis, Philosophy, and the Order of Knowledge*, 44–97. Bloomington: Indiana University Press.

Muehlmann, Shaylih. 2012. "Rhizomes and Other Uncountables: The Malaise of Enumeration in Mexico's Colorado River Delta." *American Ethnologist* 39 (2): 339–53. https://doi.org/10.1111/j.1548-1425.2012.01368.x.

Mufwene, Salikoko. 2000. "Creolization Is a Social, Not a Structural, Process." In *Degrees of Restructuring in Creole Languages*, edited by Ingrid Neumann-Holzschuh and Edgar Schneider, 65–84. Amsterdam: John Benjamins.

Mühlhäusler, Peter. 1986. *Pidgin and Creole Linguistics*. Oxford: B. Blackwell.

Mühlhäusler, Peter. 1996. *Linguistic Ecology: Language Change and Linguistic Imperialism in the Pacific Region*. New York: Routledge. https://doi.org/10.4324/9780203211281.

Mühlhäusler, Peter, and Adrian Peace. 2006. "Environmental Discourses." *Annual Review of Anthropology* 35 (1): 457–79. https://doi.org/10.1146/annurev.anthro.35.081705.123203.

Müller, Gotelind, and Gregor Benton. 2006. "Esperanto and Chinese Anarchism in the 1920's and 1930's." *Language Problems and Language Planning* 30 (2): 173–92.

Muñoz, José Esteban. 2009. *Cruising Utopia: The Then and There of Queer Futurity*. New York: New York University Press.

Murray, Stephen O. 1998. *American Sociolinguistics: Theorists and Theory Groups*. Amsterdam: John Benjamins. https://doi.org/10.1075/z.86.

Myerson, George, and Yvonne Rydin. 1996. *The Language of Environment: A New Rhetoric*. London: University College of London Press.

Narotzky, Susana, and Niko Besnier. 2014. "Crisis, Value and Hope: Rethinking the Economy." *Current Anthropology* 55 (S9): S4–S16. https://doi.org/10.1086/676327.

Nichols, Robert. 2014. "The Colonialism of Incarceration." *Radical Philosophy Review* 17 (2): 435–55. https://doi.org/10.5840/radphilrev201491622.

Nobles, Melissa. 2008. *The Politics of Official Apologies*. Cambridge: Cambridge University Press. https://doi.org/10.1017/CBO9780511756252.

Nussbaum, Martha. 1997. *Cultivating Humanity: A Classical Defence of Reform in Liberal Education*. Cambridge, MA: Harvard University Press.

Ochs, Elinor, and Lisa Capps. 1996. "Narrating the Self." *Annual Review of Anthropology* 25 (1): 19–43. https://doi.org/10.1146/annurev.anthro.25.1.19.

Ochs, Elinor, and Bambi Schieffelin, eds. 1979. *Developmental Pragmatics*. New York: Academic Press.

Ogbu, John. 1978. *Minority Education and Caste: The American System in Cross-Cultural Perspective*. San Diego: Academic Press.

Okrent, Arika. 2009. *In the Land of Invented Languages: Esperanto Rock Stars, Klingon Poets, Loglan Lovers, and the Mad Dreamers Who Tried to Build A Perfect Language*. New York: Random House.

Olusoga, David, and Casper Erichsen. 2010. *The Kaiser's Holocaust: Germany's Forgotten Genocide and the Colonial Roots of Nazism*. London: Faber and Faber.

Ong, Walter. 1967. *Orality and Literacy: The Technologizing of the Word*. London: Routledge.

Ortner, Sherry. 1996. *Making Gender: The Politics and Erotics of Culture*. Boston: Beacon Press.

Ortner, Sherry. 2003. *New Jersey Dreaming: Capital, Culture and the Class of '58*. Durham: Duke University Press. https://doi.org/10.1215/9780822387374.

Orwell, George. 1934. *Burmese Days*. New York: Harper.

Orwell, George. (1945) 1997. "Animal Farm." In *The Complete Works of George Orwell*, vol. 8, edited by Peter Hobley Davison, Ian Angus, and Sheila Davison, 11–68. Reprint, London: Secker & Warburg.

Orwell, George. 1946. *Politics and the English Language*. London: Horizon.

Orwell, George. (1946) 1984. *Why I Write*. Reprint, London: Penguin.

Orwell, George. (1949) 1986. "Nineteen Eighty-Four." In *The Complete Works of George Orwell*, vol. 9, edited by Peter Davidson, 741–1280. Reprint, London: Secker & Warburg.

Orwell, George. 1950. "Shooting an Elephant." In *Shooting an Elephant, and Other Essays*, 31–40. New York: Harcourt, Brace.

Otero, Carlos P., ed. 1988. *Noam Chomsky: Language and Politics*. Montréal: Black Rose Books.

Outram, Dorinda. 1987. "Le langage mâle de la vertu: Women and the Discourse of the French Revolution." In *The Social History of Language*, edited by Peter Burke and Roy Porter, 120–35. Cambridge: Cambridge University Press.

Packenham, Robert. 1973. *Liberal America and the Third World: Political Development Ideas in Foreign Aid and Social Science*. Princeton: Princeton University Press.

Pardue, David. 2001. "Uma so Lingua, um so Bandeira, um so Pastor: Spiritism and Esperanto in Brazil." *Esperantologio/Esperanto Studies* 2: 11–27.

Park, Joseph Sung-Yul. 2010. *Unspeakable Tongue: Ideologies of English in South Korea*. Berlin: Mouton de Gruyter.

Park, Joseph Sung-Yul. 2011. "The Promise of English: Linguistic Capital and the Neoliberal Worker in the South Korean Job Market." *International Journal of Bilingual Education and Bilingualism* 14 (4): 443–55. https://doi.org/10.1080/13670050.2011.573067.

Park, Joseph Sung-Yul, and Adrienne Lo. 2012. "Transnational South Korea as a Site for a Sociolinguistics of Globalization: Markets, Timescales, Neoliberalism." *Journal of Sociolinguistics* 16 (2): 147–64. https://doi.org/10.1111/j.1467-9841.2011.00524.x.

Patrick, Peter. 2016. "The Impact of Sociolinguistics on Refugee Status Determination." In *Sociolinguistic Research: Application and Impact*, edited by Robert Lawson and Dave Sayers, 235–56. London: Routledge.

Pavlenko, Aneta. Forthcoming. "Superdiversity and Why It Isn't: Reflections on Terminological Innovation and Academic Branding." In *Sloganizations in Language Education Discourse*, edited by S. Breidbach, L. Küster, and B. Schmenk. Bristol, UK: Multilingual Matters.

Peck, James, ed. 1987. *The Chomsky Reader*. New York: Pantheon.

Pennycook, Alastair. 2016. "Mobile Times, Mobile Terms: The Trans-super-poly-metro Movement." In *Sociolinguistics: Theoretical Debates*, edited by Nikolas Coupland, 201–16. Cambridge: Cambridge University Press. https://doi.org/10.1017/CBO9781107449787.010.

Pfaff, Carol W. 2010. "Multilingual Development in Germany in the Crossfire of Ideology and Politics." In *Perspectives in Politics and Discourse*, edited by Urszula Okulska and Piotr Cap, 327–58. Amsterdam: John Benjamins. https://doi.org/10.1075/dapsac.36.23pfa.

Philips, Susan. 1998. "Language Ideologies in Institutions of Power: A Commentary." In *Language Ideologies: Practise and Theory*, edited by Bambi Schieffelin, Kathryn Woolard, and Paul Kroskrity, 211–28. Oxford: Oxford University Press.

Philips, Susan. 2010. "The Feminization of Anthropology: Moving Private Discourses into the Public Sphere." *Gender and Language* 4 (1): 1–31. https://doi.org/10.1558/genl.v4i1.1.

Phillipson, Robert. 2008. "The Linguistic Imperialism of Neoliberal Empire." *Critical Inquiry in Language Studies* 5 (1): 1–43. https://doi.org/10.1080/15427580701696886.

Pietikäinen, Sari. 2014. "Circulation of Indigenous Sámi Resources across Media Spaces. A Rhizomatic Discourse Approach." In *Mediatization and Sociolinguistic Change*, edited by Jannis Androutsopoulos, 515–38. Berlin: Walter de Gruyter. https://doi.org/10.1515/9783110346831.515.

Piller, Ingrid, and Kimie Takahashi. 2011. "Linguistic Diversity and Social Inclusion." *International Journal of Bilingual Education and Bilingualism* 14 (4): 371–81. https://doi.org/10.1080/13670050.2011.573062.

Pratt, Richard. (1892) 1973. Official Report of the Nineteenth Annual Conference of Charities and Correction. In "The Advantages of Mingling Indians with Whites," in *Americanizing the American Indians: Writings by the "Friends of the Indian" 1880–1900*, 260–271. Reprint, Cambridge, MA: Harvard University Press.

Price, David H. 2004. *Threatening Anthropology: McCarthyism and the FBI's Surveillance of Activist Anthropologists*. Durham: Duke University Press. https://doi.org/10.1215/9780822385684.

Prudent, Lambert-Félix, and Georges Merida. 1984. "'… An langaj kréyòl dimi-panaché…': interlecte et dynamique conversationnelle." *Langages* 74: 31–45.

Pujolar, Joan. 2001. *Gender, Heteroglossia and Power: A Sociolinguistic Study of Youth Culture*. Berlin: Mouton de Gruyter. https://doi.org/10.1515/9783110809121.

Pujolar, Joan. 2007. "African Women in Catalan Language Courses: Struggles over Class, Gender and Ethnicity in Advanced Liberalism." In *Words, Worlds and Material Girls: Language, Gender and Globalization*, edited by Bonnie McElhinny, 305–48. Berlin: Mouton de Gruyter.

Rafael, Vicente. 1988. *Contracting Colonialism: Translation and Christian Conversion in Tagalog Society under Early Spanish Rule*. Ithaca: Cornell University Press.

Rafael, Vicente. 2014. "Translation, American English and the National Insecurities of Empire." In *Formations of the American Empire*, edited by Alyosha Goldstein, 335–59. Durham: Duke University Press. https://doi.org/10.1215/9780822375968-014.

Rafael, Vicente. 2015. "Betraying Empire: Translation and the Ideology of Conquest." *Translation Studies* 8 (1): 82–93. https://doi.org/10.1080/14781700.2014.928649.

Rafael, Vincente. 2016. *Motherless Tongues: The Insurgency of Language amid Wars of Translation*. Durham: Duke University Press. https://doi.org/10.1215/9780822374572.

Ramirez, Renya. 2007. *Native Hubs: Culture, Community and Belonging in Silicon Valley and Beyond*. Durham: Duke University Press.

Rampton, Ben. 2001. "Critique in Interaction." *Critique of Anthropology* 21 (1): 83–107. https://doi.org/10.1177/0308275X0102100105.

Rampton, Ben, Janet Maybin, and Karen Tusting. 2007. "Linguistic Ethnography." Special issue, *Journal of Sociolinguistics* 1 (5): 575–716.

Renzi, Alessandra. 2008. "The Space of Tactical Media." In *Tactics in Hard Times: Practices and Spaces of New Media*, edited by Megan Boler, 71–100. Cambridge, MA: MIT Press.

Reyes, Angela, and Adrienne Lo, eds. 2009. *Beyond Yellow English*. Oxford: Oxford University Press. https://doi.org/10.1093/acprof:oso/9780195327359.001.0001.

Richard, Analiese, and Daromir Rudnyckyj. 2009. "Economies of Affect." *Journal of the Royal Anthropological Institute* 15 (1): 57–77. https://doi.org/10.1111/j.1467-9655.2008.01530.x.

Richards, Robert W. 2008. *The Tragic Sense of Life: Ernst Haeckel and the Struggle over Evolutionary Thought*. Chicago: University of Chicago Press. https://doi.org/10.7208/chicago/9780226712192.001.0001.

Rickford, John. 1993. "Concord and Conflict in the Speech Community." Revised version of "Concord and Contrast in the Characterization of the Speech Community," 1986, prepared for the Dean's Symposium on Competition and Cooperation in the Context of the Social Sciences, University of Chicago. *Sheffield Working Papers in Language and Linguistics* 3: 87–119. http://www.johnrickford.com/Writings/OnlinePapers/tabid/1127/Default.aspx.

Rickford, John. 1999. *African American Vernacular English: Features, Evolution, Educational Implications*. London: Blackwell.

Rickford, John, and Russell Rickford. 2000. *Spoken Soul: The Story of Black English*. New York: John Wiley and Sons.

Roberge, Paul T. 2006. "The Development of Creolistics and the Study of Pidgin Languages: An Overview." In *History of the Language Sciences*, vol. 3, edited by S. Auroux, E.F.K. Koerner, H.J. Niederehe, and K. Versteegh, 2398–412. Berlin: Walter de Gruyter.

Robinson, Pearl. 2004. "Area Studies in Search of Africa." In *The Politics of Knowledge: Area Studies and the Disciplines*, edited by David Szanton, 119–83. Berkeley: University of California Press.

Rocher, Rosane. 1995. "Sir William Jones and Indian Pandits." In *Objects of Enquiry: The Life, Contributions, and Influences of Sir William Jones (1746–1794)*, edited by Garland Cannon and Kevin Brine, 51–82. New York: New York University Press.

Rocher, Rosane. 2004. "Hamilton, Alexander (1762–1824)," *The Oxford Dictionary of National Biography*, 2008 online edition.

Rollins, Peter C. 1980. *Benjamin Lee Whorf: Lost Generation Theories of Mind, Language, and Religion*. Ann Arbor, MI: Published for Popular Culture Association by University Microfilms International.

Romaine, Suzanne. 1988. *Pidgin and Creole Languages*. London: Longman.

Rosa, Jonathan. 2016. "Standardization, Racialization, Languagelessness: Sociolinguistic Ideologies across Communicative Contexts." *Journal of Linguistic Anthropology* 26 (2): 162–83. https://doi.org/10.1111/jola.12116.

Rosa, Jonathan, and Christa Burdick. Forthcoming. "Language Ideologies." In *Oxford Handbook of Language and Society*, edited by Ofelia Garcia, Nelson Flores, and Massimiliano Spotti. New York: Oxford University Press.

Rose, Christine M. 2005. "Margaret Schlauch (1898–1986)." In *Women Medievalists and the Academy*, edited by Jane Chance, 523–39. Madison: University of Wisconsin Press.

Rose, Nikolas. 1999. *Powers of Freedom: Reframing Political Thought*. Cambridge: Cambridge University Press. https://doi.org/10.1017/CBO9780511488856.

Rosoff, Sonia Branca. 1994. *L'écriture des citoyens: une analyse linguistique de l'écriture des peu-lettrés pendant la période révolutionnaire*. Paris: Klincksieck.

Rossi-Landi, Ferruccio. 1973. *Ideologies of Linguistic Relativity*. The Hague: Mouton.

Rotsaert, Marie-Louise. 1979. "Étymologie et idéologie. Des reflets du nationalisme sur la lexicologie allemande, 1830–1914." *Historiographia Linguistica* 6 (3): 309–38. https://doi.org/10.1075/hl.6.3.04rot.

Roy, Sylvie. 2003. "Bilingualism and Standardization in a Canadian Call Center: Challenges for a Linguistic Minority Community." In *Language Socialization in Multilingual Societies*, edited by Robert Bayley and Sandra Schecter, 267–87. Clevedon, UK: Multilingual Matters.

Rudy, Stephen. 1985. "Preface." In *Part 1: Comparative Slavic Studies. The Cyrillo-Methodian Tradition of Roman Jakobson: Selected Writings*, vol. VI: *Early Slavic Paths and Crossroads*, ix–xxiii. Berlin: De Gruyter.

Said, Edward. 1978. *Orientalism*. New York: Vintage.

Said, Edward. 1993. *Culture and Imperialism*. London: Chatto and Windus.

Said, Edward. 2000. *Out of Place: A Memoir*. New York: Vintage Books.

Salonga, Aileen Olimba. 2010. "Language and Situated Agency: An Exploration of the Dominant Linguistic and Communication Practices in the Philippine Offshore Call Centers." PhD diss., National University of Singapore.

San Diego Bakhtin Circle, ed. 2000. *Bakhtin and the Nation*. Lewisburg, PA: Bucknell University Press.

Sandfeld, Kristian. 1930. *Linguistique balkanique. Problèmes et résultats*. Paris: Champion.

Sapir, Edward. 1925. "Memorandum on the Problem of an International Auxiliary Language, and Signed by Leonard Bloomfield, Franz Boas, J.L. Gerig, George Phillip Krapp." *Romanic Review* 16: 244–56.

Sarangi, Srikant. 1994. "Intercultural or Not? Beyond Celebration of Cultural Differences in Miscommunication Analysis." *Pragmatics* 4 (3): 409–27. https://doi.org/10.1075/prag.4.3.05sar.

Schacter, Harvey. 2016. "Review of *Big Insights from Small Data: Observations, Anecdotes and Hunches Can Often Shine a Light on Areas Not Illuminated by Numbers*, by Martin Lindstrom." *Globe and Mail*, May 25, B14.

Schieffelin, Bambi, and Rachelle Charlier Doucet. 1998. "The 'Real' Haitian Creole: Ideology, Metalinguistics and Orthographic Choice." In *Language Ideologies: Practice and Theory*, edited by Bambi Schieffelin, Kathryn Woolard, and Paul Kroskrity, 285–316. New York: Oxford University Press.

Schieffelin, Bambi B., and Elinor Ochs, eds. 1986. *Language Socialization across Cultures*. Cambridge: Cambridge University Press.

Schieffelin, Bambi, Kathryn Woolard, and Paul Kroskrity, eds. 1998. *Language Ideologies: Practice and Theory*. Oxford: Oxford University Press.

Schlauch, Margaret. 1955. *The Gift of Language*. New York: Dover.

Schleicher, August. 1869. *Darwinism Tested by the Science of Language. Translated from the German with Preface and Additional Notes by Dr. Alex. V.W. Bikkers*. London: John Camden Hotten.

Schrambke, Renate. 2010. "Language and Space: Traditional Dialect Geography." In *Language and Space*, edited by Peter Auer and Jürgen Schmidt, 87–107. Berlin: Walter de Gruyter.

Schrecker, Ellen. 1986. *No Ivory Tower: McCarthyism and the Universities*. New York: Oxford University Press.

Schultz, Emily A. 1990. *Dialogue at the Margins: Whorf, Bakhtin, and Linguistic Relativity*. Madison, WI: University of Wisconsin Press.

Shankar, Shalini, and Jillian Cavanaugh. 2012. "Language and Materiality in Global Capitalism." *Annual Review of Anthropology* 41 (1): 355–69. https://doi.org/10.1146/annurev-anthro-092611-145811.

Sheppard, Emily. 2014. "Making Sense of National Socialism: Linguistic Ideology and Linguistic Practices in Germany, 1933–1939." MA thesis, Department of Social Justice Education, University of Toronto.

Shohamy, Elana. 2009. "Language Tests for Immigrants: Why Language? Why Tests? Why Citizenship?" In *Discourses on Language and Integration: Critical Perspectives on Language Testing Regimes in Europe*, edited by Gabrielle Hogan-Brun, Clare Mar-Molinero, and Patrick Stevenson, 45–60. Amsterdam: John Benjamins. https://doi.org/10.1075/dapsac.33.07sho.

Silva, Emanuel da, and Monica Heller. 2009. "From Protector to Producer: The Role of the State in the Discursive Shift from Minority Rights to Economic Development." *Language Policy* 8 (2): 95–116. https://doi.org/10.1007/s10993-009-9127-x.

Silverstein, Michael. 2000. "Whorfianism and the Linguistic Imagination of Nationality." In *Regimes of Language: Ideologies, Polities, Identities*, edited by Paul Kroskrity, 85–138. Santa Fe: School of American Research Press.

Simpson, Audra. 2007. "On Ethnographic Refusal: Indigeneity, 'Voice' and Colonial Citizenship." *Junctures* 9: 67–80.

Simpson, Audra. 2014. *Mohawk Interruptus: Political Life across the Borders of Settler States*. Durham: Duke University Press. https://doi.org/10.1215/9780822376781.

Simpson, Christopher. 1988. *Blowback: America's Recruitment of Nazis and Its Effects on the Cold War*. New York: Weidenfield and Nicolson.

Simpson, Christopher. 1993. "U.S. Mass Communications Research and Counterinsurgency after 1945." In *Ruthless Criticism: New Perspectives in US Communication History*, edited by William Sloman and Robert McChesne, 313–48. Minneapolis: University of Minnesota Press.

Simpson, Christopher. 1995. *Science of Coercion: Communication Research and Psychological Warfare 1945–1960*. Oxford: Oxford University Press.

Simpson, Leanne Betasamosake. 2008. *Lighting the Eighth Fire: The Liberation, Resurgence and Protection of Indigenous Nations*. Winnipeg: Arbeiter Ring Press.

Simpson, Leanne Betasamosake. 2011. *Dancing on Our Turtle's Back: Stories of Nishnaabeg Re-Creation, Resurgence, and a New Emergence*. Winnipeg: Arbeiter Ring.

Simpson, Leanne Betasamosake. 2013. *Islands of Decolonial Love*. Winnipeg: Arbeiter Ring.

Simpson, Leanne Betasamosake. 2014. "Land as Pedagogy: Nishnaabeg Intelligence and Rebellious Transformation." *Decolonization* 3 (3): 1–25.

Simpson, Leanne Betasamosake. 2016. *Land & Reconciliation: Having the Right Conversations*. Peterborough, ON: Electric City Magazine.

Singh, Michael, and Jinghe Han. 2008. "The Commoditization of English and the Bologna Process: Global Products and Services, Exchange Mechanisms and Trans-National Labour." In *Language as Commodity: Global Structures, Local Marketplaces*, edited by Peter K.W. Tan and Rani Rubdy, 204–24. London: Continuum.

Singh, Rajendra, J.K. Lele, and G. Martohardjono. 1988. "Communication in a Multilingual Society: Some Missed Opportunities." *Language in Society* 17 (1): 43–59. https://doi.org/10.1017/S0047404500012586.

Slembrouck, Stef. 2001. "Explanation, Interpretation and Critique in the Analysis of Discourse." *Critique of Anthropology* 21 (1): 33–57. https://doi.org/10.1177/0308275X0102100103.

Slezkine, Yuri. 1994. "The USSR as a Communal Apartment, or How a Socialist State Promoted Ethnic Particularism." *Slavic Review* 53 (2): 414–52. https://doi.org/10.2307/2501300.

Slezkine, Yuri. 1996. "N. la. Marr and the National Origins of Soviet Ethnogenetics." *Slavic Review* 55 (4): 826–62. https://doi.org/10.2307/2501240.

Slobin, Dan, ed. 1967. *A Field Manual for Cross-Cultural Study of the Acquisition of Communicative Competence*. Berkeley: University of California.

Smith, Michael G. 1993. "The Eurasian Imperative in Early Soviet Language Planning: Russian Linguists at the Service of the Nationalities." In *Beyond Sovietology: Essays in Politics and History*, edited by Susan Gross Solomon, 159–91. Armonk, NY: M.E. Sharpe.

Smith, Michael G. 1998. *Language and Power in the Creation of the USSR, 1917–1953*. Berlin: Mouton de Gruyter. https://doi.org/10.1515/9783110805581.

Smitherman, Geneva. 2000. *Talkin That Talk: Language, Culture and Education in African America*. London: Routledge.

Sokolovska, Zorana. 2016. "Languages in 'the United Nations of Europe': Debating a Post-War Language Policy for Europe." *Language Policy*, October 5. https://doi.org/10.1007/s10993-016-9417-z.

Solovey, Mark, ed. 2012. *Cold War Social Science: Knowledge Production, Liberal Democracy and Human Nature*. New York: Palgrave Macmillan. https://doi.org/10.1057/9781137013224.

Solovey, Mark. 2013. *Shaky Foundations: The Politics-Patronage-Social Science Nexus in Cold War America*. New Brunswick, NJ: Rutgers University Press.

Somerville, Margaret. 2013. *Water in a Dry Land: Place-Learning through Art and Story*. New York: Routledge.

Spears, Arthur, ed. 1999. *Race and Ideology: Language, Symbolism, and Popular Culture.* Detroit: Wayne State University Press.

Spivey, Donald. 1978. *Schooling for the New Slavery: Black Industrial Education, 1868–1915.* Westport, CT: Greenwood Press.

Stalin, Joseph. 1951. *Marxism and Linguistics.* New York: International Publishers.

Stead, Sylvia. 2016. "We Must Call the 'Alt-Right' What It Is: Fascist, Racist, White Supremacist." *Globe and Mail,* November 25. http://www.theglobeandmail.com/community/inside-the-globe/we-must-call-the-alt-right-what-it-is-fascist-racist-white-supremacist/article33050627/.

St-Hilaire, Aonghas. 2009. "Postcolonial Identity Politics, Language and the Schools in St. Lucia." *International Journal of Bilingualism and Bilingual Education* 12 (1): 31–46. https://doi.org/10.1080/13670050802149507.

Stoler, Ann Laura. 1991. "Carnal Knowledge and Imperial Power: Gender, Race and Morality in Colonial Asia." In *Gender at the Crossroads of Knowledge: Feminist Anthropology in the Postmodern Era,* edited by Micaela Di Leonardo, 51–102. Berkeley: University of California Press.

Stoler, Ann Laura, and Carole McGranahan. 2007. "Introduction: Refiguring Imperial Terrain." In *Imperial Formations,* edited by Ann Laura Stoler, Carole McGranahan, and Peter Perdue, 3–45. Santa Fe: School for Advanced Research Press,

Stoler, Ann Laura, Carole McGranahan, and Peter Perdue, eds. 2007. *Imperial Formations.* Santa Fe: School for Advanced Research Press.

Strang, Veronica. 2004. *The Meaning of Water.* Oxford: Berg.

Strathern, Marilyn. 2000. "Introduction: New Accountabilities." In *Audit Cultures: Anthropological Studies in Accountability, Ethics and the Academy,* edited by Marilyn Strathern, 1–18. London: Routledge. https://doi.org/10.4324/9780203449721.

Street, Brian. 1984. *Literacy in Theory and Practice.* Cambridge: Cambridge University Press.

Swiggers, Pierre. 1990. "Ideology and the 'Clarity' of French." In *Ideologies of Language,* edited by John Joseph and Talbot Taylor, 112–30. London: Routledge.

Szabó, Zoltán Gendler. 2004. "Noam Chomsky." In *Dictionary of Modern American Philosophers, 1860–1960,* edited by Ernest LePore, 480–86. Bristol: Multilingual Matters.

Szanton, David. 2004. "The Origin, Nature and Challenges of Area Studies in the United States." In *The Politics of Knowledge: Area Studies and the Disciplines,* edited by David Szanton, 1-31. Berkeley: University of California Press.

Tabouret-Keller, Andrée. 2011. *Le bilinguisme en procès (1840–1940).* Limoges: Lambert-Lucas.

Tabouret-Keller, Andrée, and Robert Le Page. 1985. *Acts of Identity: Creole-Based Approaches to Language and Ethnicity.* Cambridge: Cambridge University Press.

Tannen, Deborah. 1990. *You Just Don't Understand.* New York: Morrow.

Tansman, Alan. 2004. "Japanese Studies: The Intangible Act of Translation." In *The Politics of Knowledge: Area Studies and the Disciplines,* edited by David Szanton, 184–216. Berkeley: University of California Press.

Taylor, Keeanga-Yamahtta. 2016. *From #BlackLivesMatter to Black Liberation.* Chicago: Haymarket.

Theodossopoulos, Dimitrios. 2014. "The Ambivalence of Anti-Austerity Indignation in Greece: Resistance, Hegemony and Complicity." *History and Anthropology* 25 (4): 488–506. https://doi.org/10.1080/02757206.2014.917086.

Thomas, Julia Adeney. 2014. "Visualizing Fascism: Japan's State of Unexception." Paper presented at "Visualizing Fascism" workshop, November 21, University of Toronto, Toronto, ON.

Thompson, E.P. 1974. "Inside *Which* Whale?" In *George Orwell: A Collection of Critical Essays*, edited by Raymond Williams, 80–88. Englewood Cliffs, NJ: Prentice-Hall.

Todd, Zoe. 2014. "Fish Pluralities: Human-Animal Relations and Sites of Engagement in Paulatuuq, Arctic Canada." *Études/Inuit/Studies* 38 (1–2): 217–38. https://doi.org/10.7202/1028861ar.

Todd, Zoe. 2016. "From a Fishy Place: Examining Canadian State Law Applied in the *Daniels* Decision from the Perspective of Métis Legal Orders." *Topia* 36: 43–57.

Todorov, Tzvetan. 1984. *Mikhail Bakhtin: The Dialogical Principle*, translated by Wlad Godzich. Minneapolis: University of Minnesota Press.

Toman, Jindrich. 1995. *The Magic of a Common Language: Jakobson, Mathesius, Trubetzkoy, and the Prague Linguistic Circle*. Cambridge, MA: MIT Press.

Tonkin, Humphrey. 2011. "Chaos in Esperanto-Land: Echoes of the Holocaust." *Language Problems and Language Planning* 35 (2): 161–71. https://doi.org/10.1075/lplp.35.2.04ton.

Townson, Michael. 1992. *Mother-Tongue and Fatherland: Language and Politics in Germany*. Manchester: Manchester University Press.

Trautmann, Thomas. 1997. *Aryans and British India*. Berkeley: University of California Press. https://doi.org/10.1525/california/9780520205468.001.0001.

Trautmann, Thomas, ed. 2005. *The Aryan Debate*. New Delhi: Oxford.

Trautmann, Thomas. 2006. *Languages and Nations: The Dravidian Proof in Colonial Madras*. Berkeley: University of California Press.

Trechter, Sara, and Mary Bucholtz. 2001. "White Noise: Bringing Language into Whiteness Studies." *Journal of Linguistic Anthropology* 11 (1): 3–21. https://doi.org/10.1525/jlin.2001.11.1.3.

Trilling, Lionel. 1974. "George Orwell and the Politics of Truth." In *George Orwell: A Collection of Critical Essays*, edited by Raymond Williams, 62–79. Englewood Cliffs, NJ: Prentice-Hall.

Trubetzkoy, Nikolai. 1921. "Preface." In *Rossiia vo mgle [Russia in the Shadows]* by H.G. Wells, iii–xvi. Sofia: Rossijsko-bolgarskoe knigoizdatel'stvo.

Trudgill, Peter. 1974. *Sociolinguistics: An Introduction*. Harmondsworth: Penguin.

Truth and Reconciliation Commission of Canada. 2015. *Honouring the Truth, Reconciling for the Future: Summary of the Final Report of the Truth and Reconciliation Commission of Canada*. Ottawa: Truth and Reconciliation Commission of Canada.

Tsing, Anna. 1994. *In the Realm of the Diamond Queen*. Princeton: Princeton University Press.

Tsitsipis, Lukas. 2007. "Bilingualism, Praxis and Linguistic Description." In *Bilingualism: A Social Approach*, edited by Monica Heller, 277–96. London: Palgrave. https://doi.org/10.1057/9780230596047_13.

Tuck, Eve. 2009. "Suspending Damage: A Letter to Communities." *Harvard Educational Review* 79 (3): 409–27. https://doi.org/10.17763/haer.79.3.n0016675661t3n15.

Tuck, Eve, and K. Wayne Yang. 2012. "Decolonization Is Not a Metaphor." *Decolonization* 1 (1): 1–40.

Tuck, Eve, and K. Wayne Yang. 2014. "R-words: Refusing Research." In *Humanizing Research: Decolonizing Qualitative Inquiry with Youth and Communities*, edited by D. Paris and M.T. Winn, 223–40. Thousand Oaks, CA: Sage.

Tuhiwai Smith, Linda. 1999. *Decolonizing Methodologies: Research and Indigenous Peoples*. London: Zed Books.

Uchida, Aki. 1992. "When 'Difference' is 'Dominance': A Critique of the 'Anti-Power-Based' Cultural Approach to Sex Differences." *Language in Society* 21 (4): 547–68. https://doi.org/10.1017/S0047404500015724.

Urciuoli, Bonnie. 2008. "Skills and Selves in the New Workplace." *American Ethnologist* 35 (2): 211–28. https://doi.org/10.1111/j.1548-1425.2008.00031.x.

Urciuoli, Bonnie, and Chaise LaDousa. 2013. "Language Management/Labour." *Annual Review of Anthropology* 42 (1): 175–90. https://doi.org/10.1146/annurev-anthro-092412-155524.

Usui, Hiroyuki. 2008. "Interlinguistics and Esperanto Studies in the Social Context of Modern Japan." *Language Problems and Language Planning* 32 (2): 181–202. https://doi.org/10.1075/lplp.32.2.06usu.

van Avermaet, Piet. 2009. "Fortress Europe? Language Policy Regimes for Immigration and Citizenship." In *Discourses on Language and Integration: Critical Perspectives on Language Testing Regimes in Europe*, edited by Gabrielle Hogan-Brun, Clare Mar-Molinero, and Patrick Stevenson, 15–44. Amsterdam: John Benjamins. https://doi.org/10.1075/dapsac.33.06ave.

van Dijk, Teun. 1991. *Racism and the Press*. London: Routledge.

Velleman, Barry. 2008. "The 'Scientific Linguist' Goes to War: The United States A.S.T. Program in Foreign Languages." *Historiographia Linguistica* 35 (3): 385–416. https://doi.org/10.1075/hl.35.3.05vel.

Veracini, Lorenzo. 2011. "Introducing Settler Colonial Studies." *Settler Colonial Studies* 1 (1): 1–12. https://doi.org/10.1080/2201473X.2011.10648799.

Vice, Sue. 1997. *Introducing Bakhtin*. Manchester: Manchester University Press.

Vidal, Dominique. 2002. *Les historiens allemands relisent la Shoah*. Bruxelles: Éditions Complexe.

Visweswaran, Kamala. 1998. "Race and the Culture of Anthropology." *American Anthropologist* 100 (1): 70–83. https://doi.org/10.1525/aa.1998.100.1.70.

Vološinov, Valentin N. 1973. *Marxism and the Philosophy of Language*, translated by Ladislav Matejka and I.R. Titunik. New York: Seminar Press. Originally published as *Marksizm i filosofiiâ iâzyka* (1929).

Vossler, Otto, ed. 1955. *Briefwechsel: Benedetto Croce-Karl Vossler*, translated by Emily Sheppard. Berlin: Suhrkamp.

Vygotsky, Lev S. 1978. *Mind in Society: The Development of Higher Psychological Processes*. Edited by Michael Cole, Sylvia Scribner Vera John-Steiner, and Ellen Souberman. Cambridge, MA: Harvard University Press.

Wacquant, Loïc. (1998) 2006. "Pierre Bourdieu." In *Key Sociological Thinkers*, edited by Rob Stones, 261–77. London: Palgrave Macmillan.

Wacquant, Loïc. 2012. "Three Steps to a Historical Anthropology of Actually Existing Neoliberalism." *Social Anthropology* 20 (1): 66–79. https://doi.org/10.1111/j.1469-8676.2011.00189.x.

Wade, Mathieu. 2016. "Langues publiques et publics linguistiques: enquête sur un effet structurant du régime linguistique néo-brunswickois sur les sciences sociales et la société civile acadiennes." PhD diss., Université du Québec à Montréal.

Wald, Alan M. 2012. *American Night: The Literary Left in the Era of the Cold War.* Chapel Hill: University of North Carolina Press.

Walder, Andrew. 2004. "The Transformation of Contemporary China Studies." In *The Politics of Knowledge: Area Studies and the Disciplines,* edited by David Szanton, 314–40. Berkeley: University of California Press.

Wallerstein, Immanuel. 1974. *Capitalist Agriculture and the Origins of the European World-Economy in the Sixteenth Century.* Vol. I of *The Modern World-System.* New York: Academic Press.

Wallerstein, Immanuel. 1980. *Mercantilism and the Consolidation of the European World-Economy, 1600–1750.* Vol. II of *The Modern World-System.* New York: Academic Press.

Wallerstein, Immanuel. 1989. *The Second Great Expansion of the Capitalist World-Economy, 1730–1840s.* Vol. III of *The Modern World-System.* New York: Academic Press.

Wallerstein, Immanuel. 2011. *Centrist Liberalism Triumphant, 1789–1914.* Vol. IV of *The Modern World-System.* Berkeley: University of California Press.

Wall Zimmerer, Robin. 2003. *Gathering Moss: A Natural and Cultural History of Mosses.* Corvallis: Oregon State University.

Wall Zimmerer, Robin. 2013. *Braiding Sweetgrass: Indigenous Wisdom, Scientific Knowledge, and the Teachings of Plants.* Minneapolis: Milkweed Press.

Wax, Dustin, ed. 2008. *Anthropology at the Dawn of the Cold War: The Influence of Foundations, McCarthyism and the CIA.* London: Pluto Press.

Weber, Eugene. 1976. *Peasants into Frenchmen.* Stanford: Stanford University Press.

Wee, Lionel. 2008. "Linguistic Instrumentalism in Singapore." In *Language as Commodity: Global Structures, Local Marketplaces,* edited by P.K. Tan and R. Rubdy, 31–43. London: Continuum.

Whorf, Benjamin. 1942. "Language, Mind and Reality." *Theosophist* (Madras, India), January and April issues.

Widdowson, H. 1995. "Discourse Analysis: A Critical View." *Language and Literature* 4 (3): 157–72. https://doi.org/10.1177/096394709500400301.

Wilce, James, and Janina Fenigsen. 2016. "Special Issue: Emotion Pedagogies." *Ethos* 44 (2): 79–192, E4–E9.

Willemyns, Roland. 2002. "The Dutch-French Language Border in Belgium." *Journal of Multilingual and Multicultural Development* 23 (1–2): 36–49. https://doi.org/10.1080/01434630208666453.

Williams, Glyn. 1992. *Sociolinguistics: A Sociological Critique.* London: Routledge.

Williams, Quentin. 2016. "AfriKaaps Is an Act of Reclamation." *Mail and Guardian,* December 15. https://mg.co.za/article/2016-12-15-00-afrikaaps-is-an-act-of-reclamation/.

Williams, Raymond. 1973. *The Country and the City.* London: Chatto and Windus.

Williams, Raymond. (1976) 1983. *Keywords: A Vocabulary of Culture and Society.* Oxford: Oxford University Press.

Williams, Raymond. 1977. *Marxism and Literature.* Oxford: Oxford University Press.

Williams, Raymond. 1989. "Walking Backwards into the Future." In *Resources of Hope: Culture, Democracy, Socialism,* 281–287. London: Verso.

Williams, Vernon. 1996. *Rethinking Race: Franz Boas and His Contemporaries*. Lexington: University of Kentucky.

Winford, Don. 2003. *An Introduction to Contact Linguistics*. Oxford: Blackwell.

Wodak, Ruth. 1996. *Disorders of Discourse*. London: Longman.

Wodak, Ruth, and John Richardson, eds. 2013. *Analysing Fascist Discourse: European Fascism in Talk and Text*. London: Routledge.

Wohlleben, Peter. 2015. *The Hidden Life of Trees: What They Feel, How They Communicate*. Vancouver: Greystone Books.

Wolf, Eric. (1982) 1997. *Europe and the People without History*. Berkeley: University of California Press.

Wolfe, Patrick. 2006. "Settler Colonialism and the Elimination of the Native." *Journal of Genocide Research* 8 (4): 387–409. https://doi.org/10.1080/14623520601056240.

Woolard, Kathryn. 1998. "Language Ideology as a Field of Inquiry." In *Language Ideologies: Practice and Theory*, edited by Bambi Schieffelin, Kathryn Woolard, and Paul Kroskrity, 3–49. New York: Oxford University Press.

Wright, Michelle. 1999. "Nigger Peasants from France: Missing Translations of American Anxieties on Race and the Nation." *Callaloo* 22 (4): 831–52. https://doi.org/10.1353/cal.1999.0206.

Wynter, Sylvia, and Katherine McKittrick. 2015. "Unparallelled Catastrophe for Our Species? Or, To Give Humanness a Different Future: Conversations." In *Sylvia Wynter: On Being Human as Praxis*, edited by Katherine McKittrick, 9–89. Durham: Duke University Press.

Yang, Jie. 2007. "'Re-Employment Stars': Language, Gender and Neoliberal Restructuring in China." In *Words, Worlds, Material Girls: Language, Gender and Global Economies*, edited by Bonnie McElhinny, 77–102. Berlin: Mouton de Gruyter. https://doi.org/10.1515/9783110198805.1.77.

Yang, Sunyoung. 2015. "The Korean Internet Freak Community and Its Cultural Politics, 2002–2011." PhD diss., University of Toronto.

Yankah, Kwesi. 1998. *Free Speech in Traditional Society: The Cultural Foundations of Communication in Contemporary Ghana*. Accra: University of Ghana Press.

Yeung, Shirley, and Mi-Cha Flubacher. 2016. "Discourses of Integration: Language, Skills and the Politics of Difference." *Multilingua* 35 (6): 599–616.

Young, Robert J.C. 1995. *Colonial Desire: Hybridity in Theory, Culture and Race*. London: Routledge.

Zentella, Ana Celia. 1997. *Growing Up Bilingual: Puerto Rican Children in New York*. Cambridge: Blackwell.

INDEX

Aboriginal languages. *See* Indigenous languages
Abstand languages, 203–4
accountability, 232
accumulation by dispossession, 252
Adam, Lucien, *Les idiomes négro-aryen et maléo-aryen*, 75
advertising, 154, 162, 245–46, 248–49, 252
aesthetic/poetic function, 170
affect, 246–47
African American English (AAE), 20, 209, 214–15, 217–19
African Americans, 18, 77–78, 80, 200, 205, 209
  Boas's views on, 115
  claims for rights and recognition, 212
  education, 114–15
African languages, 75, 219
African studies, 178–79
Africans, 15
agglutinating languages, 67, 70
Albanian, 59
Alliance française, 194
Allsopp, Richard, 219
Alsace, 70, 104, 119
"alt-left," 5
"alt-right," xv, 5–6, 235
amalgamation, 74
American Anthropological Association, 58, 78–79, 165
American Anthropologist, 78–79
American Council of Learned Societies, 176
American Indian languages, 81–82, 84–85. *See also* Indigenous languages
American public health regime, 116
American Revolution, 43, 54
American structural linguistics, 180
American tradition in anthropology, 76–80

ancien régime, 108
Anderson, Benedict, 97
Anglicists, 55–56
Animal Farm (Orwell), 19, 188–89
Anishinaabe people, 15
Anishinaabe people, migration history, 14–15
Anishinaabe philosophers linked to the Great Lakes, 2
anthropological comparative method of human evolution, 59
anthropology, 6, 64, 69, 168
  psychological approach to, 163
  role in South and Southeast Asian Studies, 179
anthropology of education, 207
anti-capitalist work, 167
anti-colonial critiques, 220
anti-fascist and anti-capitalist political positions, 182
anti-Semitism, 79–80, 145, 147–48, 165–66, 180, 187, 196
apartheid, 115
apologies, 255–56
applied linguistics, 133, 161, 176
Arabic language, 67
Aracil, Lluis, 221
area studies, 19, 161, 163, 176, 178, 181
Arendt, Hannah, xiv, xv, 11, 21–22, 124–25, 145, 190
Armstrong, Samuel Chapman, 114
artificial language, 19
Aryan, 53–54
Aryan superiority, 148
Aryanism, 80
"Asiatic," 43
Aspects of the Theory of Syntax (Chomsky), 187
Association of Language Testers in Europe (ALTE), 239

audit, 232, 239
Ausbau languages, 203–4
authentic language, 245
authenticity, 230, 247–49
authoritative knowledge, 117
auxiliary language movement, 202
awareness, 7–8

Bacon, Francis, 11
Bakhtin Circle, 141–42
Bally, Charles, 120
Bantu, 68
Basque language, 67–68, 76, 221
Baugh, John, 237
Bauman, Richard, 11
  Voices of Modernity, 10
baybayin, 42
Béarnais dialect, 223
Benedict, Ruth, 79, 173
Bengalis, 51, 125
Berardi, "Bifo," 232
Bernstein, Basil, 206–7
Bible, historical veracity, 68
Bible translation into Indigenous languages, 28
biblical accounts of flood and the Tower of
    Babel, 47–48
biblical forms of genealogy, 49
biblical traditional focus on fall from grace, 53
bilingualism, 105, 114, 202, 204, 243
Billig, Michael, 122
biological determinism, 83
biological mixing of races. *See* hybridity
biology, 64
Birmingham School of Cultural Studies, 235
Black Skin, White Masks (Fanon), 251
Blair, Hugh, 11
Bleek, Wilhelm Heinrich Immanuel, 68–69
  *Comparative Grammar of South African
    Languages,* 68
Bloch, Bernard, 180
Bloomfield, Leonard, 46, 86, 171, 180
Boas, Franz, 11, 18, 59, 76, 78, 85–87, 89, 133,
    164, 171
  approach to Blackness and Indigeneity, 82, 84
  approach to race and racism, 83
  challenged evolutionary ideas of primitive
    language, 84
  commitment to ideas of progress and
    modernity, 80
  focus on culture, 82
  The Handbook of American Languages, 84
  interest in Indigenous issues in the
    Americas, 79
  "The Limitations of the Comparative
    Method of Anthropology," 81

preservation of Indigenous languages, 115
professionalization of anthropology, 79
  "Race and Nationality," 87
Boasian thought, 175
Bopp, Franz, 120
boundary-crossing, 229
Bourdieu, Pierre, 9, 107, 111–12, 210, 223–24
bourgeois capitalism, 99
bourgeois nation-state, 108
bourgeois nationalism, 18, 137
bourgeoisie, 94, 96–98, 100, 108, 110
Boutet, Josiane, 11
branding, 249
Brazeau, Jacques, 213
Brébeuf, Jean de, 41
Brès, Jacques, 11, 223
Breton, 94, 151, 221
Briggs, Charles, 10–11
Britain, 17, 33, 61–62, 197
Britain's vote to leave EU, 234
British conquest of the Indian subcontinent, 46
British Council, 194
British East India Company, 29, 34, 42–43, 56
British Empire, 40
British sociolinguistics, 197, 223
brotherhood, 15
bureaucracy, 97–98, 101
Burmese, 67
Burmese Days (Orwell), 190
Butler, Judith, 217

Cahiers de linguistique sociale, 222
Canada
  census, 103
  federal language policy, 243
  settler colonialism, 32
Canadian Bible Society, 28, 39, 41
capitalism, 3–4, 11, 16, 99, 179, 230–31. *See also*
    industrial capitalism
  late (*See* late capitalism)
  mercantile (*See* mercantile capitalism)
  unequal access to control over production
    and distribution of resources, 100
  unequal distribution of wealth, 107
capitalism/communism competition, 162
capitalist ideologies, 62
Caribbean, 13, 61
Caribbean creole speakers, 74
Caribbean language, 20
Carnegie Foundation, 178
Castilian grammar, 35–36
Catalan linguistic minority movement, 221
Catholic Church, 28, 41
Celtic languages, 151–52
  German interest in, 151

censuses, 18, 95, 102, 128
  language questions on, 99, 103, 109
Center for Applied Linguistics, 202
Centre international de recherche sur le bilinguisme (CIRB) at Laval, 202–3
Chakrabarty, Dipesh, 11
Chatterjee, Partha, 11
Chicano claims for rights and recognition, 212
"Chicanos in the United States," 205
Chikobava, Arnold, 142
China, 133–34, 168
  economic reforms, 231
  literacy campaign, 144, 166
  shared writing system, 144
China experts
  low level of Chinese literacy, 179
Chinese colonialism in Vietnam, 167
Chinese cosmological system, 120
Chinese language, 37, 67, 69–70, 72
Chippewa, 72
Chomsky, Noam, xxi, 19, 162, 182–86, 190, 198, 236, 253
  Aspects of the Theory of Syntax, 187
  Manufacturing Consent, 185
Chomskyan linguistics, 208
Christian conversion, 17, 29, 36–37, 41
Christian encounter with religious traditions in India, 48
Christian faith, 88
Christian ideals of the fall of man, 2
Christian ideas about Adam and Eve, 66
Christian supernaturalism, 44
Church and monarchy
  challenges to, 95–96
citizenship, 18, 20, 95, 98, 101–2, 239
  differentiated, 100, 108
  eligibility linked to labour, 230
  language as path to, 194
  racialized hierarchies of, 239
  speaking national language, 104–5
civil rights movement, 6, 13, 204
civilization, 18, 62, 66, 69
civilizational hierarchy of languages, 18, 37–38, 54, 64–65, 67–69, 88, 119, 203
class, 100, 139, 161
  class stratification in industrial Revolution, 135
  higher education and, 223
class conflict, 62, 221, 223
classification, 44
classless society, 136
cleanliness, 116
codification of languages, 35
coercion, 8–9, 98, 102, 146
cognitive science, 198

Cohen, Marcel, 222
Cold War, 7, 19, 143, 155, 160, 175–76, 182–83
  academic knowledge production, 163
  ideological competition (capitalism or communism), 162
  intellectual legacies in US, 237
  language-related fields relevant to, 176
  Nazis hired by US as counterintelligence experts, 177
  Soviet Union/United State competition, 162
  work critical of capitalism suppressed, 161
Cold War figures, 187–88
Cold War politics, 185
Cold War welfare state, 16
collective forms of sociability, 252
colonialism, 3–4, 12–14, 29–31, 113. *See also* decolonization
  consolidation and institutionalization, 58
  intimacy and hierarchy, 17
  justified as rescuing women from traditional or barbaric practices, 109
  linguistic distinctions used to justify colonial policies, 69
  Marxist resistance to colonial state, 167
  military enforcement, 13
  mixing and perceived contamination associated with, 19 (*See also* miscegenation)
commensuration, 40
Committee on Sociolinguistics, 197, 202–3, 205, 207, 212, 215, 237
"common sense" ideas, 8
commonalities, 99, 101
commons, 21, 230, 252, 591
the Commonwealth, 194
communication across linguistic boundaries, 125
communication and affect, 245
communication studies, 161–62, 176–77, 181
communicative competence, 198
communicative labour, 246
communicative styles, 206
communism, 11, 125, 144, 168, 178, 229
Communist Party, 11, 160, 165
"Comparative Ethnographic Analysis of Patterns of Speech in the United States," 205
Comparative Grammar of South African Languages (Bleek), 68
comparative linguistics, 56
comparative method, 147
comparative philology, 17, 19, 29, 53, 64, 68, 164
  of "Oriental languages," 45
competition, 62
compulsory language instruction, 239

compulsory military service, 101
compulsory schooling, 113
conative function, 170
conflict analysis, 214
conflict perspective in analysing language, 199
conquista pacifica (peaceful conquest), 36
consensus theory, 163
consent, 8–9, 146
constructed languages, 130, 134
"contemporary primitives"
  insight into human evolution, 68
contextualization cues, 210
contrapuntally, 16
A Contribution to the Critique of Political Economy (Marx), 138
Converting Words (Hanks), 40
Cornish, 151
corpus planning, 203–4
Corsican linguistic minority movement, 221
Cours de linguistique général (Saussure), 120–21
Cree language, 28, 39
creoles, 17, 59, 71–76, 106, 214, 219–20, 225
critical discourse analysis (CDA), 6, 183, 235–36, 252
Croce, Benedetto, 148
cross-cultural communication, 210–11
cross-racial contact, 72
Crosstalk (BBC documentary), 210
Cruising Utopia, 257
Cuba, 61, 162
cultural and linguistic imperialism, 240
cultural deficit theorists, 206
cultural hegemony, 8
cultural relativism, 164
cultural tourism, 245
culture, 6
Czechoslovakia, 169–71

Darwin, Charles, 64–66
  The Descent of Man, 63
  The Origin of Species, 63
Darwinian perspectives and comparative linguistics, 66
Darwinism Tested by the Science of Language (Schleicher), 65
Dave, Naisargi, 250
Davenport, C.B., 74
De Loria, Ella, 86
The Decolonial Atlas, 228
decolonial love, 260
decolonization, 19–20, 30–31, 185, 193, 196, 203, 219
  civil rights movements in Africa and Asia, 194

  discourses of, 11
  Indigenous groups in settler countries, 194
  linguistic minorities in France, Britain, Spain, Canada, 194
decolonization movement, 6–7
deficit
  women's language seen through lens of, 216
deficit hypothesis, 206–7
  counter arguments, 209
DeFrancis, John, 164, 166–67
DeGraff, Michel, 73
Deleuze, Gilles, 253–54
democracy, 83, 87, 99, 179, 194
democratic cosmopolitanism, 234
democratization of access to higher education, 196
Descartes, René, 96
The Descent of Man (Darwin), 63
development, 20, 193, 195, 201
  focus on democracy, 194
development discourses, 200
development theory, 219
diachronic analysis of language, 121
dialect boundaries, 118
dialect geography, 118
dialectology, 118–19, 193, 221, 223
dialogism, 141
Diaz, Junot, xiv, xv, 260
dictatorial regimes, 21
dictionaries, 18, 95, 107, 253
difference, 31, 60, 64
difference, theories of, 220
difference hypothesis, 207, 214, 216
differential citizenship, 108, 112
differentiation, axes of, 14
diffusion theory of social and linguistic change, 59–60, 81, 118
diglossia, 204
Dijk, Teun van, 235
discourse analysis. *See* critical discourse analysis (CDA)
Discourse & Society, 235
distribution of resources/regulation of capitalism, 230
D'Olivet, Antoine Fabre, 88
dominance, 214
dominant language literacy, 9
domination, 31
Donovan, William, 178
Doucet, Rachelle, 237
Dravidian family, 52
Du Bois, W.E.B., 80, 115
Durkheim, Émile, 121
Dutch East India Company, 34, 42

INDEX 299

Eagleton, Terry, 7
East, 52–53
East India Company, 42–43
Ebonics debate, 237
Eckert, Penny, xix
eco-linguistics, 21
École de Rouen, 222
ecological catastrophe, 90
economic crisis (2008), 232, 237
ecotourism, 245
education, 39, 193–94, 196, 207, 223, 251.
    See also schooling
  African Americans, 114–15
  communicative competence gap, 206
  Froebel Kindergarten, 78
  languages of, 114, 193
  mass education, 114–15
eighth fire, 15, 22
elaborated code (communicative style), 206
emotive function, 170
Encrevé, Pierre, 208
Engel, Jordan, 228
Engels, Friedrich, 3, 138
English
  contributing to status, 220
  cultural and linguistic imperialism, 240
  as global language of democracy and power, 202
  "good English," 241
  ideas of capitalism and democracy, 179
  instruction of select elites in, 55, 65
  language of globalization, 134
  learning to speak like an English person, 111
  spread of in English colonies, 56
English as a Foreign Language (EFL), 202
English as a Second Language, 205
Enlightenment, 18, 44, 95–96, 100, 130
Enlightenment rationalism and secularism, 79
enslavement of Africans, 13
enslavement of Africans for labour, 33
environmental commons, 21
environmental devastation/language endangerment, 253
environmental issue, 252
environmental movements, 13, 234
environmentalists, 63
Ervin-Tripp, Susan, xxi, 197, 207, 215
Esperanto, 76, 120, 124, 127–34, 144, 240
  adherents in South Korea, 134
  as Jewish language, 150
Esperanto brand names, 128
Esperanto (Zamenhof), 127
ethnicity, 100, 112
ethnography of communications, 211

ethnonationalism questions in census, 103
eugenics, 64, 74, 78, 80
Europe and "the Orient" interactions, 33
European imperialism, 18, 33, 133, 145
European linguistics, 67
European nationalism, 33
European state nationalism, 96
European substrate, 76
evolution, 125
evolutionary theory, 17, 53, 56, 58, 62, 118
  in American anthropology, 78
  eclipsed comparative philology as theoretical model for colonial expansion, 71
  pidgins and creoles challenge to, 76
expert knowledge, 8, 196

Fairclough, Norman, 235
family tree. *See* tree diagrams
Fanon, Frantz, *Black Skin, White Masks*, 251
fascism, 11, 19, 124–25, 145–46, 155, 161, 235
fascism as modernist progress, 154
fascist language ideology, 152
fashions of speaking, 89
FBI, 168, 171–74
feminist critiques, 196, 220, 237
feminist linguistics, 20, 175, 215–17
feminist movement, 13
feminist sociolinguistics, 244
feminist work, 167
feminization, 110, 246
Ferguson, Charles, 180, 202, 204, 207
Fillmore, Charles, xxi
finance capitalism, 231
Finnish, 68
Fishman, Joshua, 203, 207
flexibility, 250
flexible workforce, 232, 244
  language skills, 242
Folk-Lore Journal, 79
For the Earth and Water Walk, 260
Ford Foundation, 20, 178, 193, 201, 203, 205, 208
Foreign Language and Area Studies (FLAS), 178
foreign or second language learning, 181
formalist linguistics, 161
former Soviet bloc
  market reforms, 231
Foucault, Michel, 101, 114, 235
Frame of Reference Project, 184
France, 33, 61–62
  emergence of nation state, 95
  military service, 102
  sociolinguistics research, 197
  state-led disciplining of linguistic form, 107

300 INDEX

Francophone Canada, 197, 213. *See also* Québec
  discouraging students from using dominant language of English, 94
la Francophonie, 194
Frankfurt school of critical media analysis, 235
Franklin, Benjamin, 43
Fraser, Marian Botsford, 5
French colonialism in Vietnam, 69, 167
French *coopération*, 200
French Empire, 40
French-English bilingualism
  "added value," 243
French language, 70
  as language of international relations, 134
French Revolution, 18, 54, 63, 99–100, 108
Froebel Kindergarten, 78
functionalism, 199, 204
fur trade, 33, 40

Gal, Susan, 9
Galton, Francis, 74, 83
game theory, 163
Gardès-Madray, Françoise, 223
Gardin, Bernard, 11, 222–23
gender, 18, 100, 108, 110, 112, 161, 214, 223, 244
gender and sexuality as performance, 217
genealogies, 4, 10, 14, 17, 29, 45, 47–50, 60, 137
General Anthropology (Stern), 165
generative grammar, 161, 185–86, 221
generative linguistics, 163, 198–99
generative semantics, 216
German language, 67, 70
German linguists, 150
German philology, 151
Germany, 61–62, 145
The Gift of Language (Schlauch), 167
global movements for Indigenous rights, 234
Global North, 233–34, 238, 247
  efforts to democratize access to education, 194
  end of the welfare state, 20
  outsourcing or offshoring, 231
  privatization of health, elder care, and child care, 246
globalization, 134, 231
globalized economy, 20
Gobineau, Arthur de, 54
Goebbels, Josef, 176
Good Manners and Right Conduct, 116
Google Translate, 241
governance, 193
Government of India Act (1833), 56
grammars, 18, 29, 40, 95, 107, 113
  Castilian, 35–36
  Latin, 35–36

Mayan grammar, 40
Pāṇini's grammar, 46
Universal Grammar (UG), 162, 182, 186
  in vernacular language, 35
grammatical gender, 69
Gramsci, Antonio, 9–10, 98, 146, 235, 250
  The Prison Notebooks, 8
Greek, 37, 43, 45, 50, 53, 59, 67, 72, 84, 106, 180
Greenfield, Patricia, 200
Grégoire, Henri, 100
Grimm, Jakob, 11, 120
Grimm, Wilhelm, 11
Grimshaw, Allan, 212–13
Grosjean, Mireille, 120, 127–28
Guam, 61, 78
Guattari, Félix, 253–54
Gumperz, John, xxi, 193–96, 198, 201, 207–10, 212, 217
Guy, Gregory, xix

Haas, Mary, 180, 197
Haeckel, Ernst, 65, 68
  On the Origin of Language, 68
Hall, Catherine, 30, 34
Hall, Robert, 180
Hall, Stuart, 235
Halle, Morris, 171
Halliday, Michael, 235
Hamilton, Alexander (1762–1824), 55
Hampton Institute, 114–15
The Handbook of American Languages (Boas), 84
Hanks, William, *Converting Words*, 40
Harris, Randy, 236
  The Linguistics Wars, 187
Harris, Zellig, 19, 182–84, 187
  Language and Information, 183
  Mathematical Structures of Language, 183
  Methods in Structural Linguistics, 182
Harvey, David, 252
Haugen, Einar, 180
Heath, Shirley Brice, xix, 207
Hebrew, 88, 149, 182
Hechter, Michael, 111
hegemonies, 4, 8–9, 11, 98, 151
Heller, Monica, xx–xxii
Hémon, Roparz, 151
Herder, Johann Gottfried, 10–11
Hernandez-Chavez, Eduardo, 215
Herskovits, Melville, 79, 83
heteroglossia, 9, 141–42
heterosexuality, 146
The Hidden Life of Trees, 259
hierarchies of language. *See* civilizational hierarchy of languages

Higonnet, Patrice, 99
Hildegard of Bingen, 130
Hindu, 48, 53, 55
historical linguistics, 169
historical particularism, 59, 80, 82–83, 89, 165
History of British India (Mill), 55
Hitler, Adolf, 151
  Mein Kampf, 149
Hobbes, Thomas, 10, 21
Hockett, Charles, 180
homosexual practices, 160
Hook, Sidney, 183
Hoover, J. Edgar, 165
hope. *See* radical hope
Hopi, 89
House UnAmerican Activities Committee (HUAC), 160, 167, 172
How Forests Think, 259
Hudson's Bay Company, 34, 42
human agency and social reality, 141
human evolution, 59, 63, 68
human universality, 155
human *versus* nature, 14, 89
humanitarian enslavement, 66
Humboldt, Wilhelm von, 67
Hunt, George, 86–87
Huron/Wendat texts, 41
Hurston, Zora Neale, 79
hybridity, 60, 62, 66, 72, 74, 80, 146. *See also* interracial marriage
Hymes, Dell, 175, 196, 198, 205, 207–9, 211, 215, 236
  Reinventing Anthropology, 212

Iakubinskii, Lev, 139
Ichishkiin language, 208
idealism, 78
ideologies, 4, 6–7, 9, 16, 19, 32, 62
Les idiomes négro-aryen et maléo-aryen (Adam), 75
Ido, 131, 134
Ido schism, 132
immigrants, 82, 84, 101, 104, 180, 205, 210, 233, 238–40
immigrants from southern and eastern Europe in US, 77–78, 80, 179
imperial ideology, 32
imperialism, 16, 18–19, 31, 33, 60–62, 65, 124–25, 133, 145
  definitions, 30
indexes, 210
India, 17
  cultural diversity, 201
  enigma of dark-skinned people who were civilized, 51

instruction in English, 54
sociolinguistics, 195
Indian Rebellion (1857), 56
Indigenous languages, 41, 67–68, 86, 89, 164, 208
  attempts to eliminate, 28, 94, 115
  in Christian conversion, 17, 37, 40
  decay of, 65
  missionaries worked with, 28
  as windows into primitive thought, 59–60
  writing grammars and dictionaries for, 17, 29
Indigenous peoples, 15, 18, 82, 201
  appropriations of Christian and colonial discourse, 40
  European diseases, 35
  incarceration, 233
  learning of European languages, 39
  missing and murdered Indigenous women, 22
  US military wars, 78
Indigenous perspectives on watershed of the Great Lakes, 14
Indigenous resurgence, 90
Indigenous rights, 234
Indigenous sovereignty, 252
Indigenous studies, 252
individual and the collective, 141
individual freedom, 232
individuation, 250
Indo-European languages, 64, 68, 89
Indo-Germanic, 53
Indo-Germanic speakers, 65
Indophilia, 53, 55
Indophobia, 53, 55
industrial capitalism, 3, 16, 18, 56, 60–61, 63, 77, 89, 94, 96–98, 110
  regulating relations in, 113–17
industrial education in the Philippines, 115–16
Industrial Revolution, 56
  class stratification in, 135
industrialism, 127
inequalities, 2, 4, 61–62, 95, 200, 204, 206, 211, 219, 235
  social (*See* social inequality)
inflectional language, 67, 70, 72
Institute of Slavic Studies, 178
integration, 129, 145, 238–39
  language training as strategy for, 104
intellectual elites of developing countries, 195
Intensive Language Program, 176
interactional sociolinguistics, 209–10
interbreeding. *See* hybridity
Interlingua, 132–33, 164, 171, 202
internal colonialism, 30–31
International Auxiliary Language Association, 164

International Auxiliary Languages (IALs), 18, 76, 128–30, 132–35, 170–71, 201
international communication, 124
International Communication and Political Opinion, 177
international decolonization, 205
International Journal of American Linguistics, 79
international language, 164
International Monetary Fund, 231
International Propaganda and Psychological Warfare, 177
internationalism, 18–19
internment of Japanese Americans, 165
interracial marriage, 165
interracial procreation, 74. *See also* hybridity
interracial relationships, 55
intersectional analysis, 255
Islam, 16, 43–44, 137
isoglosses, 118
isolates, 59, 67, 70, 76

Jacobs, Melville, 164–66
Jakobson, Roman, 46, 120, 143, 168–71, 173, 175, 178, 198, 211, 236
 FBI file, 160, 163, 167, 171–74
 structuralism, 174
Japan, 61, 133
Japan Foundation, 194
Japanese, 133
Japhetic languages, 53, 140
Jefferson, Thomas, 49
Jespersen, Otto, 132–33
Jewish scholars
 sociolinguistics, 196
Jewish speakers, 75
Jews, 13, 15, 124–25, 129, 133, 145, 152, 165, 184
 as alien and inferior, 149
 disenfranchisement as German citizens, 147
 multilingualism, 149
 propaganda about, 153–54
Jones, Sir William, 17, 42, 45–46, 48–49, 55

key ideas about language, 2
keywords, 4–6, 8–9, 73, 130, 235
Kiksht language, 208
kinship, 48, 51
kinship tree models, 58
Klein, Naomi, 249
Klemperer, Victor, 126, 152, 154
 Lingua Tertii Imperii, 153
Klingon, 134
Kloss, Heinz, 203–4
knowledge
 "neutral" or "universal" or "objective," 7

knowledge and culture, 12
knowledge production from developing countries, 219
knowledge socially produced, 10
Kroeber, Alfred, 79
Kwakiutl (Kwakwaka'wakw) texts, 82, 86–87

Labov, William, 196, 207–10, 218, 224, 236
Lafont, Robert, 222
Lakoff, Robin, xxi, 215
 Language and Woman's Place, 216
Lambert, Wallace, 197
Lancaster, Roger, 250
language, 3, 8, 16, 68, 114, 161, 186, 223, 249
 of command, 34
 commodification of, 21
 to delimit territorial boundaries, 104
 diasporic perspective, 13
 and differential citizenship, 108–10, 194
 for diplomatic communications and military intelligence, 180
 of education, 200, 209
 as empirical, scientific object, 132
 endangerment, 253
 evolution toward perfection (*See* civilizational hierarchy of languages)
 as a form of social action connected to labour, 142–43
 grounds for exclusion, 238
 idea of a single language spoken in Eden, then diversifying, 50
 making subjects through language, 98–104
 for nation-building, 19, 107, 144
 as national soul, 150
 natural scientific object, 117, 121, 133
 place in Marxist social theory, 125
 political status of languages in empires and nation-states, 119
 and race, 19, 149–50
 rainbow-like, 171
 regulation of, 39, 195
 and religion, 29
 role in making European nations, 95
 science of, 19, 117, 183
 scientific basis for grouping languages into categories, 65
 separate system requiring study on its own terms, 86
 shaping of thought, 89
 in social difference and social inequality, 2–4, 95, 219
 superstructural phenomenon, 138
 synchronic forms of, 121
 as technology, 143, 150, 155
 in "the new work order," 233

tool of empire, 12, 36
vernacular (*See* vernacular languages)
what distinguishes humans from nonhumans, 63
of youth, 224
Language, 86
language and fascism, 144–46
Language and Information (Harris), 183
Language and Politics, 235
Language and Woman's Place (Lakoff), 216
language-based forms of measurement, 239
Langage et travail, 222
language ideologies, 7, 11, 236, 251–52
Language in Society, 197
language industries, 233
The Language of the Third Reich, 152
language planning and language policy, 201, 203–4
language practices of union members, 223
Language Problems and Language Planning, 135
"Language Problems of Developing Nations," 203
language reclamation, 255
language revitalization, 253, 255, 257
language socialization, 207
language standardization, 18, 96, 104–7
language testing, 238–39
languages as related, 49
languages of power, xv, 74, 113, 116, 200, 223
late capitalism, 3, 21, 229–30, 257
destabilizations of, 235
Latin, 67, 72, 84
Latin grammars, 35–36, 40
Latin text of the Bible, 17
Lattimore, Owen, 167
Lear, Jonathan, xiv–xv
legitimation, 3
legitimation of inequity, 6
legitimation of power, 7
Leibniz, Gottfried Wilhelm, 49, 96
Lenin, Vladimir, 136, 139
Leont'iev, Alexis, 141
LePage, Robert, 219
Lewis, Oscar, 165
lexicostatistics, 164
liberal democracy, 11, 19, 60, 95, 98, 122
liberal ideology, 96
"The Limitations of the Comparative Method of Anthropology" (Boas), 81
linear programming, 163
lingua franca, 131, 240
Lingua Tertii Imperii (Klemperer), 153
linguistic analysis, xxii, 253
linguistic anthropology, xv, 8, 95, 104, 252
linguistic ethnography, 237
linguistic ideologies, 235

linguistic minority nationalism, 9, 152, 221
linguistic relativity, 18, 88
Linguistic Society of America, 176, 180
linguistic structuralism, 174
linguistic taxonomies, 64
linguistic technologies (phonetic alphabet and writing), 69
linguistic variability, 119, 208
linguistics, xxi, 6, 64, 161, 169, 175–76, 181
applied linguistics, 133, 161, 176
generative (*See* generative linguistics)
The Linguistics Wars (Harris), 187
linguists investigation during McCarthy era, 164–67
linguists working for war effort, 180
Lippert, Charles, 228
literacy, 36, 111, 193, 195, 199
allows for conversion or development, 200
mass literacy in China, 166
workers/citizens, 114
literacy/orality, 38, 102
"lock her up! chants," xv
Locke, John, 10–11, 49
language as cornerstone of modernity, 96
Loftman, Beryl, 219
Lord of the Rings (Tolkien), 134

Macaulay, Thomas Babington, 55
machine translation, 19, 176, 181, 183, 187, 241
Mackey, William, 202
"Make America Great Again" slogan, 234
Malthus, Thomas, 63
Mandamin, Josephine, 260
Mandarin, 144
Manufacturing Consent (Chomsky), 185
Manx, 151
Marathi language, 110
Marcellesi, Jean-Baptiste, 222
Marr, Nikolai, 139
Marrism, 139–42, 175
Martin-Nielsen, Janet, 163, 181
Martinet, André, 133
Marx, Karl, 136, 175
A Contribution to the Critique of Political Economy, 138
Marxist analyses, 167, 199, 220
Marxist attention to language as praxis, 222
Marxist *base/superstructure* model, 138
Marxist linguistics, 137, 139
Marxist sociolinguists, 237
Marxist theory, 19, 125
masculinity, 127
mass education, 56, 114–15
mass literacy in China, 166

mass media, 162
"materiality," 237
Mathematical Structures of Language (Harris), 183
Mayan grammar, 40
McCarthy era, 160, 164–67, 178, 196
McElhinny, Bonnie, xvii–xix, xxii
McGee, William, 78
Mead, Margaret, 79
mechanical languages, 67
Medvedev, Pavel, 141
Meillet, Antoine, 76, 119, 121, 222
Mein Kampf (Hitler), 145, 149
mercantile capitalism, 3, 16, 33–34, 42
Mérida, Georges, 219
mestizos, 39
metalingual function, 170
Methods in Structural Linguistics (Harris), 182
metropole, 17, 32, 96, 142
microregulatory interventions, 233
military/industrial interest in mathematical tools, 163
military service, 101–2
Mill, James, *History of British India*, 55
Milroy, Lesley, 223
minority languages, 152, 203. *See also* linguistic minority nationalism
miscegenation, 66, 74, 80, 146. *See also* hybridity
missionaries, 37–38, 41
missionary grammars and dictionaries, 40
missionary linguists, 17, 29, 35–42
missionary use of Indigenous languages, 39
Mistral, Frédéric, 112
MIT Center for International Studies (CENIS), 177
Mitchell-Kernan, Claudia, 215, 218
mixed languages, 17, 56, 72
mixed linguistic forms, 59
mobility, 250
Mobilization for Youth, 208
modern-state, 124
modernism, 127
modernist nationalism, 125
modernity, 11, 13, 18–19, 62, 69, 80, 82–83, 89, 116, 135
  English as repository for, 55
modernization, 139, 201
modernization theory, 163
Mohawk language, 28
monogenesis, 66
monolingualism, 113, 200, 225
monopoly, 61
monosyllabic language, 69–70
Montréal, 15, 22

Morgan, Lewis Henry, 69, 217–18
morphemes, 67, 130, 140–41
morphology, 46, 67, 69, 106, 161
Morris, Alice Vanderbilt, 132
Moscow Linguistics Circle, 168
Le mot et l'art du mot, 169
Mukařovský, Jan, 169
Müller, Friedrich Max, 52
multilingualism, 113–14, 129, 135, 137, 139, 193, 195–96, 201, 233–34, 240, 251
  India, 201
  multilingual countries, 105
multiplicity, 7–8
multiracial democracy, 83, 87
Murdock, George, 165–66
Muslims, xv, 16, 53, 124, 179

narration, 211, 248, 252
nation-building, 193
nation-state, 18, 96, 98, 108, 155, 248
  bourgeois, 108
  construction of, 101
  emergence in Europe, 94–95
  if workers of the world were to unite, 135
  paradox of democracy and inequality, 107
National Association for the Advancement of Colored People, 80
National Defence Education Act, 181
National Institute for Mental Health, 208
National Institutes of Health, 180
national languages, 193, 225
national or cultural homogeneity of a state, 102–3
National Science Foundation, 180, 183
National Socialism. *See* Nazism
nationalism, 3, 19, 33, 80, 87, 96, 101, 103, 124, 147
  bourgeois, 18, 137
  linguistic minority nationalism, 9, 221
  national movements in Caribbean and Indian Ocean, 220
  new, 214, 219
  Romantic (*See* Romantic nationalism)
nationhood, racial interpretation of, 62
Native American languages of the Pacific Northwest, 164
Native North American claims for rights and recognition, 212
nativism, 21
natural differences, 125
"natural" laws, 18
nature as source of meaning and authority, 95
nature *versus* nurture, 74
Nazi concept of the *Volksgemeinschaft*, 145

Nazi ideologies of language, 203
Nazi intellectuals, 176
Nazi linguistics, 129, 148, 150
Nazi race theory, 125, 149
Nazi science, 80
Nazis hired by US as counterintelligence experts, 177
Nazism, 64, 124, 145, 149–50, 155
Nazism in Germany, 146–48
Nebrija, Antonio, 35, 40
Negroes had no culture (Boas), 84
"Negroes" in American society. *See* African Americans
neogrammarians, 121
Neogrammarians *(Junggrammatiker)*, 120
neoliberalism, 16, 20, 231–32, 235, 242
New Criticism, 163
New World, 33
  European diseases, 35
  expansion to, 35
new world creoles, 13
Neyret, Jules-Clément, 70
niche products, 248
Nineteen Eighty-Four (Orwell), 19, 162, 188–91
No Ivory Tower (Schrecker), 163
Noah, 47–48
Nobles, Melissa, 255
normalization, 221
normativization, 221
Northwest Coast Indians, 79, 85
Numu language, 208
Nussbaum, Martha, 58

objectivity, 6, 175
"Occidentalism," 45
Occitan language, 222
Occitan linguistic minority movement, 221
Ochs, Elinor, 207
Okrent, 130
operations research, 163
orality and literacy distinction, 69
orderliness, 116
organic languages, 67
Orient, 43–44
Oriental stereotypes, 179
"Oriental Studies," field of, 45
Orientalism, 147
Orientalism (Said), 12, 44
Orientalist knowledge, 44, 47
Orientalist stereotypes of Asian passivity, 67
Orientalists, 43, 45, 54, 56
Origin of Language (Haeckel), 68
The Origin of Species (Darwin), 63

Orwell, George, 153
  Animal Farm, 19, 188–89
  Burmese Days, 190
  Nineteen Eighty-Four, 19, 162, 188–91
Other, 13, 17, 53, 89
Out of Place (Said), 12
overseas colonialism, 30
Oyama, Tokio, 133

Pāṇini, linguistic tradition of, 17, 46
Pāṇini's grammar, 46
Passeron, Jean-Claude, 223–24
patois, 70, 94, 99, 104, 112
Peirce, Charles Sanders, 210
performance, 198, 217
periphery, 17, 109, 142
  Canada as, xvii
  creating peripheries, 110–12
  tourism, 248
personhood, ideologies of, 244
Philippines, 29, 36, 61, 78
  how to engineer public opinion, 177
  language diversity, 240
  sociolinguistics, 195
  structural adjustment policies, 239
Philips, Susan, 7, 215
philology, 12, 44, 147, 151, 221
philosophers of language, 198
phonetic alphabet and writing, 69
phonetics, 42, 46
phonology, 46, 170
pidgins, 17, 59, 70–72, 75–76, 106, 208, 214–15, 219
  definition, 73
Pinoy Workers of the World, 240
political ecology, 252
polygenesis, 66
polynomia, 222
Port Royal Grammarians, 96
Portugal, 33, 61
positionality, 7
possible common language of human race, 88
post-Fordist regime, 232
postcolonial sociolinguistics, 235
postcolonialism, 30, 32, 225
postwar labour migration, 196
potlatch, suppression among Kwakiutl, 82
Prague Linguistics Circle (PLC), 168–71, 174–75
Prague School structuralism, 180
Pravda, 142
praxis, 14, 222
pre-industrial empires (Spain and Portugal), 61
pre-modernity, 11

precarity, 237–38
Price, David, 164, 171–72, 175
  Threatening Anthropology, 160
primary school education, 114
primitive grammatical elements, 67
primitive groups, 69
The Prison Notebooks (Gramsci), 8
progress, 18, 58–60, 62, 80, 150, 195
  teleological hierarchies of, 62
propaganda, 19, 153, 162–63, 176–77
protectionism, 60
Protestant churches in Canada apologized for roles in residential schools, 28
proto-Indo-European (PIE), 50, 56
  kinship between Britain and northern India, 52
Proto-Indo-European language, 52–54
protolanguage, 50
provincializing the West, 11
proxy wars, 162
Prudent, Lambert-Félix, 219
psychological approach to anthropology, 163
psychological warfare, 163, 177
Puerto Rico, 61, 78

Québec, 221
  language planning and language policy, 204
queer linguistics, 250
queering, 258
queerness, 257
Quiet Revolution, xx, 213

race, 21, 80, 83, 100, 124, 161, 214, 237, 244
  immutability of, 74
  as means of creating labour forces, 61
  Nazi race theory, 125, 149
  used to legitimize relations of power, 112
"Race: Are We So Different?," 58
"Race and Nationality" (Boas), 87
"Race and the National Situation," 165
race-mixing, 80. *See also* hybridity
races, hierarchically ranked from Negro to Caucasian, 68
racial, cultural, and linguistic mixture, 59
racial hierarchy, 54, 68
racial hierarchy theories, 206
racial interpretation of nationhood, 62
racial mixing, concern about, 55
racialization, 110
racism, 63, 76, 235
  anti-Black racism, 165
  anti-racism training, 211
  anti-racist critiques, 217–20, 237
  anti-racist work, 167, 196
  Boas spoke against, 82
  critiques of, 80
  scientific, 68, 83
  strategies for challenging, 21
racist names of American sports teams, xv
radical hope, xiv, xv, 2, 260
radio, 151
rationality in French Revolution, 108
reason, 14, 95–96
recording languages for purpose of missionization, 41
red flags, 4, 6
red threads (key ideas about language), 2–4
reducción, 38, 40
reflexivity in anthropological practice, 211
refusal, 21, 255–56
reimaginings, 255, 258
Reinventing Anthropology (Hymes), 212
relationship between language and Chinese, 65
Research Commission on Sociolinguistics, 197
reserves and residential schools, 78
residential schools, 28, 41, 78, 115
Resources of Hope (Williams), 2
restricted code (communicative style), 206
rhizome, 253–54
Rhodes, Cecil, 62
Rickford, John, xix, 218, 220, 237
Rickford, Russell, 237
Robeson, Paul, 165
Rockefeller Foundation, 20, 88, 176, 178, 180, 193, 201
  sponsored the Committee on Sociolinguistics, 197
Rockefeller Foundation Archives of women, 215
Roma, 149, 154
Romance languages, 59
Romantic movement in art and literature, 95
Romantic nationalism, 101, 147
Romantic nationalist linguistics, 126
Romanticism, 18
Rubin, Joan, 197
rural hinterlands as periphery, 110–11
Russia, 61
Russian and Eastern European and China studies, 179
Russian language, 137, 142–43
Russian Revolution, 135, 138

S-P-E-A-K-I-N-G, 211
Said, Edward, 7, 45, 47, 52, 235
  Culture and Imperialism, 16
  Orientalism, 12, 44
  Out of Place, 12

Samoa, 78
Sankoff, Gillian, 213, 215
Sanskrit language, 45–46, 53, 56, 67, 88
  mother of Indo-European languages, 50
  second intellectual renaissance, 47
Sapir, Edward, 60, 79, 85–86, 88–89, 133, 164, 166
Saussure, Ferdinand de, 46, 132, 138, 168, 180
  Cours de linguistique général, 120–21
Saussure, René de, 132
Saussurean linguistics, 169
Schieffelin, Bambi, 207, 237
Schlauch, Margaret, 164
  The Gift of Language, 167
  Who Are the Aryans?, 167
Schlegel, August Wilhelm, 67
Schlegel, Friedrich, 67
Schleicher, August, 66–68, 75–76
  Darwinism Tested by the Science of Language, 65
Schleyer, Johannes, 130–31
scholars during McCarthy era, 160
  curtailment of research, 167
  FBI investigation, 160–61
Schoolcraft, Henry Rowe, 11
schooling, 18, 101–2, 113–14, 224. See also education
  language of, 99
  role in constructing spaces as monolingual, 94, 105
Schrecker, Ellen, *No Ivory Tower,* 163
Schreiner, Alfred, 70
Schuchardt, Hugo, 75–76, 118, 132, 171
science, English as repository for, 55
Science and Society, 165, 167
science and technology
  Soviet Union/United State competition, 162
science Cold War, 181
science of coercion, 176
science of language, 19, 117, 183
science of linguistics, 95, 121
"Science of the Word," 14
scientific authority, 58
scientific investigation, 60
scientific management, 60, 127
scientific observation, 78
scientific racism, 68, 83
scientific rationality and expertise, 82
scientific reason and technology, 62
scientific reasoning, 63
Scots and Irish Gaelic, 151
Searle, John, xxi
Sechehaye, Albert, 120
second intellectual renaissance, 47
secularized religion, 44

segmentary, 48
self-censorship (scholars during McCarthy era), 160, 175
Semitic languages, 52, 68
settler colonialism, 31–32
seven-fire prophecy, 14–15
sexuality, 100, 110, 161, 258
  illicit sexual relations, 160
Shuy, Roger, 205
Silverstein, Michael, 236
Simpson, Audra, 257
Simpson, C., 176
Simpson, Leanne, 15, 250, 259–60
"Skills and Selves in the New Workplace" (Urciuoli), 242
Skinner, B.F., 184
slavery, 43, 47, 66, 100
Slavic languages, 59
Smith, Adam, 62
Smitherman, Geneva, 237
Snyder, Gary, 211
Social Darwinism, 68, 206
social difference, xxii, 2, 4, 16, 125
  as natural (racial), 62
social inequality, xxii, 2, 4, 11, 16, 217
  sociolinguistics and, 195
social justice movements, 7, 104
social justice warriors, 5
social movements, 250, 258
Social Science Research Council, 88
socialism, 135, 165
sociolinguistics, xv, 11, 20, 95, 102, 197, 204
  British, 197, 223
  Canadian sociolinguistics, 197–98
  challenge to generativist linguistics, 198–99
  communicative competence, 198
  dominance, theories of, 221–25
  emergence of, 194–96
  Jewish scholars, 196
  Marxist, 222
  performance, 198
  US-based publications, 197
  working-class or regional minority scholars, 196
sociolinguistics of conflict, 222
sociolinguistics on sexuality, 258
sociological methods and theories of communication, 177
sociology of language, 203
soft diplomacy, 202
soft power, 152, 194
Somerville, Margaret, 252
sound as element of language most amenable to scientific analysis, 120
sound (or phonetics), 121

sound system, 170
South and Southeast Asian Studies, 179
South Asian studies, 179
Soviet dialect variation and multilingualism, 136
Soviet linguistics, 138, 140
Soviet Union, 18, 135–36, 155, 168
　collapse of, 20
　debates about use of one or multiple languages, 125
　decolonization and development through communism, 194
　Russification, 134, 142
　standardization of languages, 137, 139
　turn toward authoritarian centralism, 142
Spain's colonizing project in New Spain and the Philippines, 35–36, 38, 40
Spanish-American War, 61
Spanish Civil War, 154, 190
Spanish missionaries, 38, 41
　use of native languages, 38
Spears, Arthur, 237
speech act theory, 217
speech technologies for persuasion and propaganda, 19
Spencer, Herbert, 64
spirituality, 252
spoken languages, 68
Sprachbund, 171
Sputnik, 181
Stalin, 139–40
　manifesto (1913), 136
　turn toward authoritarian centralism, 142
standardization (of languages), 95, 102, 106–7, 193, 195–96, 199
　allows for shaping of nation, 104
　Soviet union, 137
standardized language, 21
standardized proficiency tests, 241
standpoint, 7
Star Trek, 134
state bureaucracies, 113
state coercion, 98
state military organizations, 113
status planning (changing the social value of a language), 203–4
Stead, Sylvia, 5
Steggerda, Morris, 74
Stern, Bernhard, *General Anthropology*, 165
structural adjustment, 234, 239
structural adjustment in the Global South, 231, 246
structural functionalism, 163
structural linguistics, 175, 182–83
structural phonology, 175

structuralism, 113, 120, 126, 132, 155, 168, 174, 204
structuralist/functionalist notion of class, race, gender, and age, 209
student mobility for higher education, 194
subjugated discourse, 9
substratist, 75
Summer Institute of Linguistics, 41
surveillance, 233
surveillance and censorship, 20
Swadesh, Morris, 164–66, 173, 175, 180
Swadesh lists, 164
syllabic orthographies for Indigenous languages, 42
symbols, 94–95, 102, 112. *See also* techniques that discipline tongues
　schooling's role in constructing spaces as monolingual, 105
symbolic domination, 9
syntax, 19, 161, 181

Tabouret-Keller, Andrée, 105
Taft, W.H., 115
Tagalog speakers, 42
Tannen, Deborah, *You Just Don't Understand*, 216
Tate, Henry, 86
taxonomies linked to family trees, 64
Taylor, F.W., 113
technicist approach to social and linguistic engineering, 200
techniques that discipline tongues, 95
technologies, 18
technology of the concentration camp, 146
Telestreet, 259
temporal migrants, 246
terrorism, 238
"terrorists," xv, 235
text analysis, 221
textbooks, 107
Theosophical Society, 88
Theosophist, 90
theosophy, 89
Third World where communists were perceived to be a threat, 178
Third World women leaving to care for wealthier households, 246–47
Thomason, Sarah, xix
Threatening Anthropology (Price), 160
Tolkien, J.R.R., *Lord of the Rings,* 134
Toman, Jindrich, 168–69, 175
tourism, 248
Trager, George, 180
The Transformation of Capitalist Society, 184
Transformational Grammar, 208
transformational linguistics, 216

translanguages, 40
translation, 28, 40, 113, 234, 240, 242
  machine (*See* machine translation)
transnational educational migration, 241
transnational language education industry, 239
transnationalization of social service provision, 250
Trautmann, Thomas, 45–47, 53
Treaty of Westphalia, 96
tree as model for organizing linguistic information, 65
tree diagrams, 17, 19, 50–51, 53, 118, 185, 253, 259
tree model of comparative philology, 59, 64, 76
Trente Glorieuses, 225
triangle trade, 97
Trubetzkoy, Nikolai, 143, 169–71
Trudgill, Peter, 223
Trump, Donald, 5
Truth and Reconciliation process for residential school survivors, 28–29
Tsimshian, 86
Tuskegee Institute, 114–15
typology, 203

United Nations, 155
United States, xvii, 61, 155
  censuses (language questions in), 104
  challenging deficit in, 205
  linguistic anthropology, 207
  miscegenation statutes, 74
  overseas colonialism, 78
  reserves and residential schools, 78
  settler colonialism, 32
United States-based sociolinguists, 204, 213–14
Universal Grammar (UG), 162, 182, 186
universal notions of fraternal citizenship, 18
universal socialism, 136
universal suffrage, 100
universalists, 19, 75, 175, 191
universalizing scientific approaches to language, 170
urban dialectology, 225
urban multilingualism, 224–25
urban sociolinguistics, 224
Urciuoli, Bonnie, "Skills and Selves in the New Workplace," 242

Vedic ritual, 46
Verdaguer, Jaume, 112
vernacular languages, 9, 29, 35, 40
  replacement of Latin, 36
Vietnamese language, 70
  classified as "monosyllabic," 69–70
voice, 141–42, 257
Voice of America broadcasts, 177
Voices of Modernity (Bauman), 10
Volapük, 130–31
Volk, 153
Vološinov, Valentin, 9, 138, 141, 235
Von Humboldt, Wilhelm, 107
Vossler, Karl, 148, 152, 154
Vygotsky, Lev, 141

walking backward into the future, 2, 4, 13–14, 260
Wall Zimmerer, Robin, 14–15
War on Terror, 238
Washington, Booker T., 114–15
Washington State Interim Committee on UnAmerican Activities, 165
water as commons, 252, 259
water walks, 260
wave theory, 76
wealth, distribution of, 21, 100, 107, 146–47, 232. *See also* inequalities
Weber, Eugene, 94
Weisgerber, Leo, 151
welfare state, 16, 19–20, 194–95, 206, 210
Welsh, 151
West, 32
West and the "other," 17
Western European imperialism, 73, 210
Western European nationalism, 60
White degeneracy, 75
White nationalism/supremacy, 21, 54, 61, 75, 234
Who Are the Aryans? (Schlauch), 167
Whorf, Benjamin, 18, 60, 88–89, 130, 148, 259
Williams, Doug, 259
Williams, Raymond, 4–5, 7, 31, 83, 110, 235
  Resources of Hope, 2
Wodak, Ruth, 235
Women and Language conferences, 216
women's language, 109–10
women's language seen through lens of deficit, 216
women's rights, 100
Word, 171
word lists, 49–50
workfare regimes, 242
workforce as wordforce, 233
working class social movements, 13
working-class way of talking, 223
workplace as site for cross-cultural encounter, 210

World Bank, 231
World War II, 19, 184
   destroyed many adherents of IAL movements, 133
   machine translation, 176
   respect for technology, 155
   watershed in political economy of language, 126
Wynter, Sylvia, 2, 13–14

Yiddish, 75, 125, 149
You Just Don't Understand (Tannen), 216

zaaganaash, 15
Zamenhof, L.L., 129–32
   Esperanto, 127
Zentella, Ana Celia, 237
Zionism, 112, 182
Zulu, 69